Volume 5, at last! Boy, there were some tight deadlines on this book, but I always make a point of drawing the cover image and filling every page. I hope that, no matter where I am in my career, I am always able to stick to my principles.

—Kentaro Yabuki, 2001

Kentaro Yabuki made his manga debut with *Yamato Gensoki*, a short series about a young empress destined to unite the warring states of ancient Japan and the boy sworn to protect her. His next series, *Black Cat*, commenced serialization in the pages of *Weekly Shonen Jump* in 2000 and quickly developed a loyal fan following. *Black Cat* has also become an animated TV series, first hitting Japan's airwaves in the fall of 2005.

BLACK CAT VOL. 5
The SHONEN JUMP Manga Edition

STORY AND ART BY
KENTARO YABUKI

English Adaptation/Kelly Sue DeConnick
Translation/JN Productions
Touch-up Art & Lettering/Gia Cam Luc
Design/Courtney Utt
Editor/Joel Enos

Managing Editor/Frances E. Wall
Editorial Director/Elizabeth Kawasaki
VP & Editor in Chief/Yumi Hoashi
Sr. Director of Acquisitions/Rika Inouye
Sr. VP of Marketing/Liza Coppola
Exec. VP of Sales & Marketing/John Easum
Publisher/Hyoe Narita

Printed in the U.S.A.

Published by VIZ Media, LLC
P.O. Box 77010
San Francisco, CA 94107

SHONEN JUMP Manga Edition
10 9 8 7 6 5 4 3 2 1
First printing, November 2006

PARENTAL ADVISORY
BLACK CAT is rated T+ for Older Teen and is recommended for ages 16 and up. This volume contains tobacco use and graphic, realistic violence.

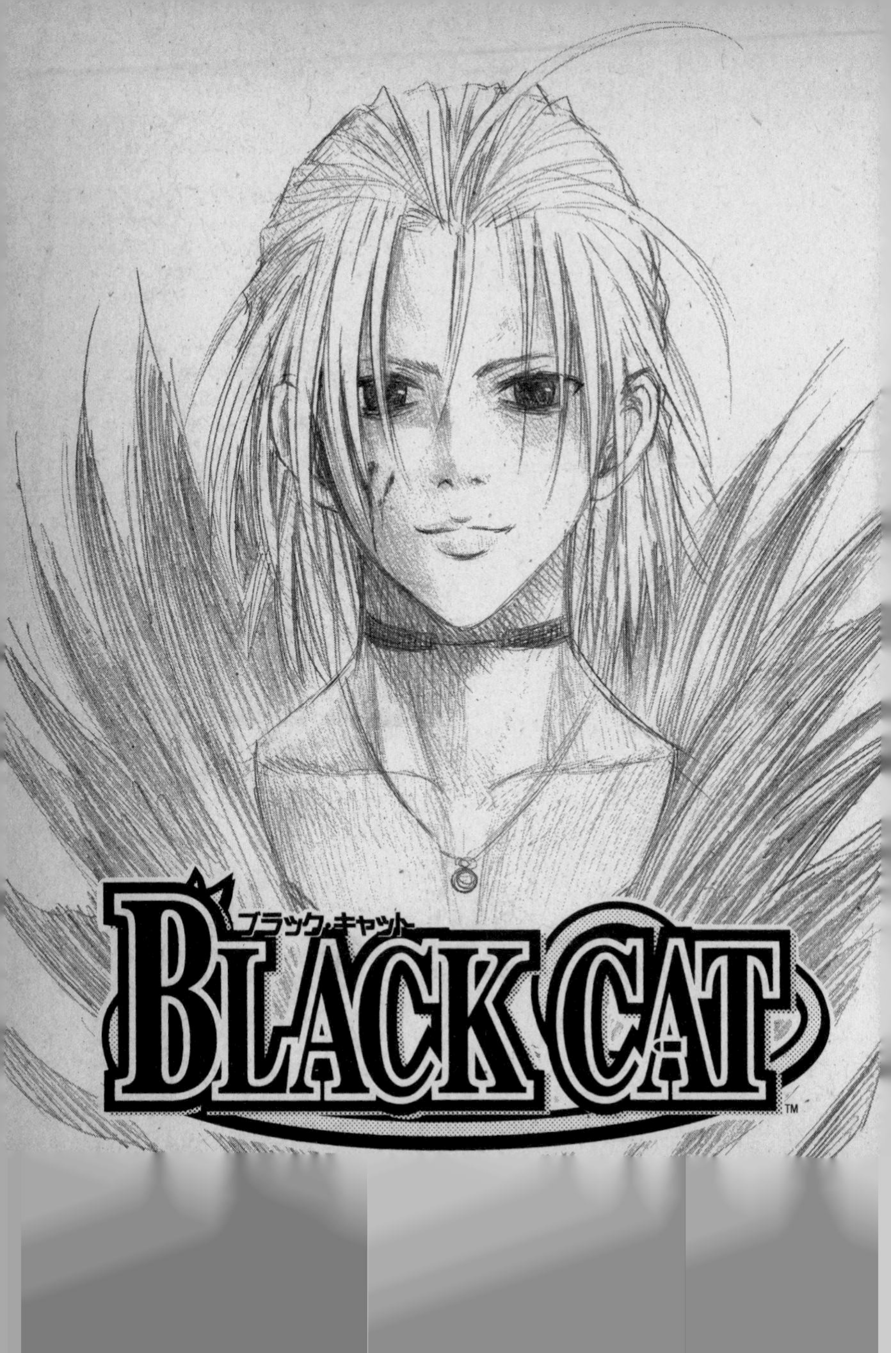
ブラック・キャット
BLACK CAT™

characters

BLACK CAT

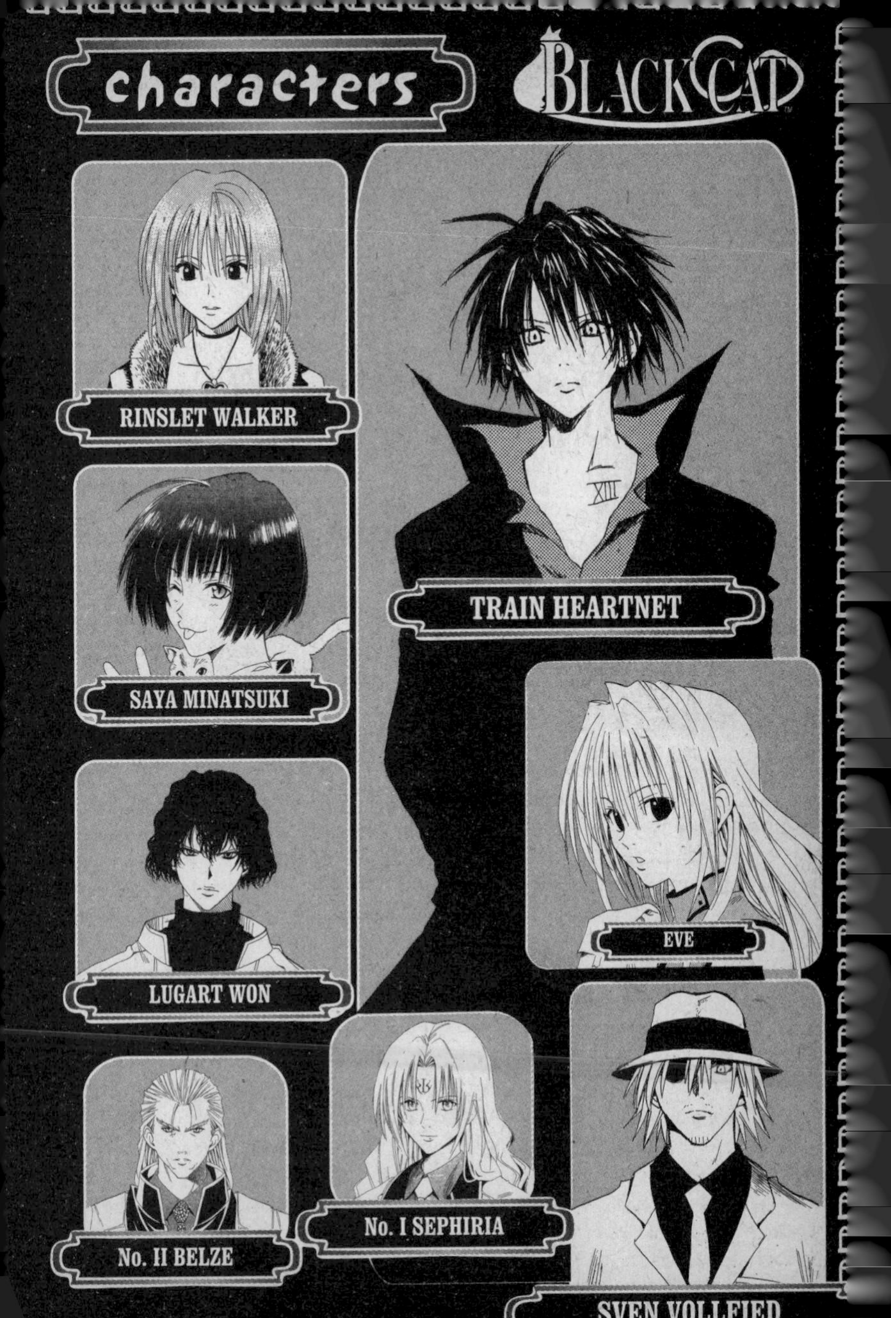
TRAIN HEARTNET
RINSLET WALKER
SAYA MINATSUKI
EVE
LUGART WON
SVEN VOLLFIED
No. I SEPHIRIA
No. II BELZE

APOSTLES of the STARS

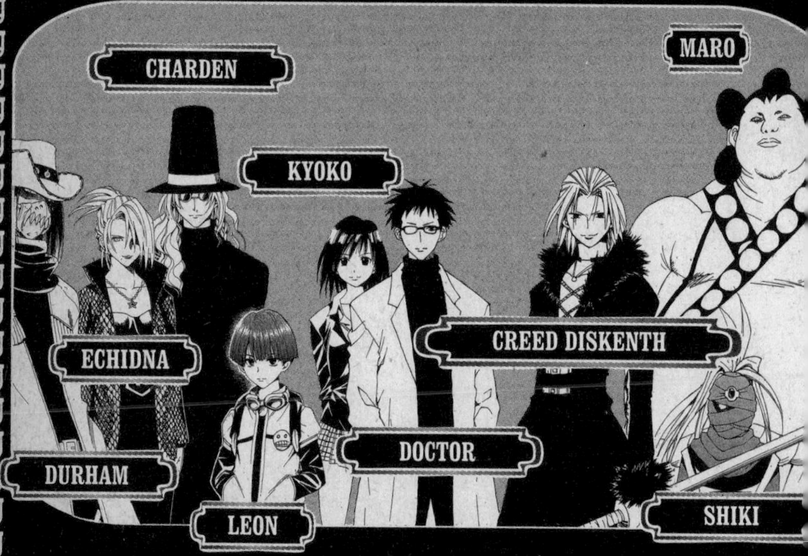
MARO
CHARDEN
KYOKO
CREED DISKENTH
ECHIDNA
DOCTOR
DURHAM
LEON
SHIKI

A fearless "eraser" responsible for the deaths of countless powerful men, Train "Black Cat" Heartnet carries an ornate pistol called "Hades." The gun is engraved with the Roman numeral XIII, his agent number as a member of Chronos, a mysterious organization that secretly controls one-third of the world's economy. Two years after his departure from Chronos, Train lives a carefree wanderer's life, working with his partner Sven as bounty hunters ("sweepers"), all the while pursuing a man who killed someone he cared for.

When Train finally found Creed, he was shocked to find that his former enemy now wanted to join him in his revolution against Chronos and the world. Train refused and they fought to a stalemate.

Recently, Sven and Train rescued Eve, a little girl who also happens to be a nanotech experiment. They also formed a loose alliance with thief-for-hire Rinslet Walker, who asked Train to help her with a caper she planned to pull at a party thrown by Madame Freesia. There, Train recognized Lugart Won, a Class-A bounty, on a mission of his own: to murder Madame Freesia.

Train confronted Won, but their battle was stopped by an unlikely foe, a dinosaur cloned as a pet for the Madame. Eve begged to save the innocent pet's life and Train obliged. But now the thwarted Lugart has a new target: Train…

BLACK CAT™

VOLUME 5 SPARK OF REVOLUTION

CONTENTS

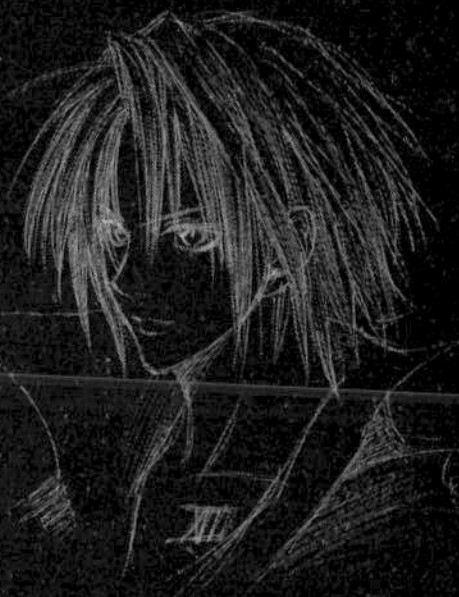

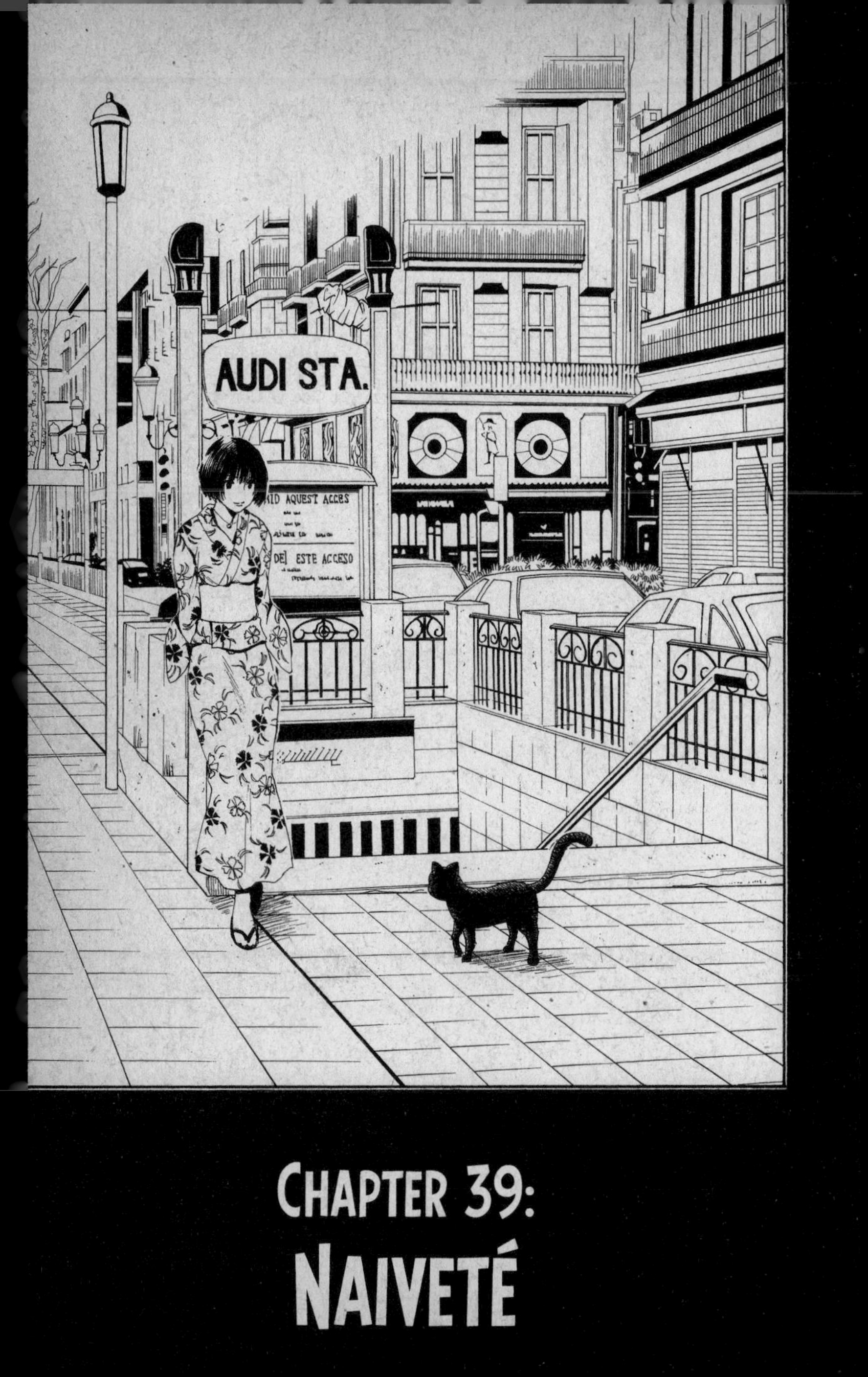
AUDI STA.

CHAPTER 39:
NAIVETÉ

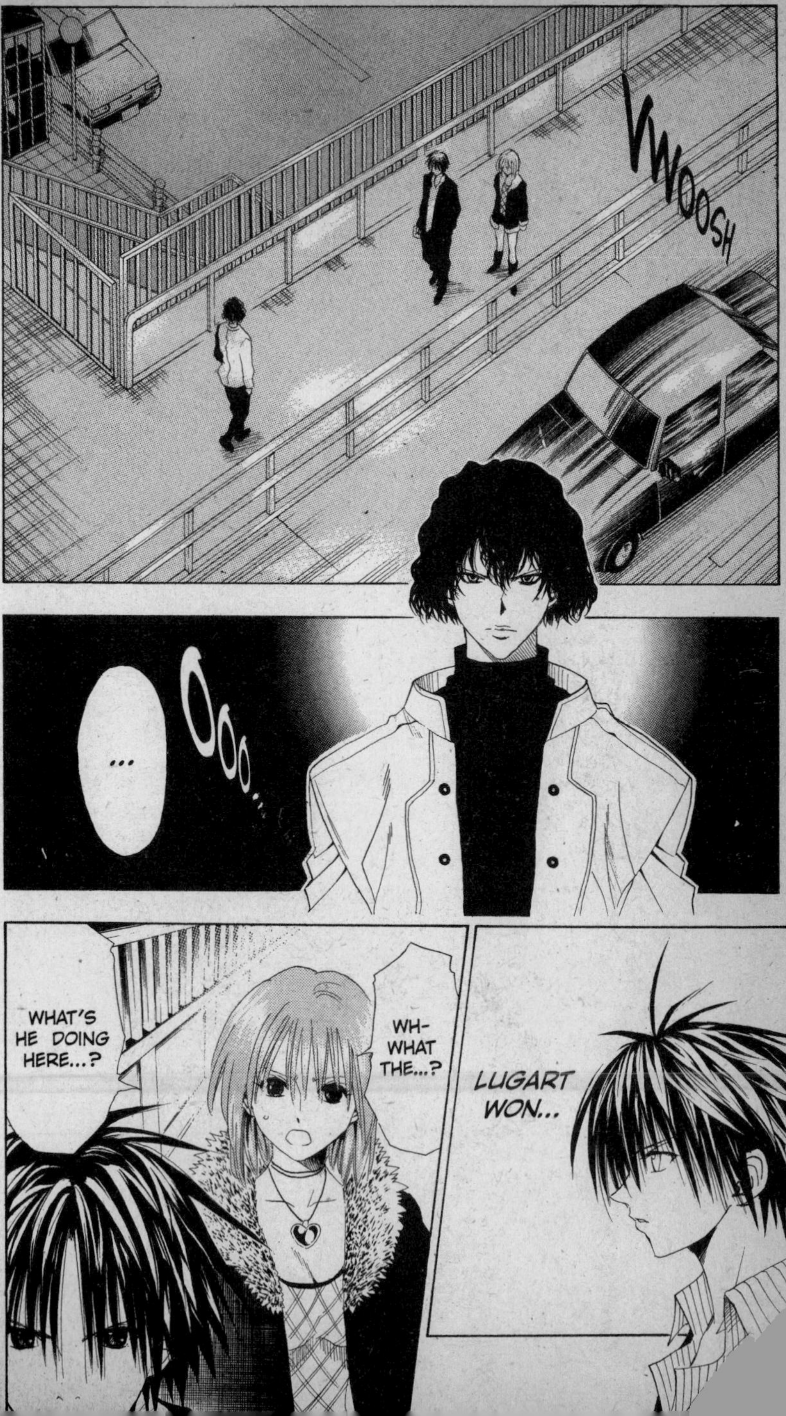
VWOOSH
...
OOO...
LUGART WON...
WH-WHAT THE...?
WHAT'S HE DOING HERE...?

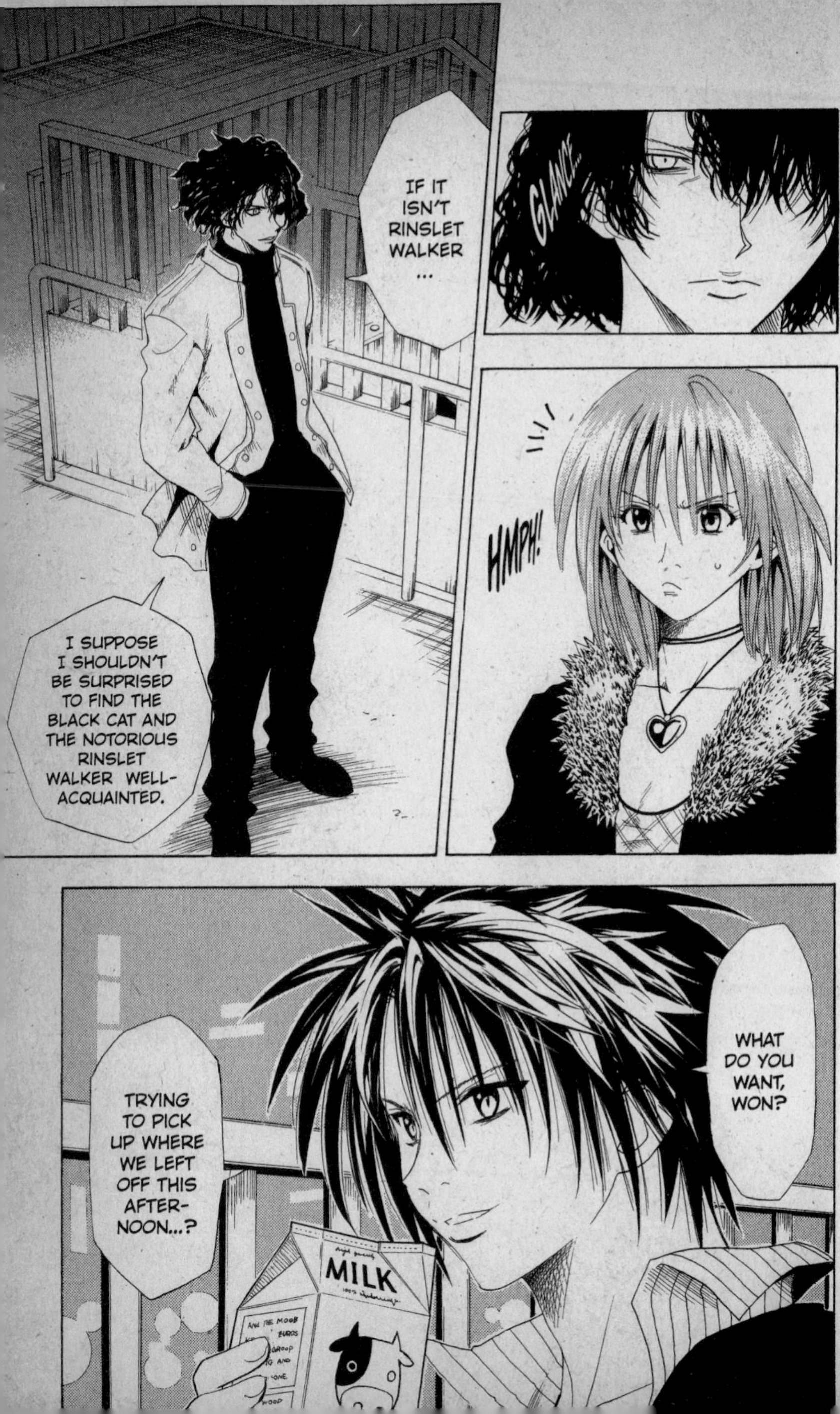
GLANCE...
HMPH!
IF IT ISN'T RINSLET WALKER ...
I SUPPOSE I SHOULDN'T BE SURPRISED TO FIND THE BLACK CAT AND THE NOTORIOUS RINSLET WALKER WELL-ACQUAINTED.
WHAT DO YOU WANT, WON?
TRYING TO PICK UP WHERE WE LEFT OFF THIS AFTER-NOON...?
MILK

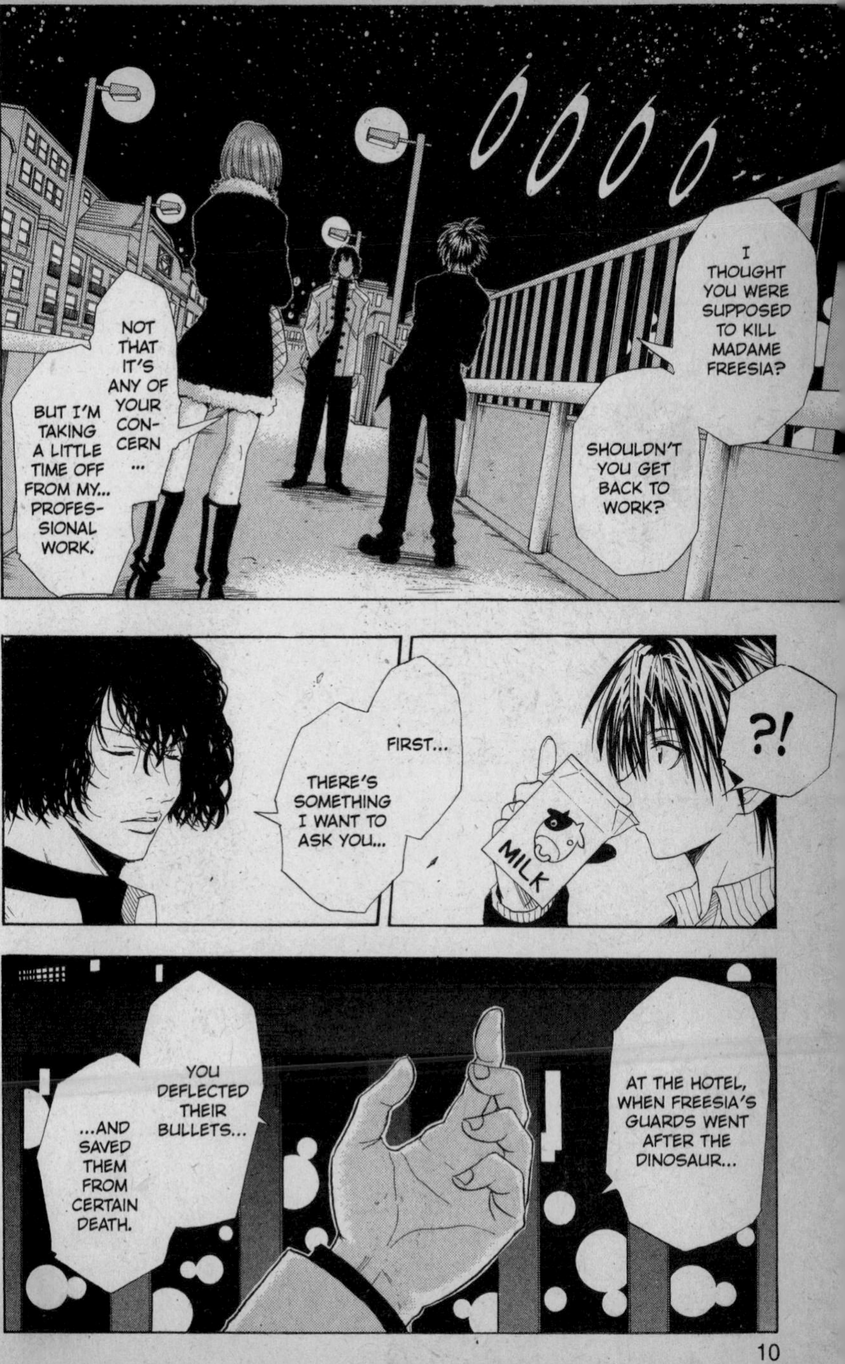
I THOUGHT YOU WERE SUPPOSED TO KILL MADAME FREESIA?
SHOULDN'T YOU GET BACK TO WORK?
NOT THAT IT'S ANY OF YOUR CONCERN...
BUT I'M TAKING A LITTLE TIME OFF FROM MY... PROFESSIONAL WORK.
?!
MILK
FIRST...
THERE'S SOMETHING I WANT TO ASK YOU...
AT THE HOTEL, WHEN FREESIA'S GUARDS WENT AFTER THE DINOSAUR...
YOU DEFLECTED THEIR BULLETS...
...AND SAVED THEM FROM CERTAIN DEATH.

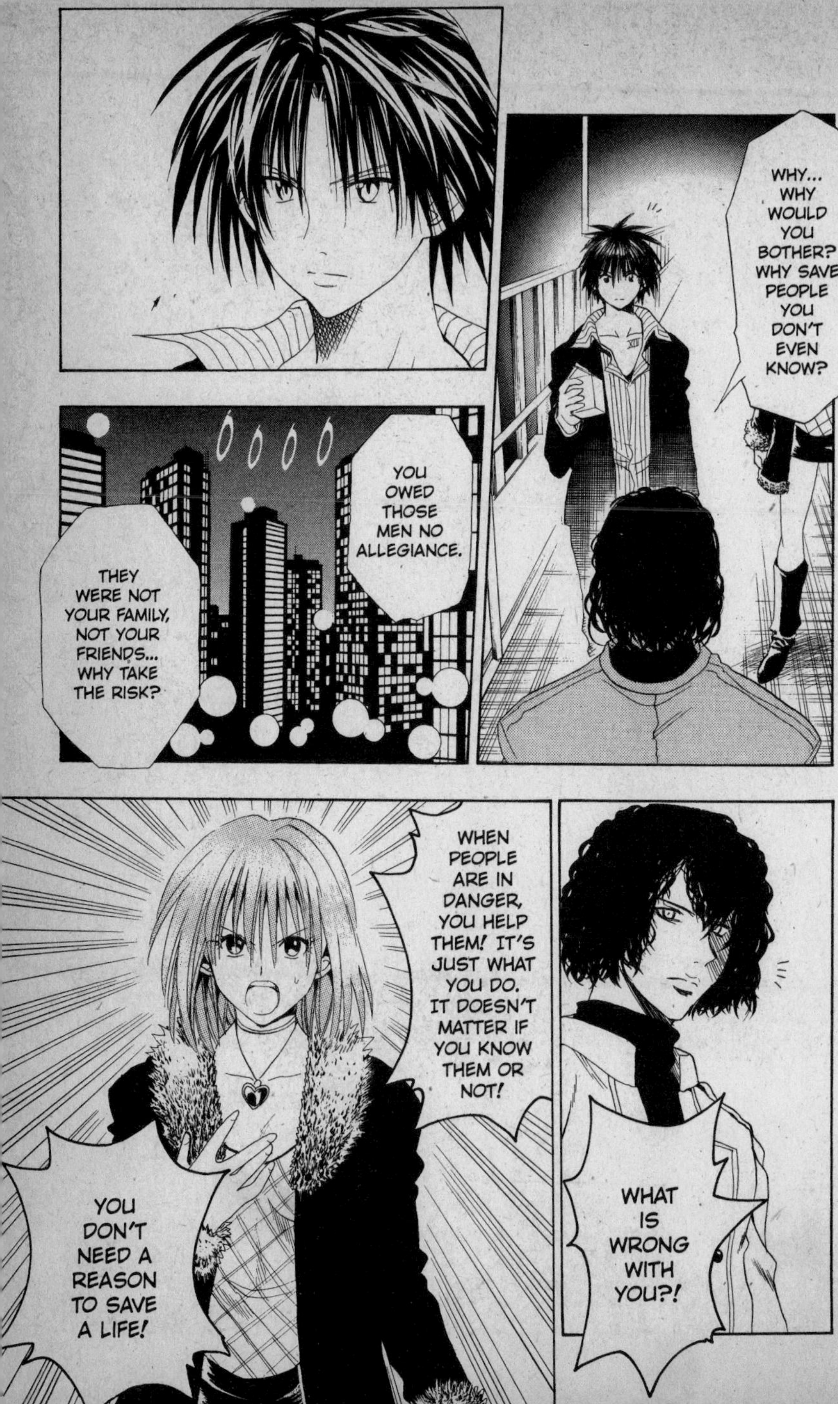
WHY... WHY WOULD YOU BOTHER? WHY SAVE PEOPLE YOU DON'T EVEN KNOW?
YOU OWED THOSE MEN NO ALLEGIANCE.
THEY WERE NOT YOUR FAMILY, NOT YOUR FRIENDS... WHY TAKE THE RISK?
WHAT IS WRONG WITH YOU?!
WHEN PEOPLE ARE IN DANGER, YOU HELP THEM! IT'S JUST WHAT YOU DO. IT DOESN'T MATTER IF YOU KNOW THEM OR NOT!
YOU DON'T NEED A REASON TO SAVE A LIFE!

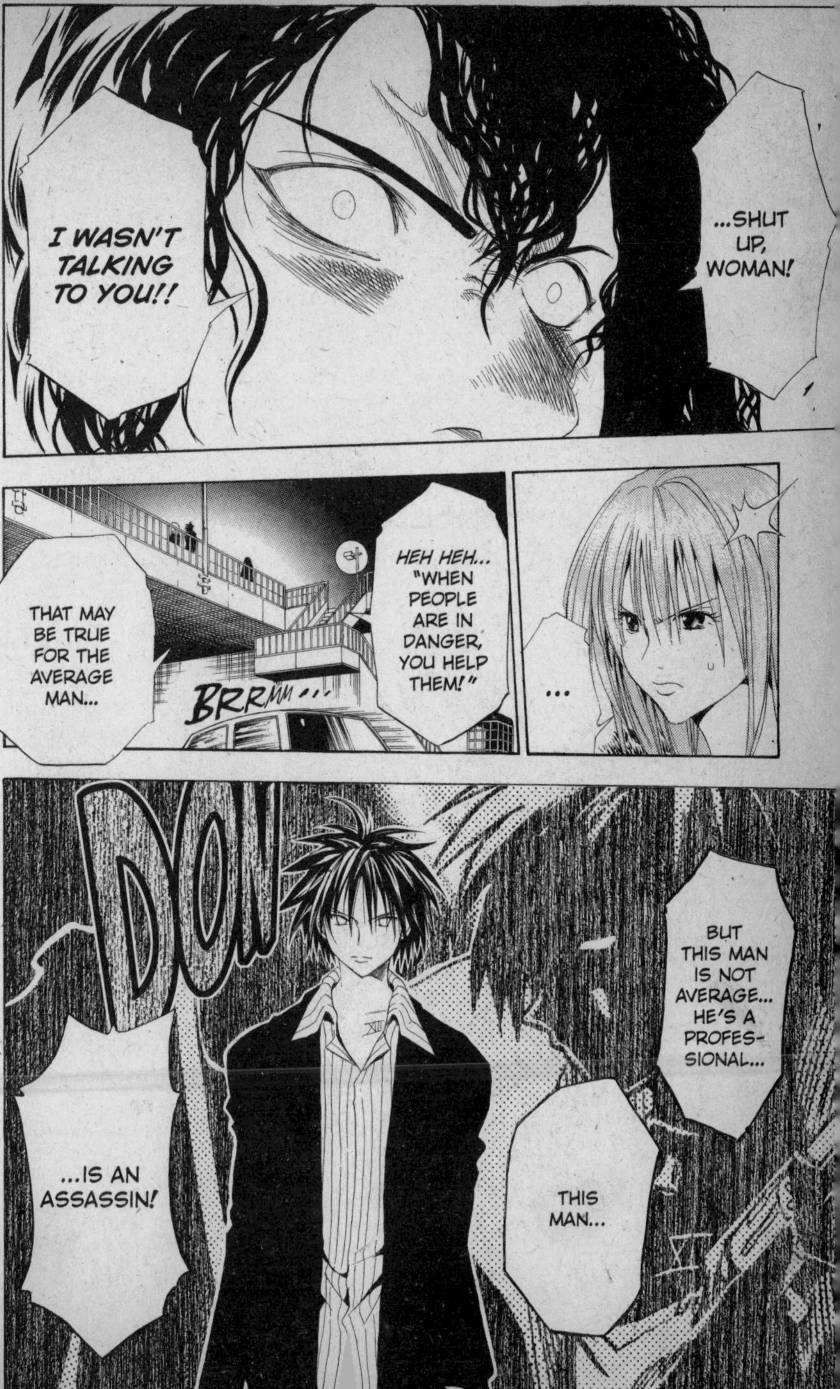
...SHUT UP, WOMAN!
I WASN'T TALKING TO YOU!!
...
HEH HEH... "WHEN PEOPLE ARE IN DANGER, YOU HELP THEM!"
BRRMM...
THAT MAY BE TRUE FOR THE AVERAGE MAN...
BUT THIS MAN IS NOT AVERAGE... HE'S A PROFES-SIONAL...
DON
THIS MAN...
...IS AN ASSASSIN!

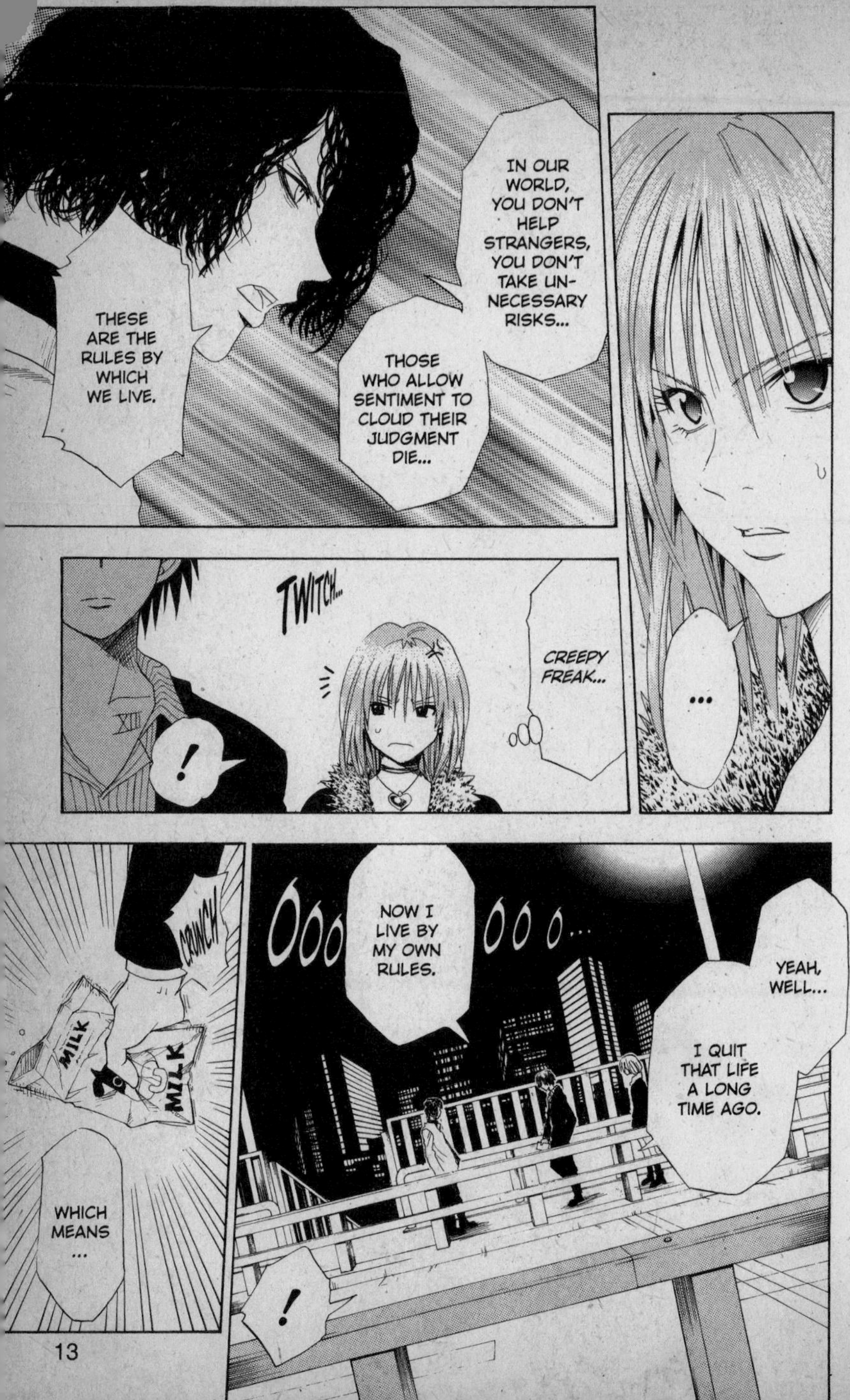
IN OUR WORLD, YOU DON'T HELP STRANGERS, YOU DON'T TAKE UN-NECESSARY RISKS...
THOSE WHO ALLOW SENTIMENT TO CLOUD THEIR JUDGMENT DIE...
THESE ARE THE RULES BY WHICH WE LIVE.
...
CREEPY FREAK...
TWITCH...
!
YEAH, WELL...
I QUIT THAT LIFE A LONG TIME AGO.
OOOOOO...
NOW I LIVE BY MY OWN RULES.
!
CRUNCH
MILK
MILK
WHICH MEANS ...

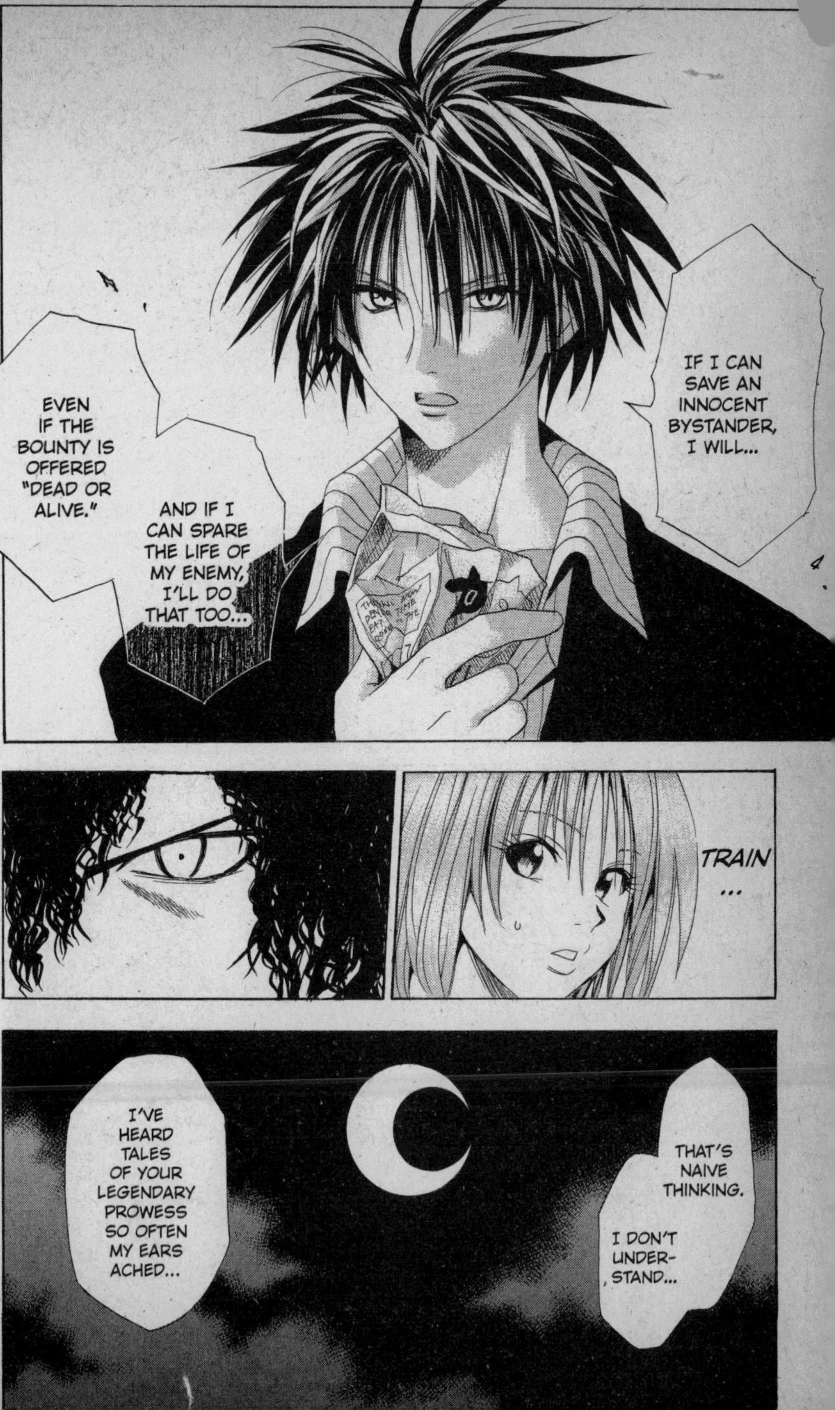
IF I CAN SAVE AN INNOCENT BYSTANDER, I WILL...
EVEN IF THE BOUNTY IS OFFERED "DEAD OR ALIVE."
AND IF I CAN SPARE THE LIFE OF MY ENEMY, I'LL DO THAT TOO...
TRAIN ...
THAT'S NAIVE THINKING.
I DON'T UNDER-STAND...
I'VE HEARD TALES OF YOUR LEGENDARY PROWESS SO OFTEN MY EARS ACHED...

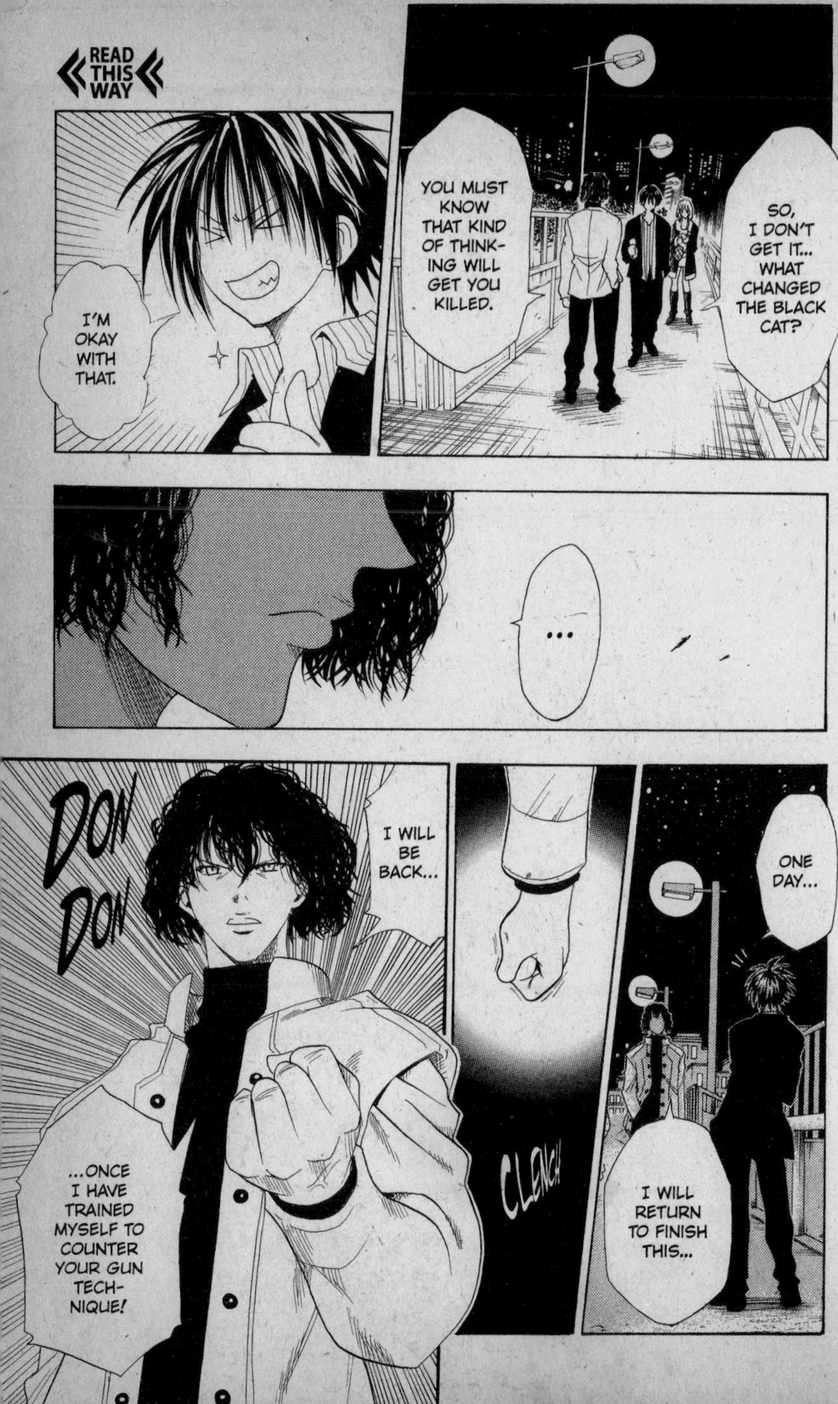
READ THIS WAY
SO, I DON'T GET IT... WHAT CHANGED THE BLACK CAT?
YOU MUST KNOW THAT KIND OF THINK-ING WILL GET YOU KILLED.
I'M OKAY WITH THAT.
...
ONE DAY...
I WILL RETURN TO FINISH THIS...
CLENCH
I WILL BE BACK...
...ONCE I HAVE TRAINED MYSELF TO COUNTER YOUR GUN TECH-NIQUE!
DON DON

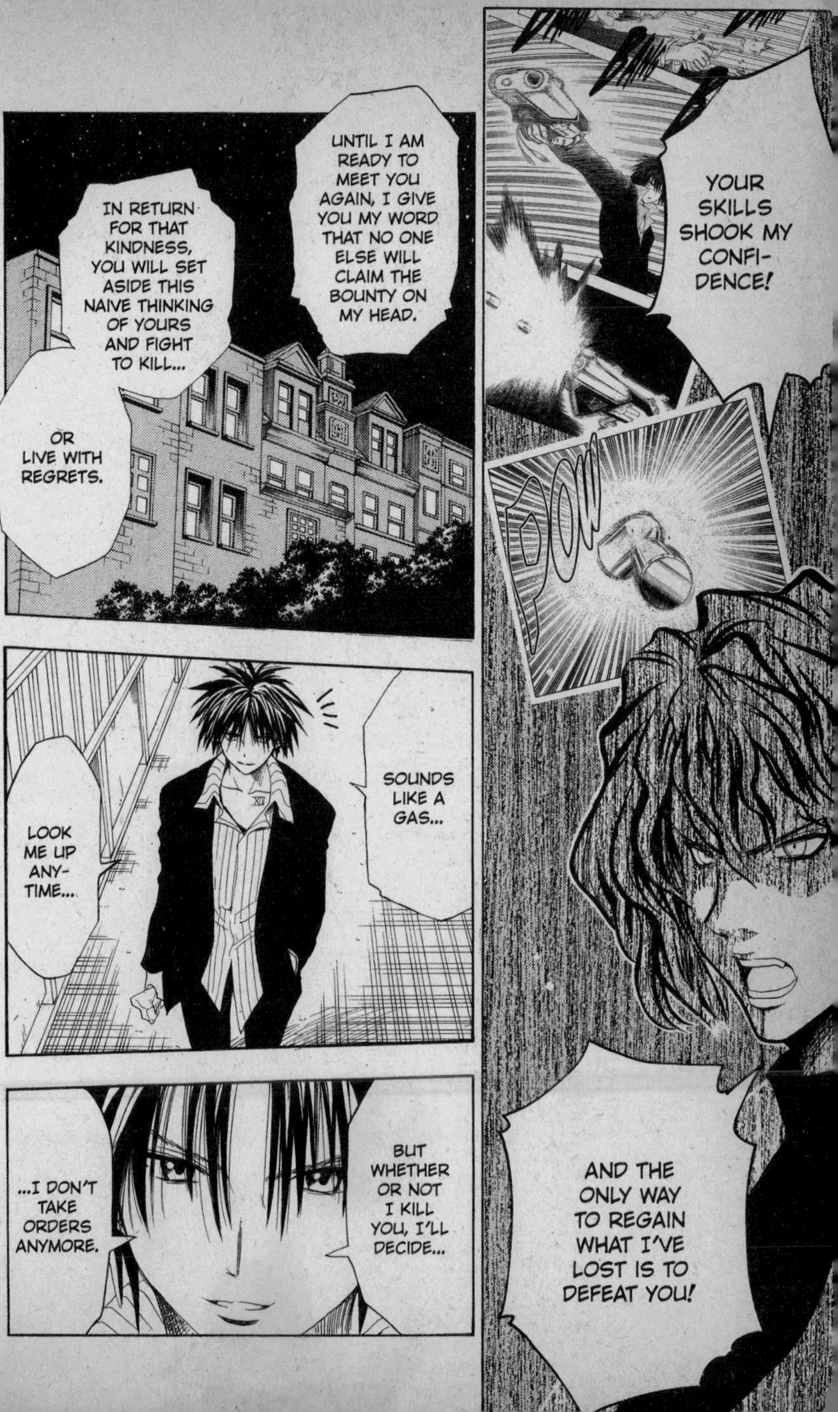
YOUR SKILLS SHOOK MY CONFI-DENCE!
POW
AND THE ONLY WAY TO REGAIN WHAT I'VE LOST IS TO DEFEAT YOU!
UNTIL I AM READY TO MEET YOU AGAIN, I GIVE YOU MY WORD THAT NO ONE ELSE WILL CLAIM THE BOUNTY ON MY HEAD.
IN RETURN FOR THAT KINDNESS, YOU WILL SET ASIDE THIS NAIVE THINKING OF YOURS AND FIGHT TO KILL...
OR LIVE WITH REGRETS.
SOUNDS LIKE A GAS...
LOOK ME UP ANY-TIME...
BUT WHETHER OR NOT I KILL YOU, I'LL DECIDE...
...I DON'T TAKE ORDERS ANYMORE.

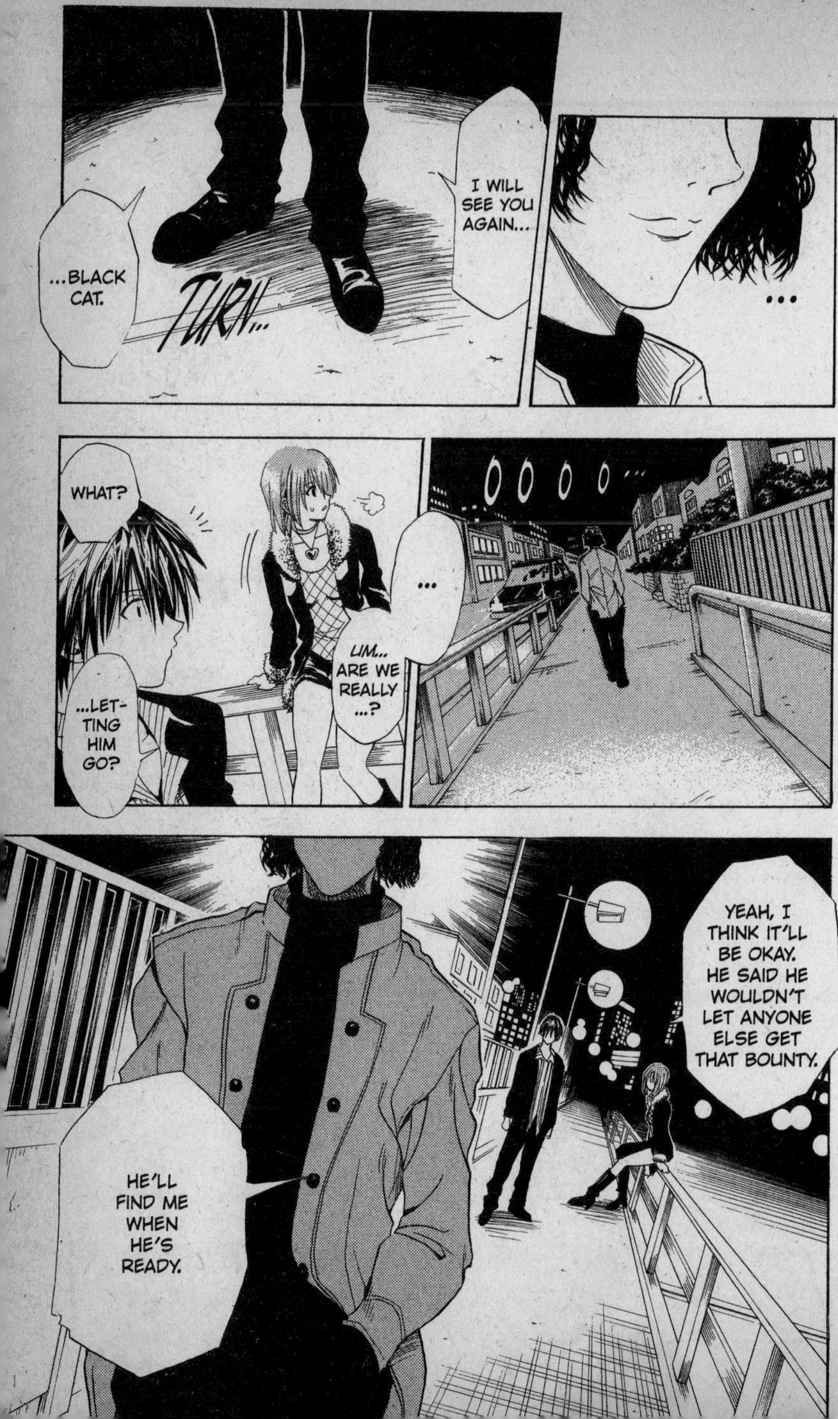
...
I WILL SEE YOU AGAIN...
TURN...
...BLACK CAT.
...
UM... ARE WE REALLY ...?
WHAT?
...LET-TING HIM GO?
YEAH, I THINK IT'LL BE OKAY. HE SAID HE WOULDN'T LET ANYONE ELSE GET THAT BOUNTY.
HE'LL FIND ME WHEN HE'S READY.

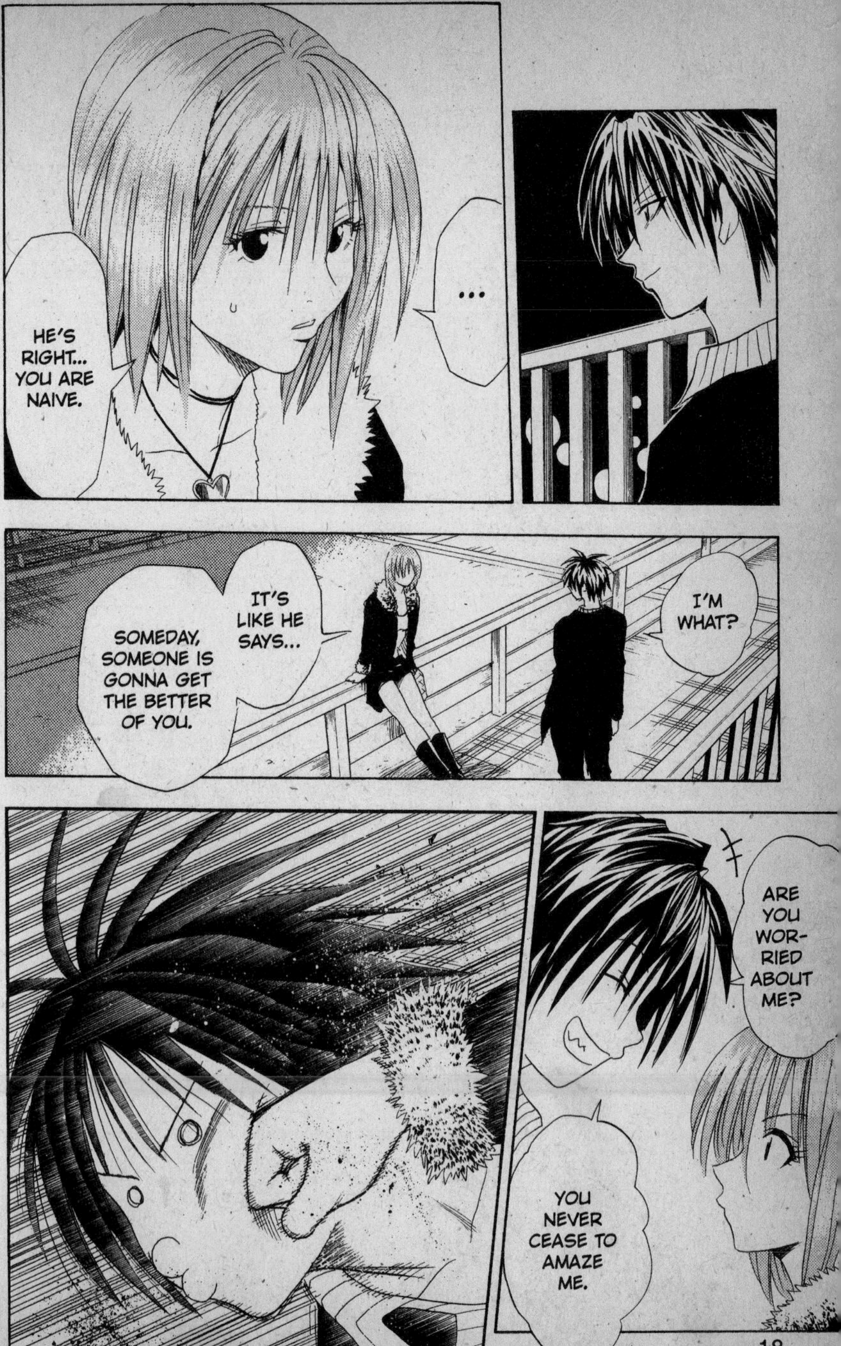
...
HE'S RIGHT... YOU ARE NAIVE.
I'M WHAT?
IT'S LIKE HE SAYS...
SOMEDAY, SOMEONE IS GONNA GET THE BETTER OF YOU.
ARE YOU WOR-RIED ABOUT ME?
YOU NEVER CEASE TO AMAZE ME.

READ THIS WAY

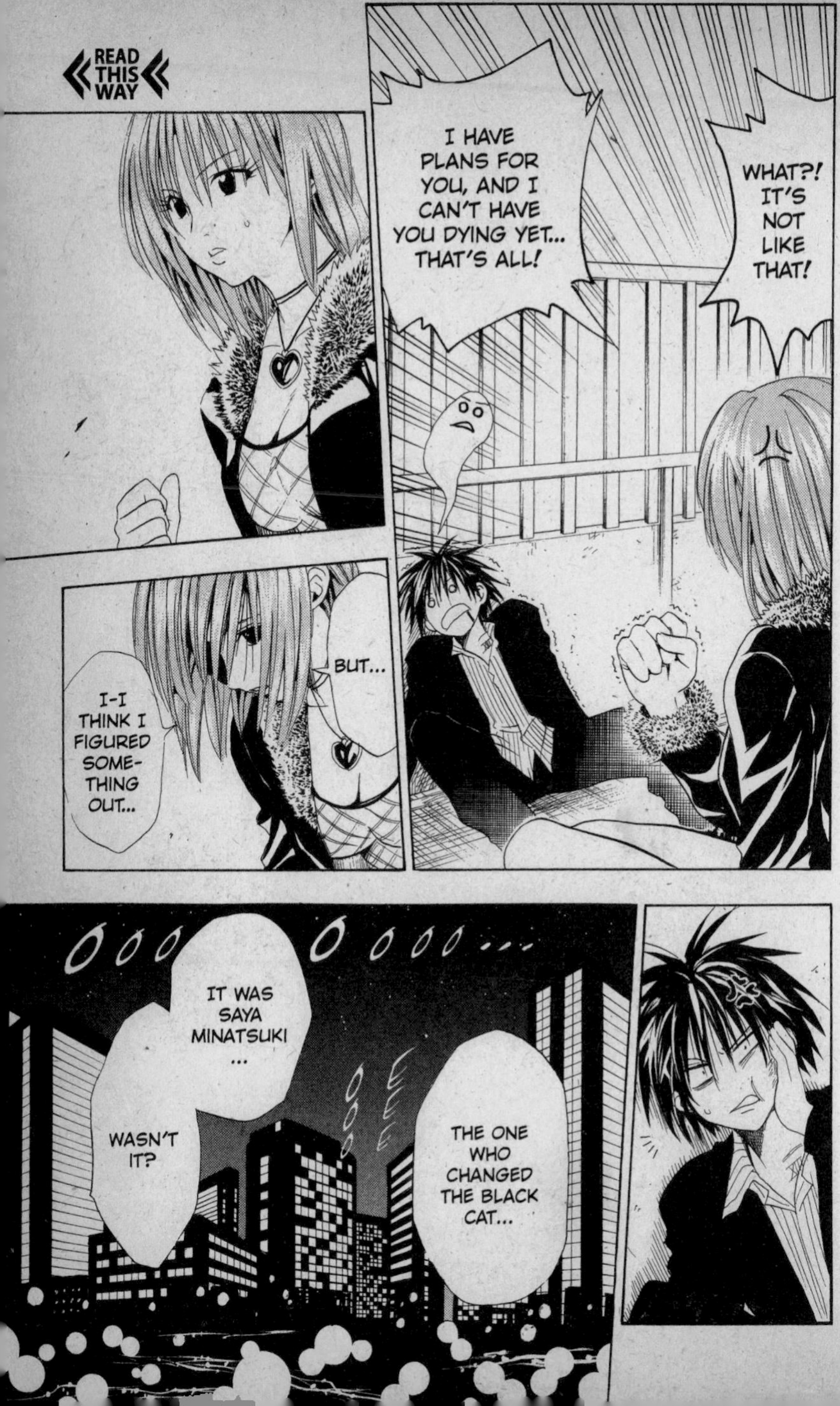
WHAT?! IT'S NOT LIKE THAT!
I HAVE PLANS FOR YOU, AND I CAN'T HAVE YOU DYING YET... THAT'S ALL!
BUT...
I-I THINK I FIGURED SOME-THING OUT...
OOO OOOO...
IT WAS SAYA MINATSUKI ...
THE ONE WHO CHANGED THE BLACK CAT...
WASN'T IT?

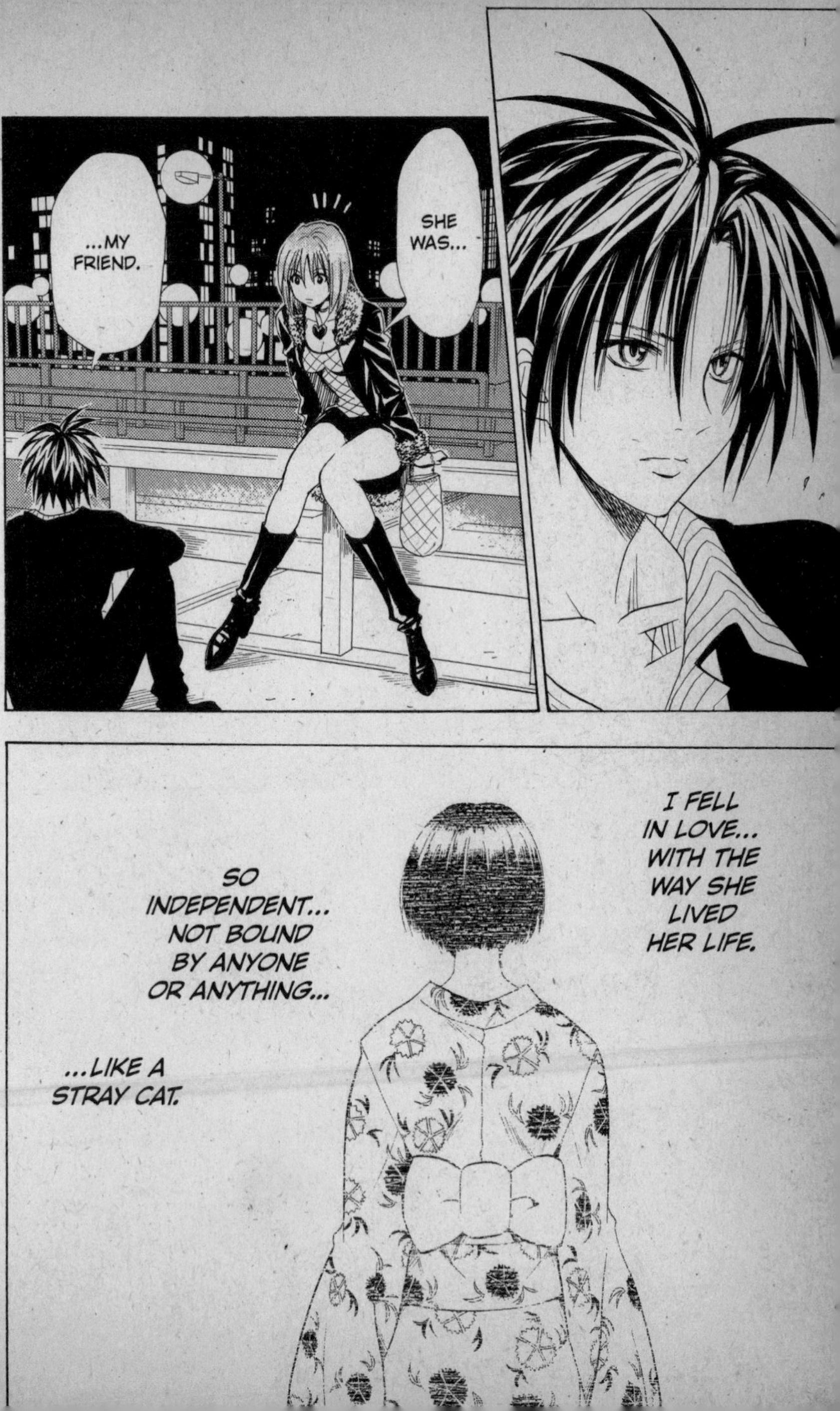
SHE WAS...
...MY FRIEND.
I FELL IN LOVE... WITH THE WAY SHE LIVED HER LIFE.
SO INDEPENDENT... NOT BOUND BY ANYONE OR ANYTHING...
...LIKE A STRAY CAT.

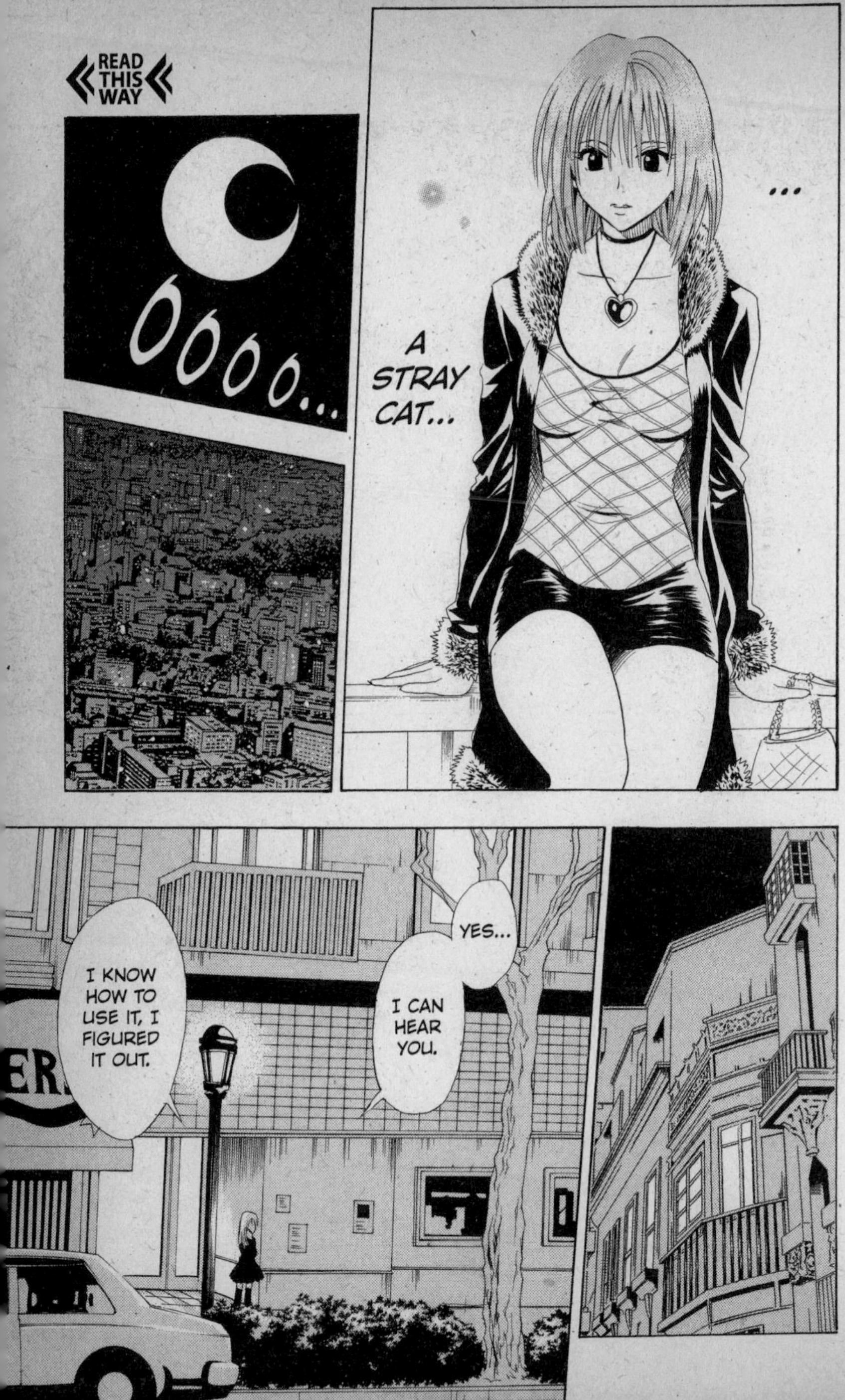
READ THIS WAY
...
A STRAY CAT...
OOOO...
YES...
I CAN HEAR YOU.
I KNOW HOW TO USE IT, I FIGURED IT OUT.

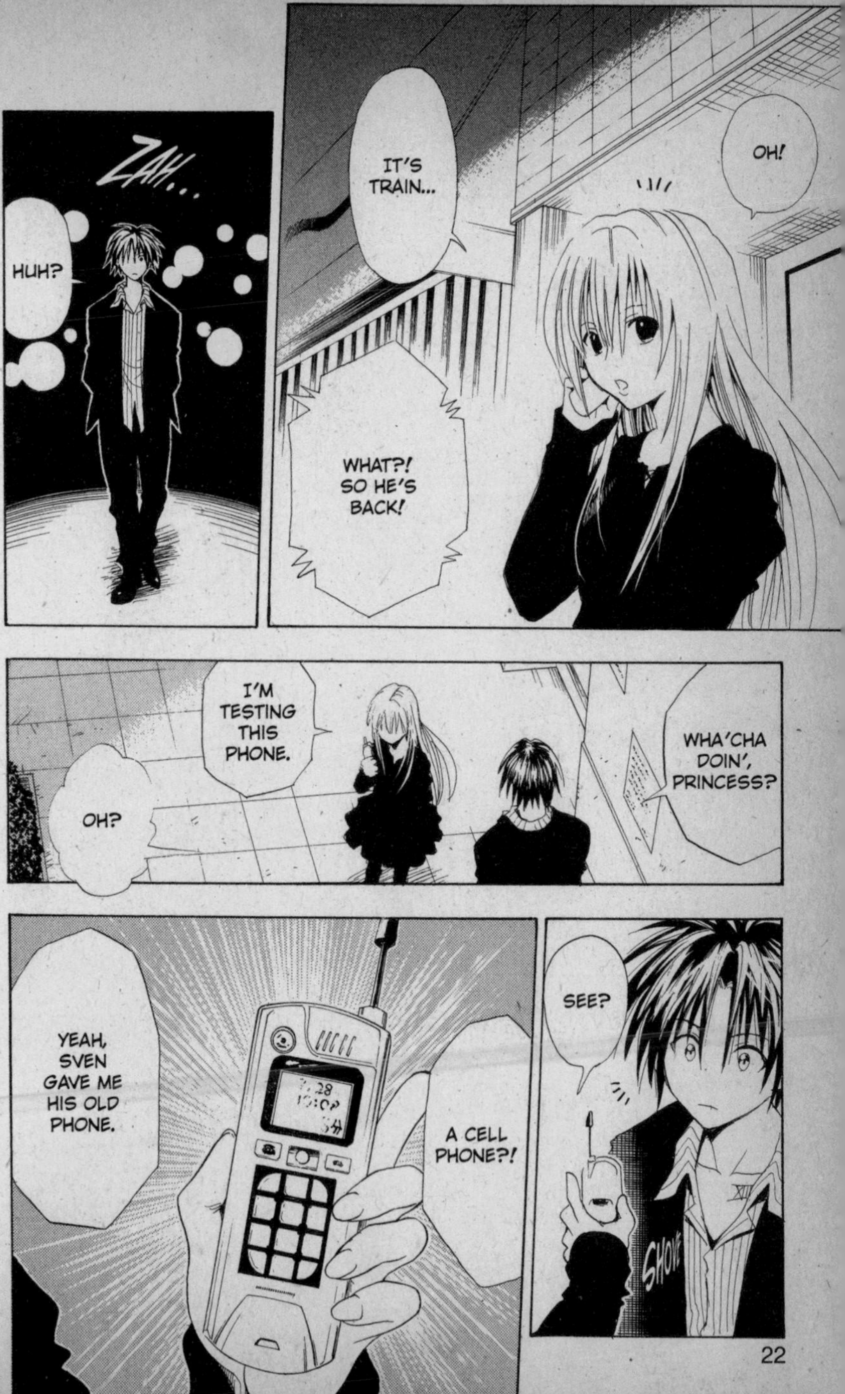
OH!
IT'S TRAIN...
WHAT?! SO HE'S BACK!
ZAH...
HUH?
WHA'CHA DOIN', PRINCESS?
I'M TESTING THIS PHONE.
OH?
SEE?
A CELL PHONE?!
YEAH, SVEN GAVE ME HIS OLD PHONE.

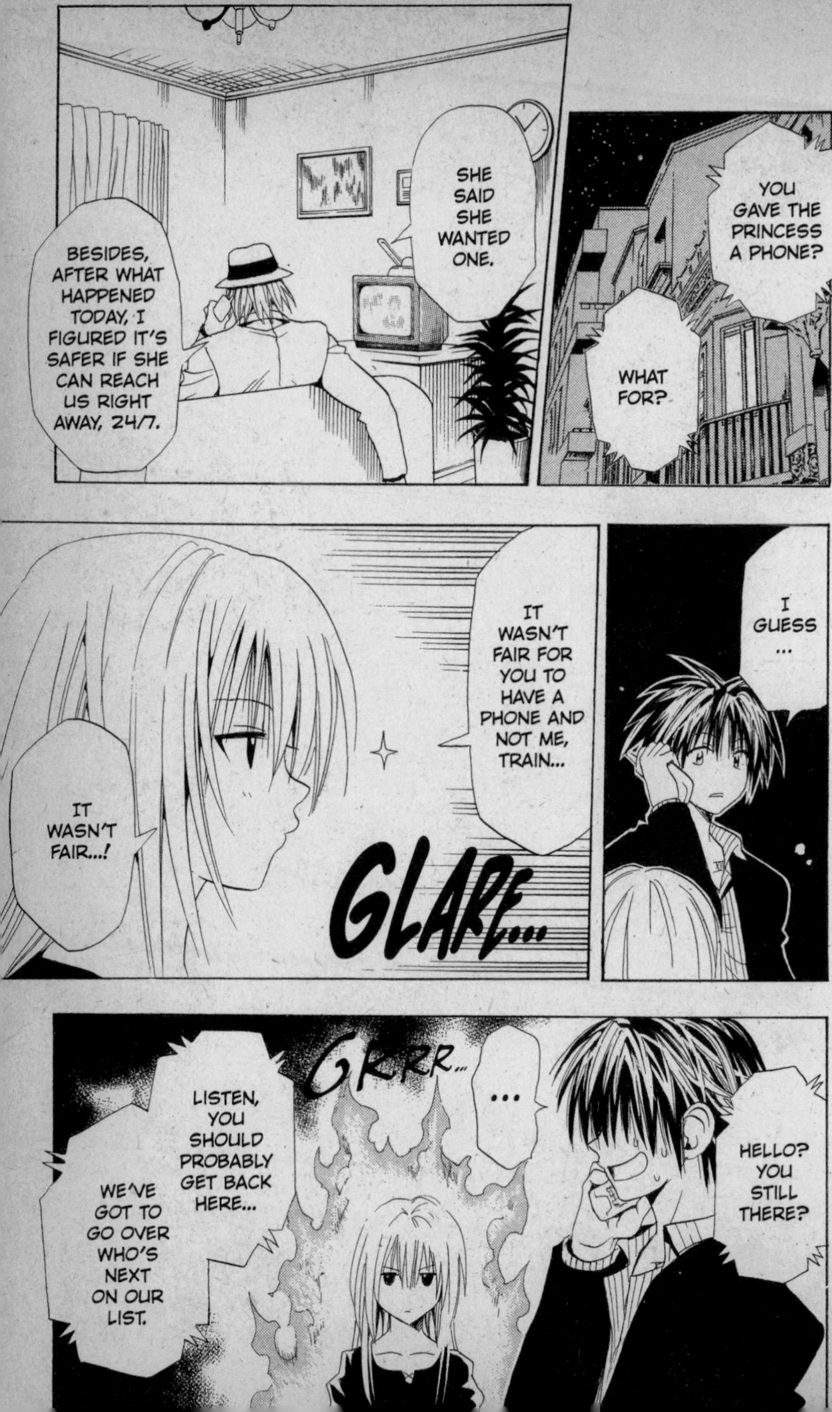
YOU GAVE THE PRINCESS A PHONE?
WHAT FOR?
SHE SAID SHE WANTED ONE.
BESIDES, AFTER WHAT HAPPENED TODAY, I FIGURED IT'S SAFER IF SHE CAN REACH US RIGHT AWAY, 24/7.
I GUESS...
IT WASN'T FAIR FOR YOU TO HAVE A PHONE AND NOT ME, TRAIN...
IT WASN'T FAIR...!
GLARE...
HELLO? YOU STILL THERE?
...
GRRR...
LISTEN, YOU SHOULD PROBABLY GET BACK HERE...
WE'VE GOT TO GO OVER WHO'S NEXT ON OUR LIST.

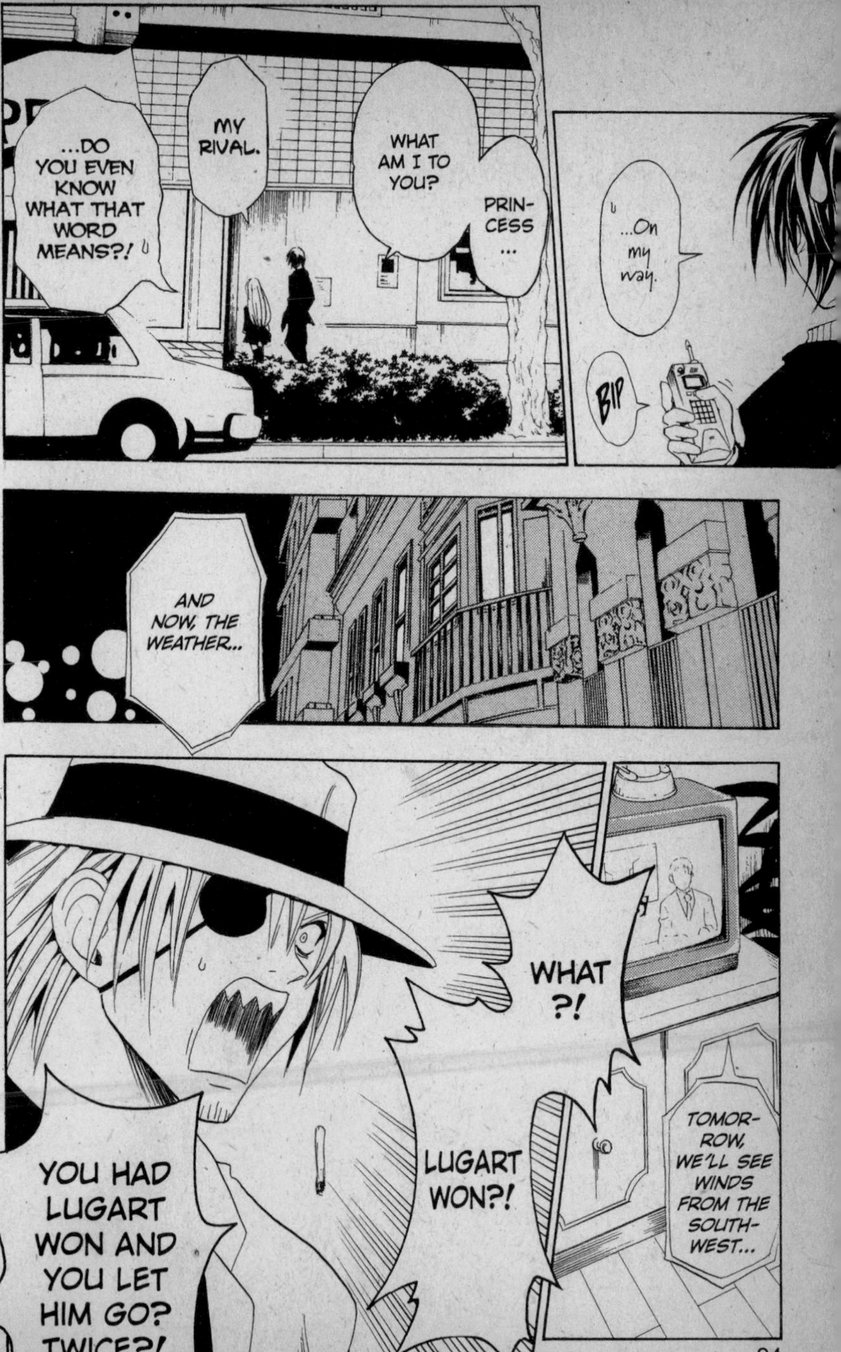
...On my way.
BIP
PRINCESS...
WHAT AM I TO YOU?
MY RIVAL.
...DO YOU EVEN KNOW WHAT THAT WORD MEANS?!
AND NOW, THE WEATHER...
TOMORROW, WE'LL SEE WINDS FROM THE SOUTHWEST...
WHAT?!
LUGART WON?!
YOU HAD LUGART WON AND YOU LET HIM GO? TWICE?!

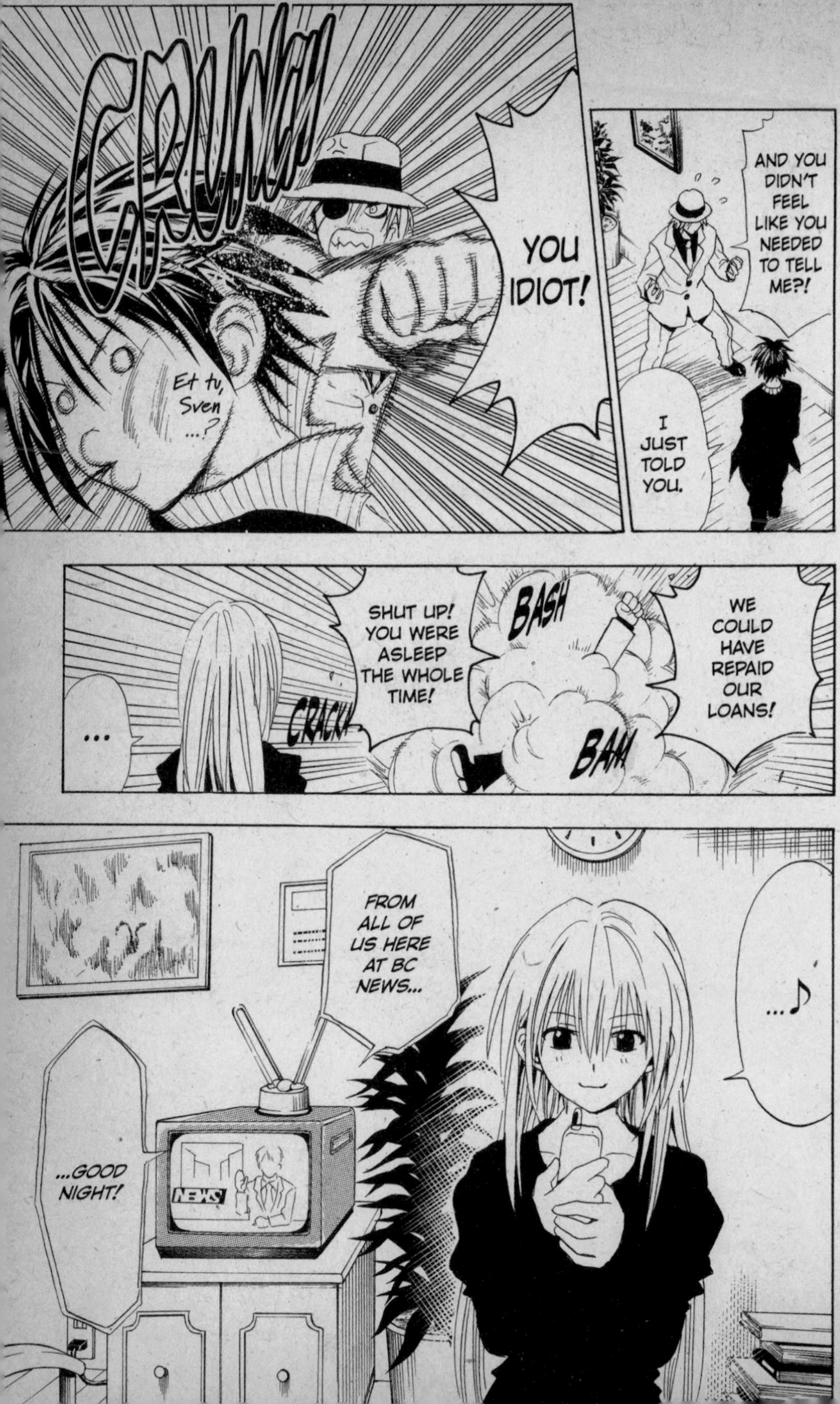

AND YOU DIDN'T FEEL LIKE YOU NEEDED TO TELL ME?!
I JUST TOLD YOU.
CRUNCH
YOU IDIOT!
Et tu, Sven ...?
WE COULD HAVE REPAID OUR LOANS!
BASH
BAM
SHUT UP! YOU WERE ASLEEP THE WHOLE TIME!
CRACK
...
...♪
FROM ALL OF US HERE AT BC NEWS...
NEWS
...GOOD NIGHT!

SKETCH NO. 1

◎ KYOKO IN THE OUTFIT ASHI REQUESTED.
I LIKE SKETCHING KYOKO IN CASUAL MODE.

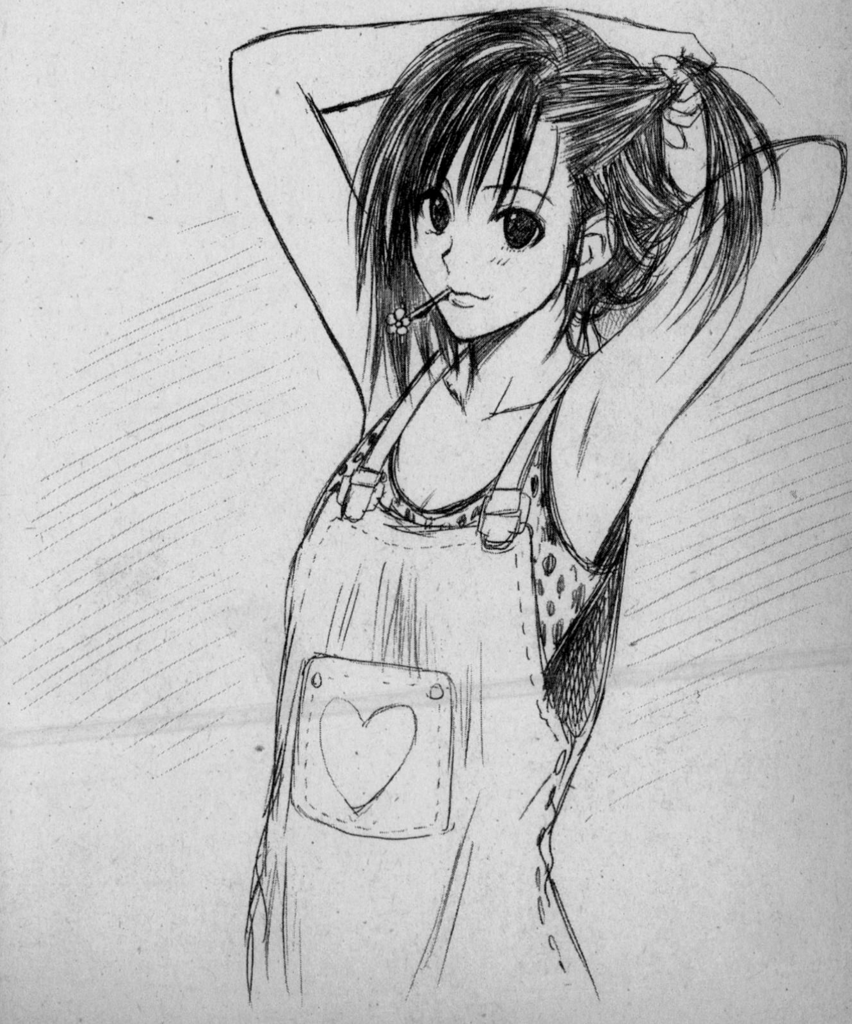

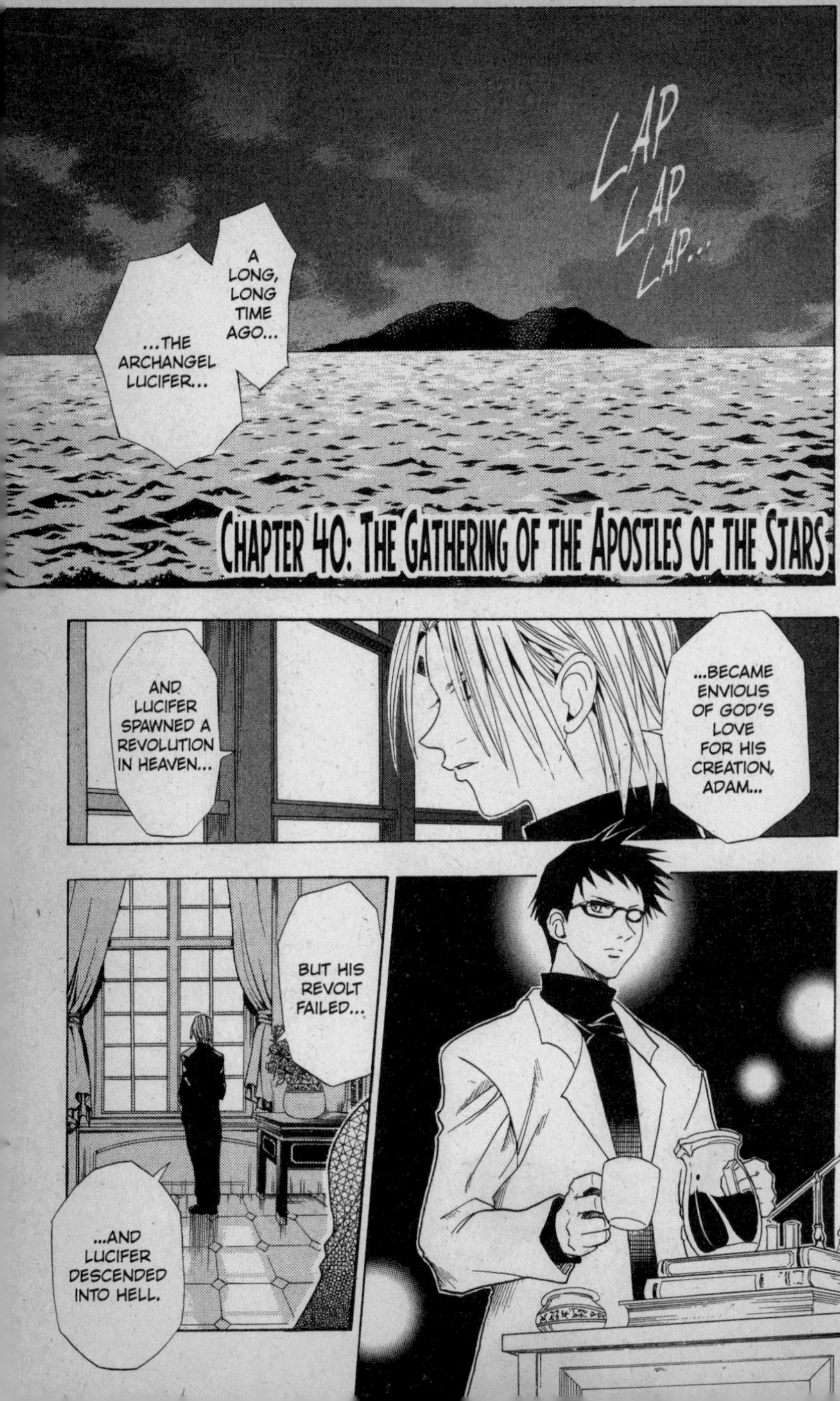
LAP LAP LAP...
A LONG, LONG TIME AGO...
...THE ARCHANGEL LUCIFER...
CHAPTER 40: THE GATHERING OF THE APOSTLES OF THE STARS
...BECAME ENVIOUS OF GOD'S LOVE FOR HIS CREATION, ADAM...
AND LUCIFER SPAWNED A REVOLUTION IN HEAVEN...
BUT HIS REVOLT FAILED...
...AND LUCIFER DESCENDED INTO HELL.

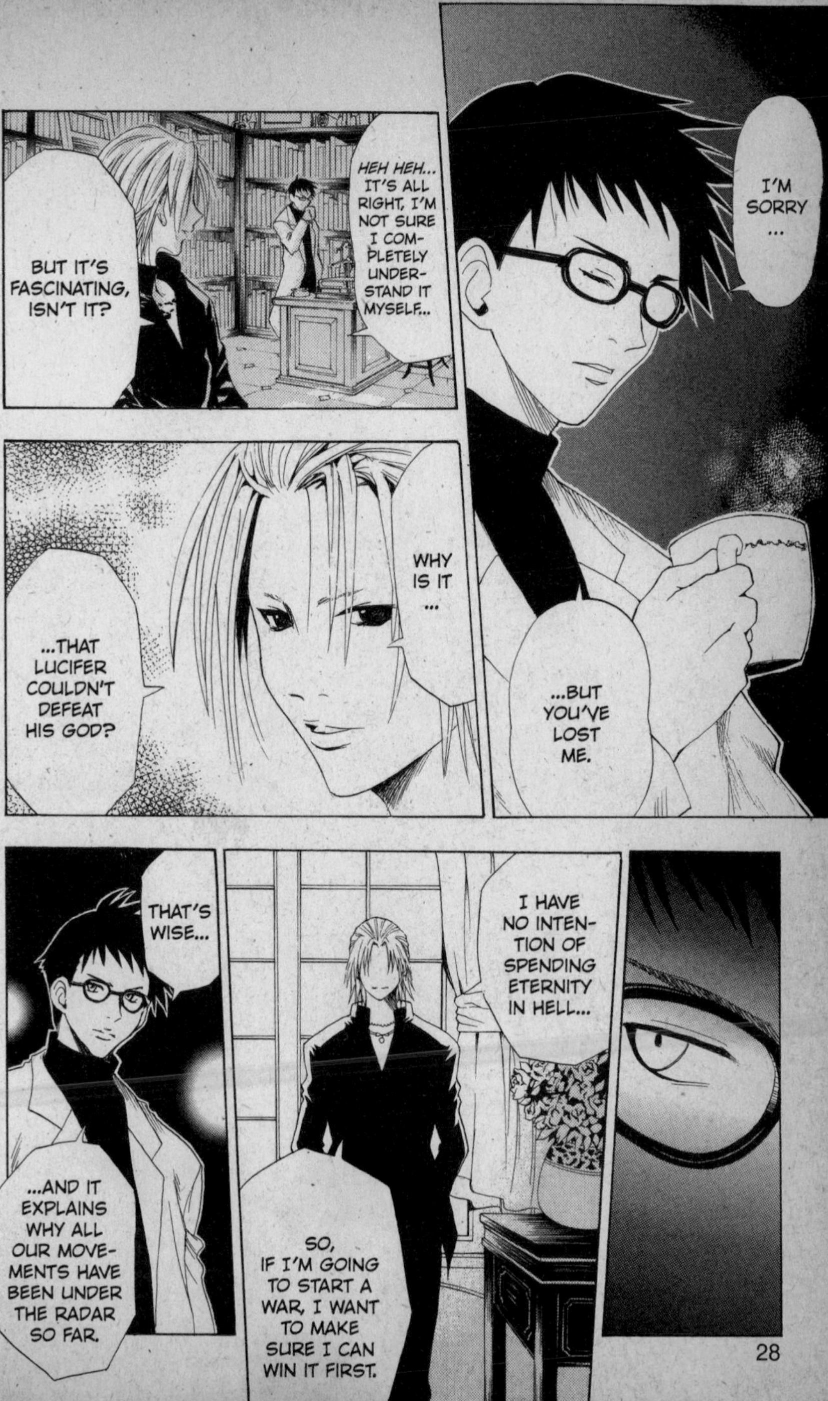
I'M SORRY...
...BUT YOU'VE LOST ME.
HEH HEH... IT'S ALL RIGHT, I'M NOT SURE I COMPLETELY UNDERSTAND IT MYSELF...
BUT IT'S FASCINATING, ISN'T IT?
WHY IS IT...
...THAT LUCIFER COULDN'T DEFEAT HIS GOD?
I HAVE NO INTENTION OF SPENDING ETERNITY IN HELL...
SO, IF I'M GOING TO START A WAR, I WANT TO MAKE SURE I CAN WIN IT FIRST.
THAT'S WISE...
...AND IT EXPLAINS WHY ALL OUR MOVEMENTS HAVE BEEN UNDER THE RADAR SO FAR.

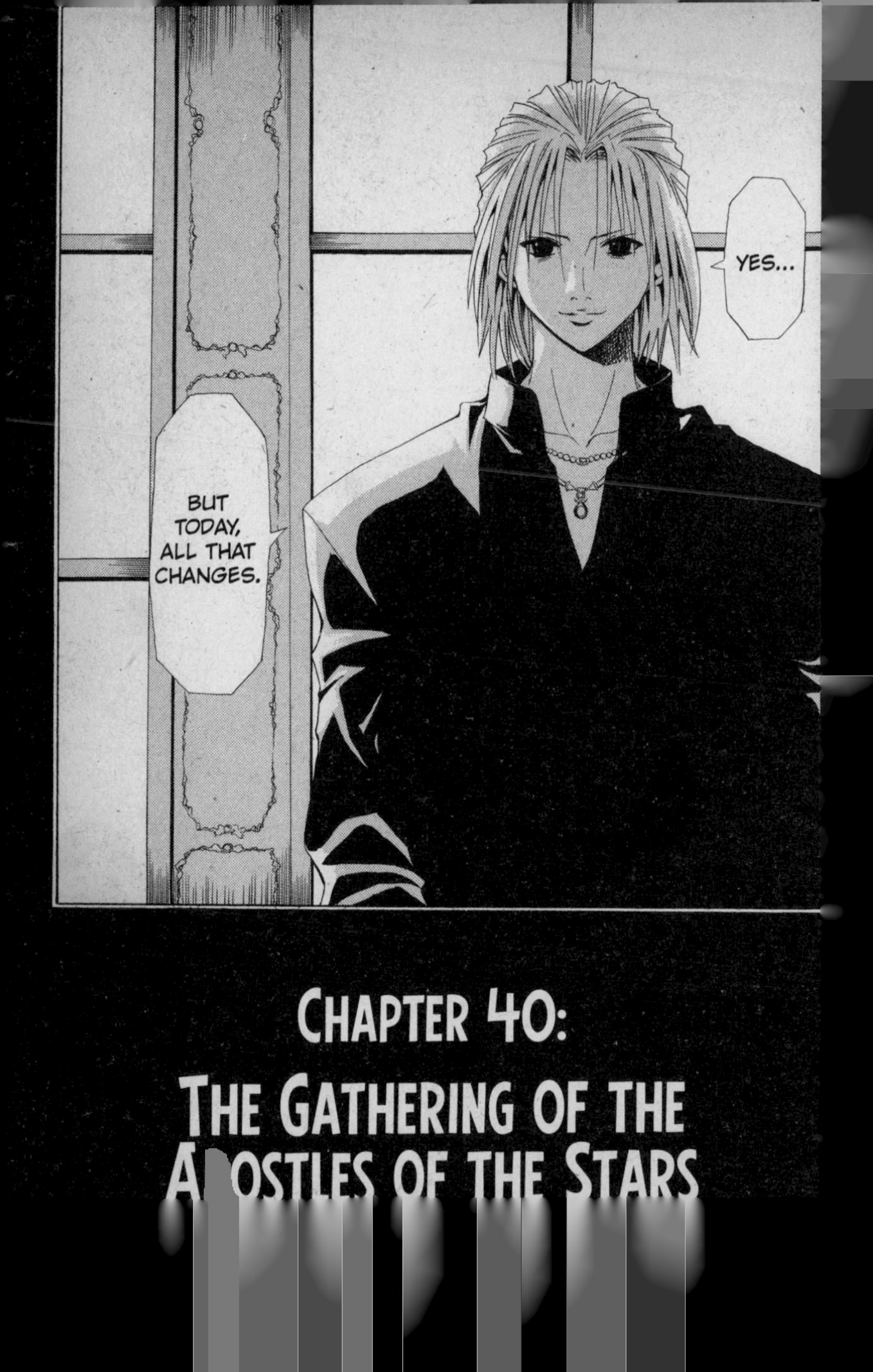
YES...
BUT TODAY, ALL THAT CHANGES.

Chapter 40:

The Gathering of the Apostles of the Stars

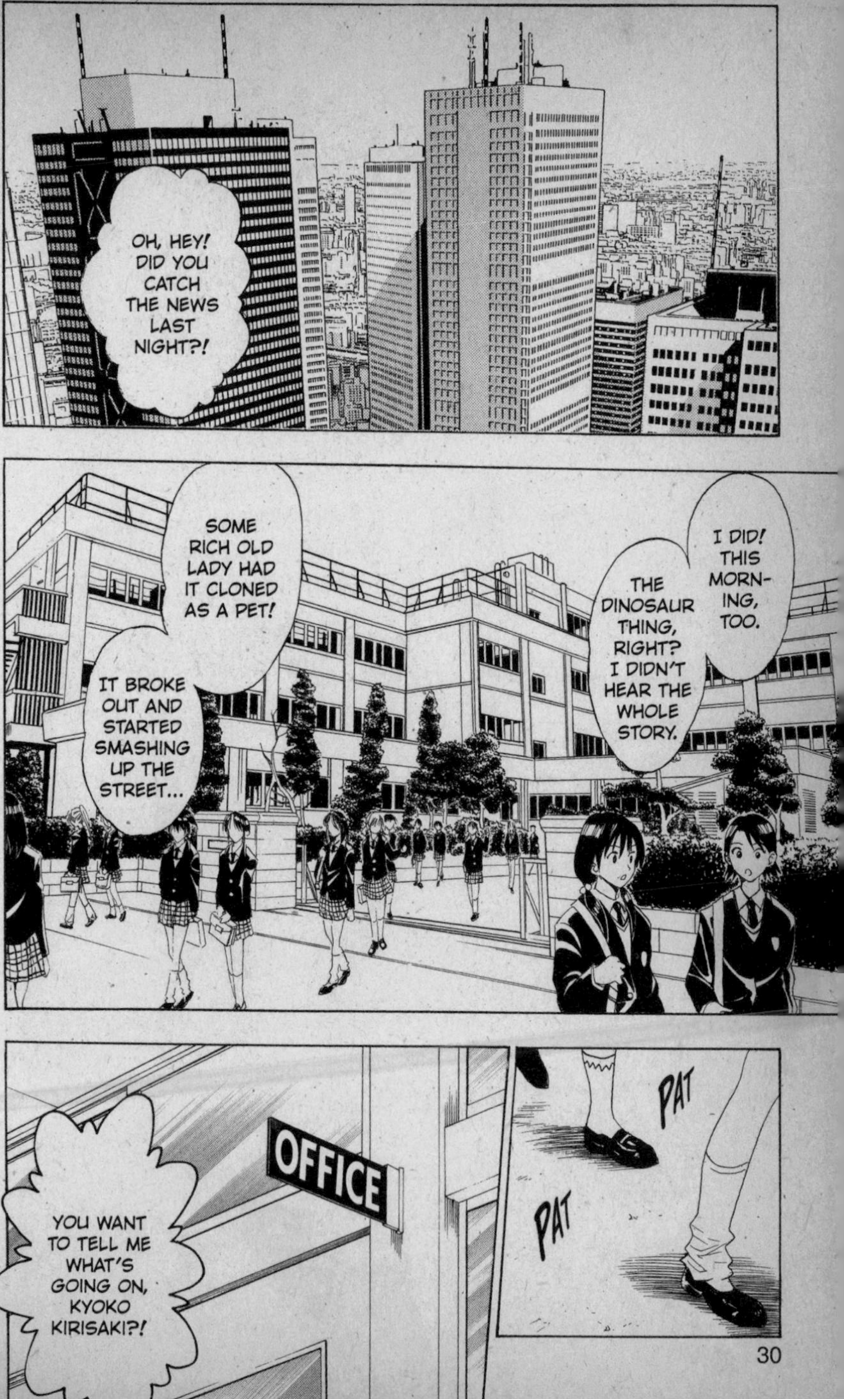
OH, HEY! DID YOU CATCH THE NEWS LAST NIGHT?!
I DID! THIS MORN-ING, TOO.
THE DINOSAUR THING, RIGHT? I DIDN'T HEAR THE WHOLE STORY.
SOME RICH OLD LADY HAD IT CLONED AS A PET!
IT BROKE OUT AND STARTED SMASHING UP THE STREET...
PAT
PAT
OFFICE
YOU WANT TO TELL ME WHAT'S GOING ON, KYOKO KIRISAKI?!

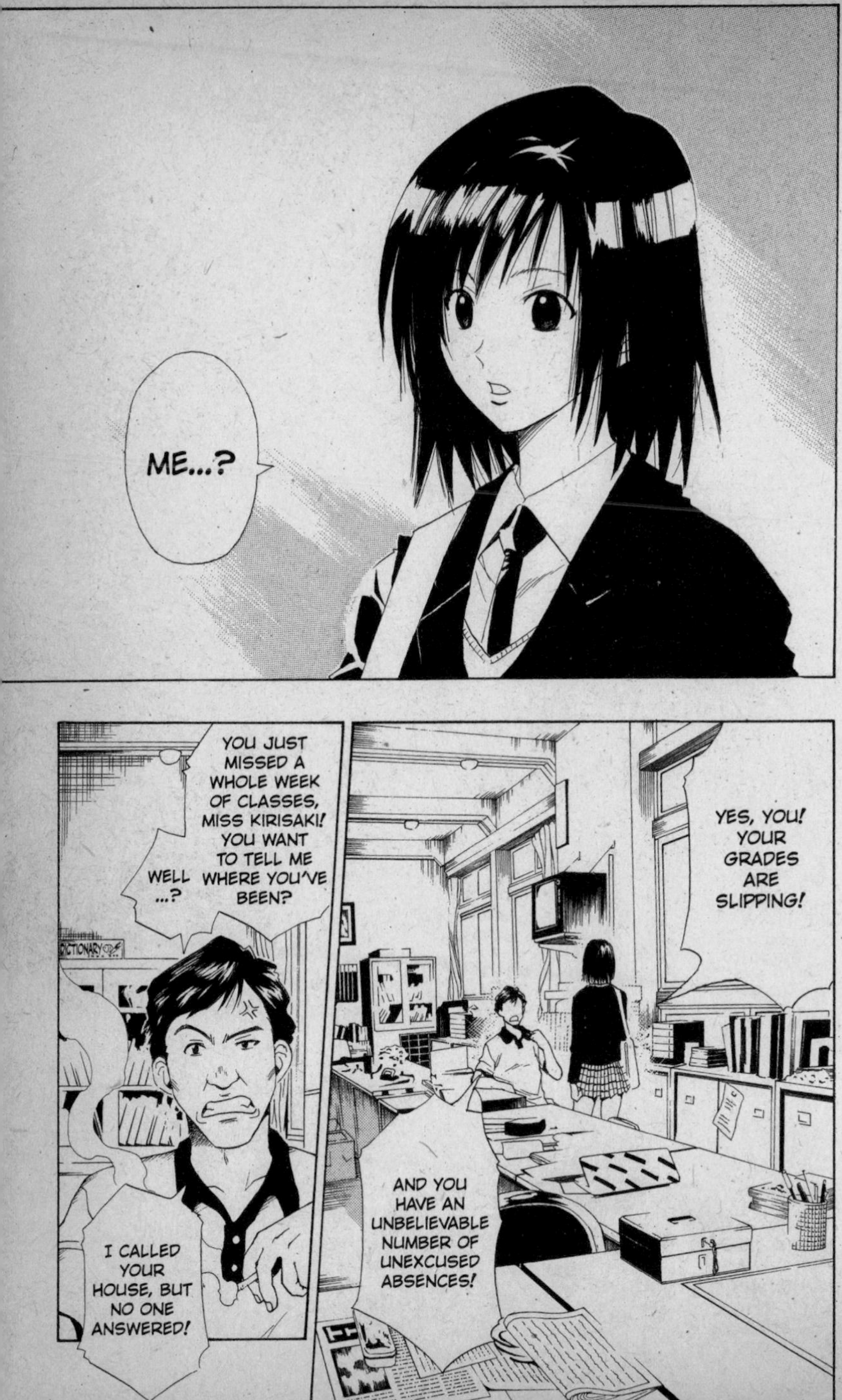
ME...?
YES, YOU! YOUR GRADES ARE SLIPPING!
AND YOU HAVE AN UNBELIEVABLE NUMBER OF UNEXCUSED ABSENCES!
YOU JUST MISSED A WHOLE WEEK OF CLASSES, MISS KIRISAKI! YOU WANT TO TELL ME WHERE YOU'VE BEEN?
WELL ...?
I CALLED YOUR HOUSE, BUT NO ONE ANSWERED!

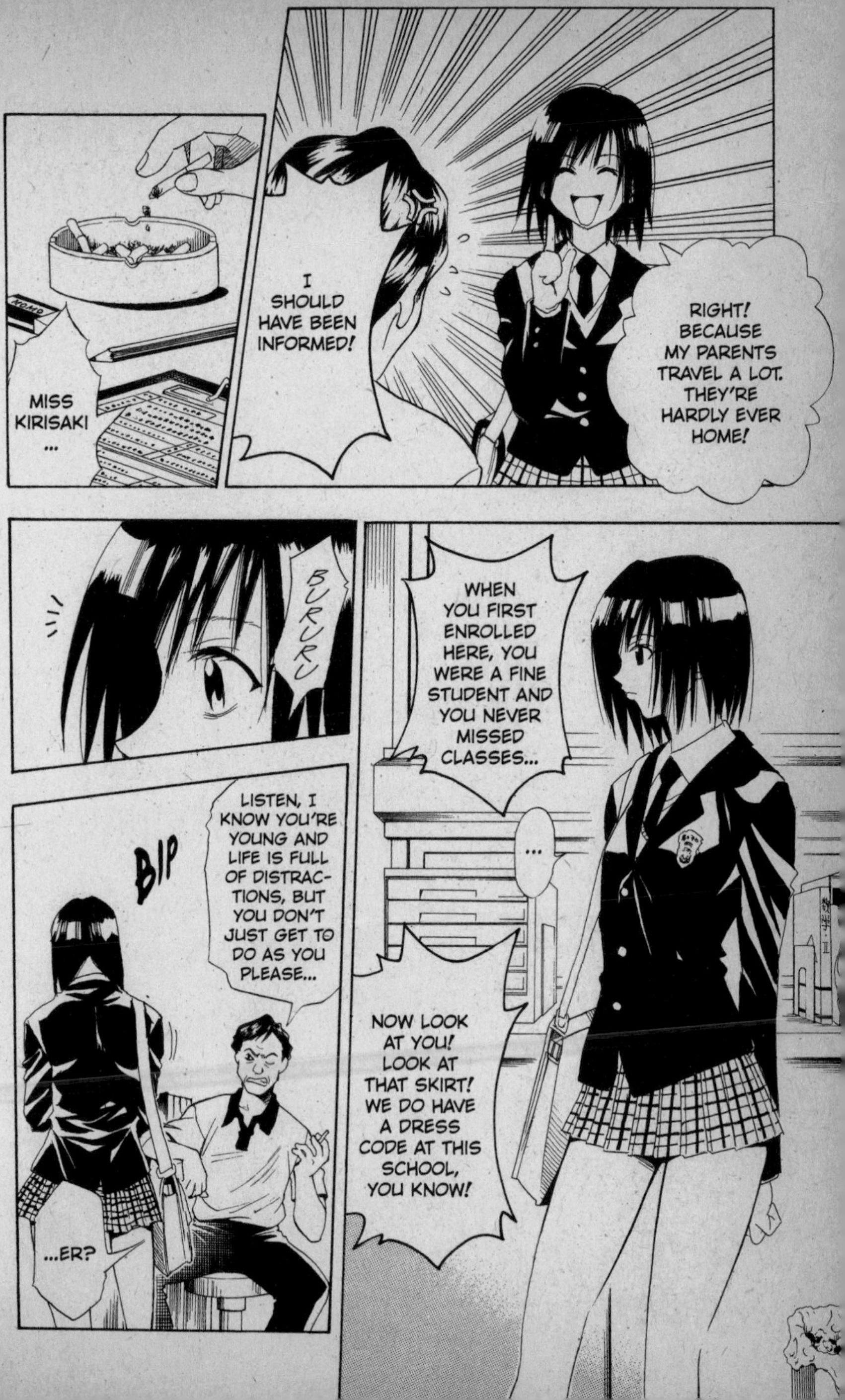
RIGHT! BECAUSE MY PARENTS TRAVEL A LOT. THEY'RE HARDLY EVER HOME!
I SHOULD HAVE BEEN INFORMED!
MISS KIRISAKI ...
WHEN YOU FIRST ENROLLED HERE, YOU WERE A FINE STUDENT AND YOU NEVER MISSED CLASSES...
...
NOW LOOK AT YOU! LOOK AT THAT SKIRT! WE DO HAVE A DRESS CODE AT THIS SCHOOL, YOU KNOW!
BURURU
LISTEN, I KNOW YOU'RE YOUNG AND LIFE IS FULL OF DISTRAC-TIONS, BUT YOU DON'T JUST GET TO DO AS YOU PLEASE...
BIP
...ER?

READ THIS WAY

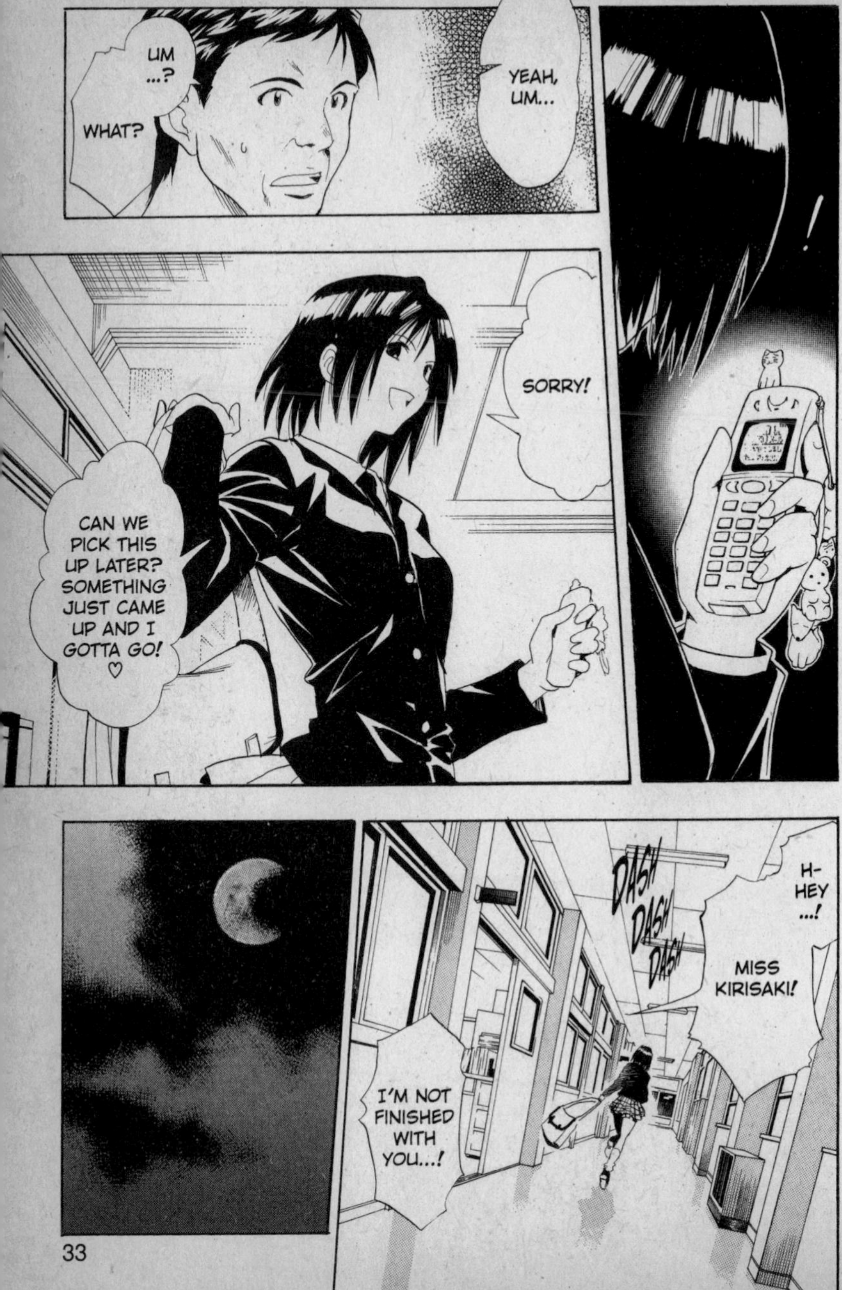
!
YEAH, UM...
UM ...?
WHAT?
SORRY!
CAN WE PICK THIS UP LATER? SOMETHING JUST CAME UP AND I GOTTA GO! ♡
DASH DASH DASH
H-HEY ...!
MISS KIRISAKI!
I'M NOT FINISHED WITH YOU...!

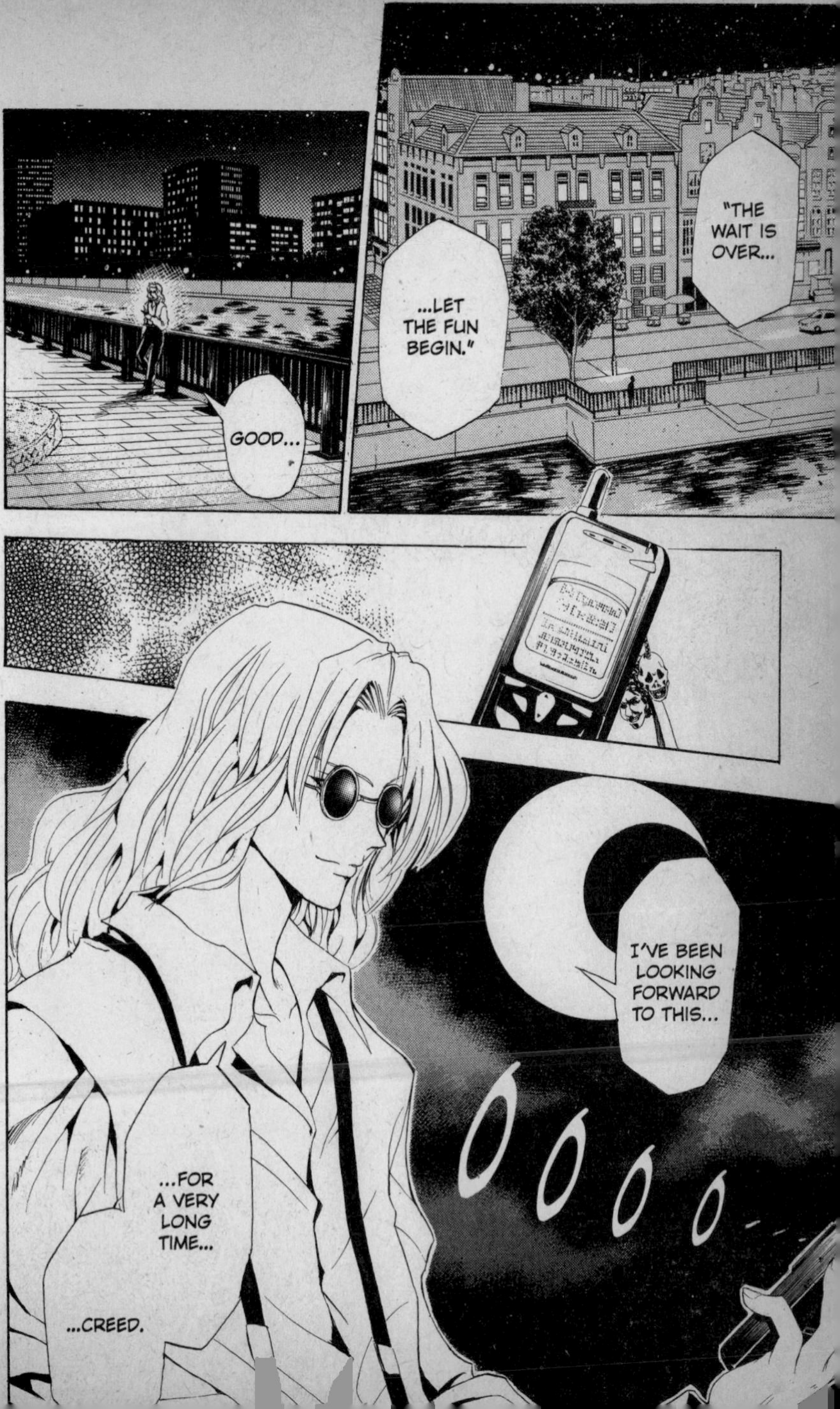
"THE WAIT IS OVER...
...LET THE FUN BEGIN."
GOOD...
I'VE BEEN LOOKING FORWARD TO THIS...
...FOR A VERY LONG TIME...
...CREED.

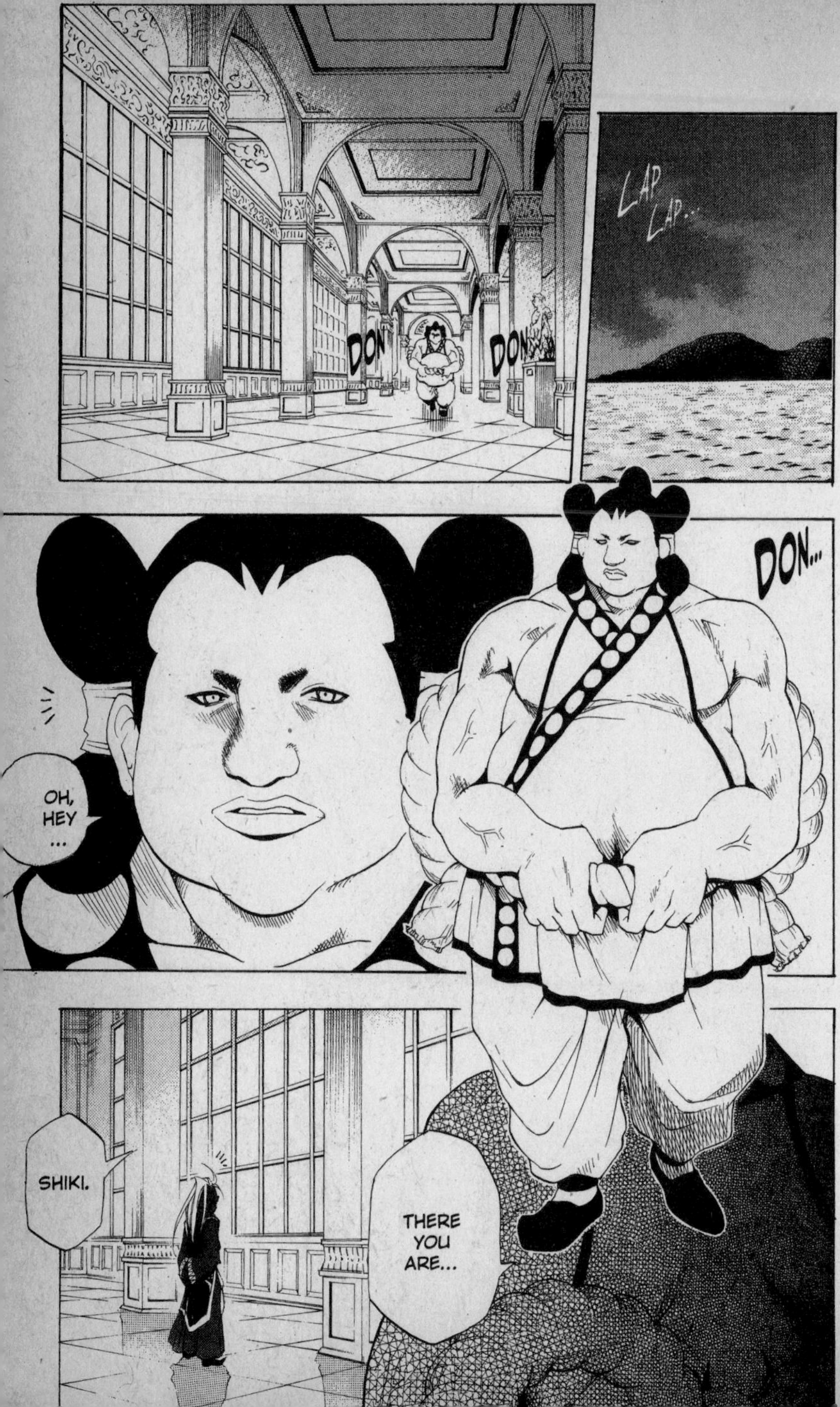

LAP LAP...
DON
DON
DON...
OH, HEY ...
THERE YOU ARE...
SHIKI.

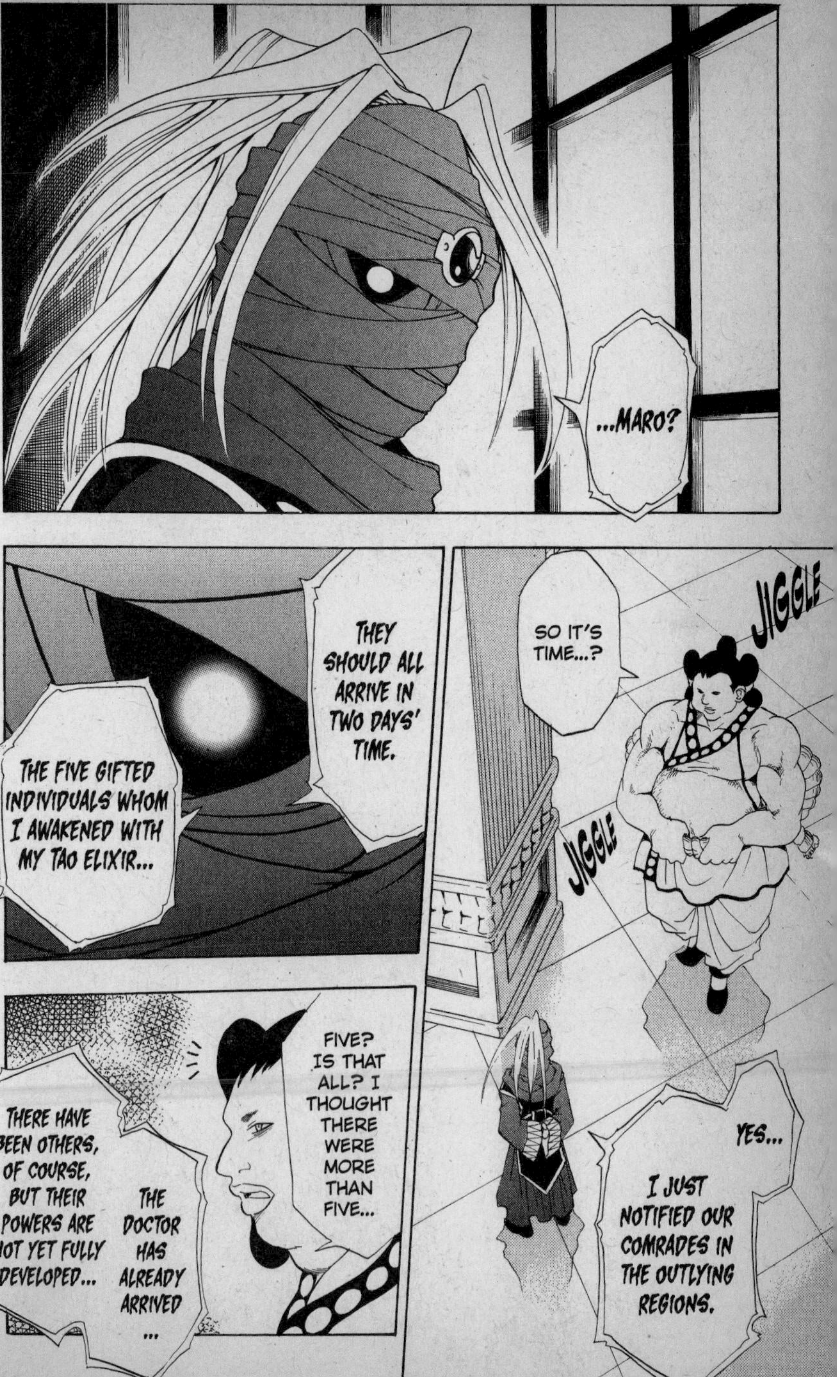
...MARO?
SO IT'S TIME...?
JIGGLE
JIGGLE
YES...
I JUST NOTIFIED OUR COMRADES IN THE OUTLYING REGIONS.
THE FIVE GIFTED INDIVIDUALS WHOM I AWAKENED WITH MY TAO ELIXIR...
THEY SHOULD ALL ARRIVE IN TWO DAYS' TIME.
FIVE? IS THAT ALL? I THOUGHT THERE WERE MORE THAN FIVE...
THERE HAVE BEEN OTHERS, OF COURSE, BUT THEIR POWERS ARE NOT YET FULLY DEVELOPED...
THE DOCTOR HAS ALREADY ARRIVED...

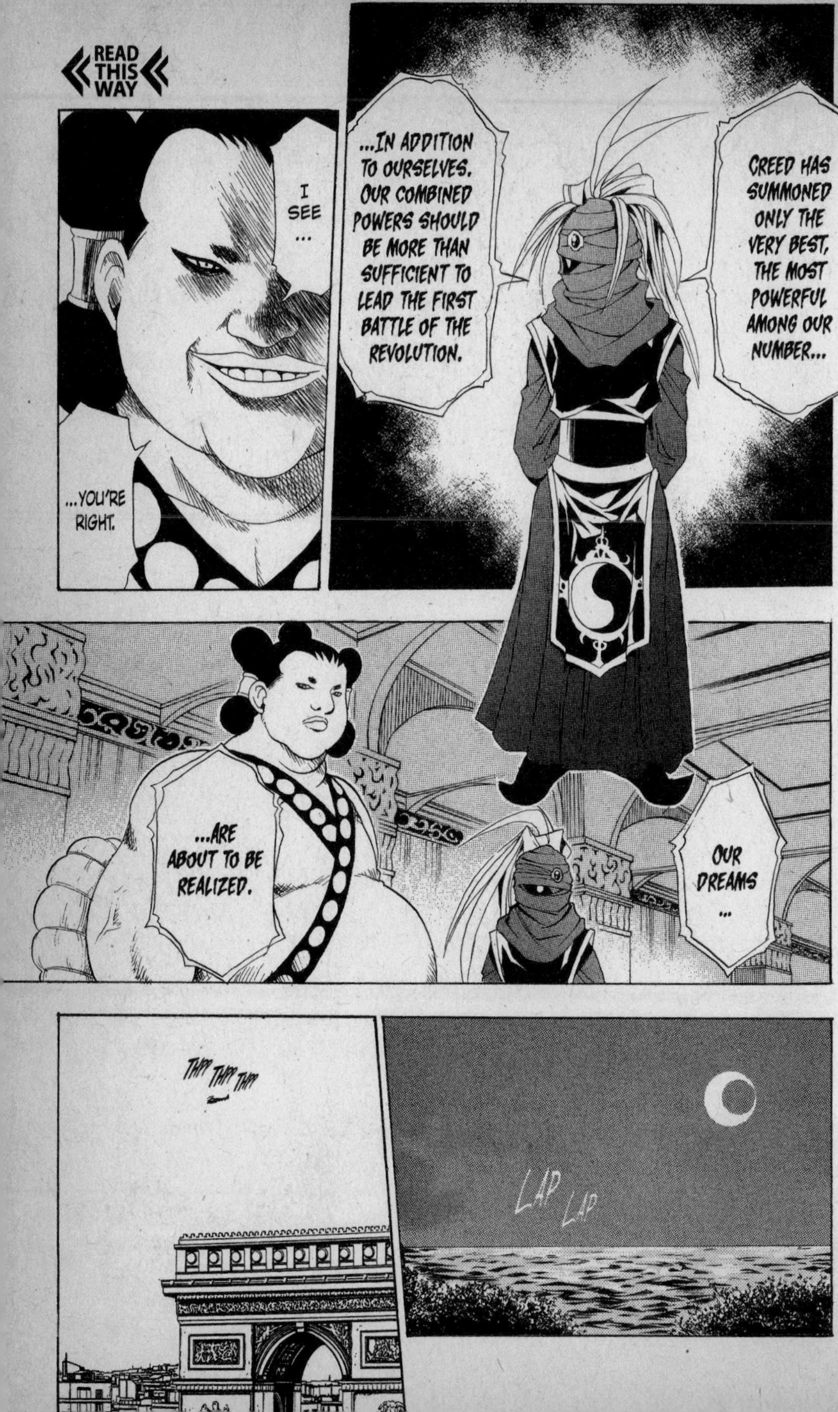
READ THIS WAY
CREED HAS SUMMONED ONLY THE VERY BEST, THE MOST POWERFUL AMONG OUR NUMBER...
...IN ADDITION TO OURSELVES. OUR COMBINED POWERS SHOULD BE MORE THAN SUFFICIENT TO LEAD THE FIRST BATTLE OF THE REVOLUTION.
I SEE ...
...YOU'RE RIGHT.
OUR DREAMS ...
...ARE ABOUT TO BE REALIZED.
LAP LAP
THPP THPP THPP

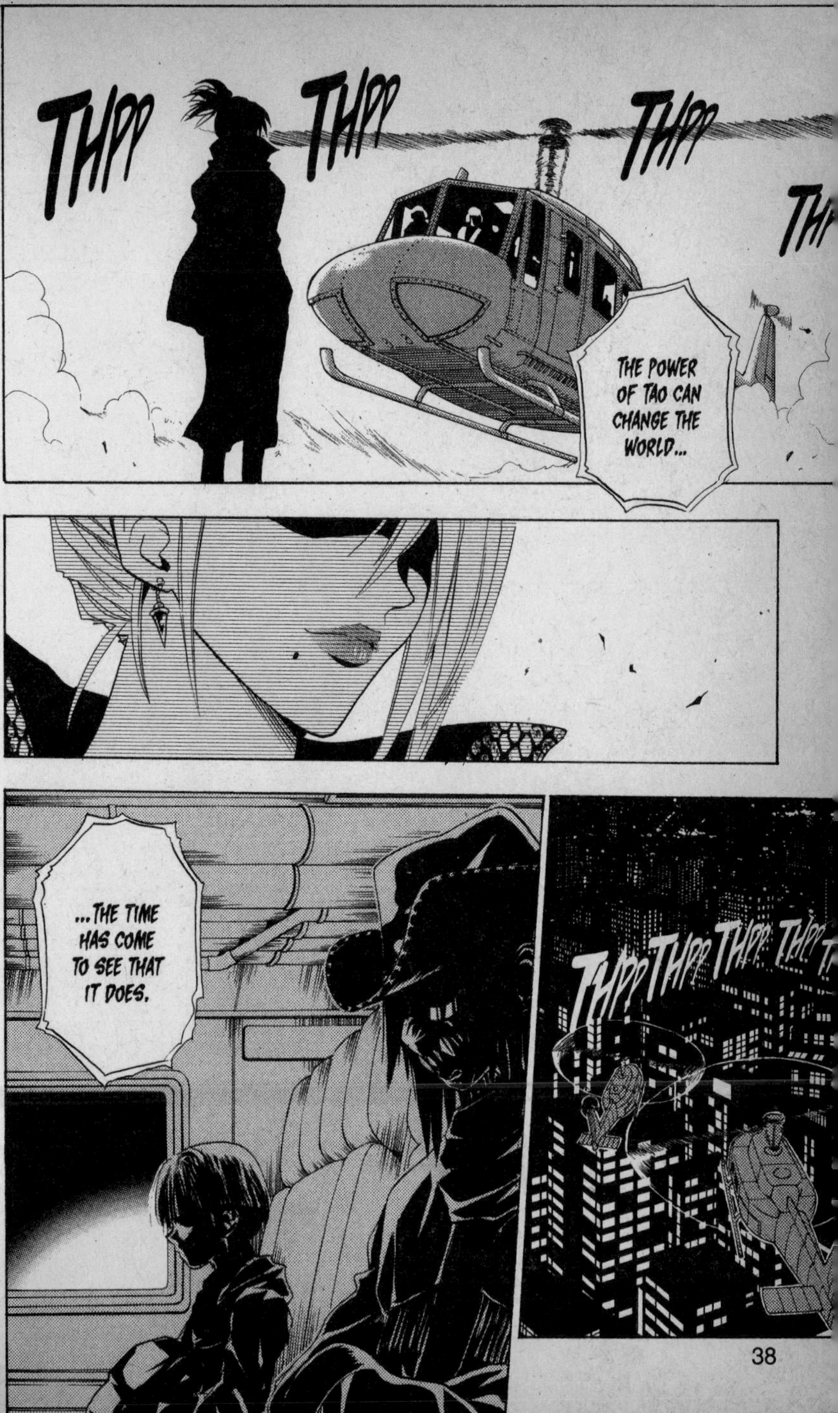
THPP
THPP
THPP
THE POWER OF TAO CAN CHANGE THE WORLD...
THPP THPP THPP THPP
...THE TIME HAS COME TO SEE THAT IT DOES.

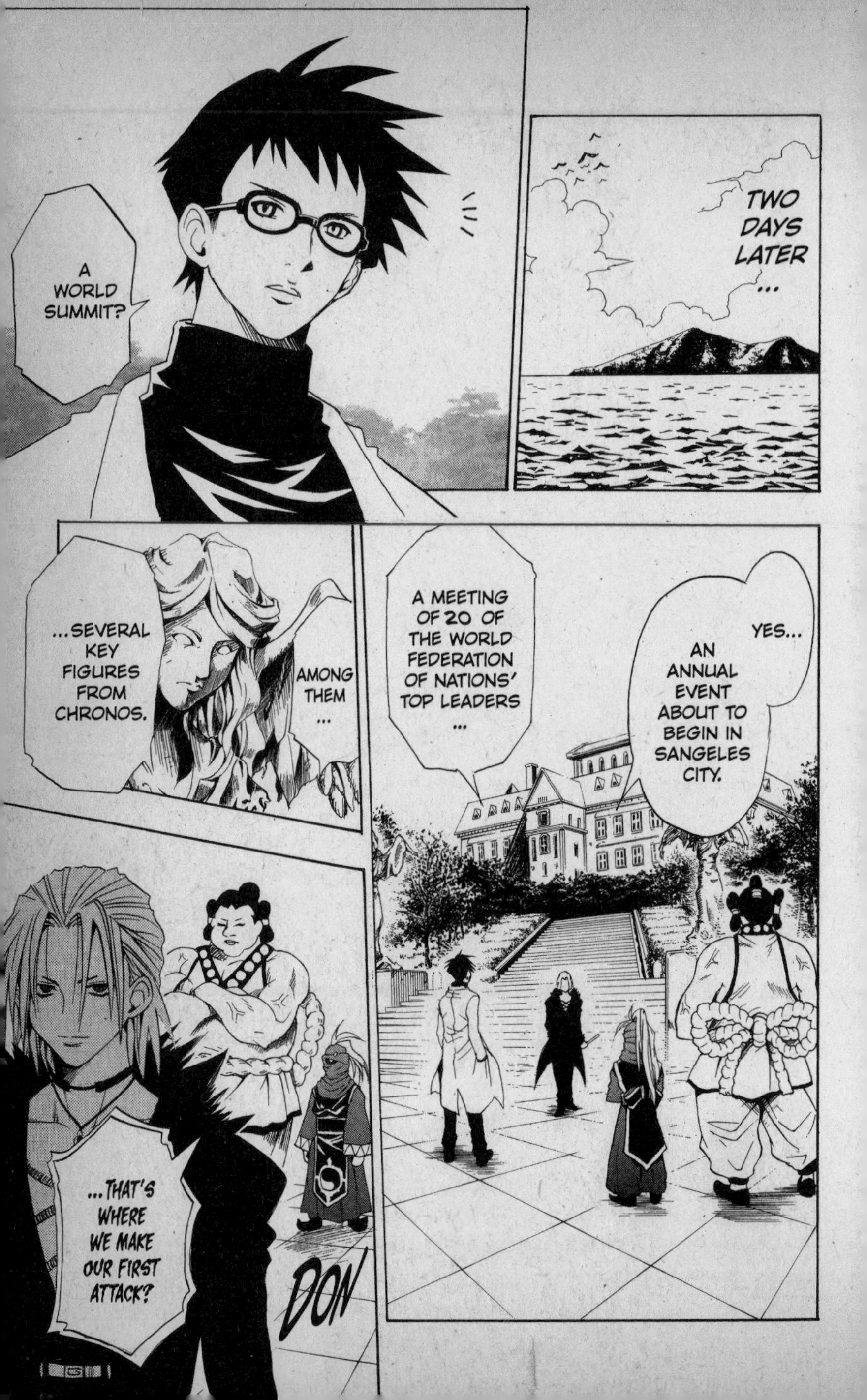
TWO DAYS LATER...
A WORLD SUMMIT?
YES... AN ANNUAL EVENT ABOUT TO BEGIN IN SANGELES CITY.
A MEETING OF 20 OF THE WORLD FEDERATION OF NATIONS' TOP LEADERS...
AMONG THEM...
...SEVERAL KEY FIGURES FROM CHRONOS.
...THAT'S WHERE WE MAKE OUR FIRST ATTACK?
DON

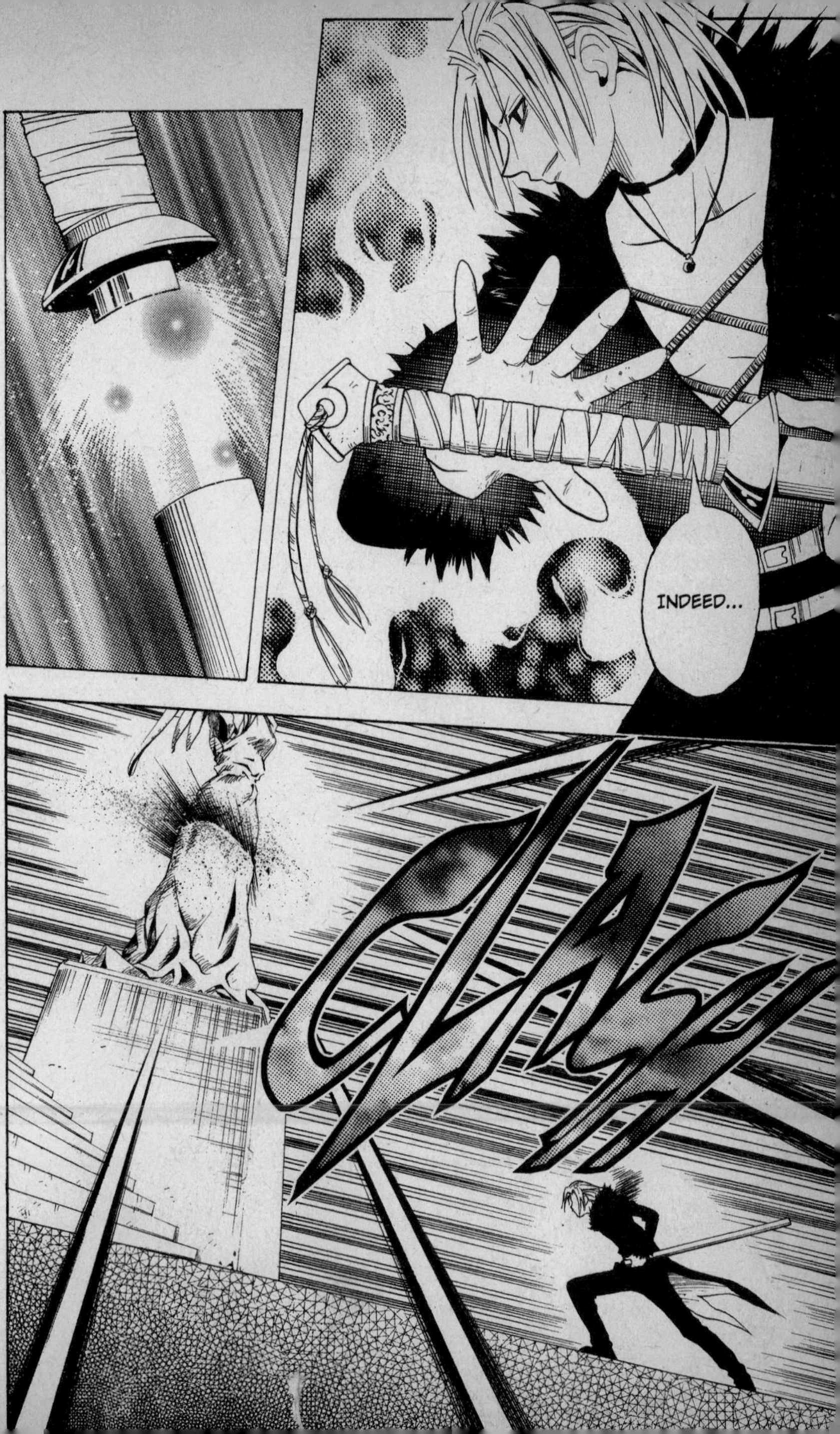
INDEED...

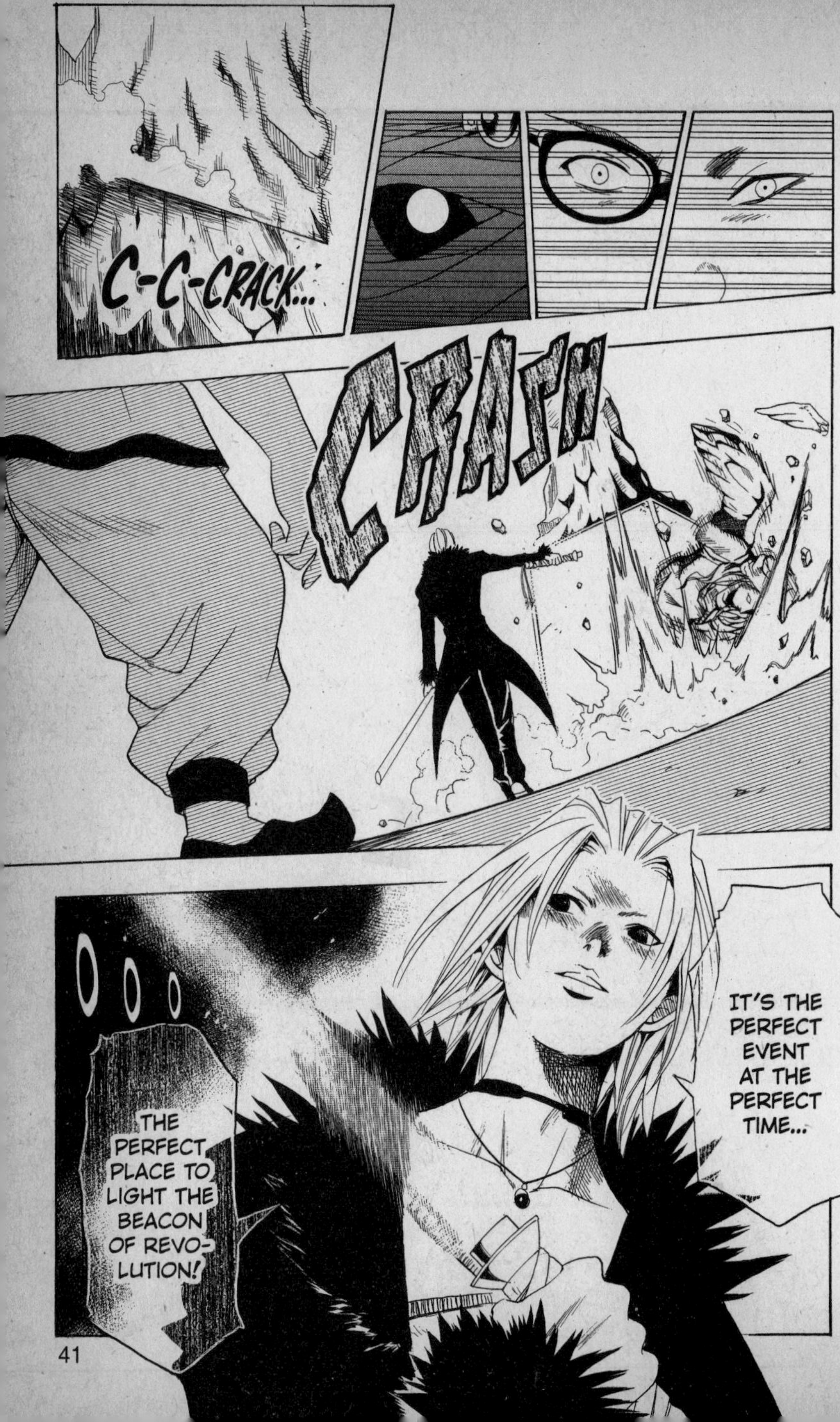
C-C-CRACK...
CRASH
IT'S THE PERFECT EVENT AT THE PERFECT TIME...
THE PERFECT PLACE TO LIGHT THE BEACON OF REVO-LUTION!

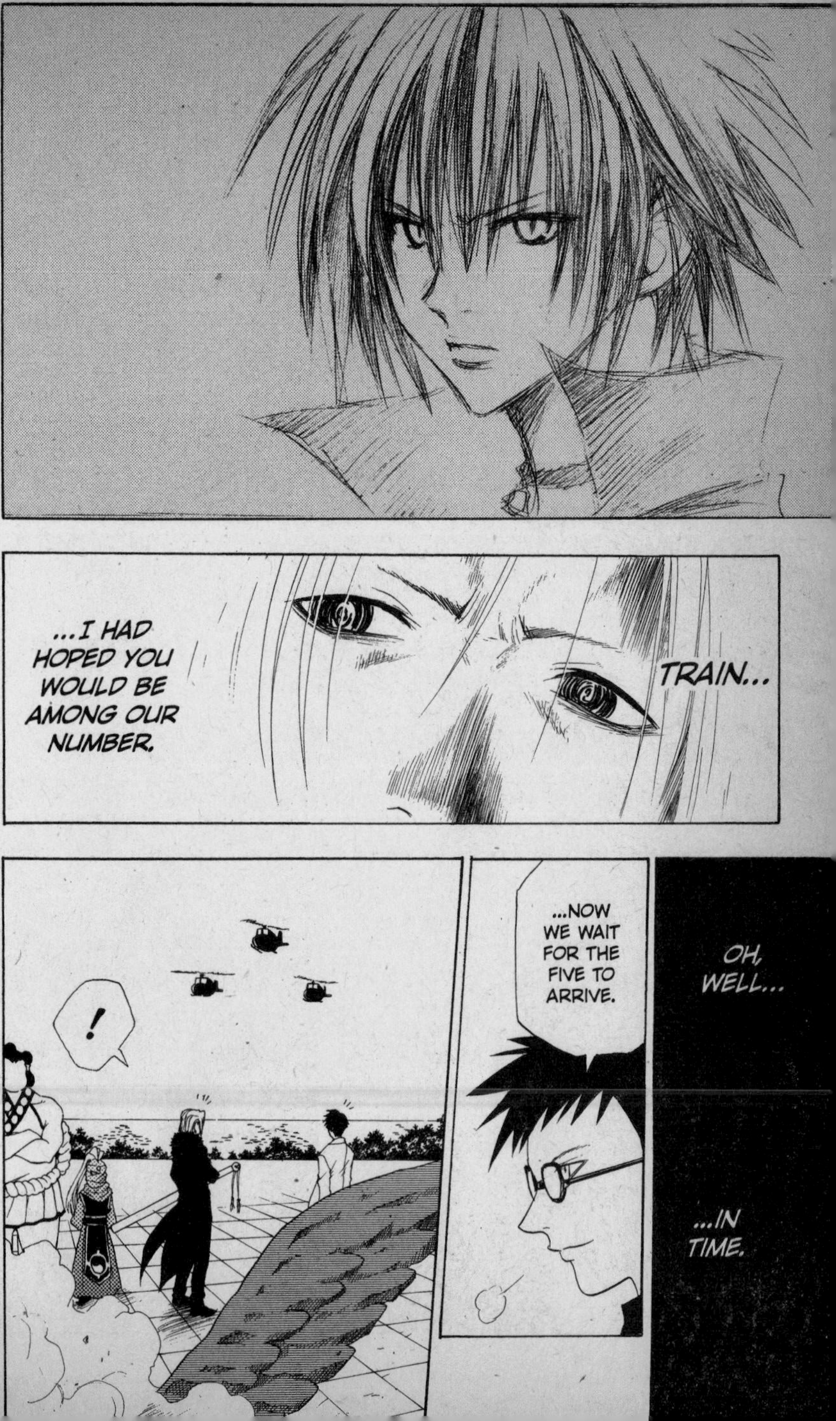
TRAIN...
...I HAD HOPED YOU WOULD BE AMONG OUR NUMBER.
OH, WELL...
...IN TIME.
...NOW WE WAIT FOR THE FIVE TO ARRIVE.
!

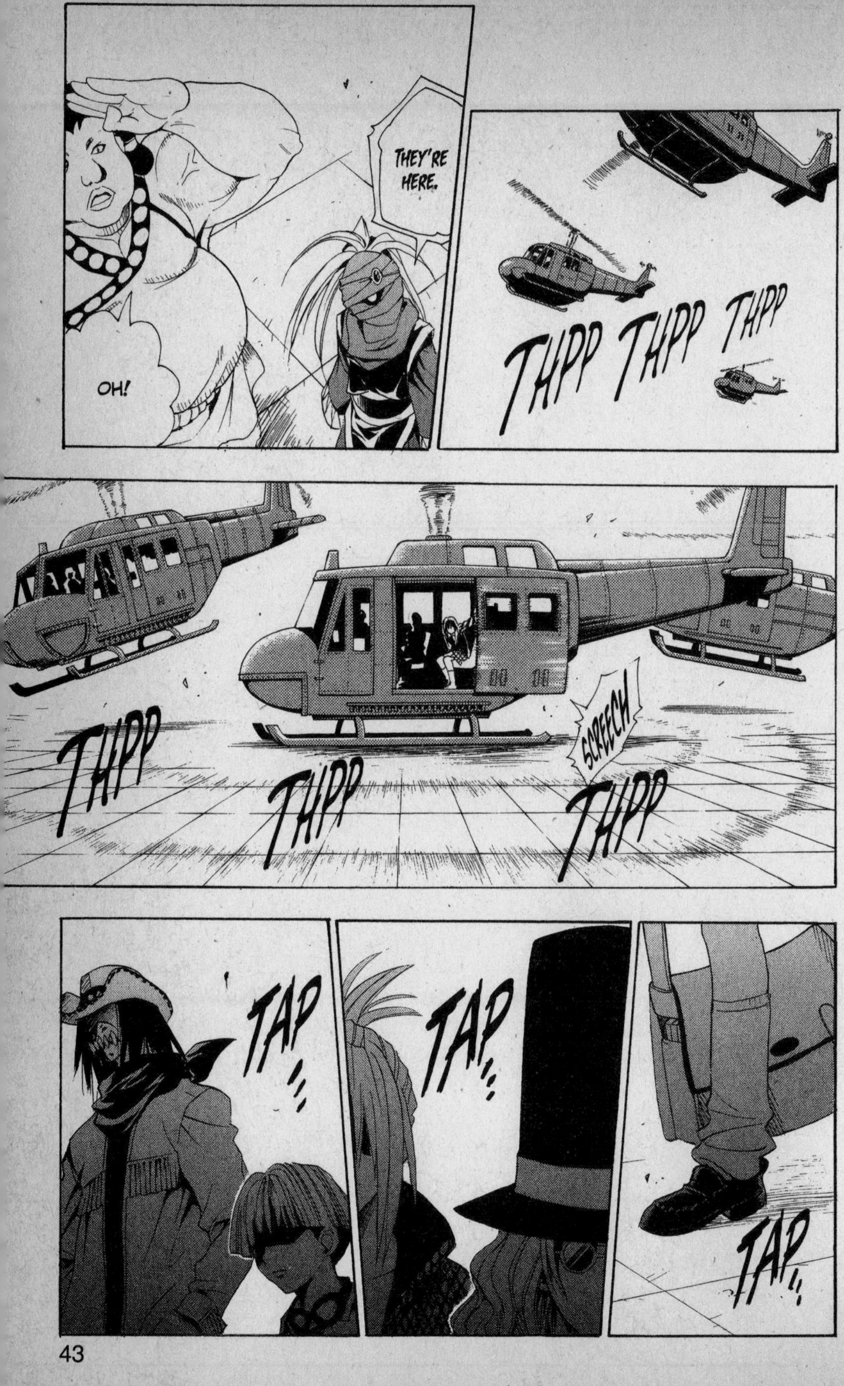
THPP THPP THPP
THEY'RE HERE.
OH!
SCREECH
THPP
THPP
THPP
TAP
TAP
TAP

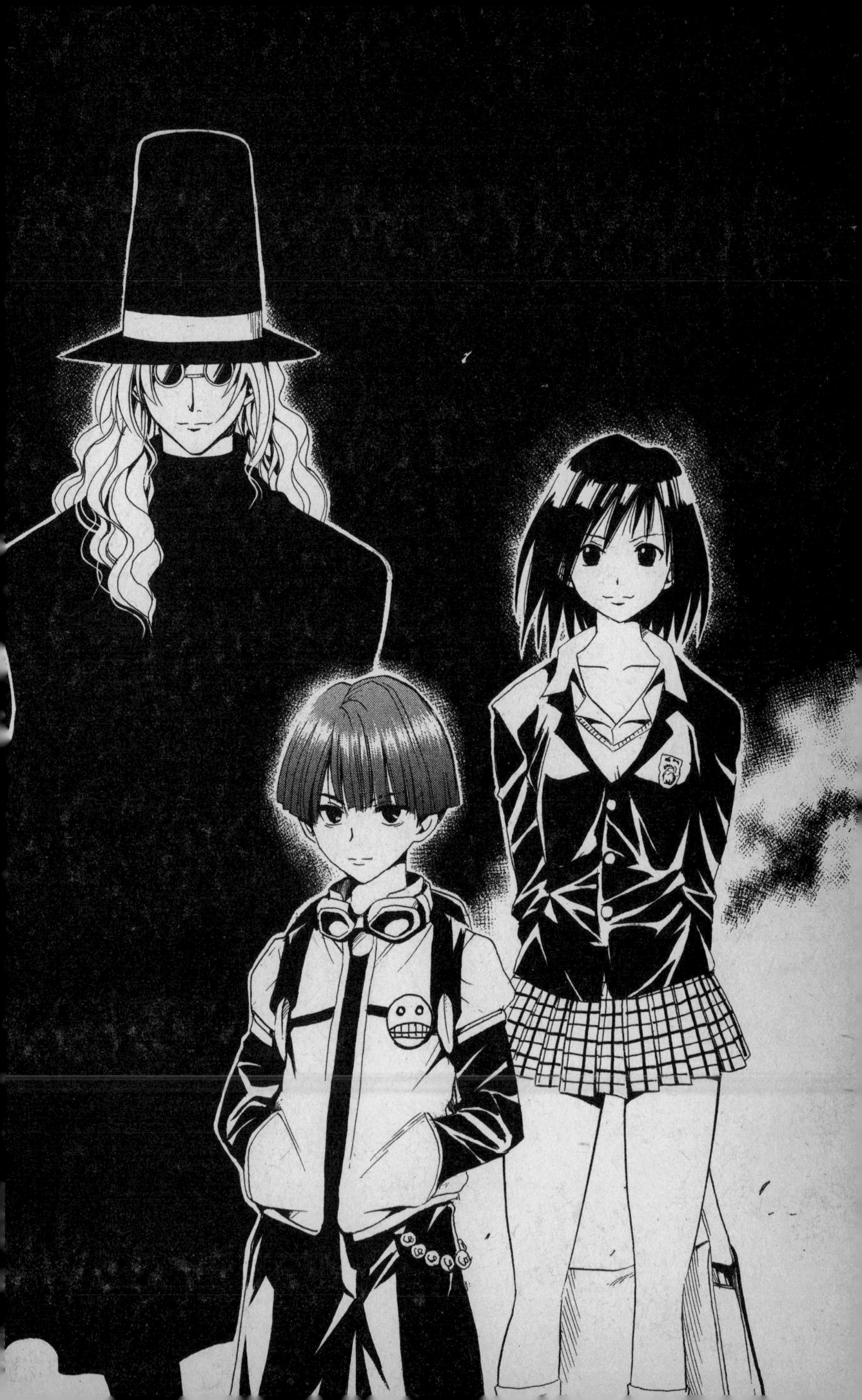

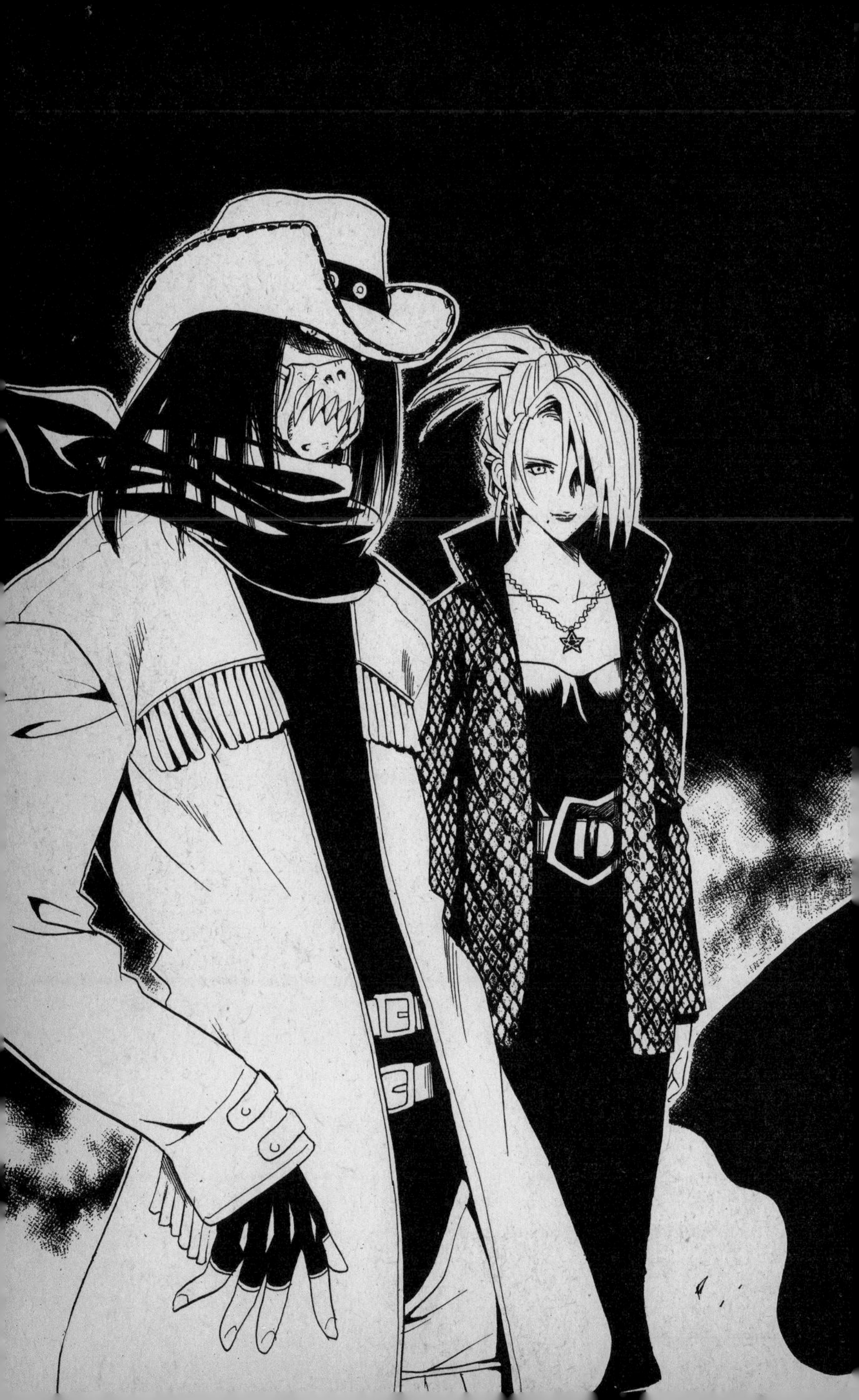

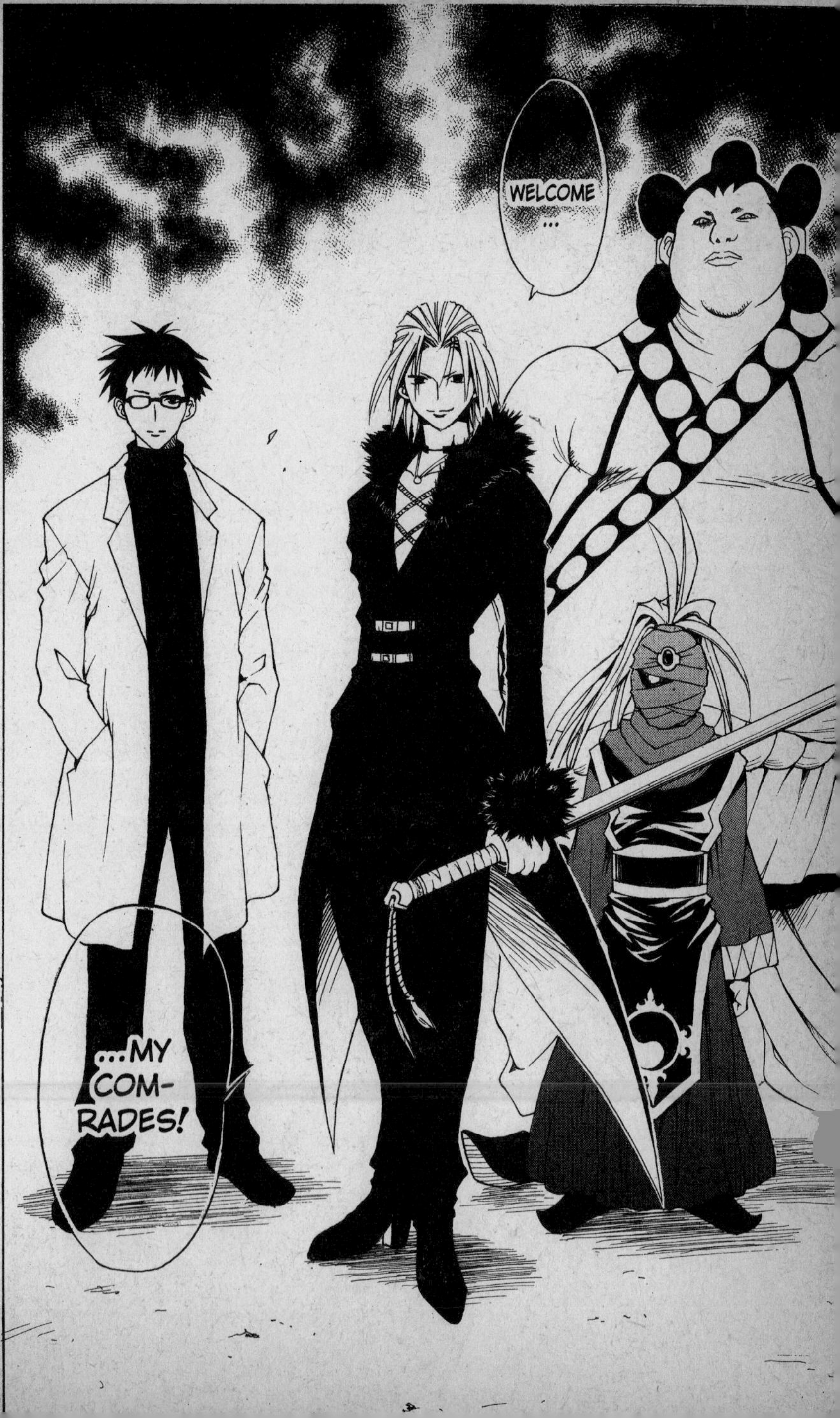
WELCOME ...
...MY COMRADES!

Chapter 41: Spark of Revolution

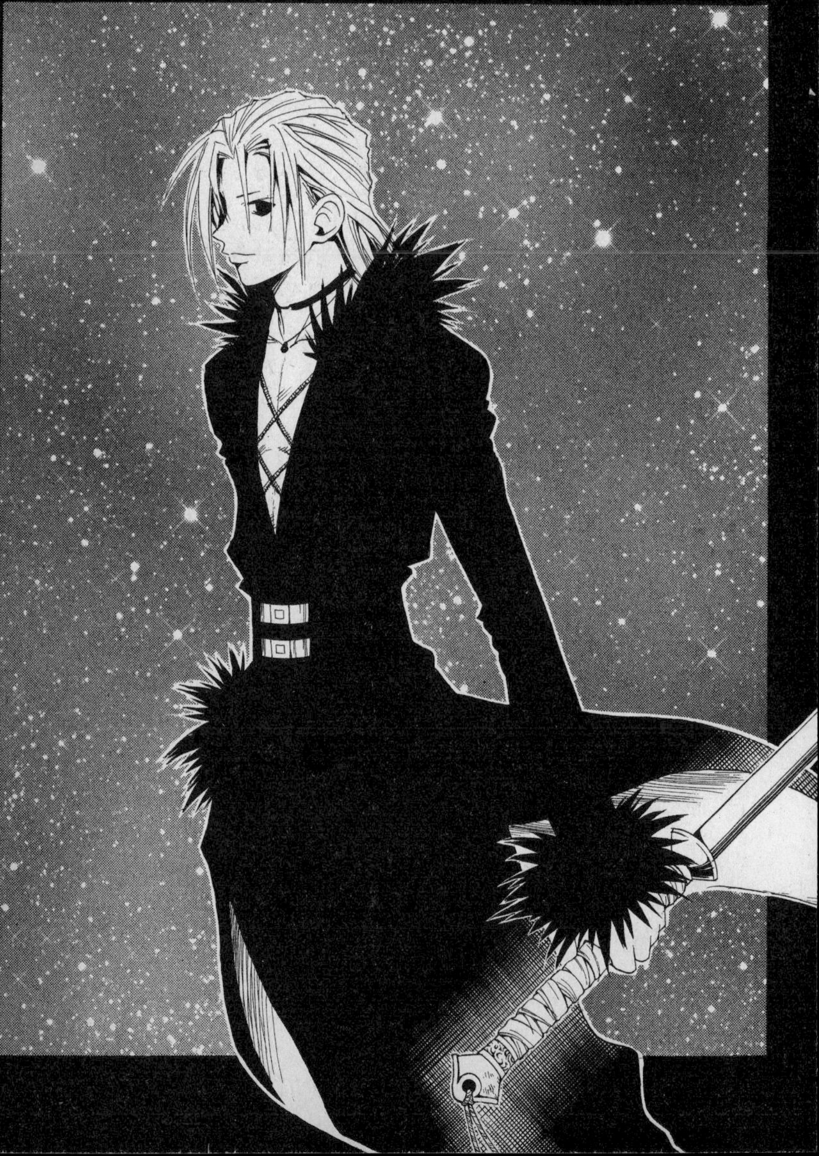

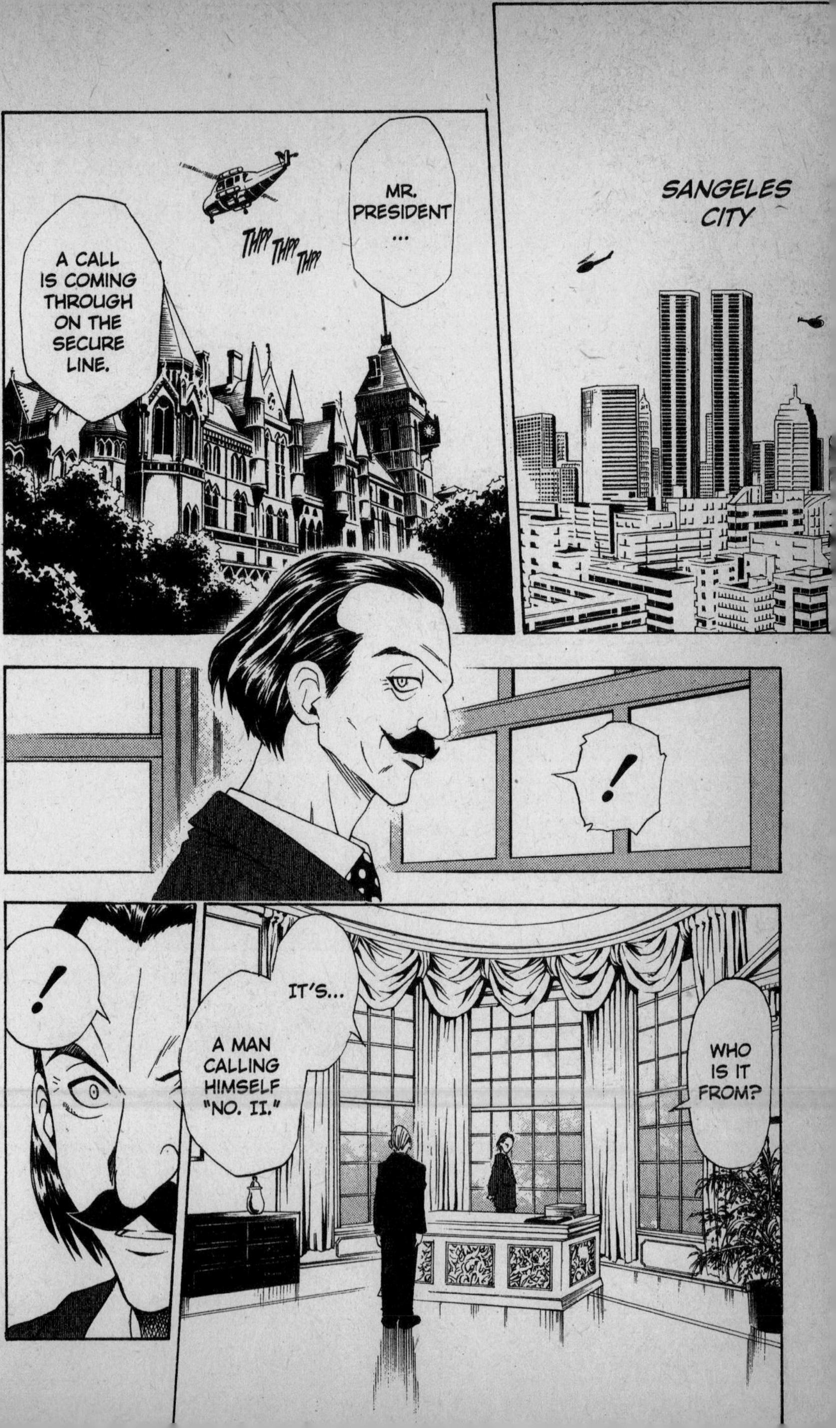
SANGELES CITY
MR. PRESIDENT ...
THPP THPP THPP
A CALL IS COMING THROUGH ON THE SECURE LINE.
!
WHO IS IT FROM?
IT'S...
A MAN CALLING HIMSELF "NO. II."
!

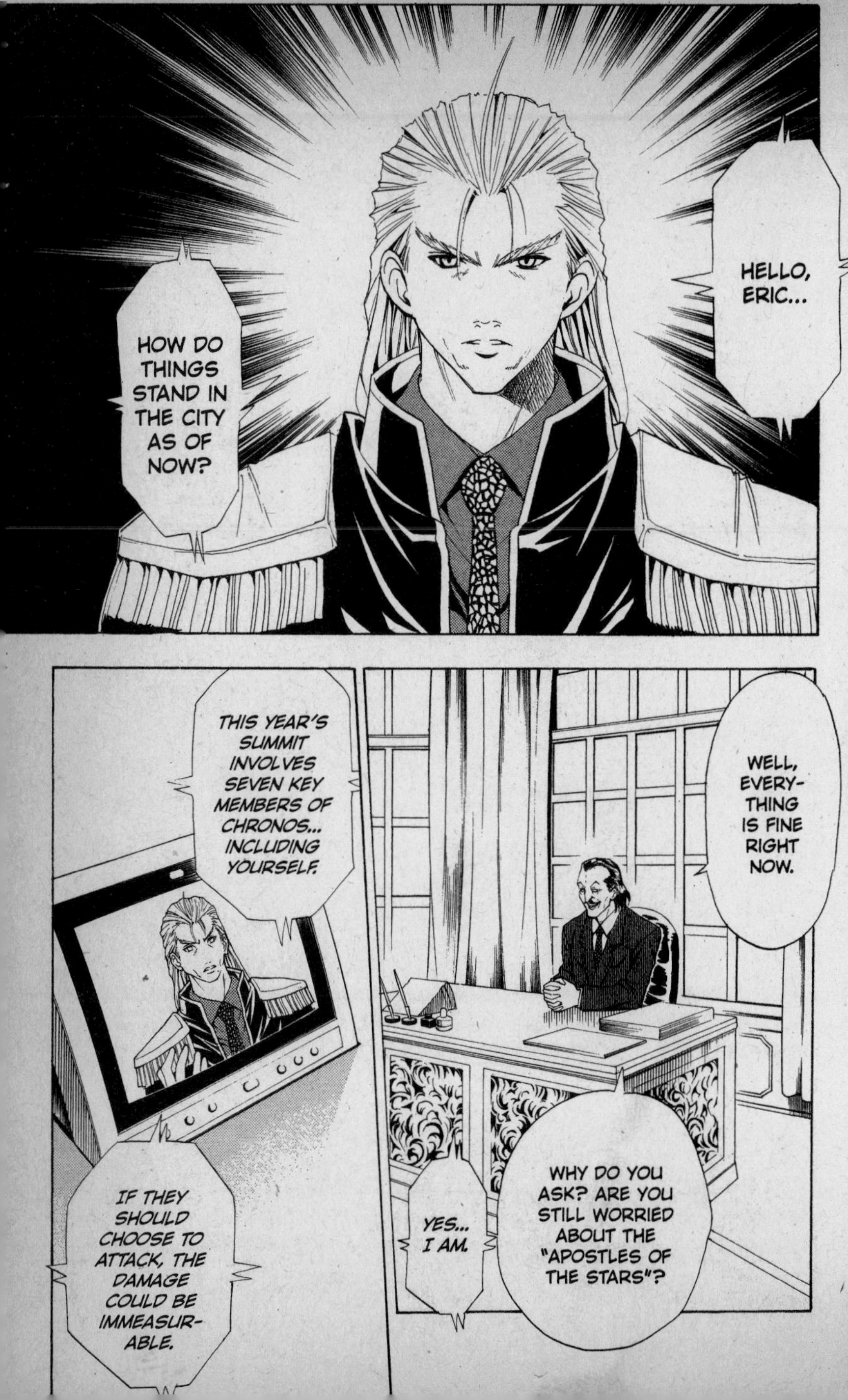
HELLO, ERIC...
HOW DO THINGS STAND IN THE CITY AS OF NOW?
WELL, EVERY-THING IS FINE RIGHT NOW.
WHY DO YOU ASK? ARE YOU STILL WORRIED ABOUT THE "APOSTLES OF THE STARS"?
YES... I AM.
THIS YEAR'S SUMMIT INVOLVES SEVEN KEY MEMBERS OF CHRONOS... INCLUDING YOURSELF.
IF THEY SHOULD CHOOSE TO ATTACK, THE DAMAGE COULD BE IMMEASUR-ABLE.

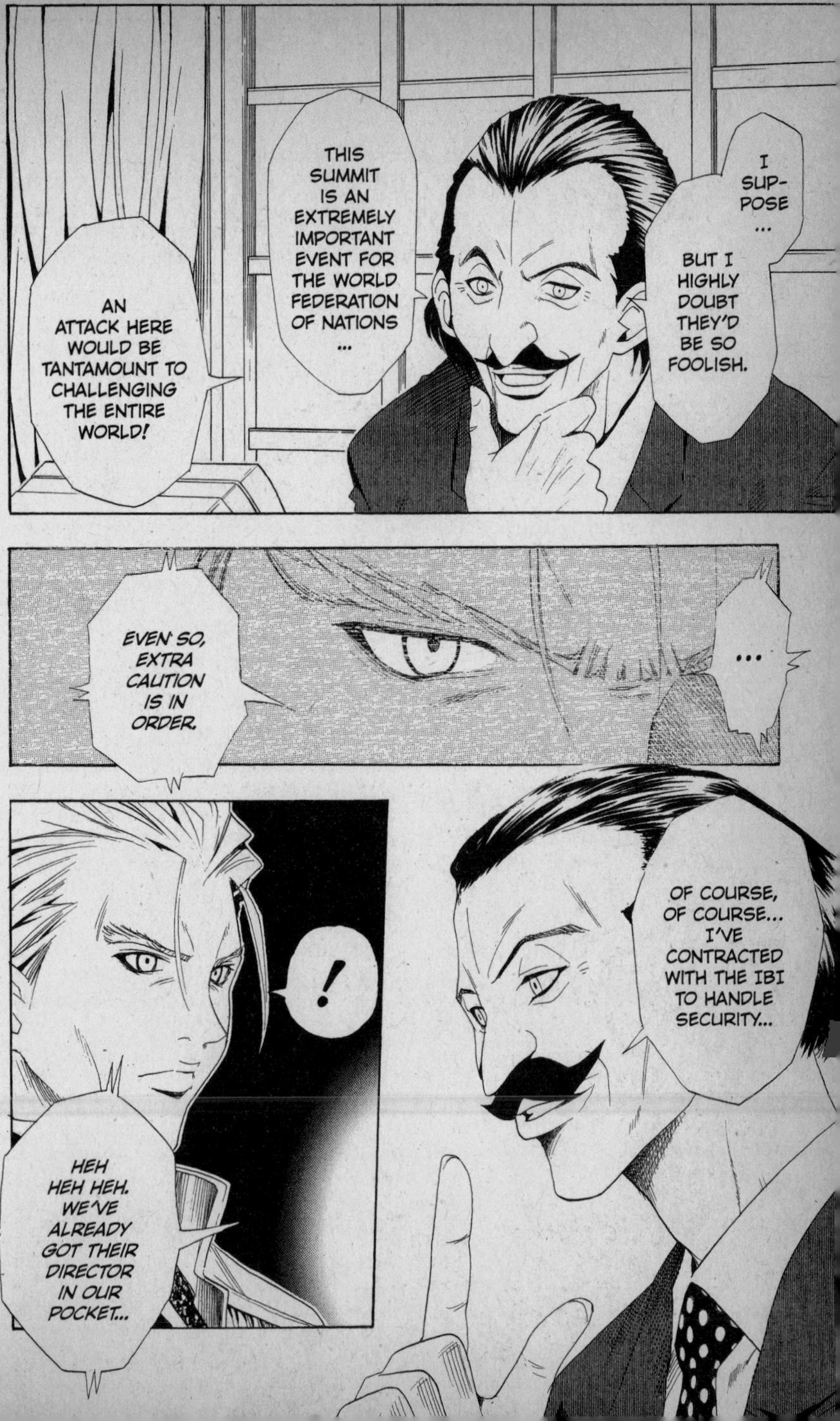
I SUP-POSE ...
BUT I HIGHLY DOUBT THEY'D BE SO FOOLISH.
THIS SUMMIT IS AN EXTREMELY IMPORTANT EVENT FOR THE WORLD FEDERATION OF NATIONS ...
AN ATTACK HERE WOULD BE TANTAMOUNT TO CHALLENGING THE ENTIRE WORLD!
...
EVEN SO, EXTRA CAUTION IS IN ORDER.
OF COURSE, OF COURSE... I'VE CONTRACTED WITH THE IBI TO HANDLE SECURITY...
!
HEH HEH HEH. WE'VE ALREADY GOT THEIR DIRECTOR IN OUR POCKET...

READ THIS WAY

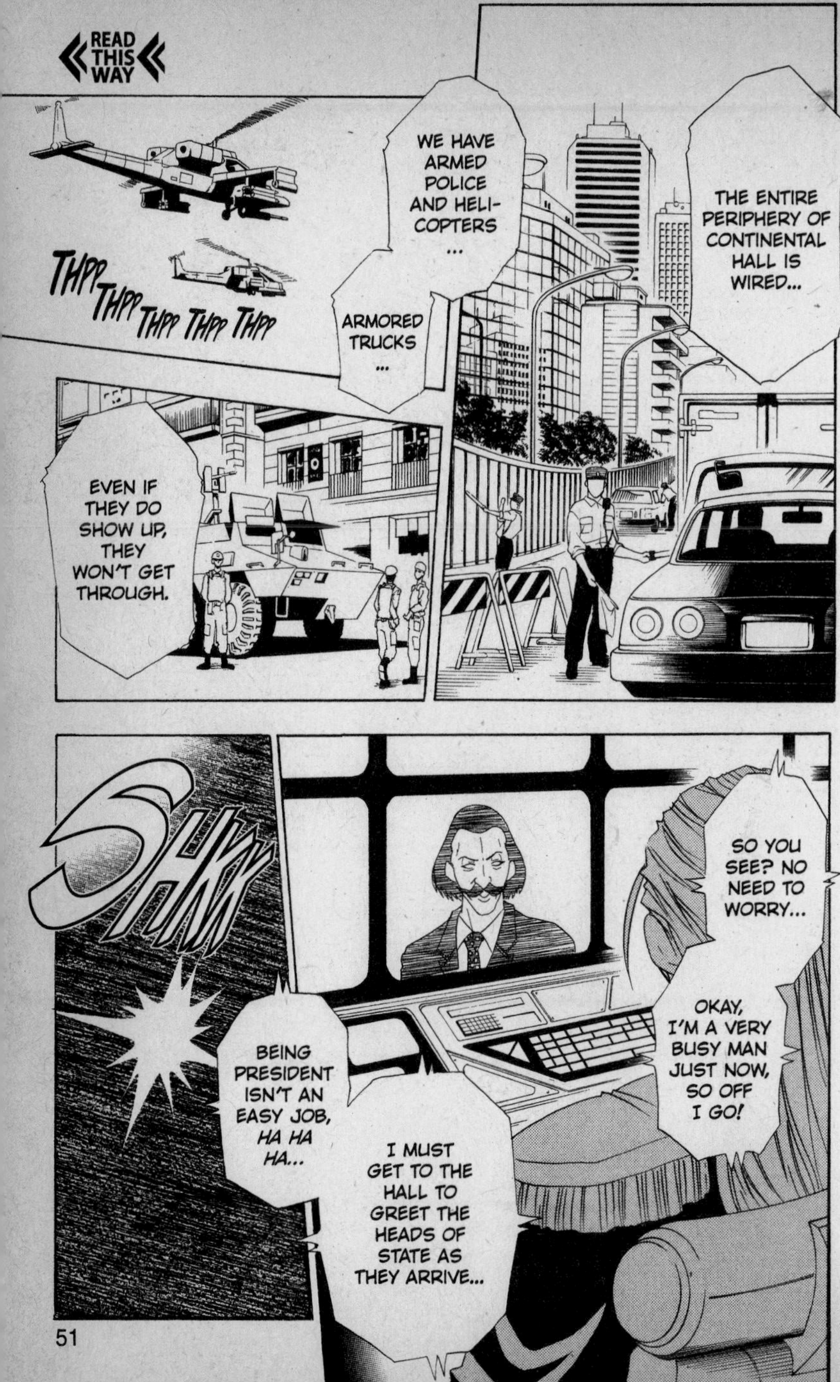

THE ENTIRE PERIPHERY OF CONTINENTAL HALL IS WIRED...
WE HAVE ARMED POLICE AND HELI-COPTERS ...
ARMORED TRUCKS ...
THPP THPP THPP THPP THPP
EVEN IF THEY DO SHOW UP, THEY WON'T GET THROUGH.
SO YOU SEE? NO NEED TO WORRY...
OKAY, I'M A VERY BUSY MAN JUST NOW, SO OFF I GO!
I MUST GET TO THE HALL TO GREET THE HEADS OF STATE AS THEY ARRIVE...
BEING PRESIDENT ISN'T AN EASY JOB, *HA HA HA*...
SHKK

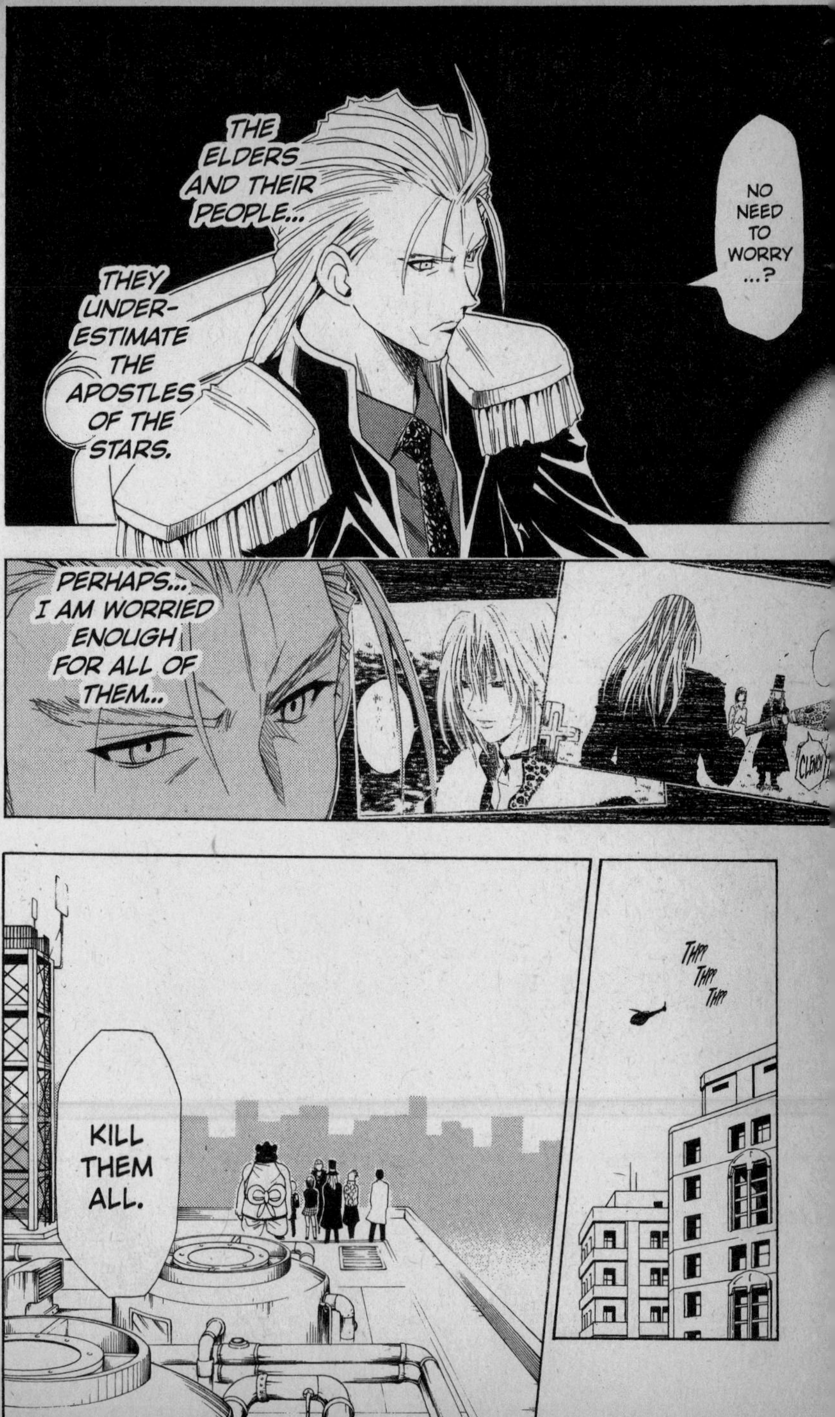
NO NEED TO WORRY ...?
THE ELDERS AND THEIR PEOPLE...
THEY UNDER-ESTIMATE THE APOSTLES OF THE STARS.
CLENCH
PERHAPS... I AM WORRIED ENOUGH FOR ALL OF THEM...
THPP THPP THPP
KILL THEM ALL.

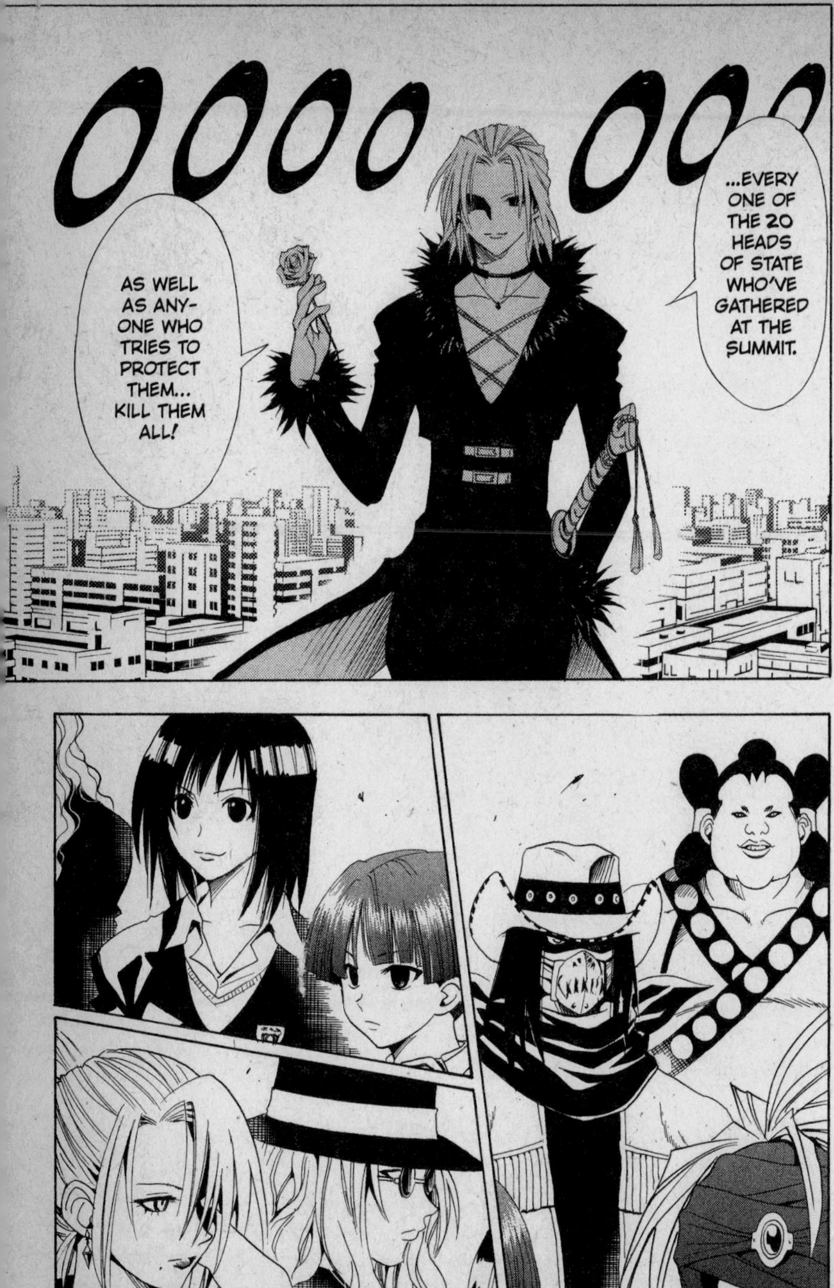
OOOO OOO
...EVERY ONE OF THE 20 HEADS OF STATE WHO'VE GATHERED AT THE SUMMIT.
AS WELL AS ANY-ONE WHO TRIES TO PROTECT THEM... KILL THEM ALL!

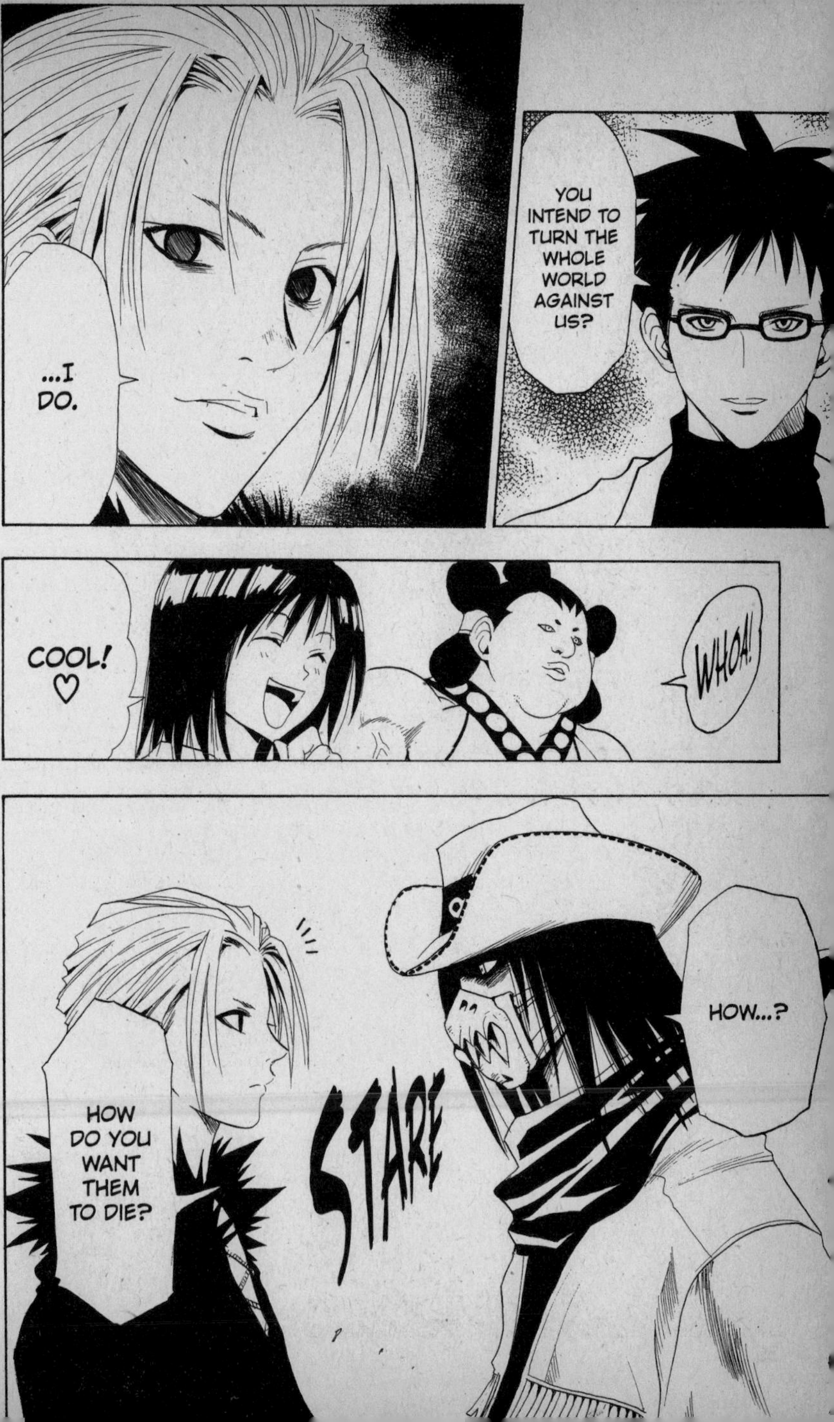
YOU INTEND TO TURN THE WHOLE WORLD AGAINST US?
...I DO.
WHOA!
COOL! ♡
HOW...?
STARE
HOW DO YOU WANT THEM TO DIE?

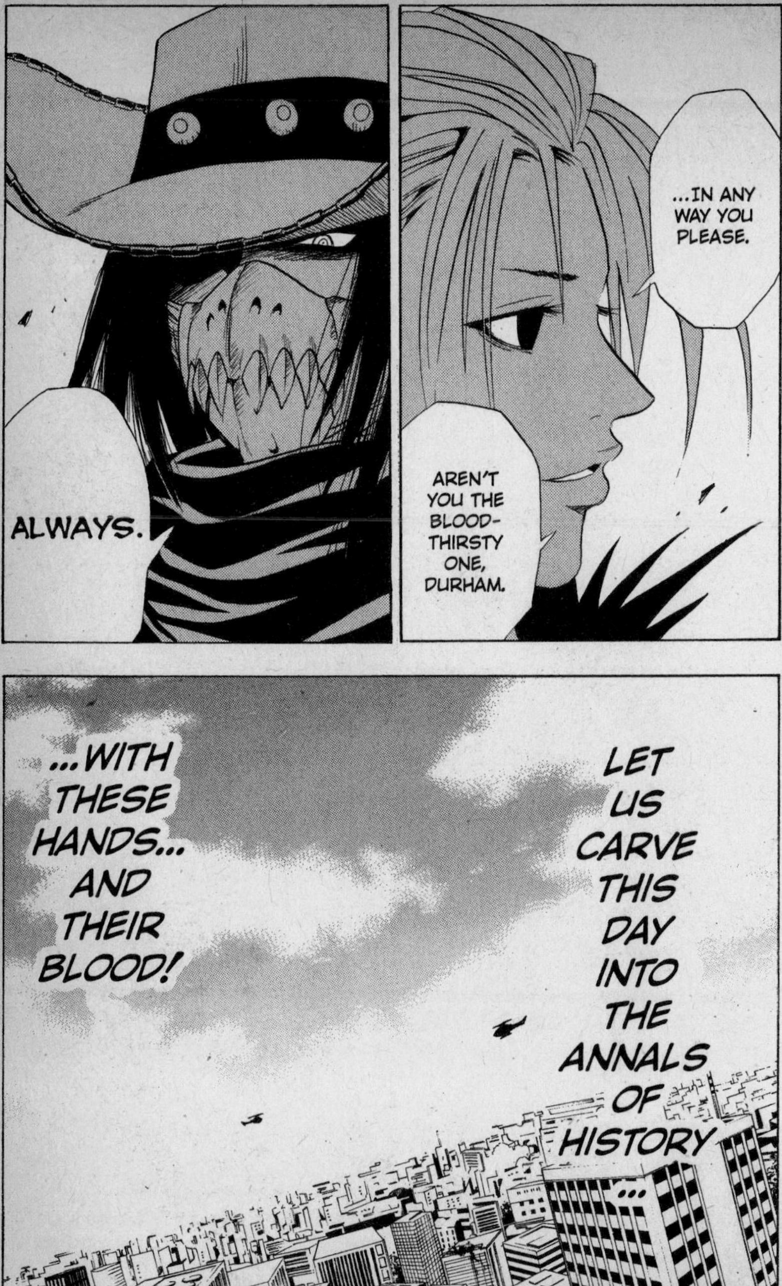
...IN ANY WAY YOU PLEASE.
AREN'T YOU THE BLOOD-THIRSTY ONE, DURHAM.
ALWAYS.
LET US CARVE THIS DAY INTO THE ANNALS OF HISTORY...
...WITH THESE HANDS... AND THEIR BLOOD!

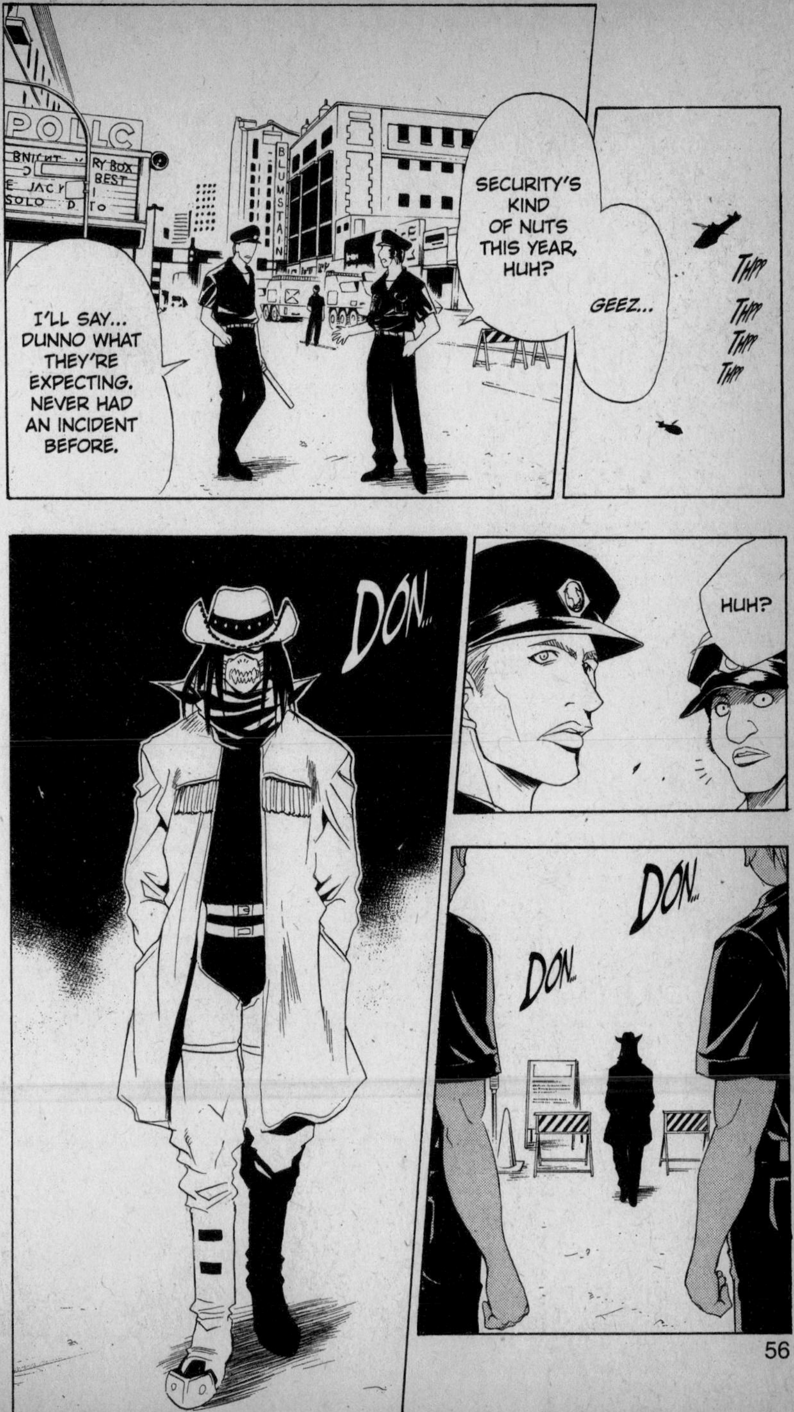
GEEZ...
THPP THPP THPP THPP
SECURITY'S KIND OF NUTS THIS YEAR, HUH?
I'LL SAY... DUNNO WHAT THEY'RE EXPECTING. NEVER HAD AN INCIDENT BEFORE.
HUH?
DON...
DON...
DON...

READ THIS WAY

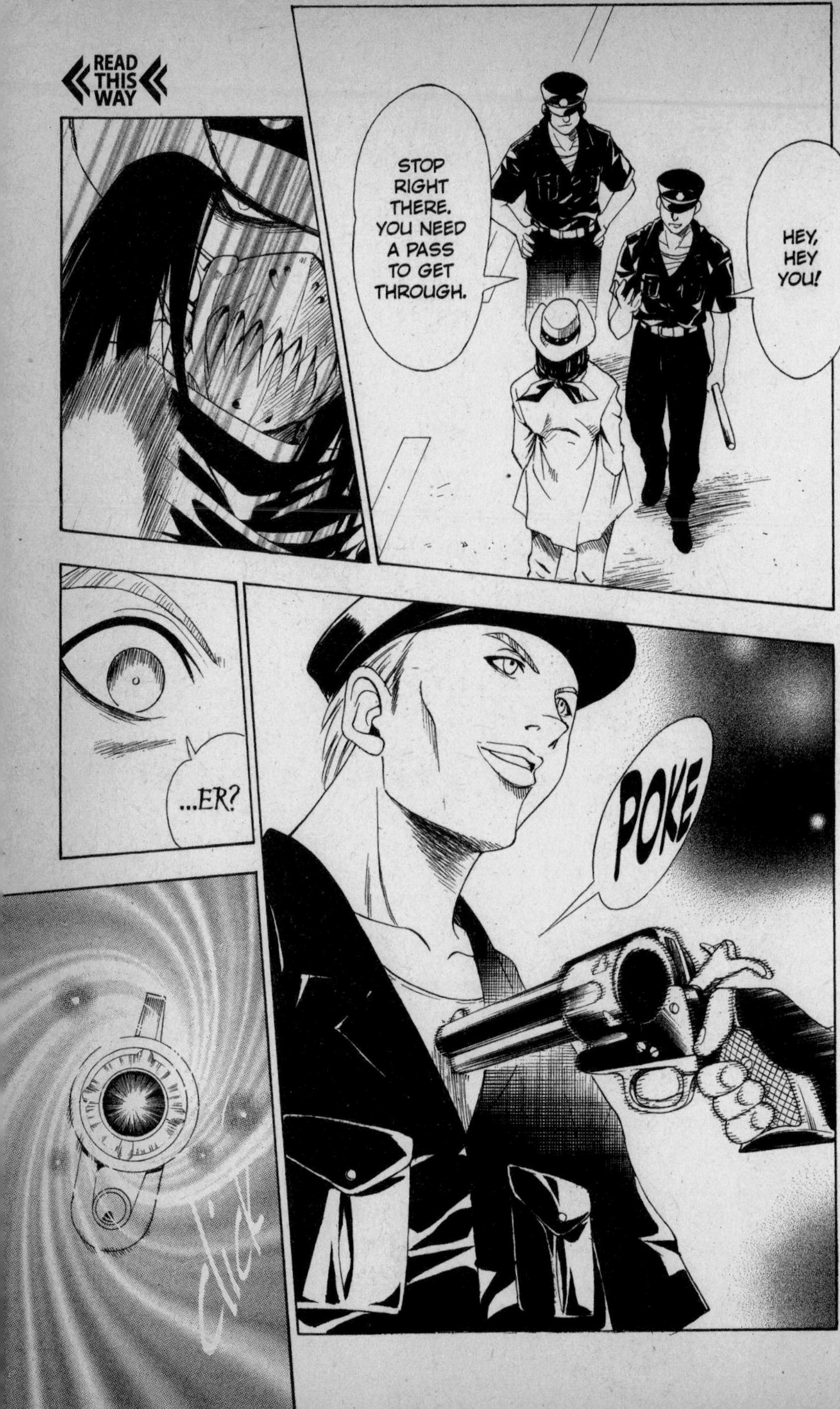
HEY, HEY YOU!
STOP RIGHT THERE. YOU NEED A PASS TO GET THROUGH.
POKE
...ER?
Click

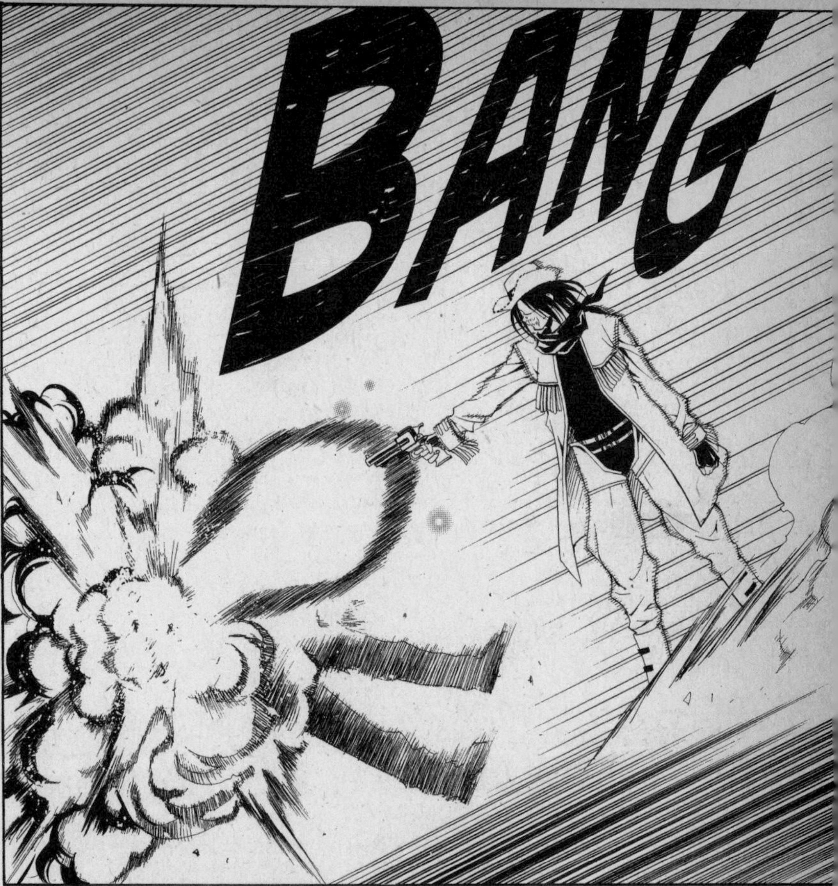
BANG
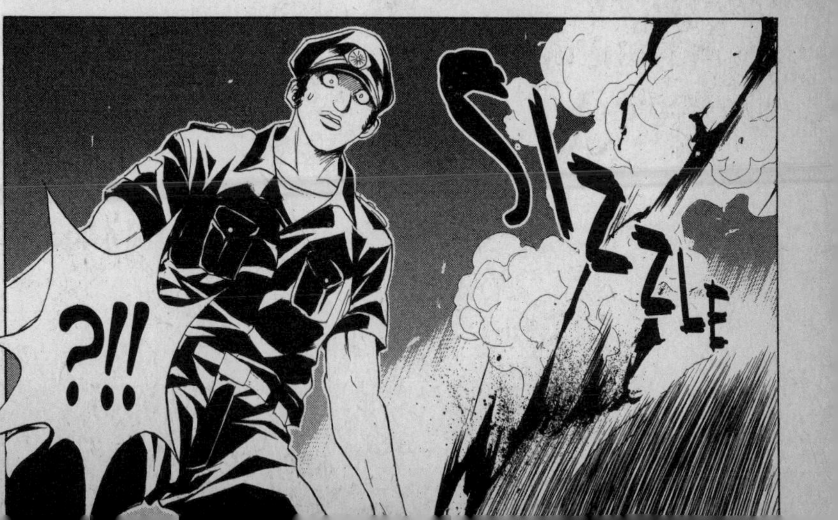
SIZZLE
?!!

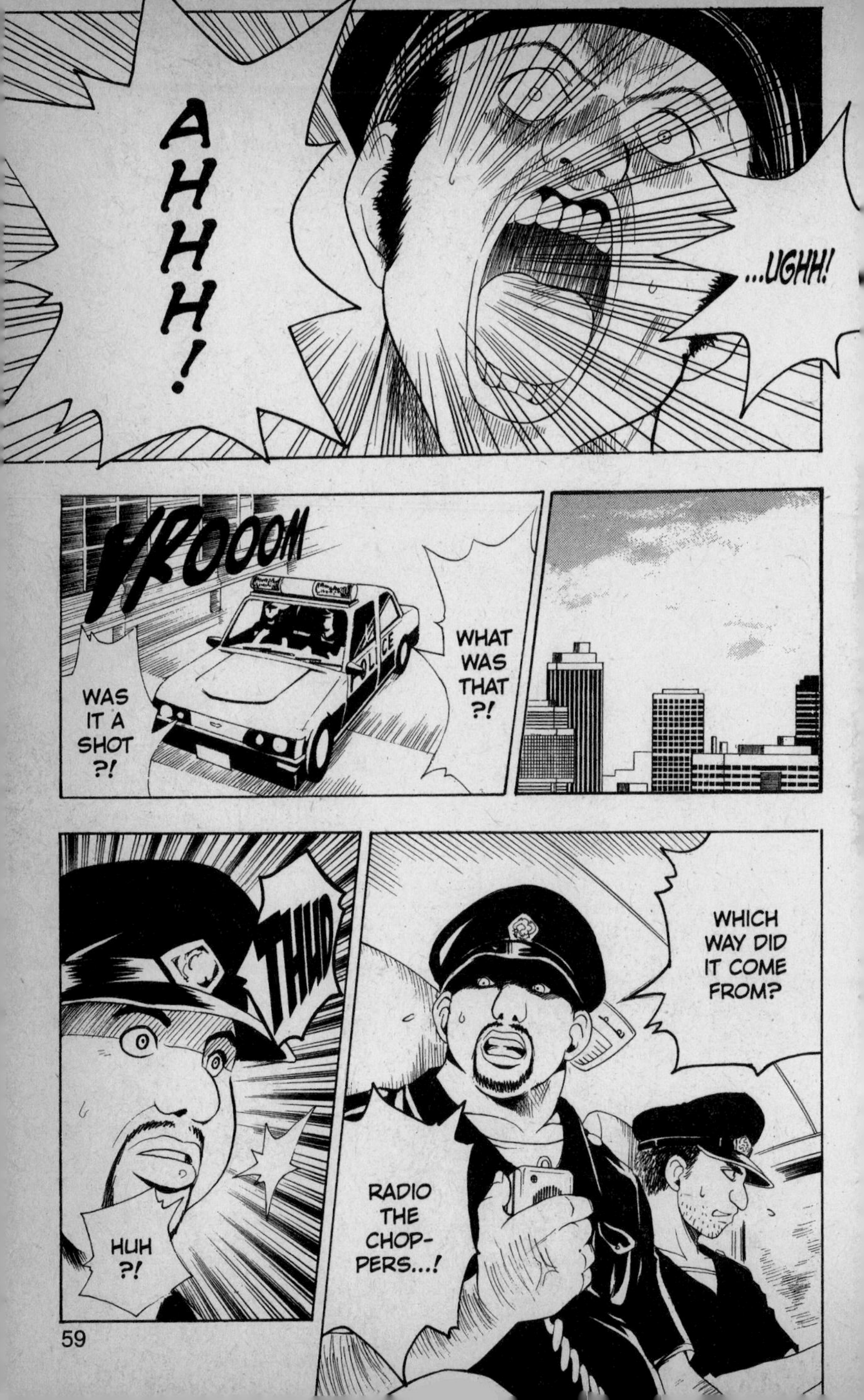
AHHHH!
...UGHH!
VROOOM
WHAT WAS THAT?!
WAS IT A SHOT?!
WHICH WAY DID IT COME FROM?
RADIO THE CHOP-PERS...!
THUD
HUH?!

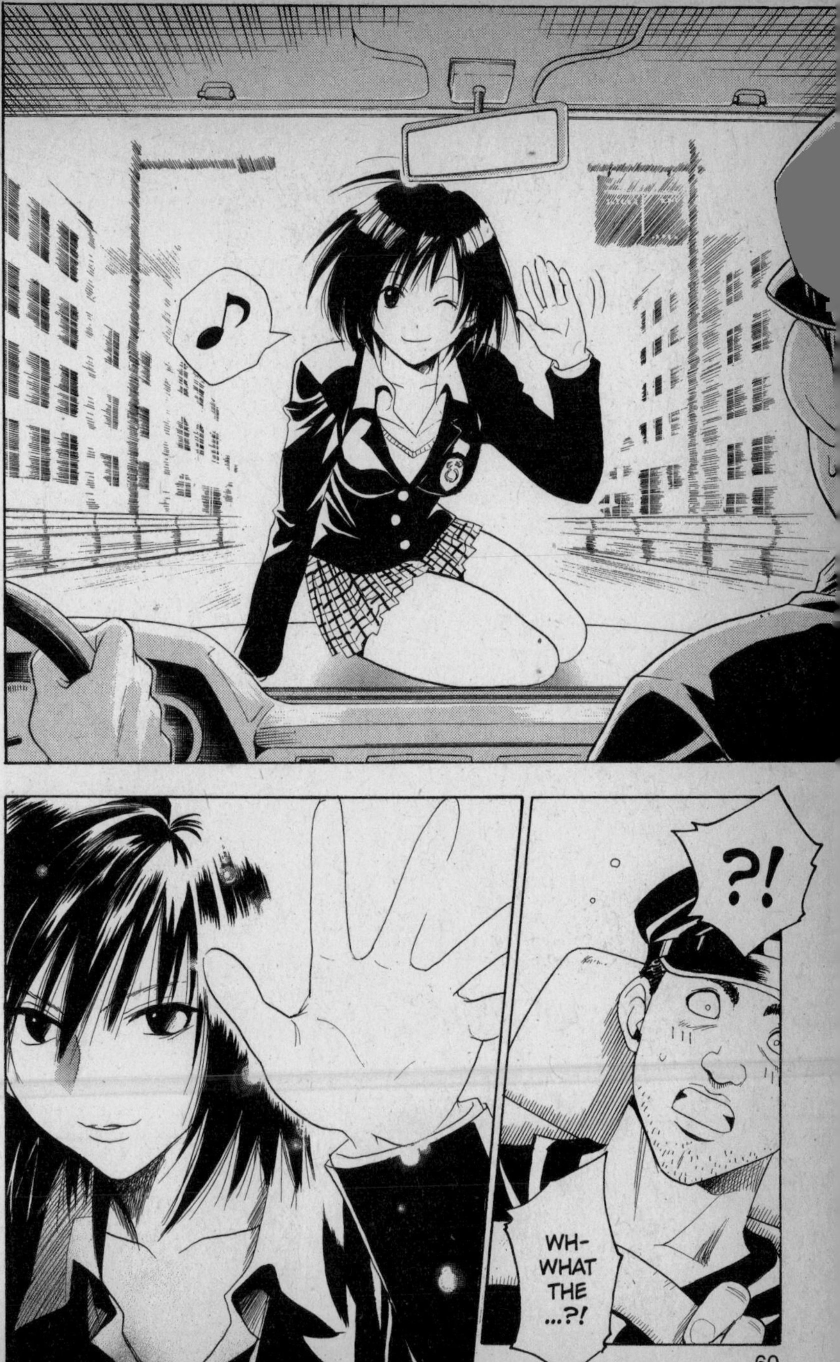
?!
WH- WHAT THE ...?!

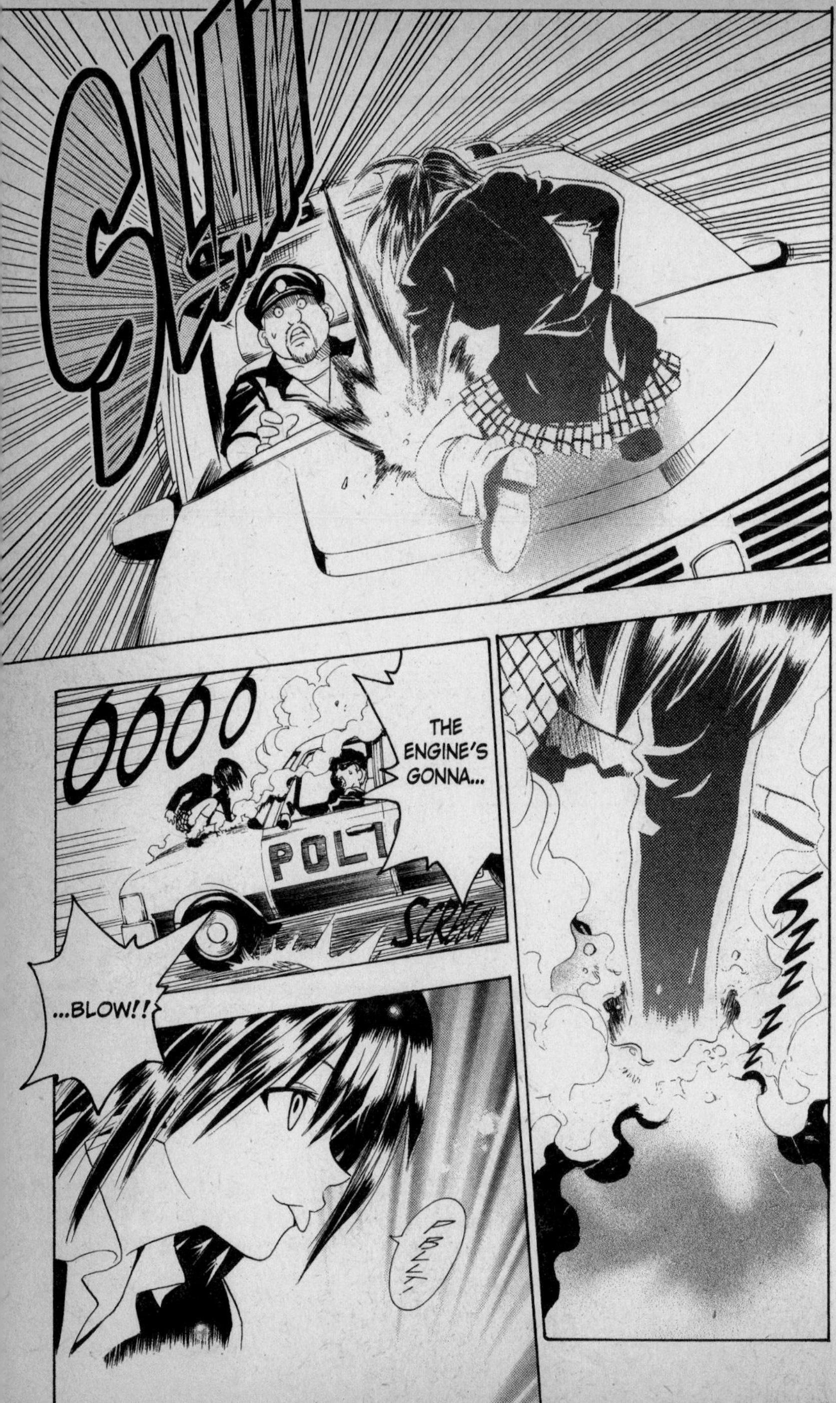
SZZZZ
OOOO
THE ENGINE'S GONNA...
POL
...BLOW!!
PBLLT!

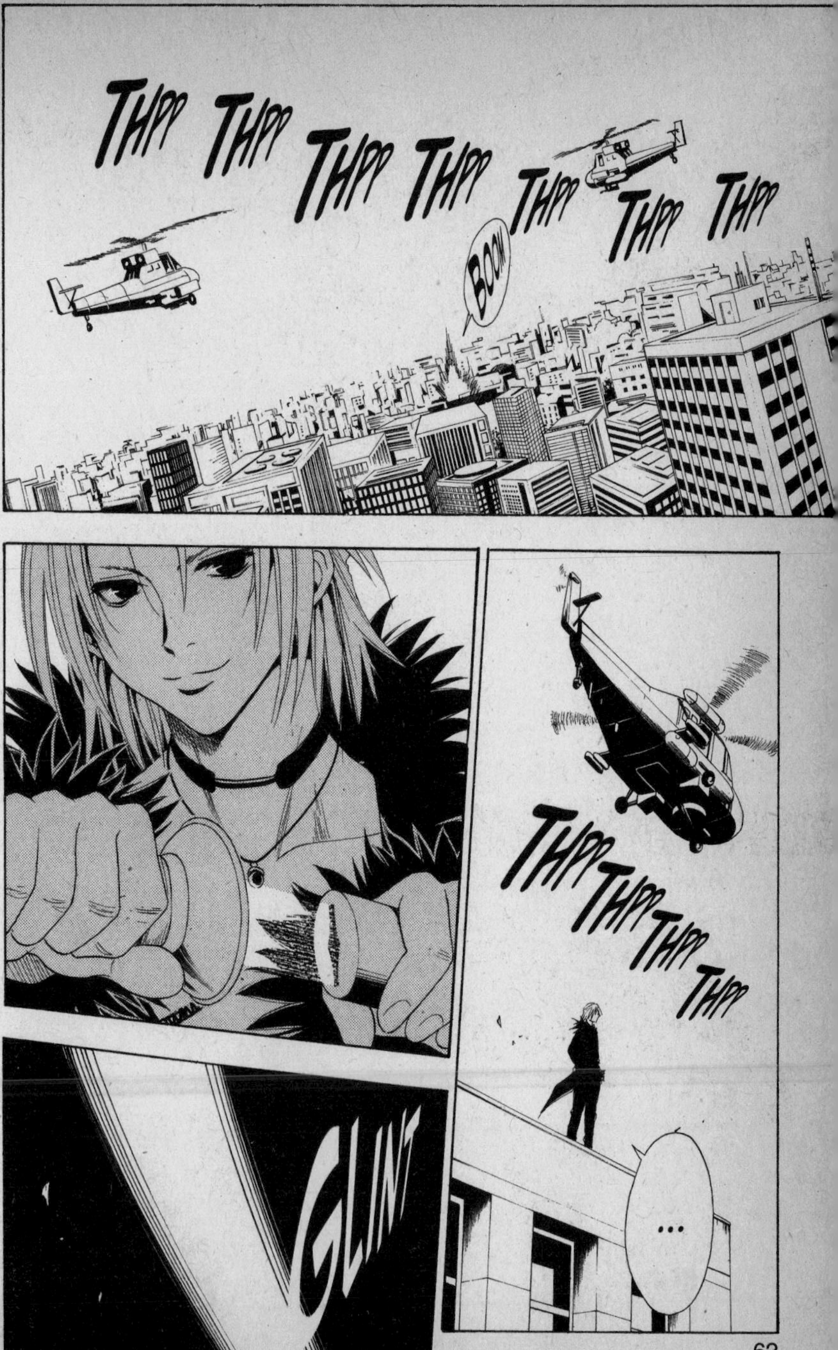
THPP THPP THPP THPP THPP THPP THPP
BOOM
THPP THPP THPP THPP
...
GLINT

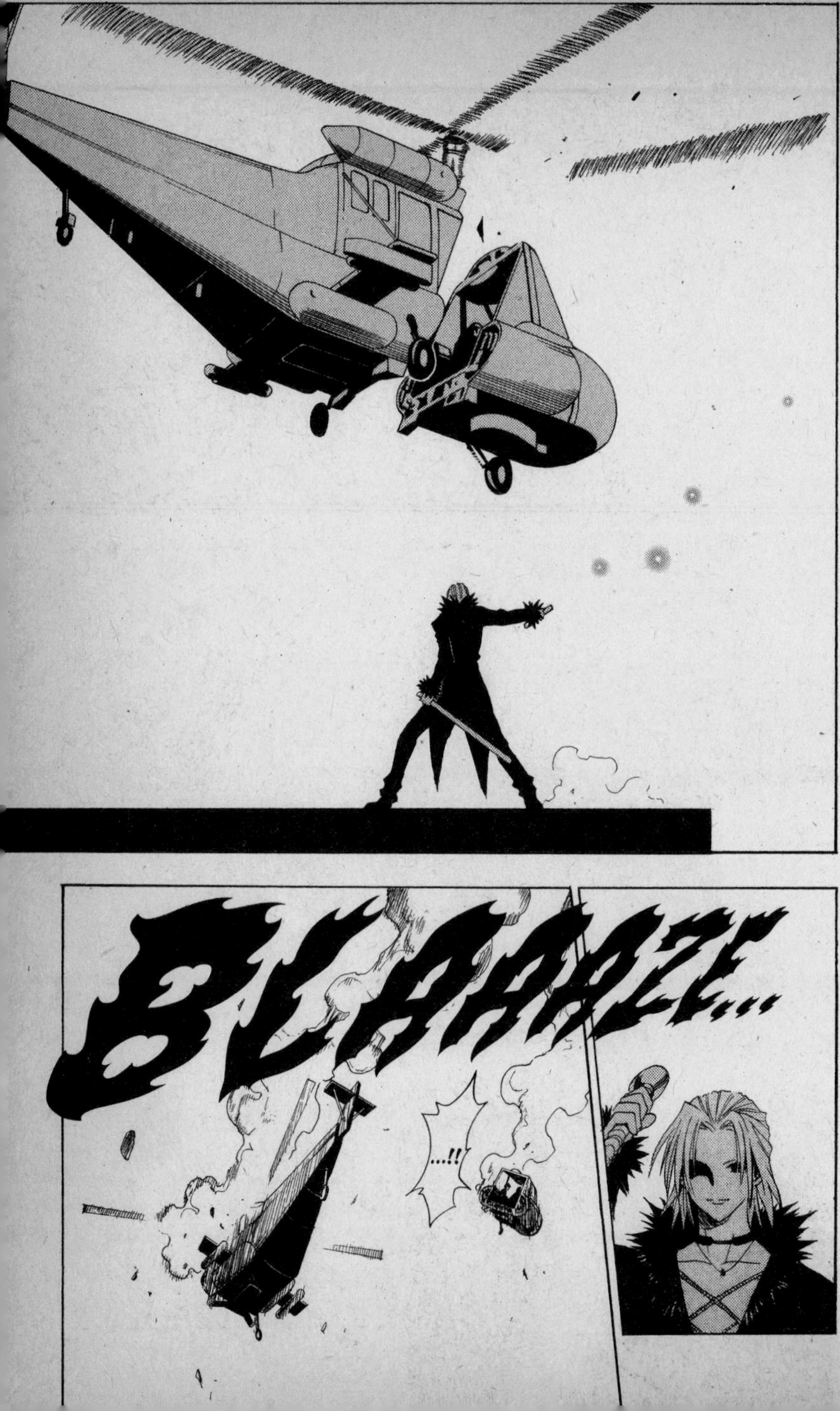
BLAAAZE...
...!!

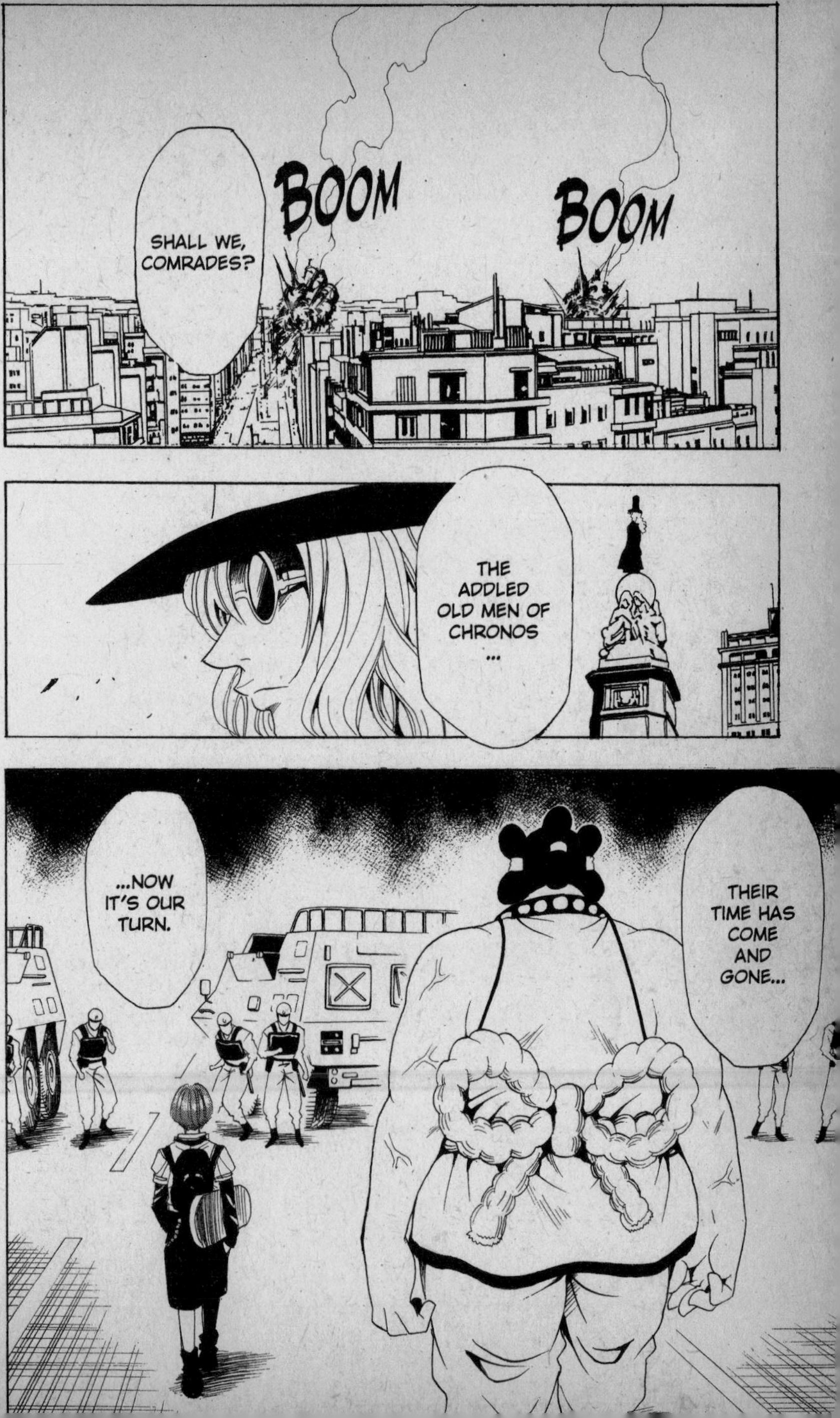
BOOM
BOOM
SHALL WE, COMRADES?
THE ADDLED OLD MEN OF CHRONOS ...
THEIR TIME HAS COME AND GONE...
...NOW IT'S OUR TURN.

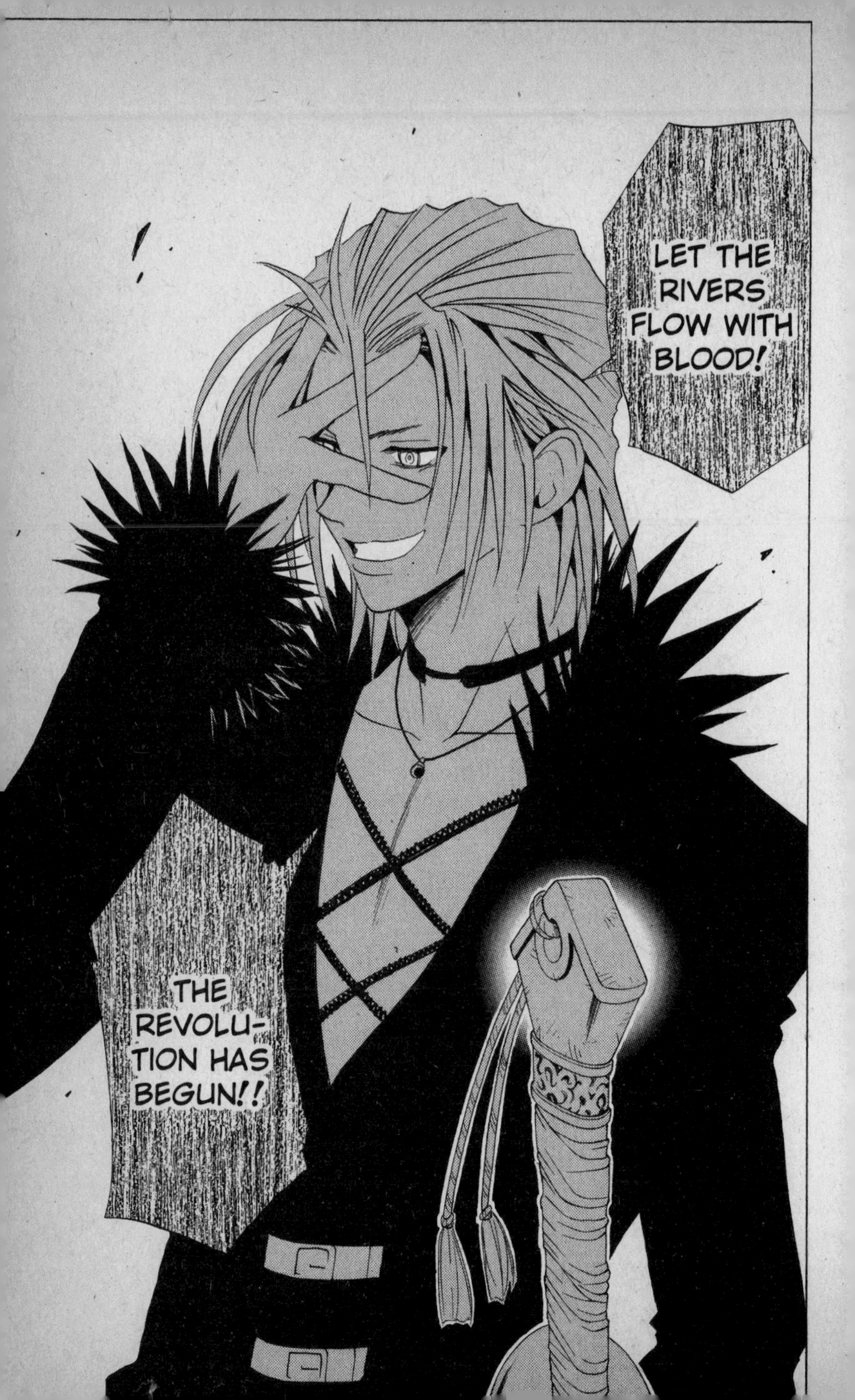
LET THE RIVERS FLOW WITH BLOOD!
THE REVOLU- TION HAS BEGUN!!

BLACK CAT

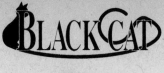

profile

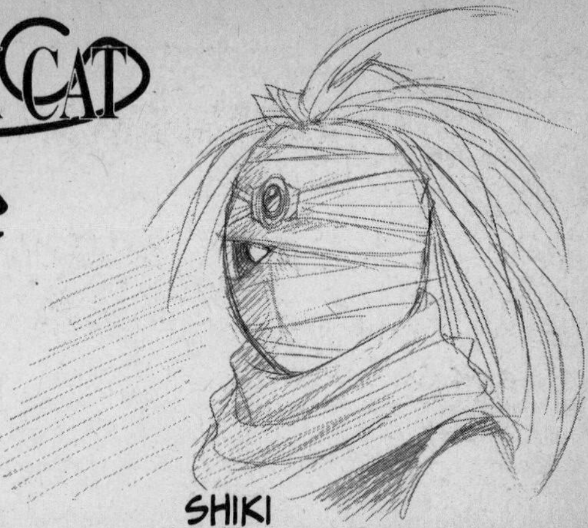

SHIKI

DATA	
BIRTHDAY:	?
AGE:	?
BLOOD TYPE:	?
HEIGHT:	144 CM
WEIGHT:	?
INTERESTS:	DEEP MEDITATION; PHARMACEUTICALS
POWER:	CREATES AND MANIPULATES INSECTS
COMMENTS:	ORIGINALLY FROM THE BIRTHPLACE OF TAO; ABLE TO DRAW THE TAO POWER OUT IN OTHERS; ABLE TO TRANSFORM HIS *CHI* INTO VARIOUS "INSECTS," WITH SPECIAL CHARACTERISTICS...BUT, THESE INSECTS SELF-DESTRUCT AFTER A CERTAIN AMOUNT OF TIME.

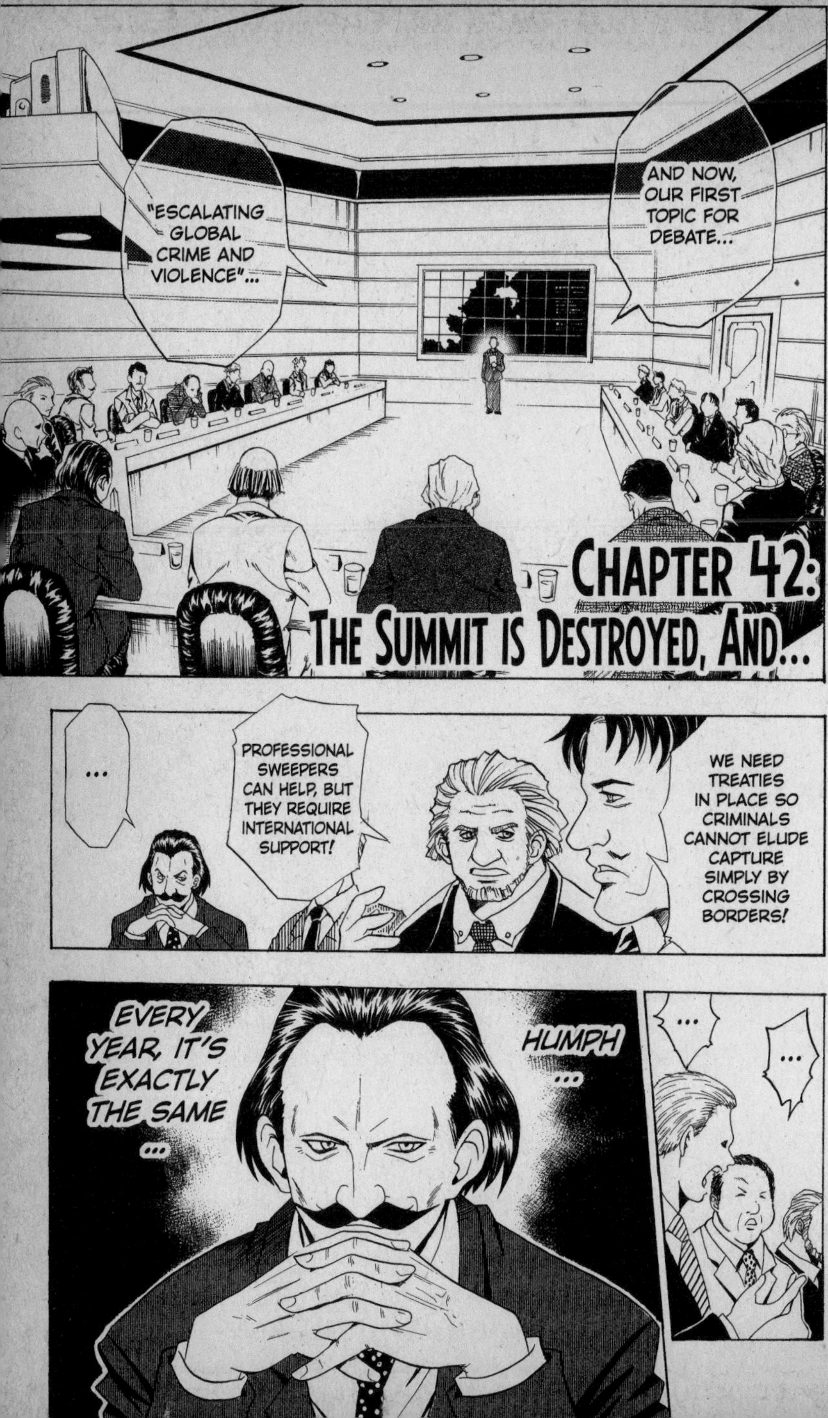
AND NOW, OUR FIRST TOPIC FOR DEBATE...
"ESCALATING GLOBAL CRIME AND VIOLENCE"...
CHAPTER 42:
THE SUMMIT IS DESTROYED, AND...
WE NEED TREATIES IN PLACE SO CRIMINALS CANNOT ELUDE CAPTURE SIMPLY BY CROSSING BORDERS!
PROFESSIONAL SWEEPERS CAN HELP, BUT THEY REQUIRE INTERNATIONAL SUPPORT!
...
...
...
HUMPH ...
EVERY YEAR, IT'S EXACTLY THE SAME ...

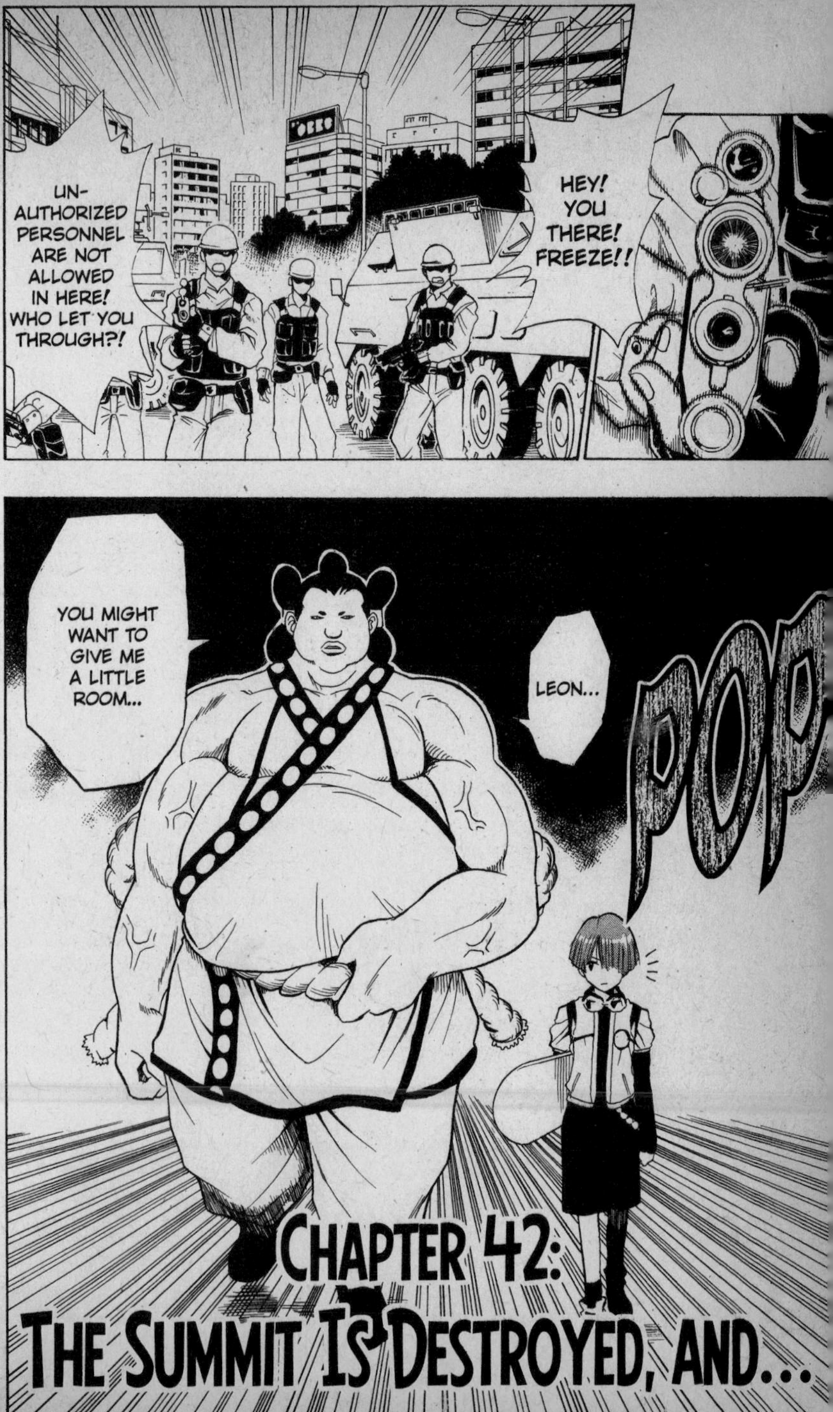
HEY! YOU THERE! FREEZE!!
UN-AUTHORIZED PERSONNEL ARE NOT ALLOWED IN HERE! WHO LET YOU THROUGH?!
POP
LEON...
YOU MIGHT WANT TO GIVE ME A LITTLE ROOM...
CHAPTER 42:
THE SUMMIT IS DESTROYED, AND...

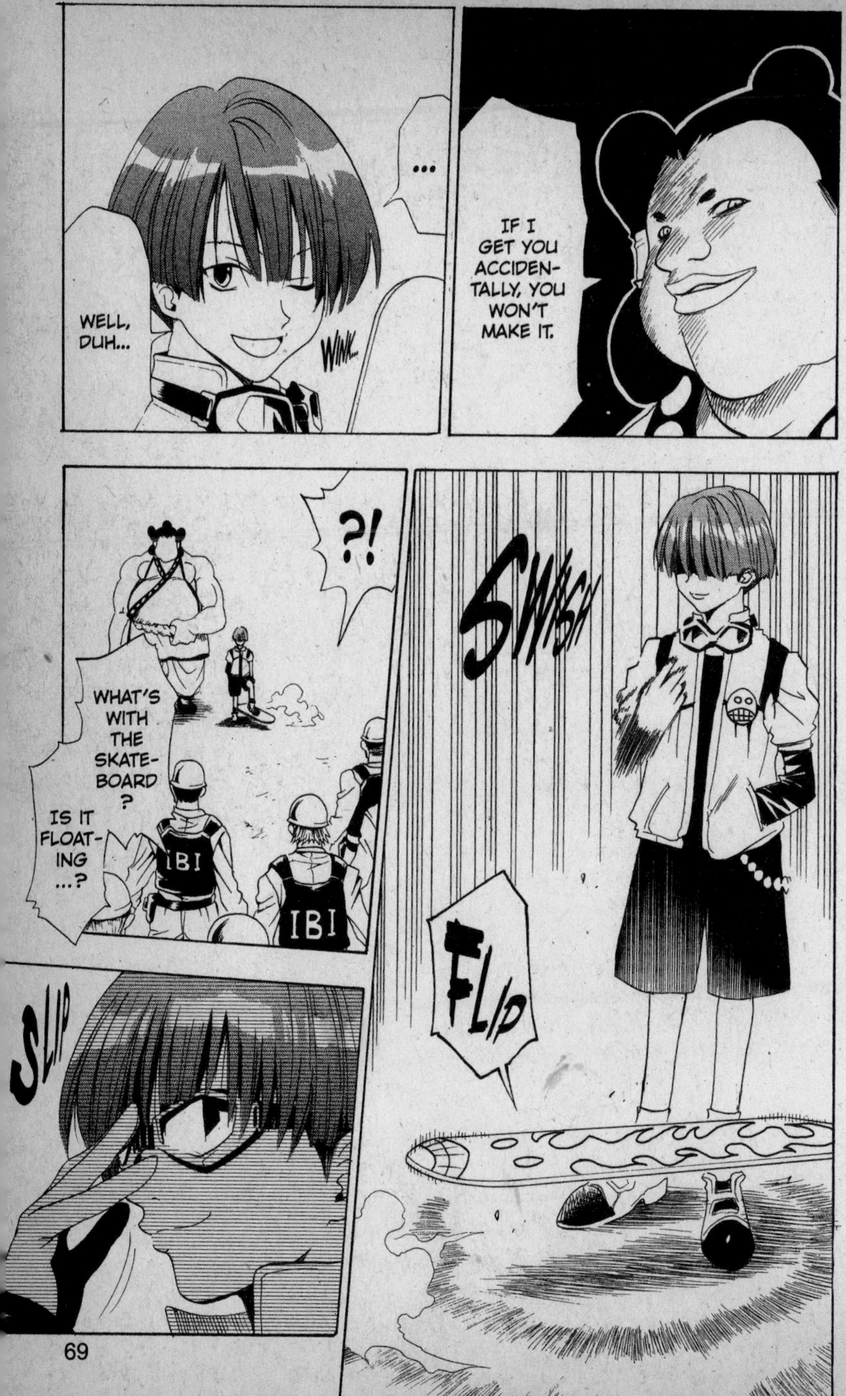
IF I GET YOU ACCIDENTALLY, YOU WON'T MAKE IT.
...
WINK...
WELL, DUH...
SWISH
FLIP
?!
WHAT'S WITH THE SKATEBOARD?
IS IT FLOATING ...?
IBI
IBI
SLIP

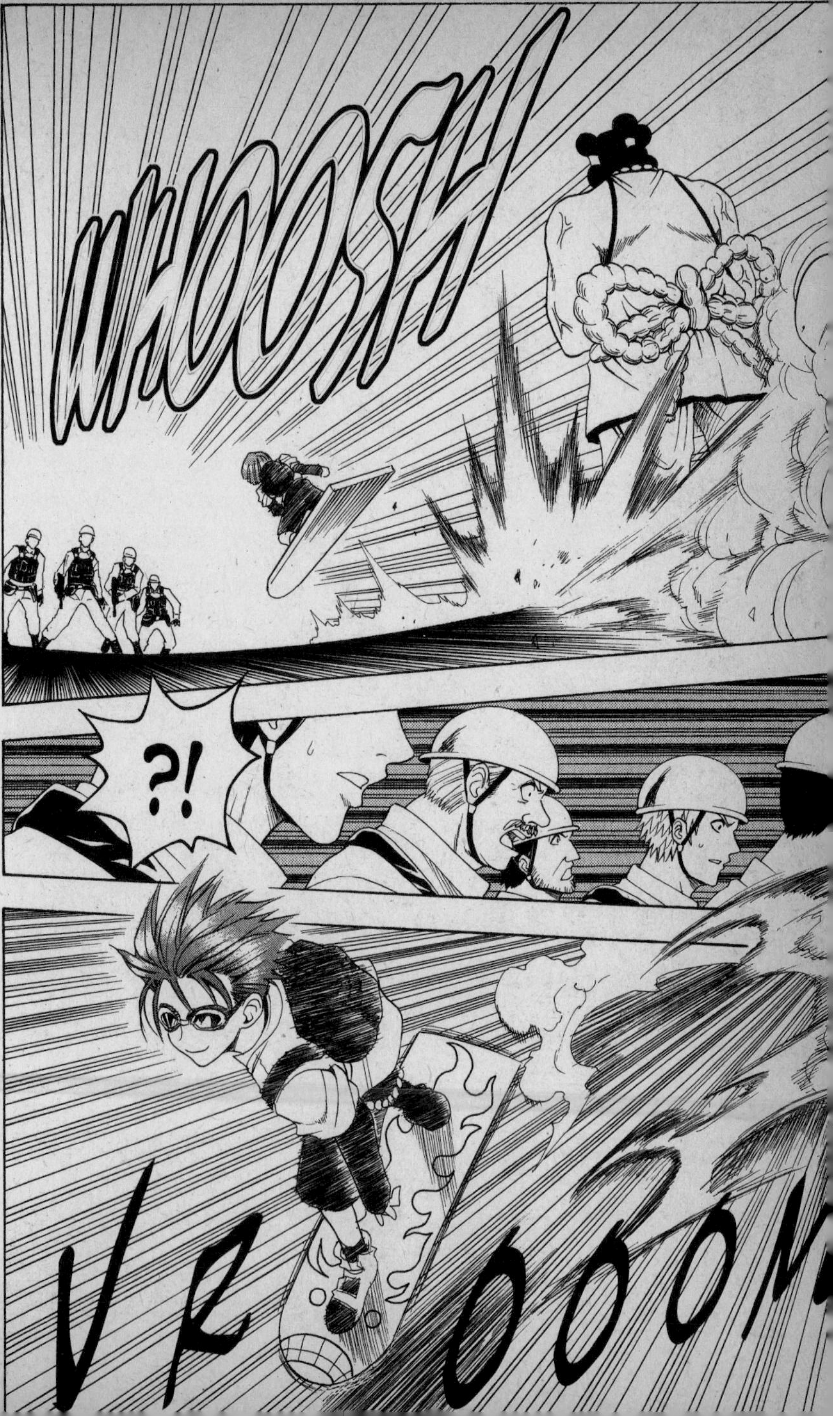
WHOOSH
?!
VROOOM

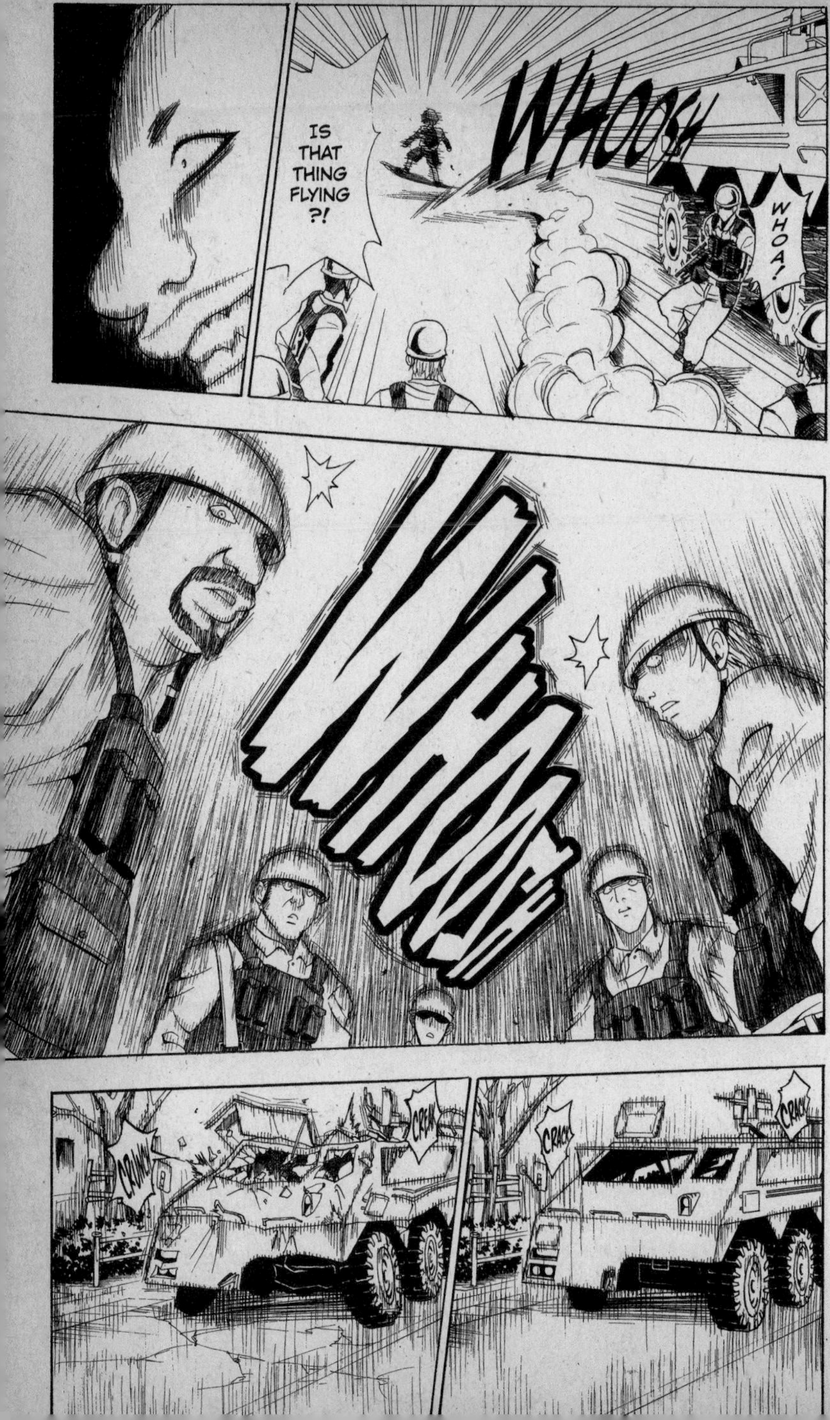
WHOOSH
WHOA!
IS THAT THING FLYING?!
CRACK
CRACK
CREAK
CRUNCH

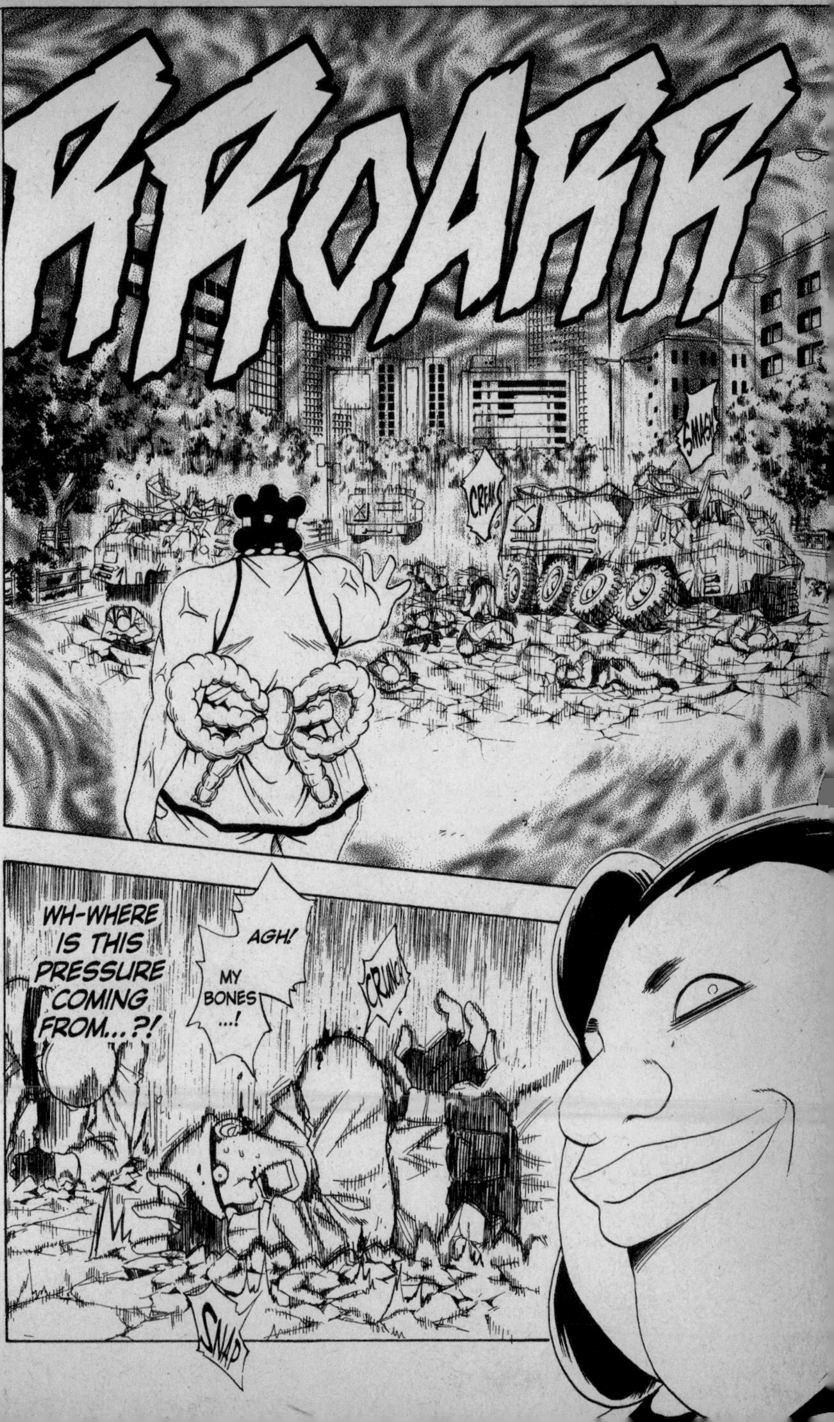
RROARR
SMASH
CREAK
CRUNCH
AGH!
MY BONES ...!
WH-WHERE IS THIS PRESSURE COMING FROM...?!
SNAP

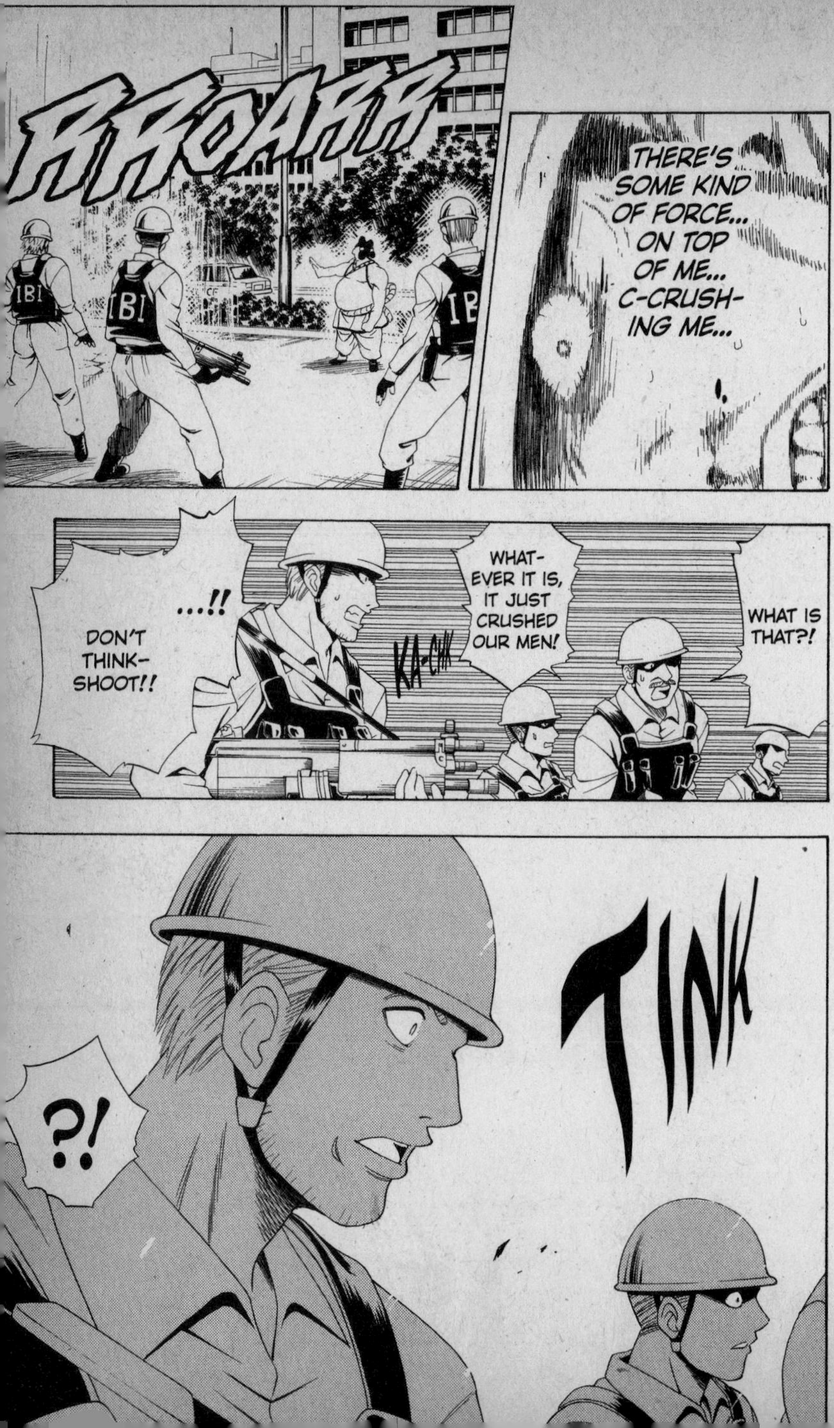
THERE'S SOME KIND OF FORCE... ON TOP OF ME... C-CRUSHING ME...
RROARR
WHAT IS THAT?!
WHAT-EVER IT IS, IT JUST CRUSHED OUR MEN!
KA-CHK
...!!
DON'T THINK-SHOOT!!
TINK
?!

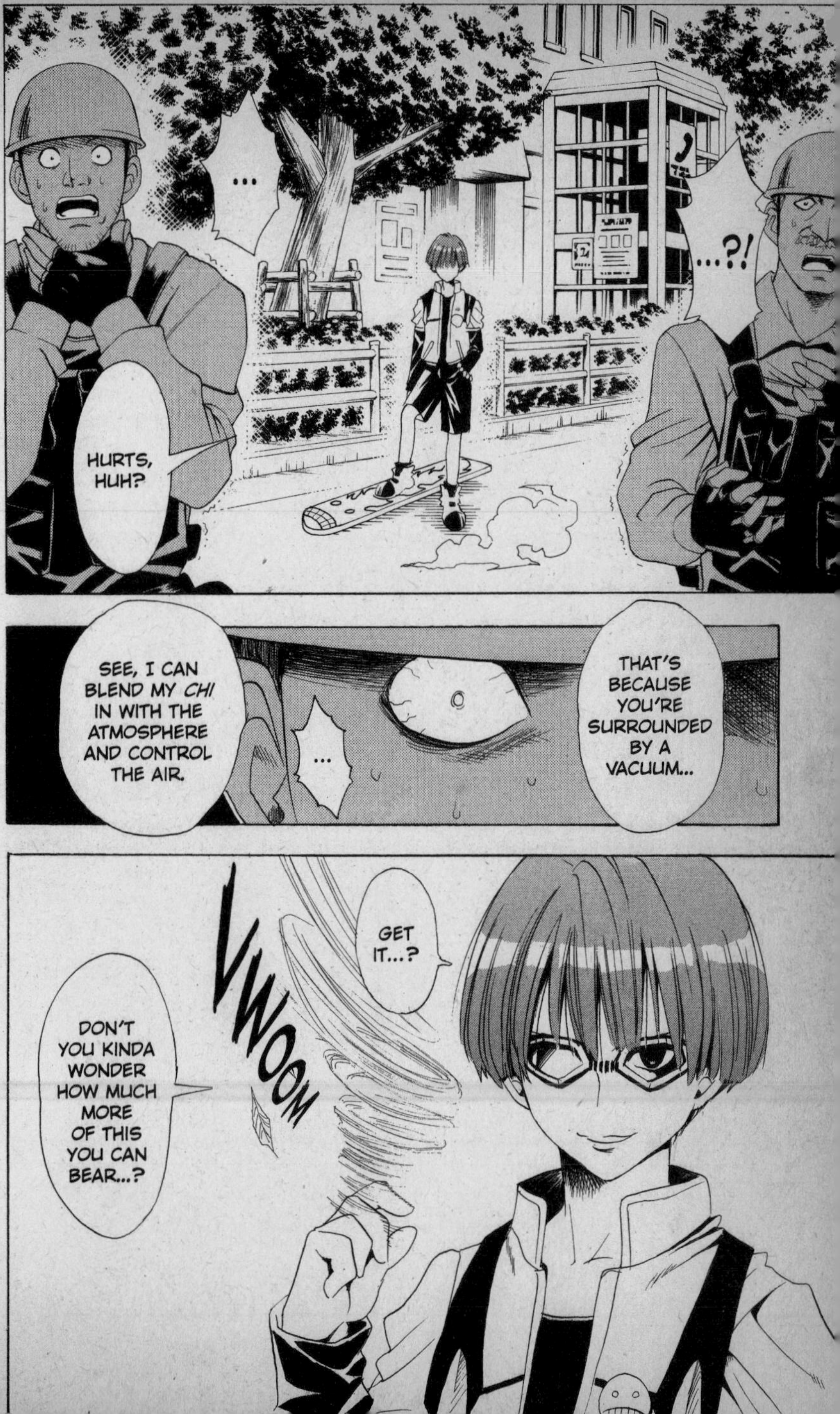

...?!
...
HURTS, HUH?
THAT'S BECAUSE YOU'RE SURROUNDED BY A VACUUM...
...
SEE, I CAN BLEND MY *CHI* IN WITH THE ATMOSPHERE AND CONTROL THE AIR.
GET IT...?
VWOOM
DON'T YOU KINDA WONDER HOW MUCH MORE OF THIS YOU CAN BEAR...?

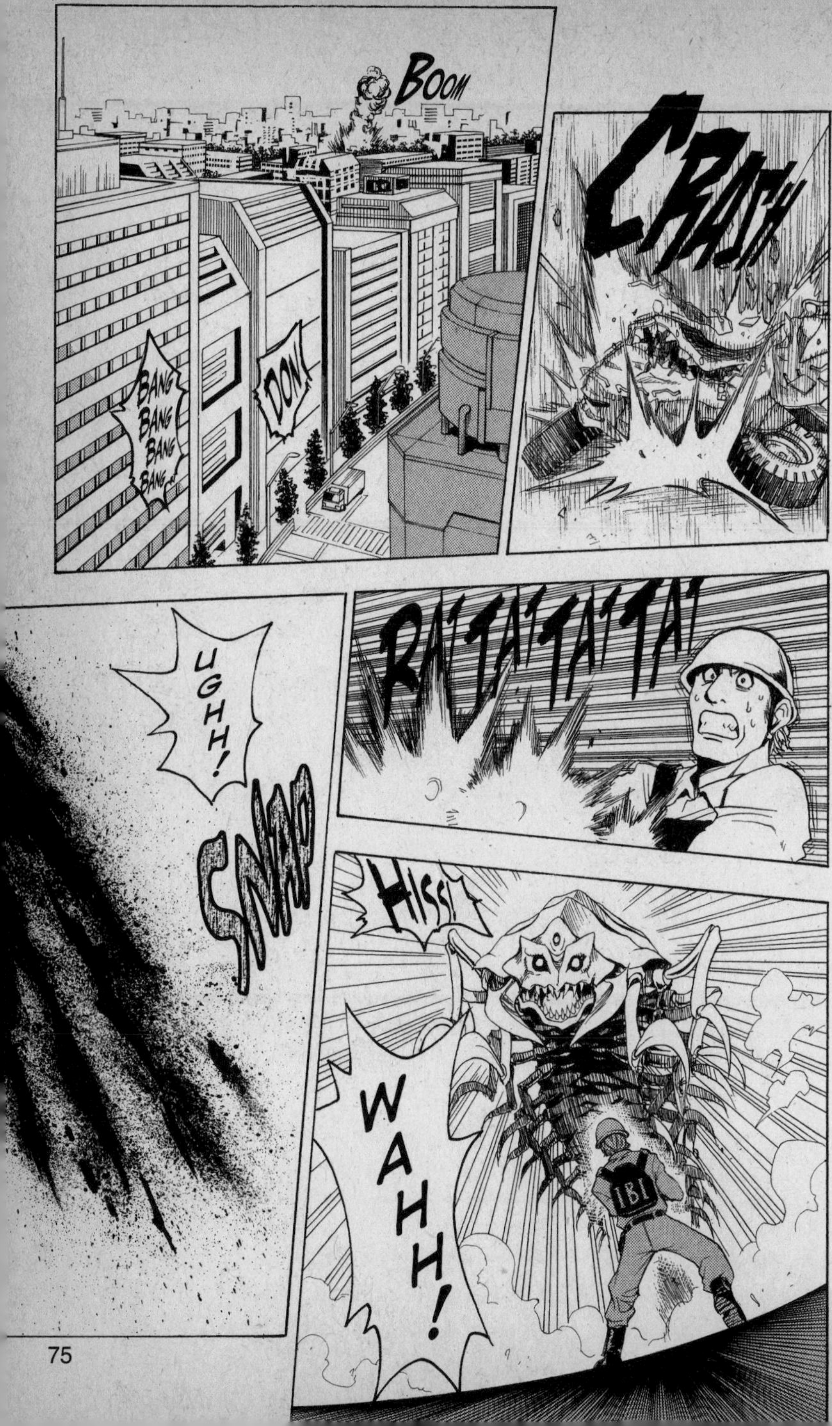
CRASH
BOOM
DON!
BANG
BANG
BANG
BANG
RATATATATA
HISS!
WAHH!
UGHH!
SNAP

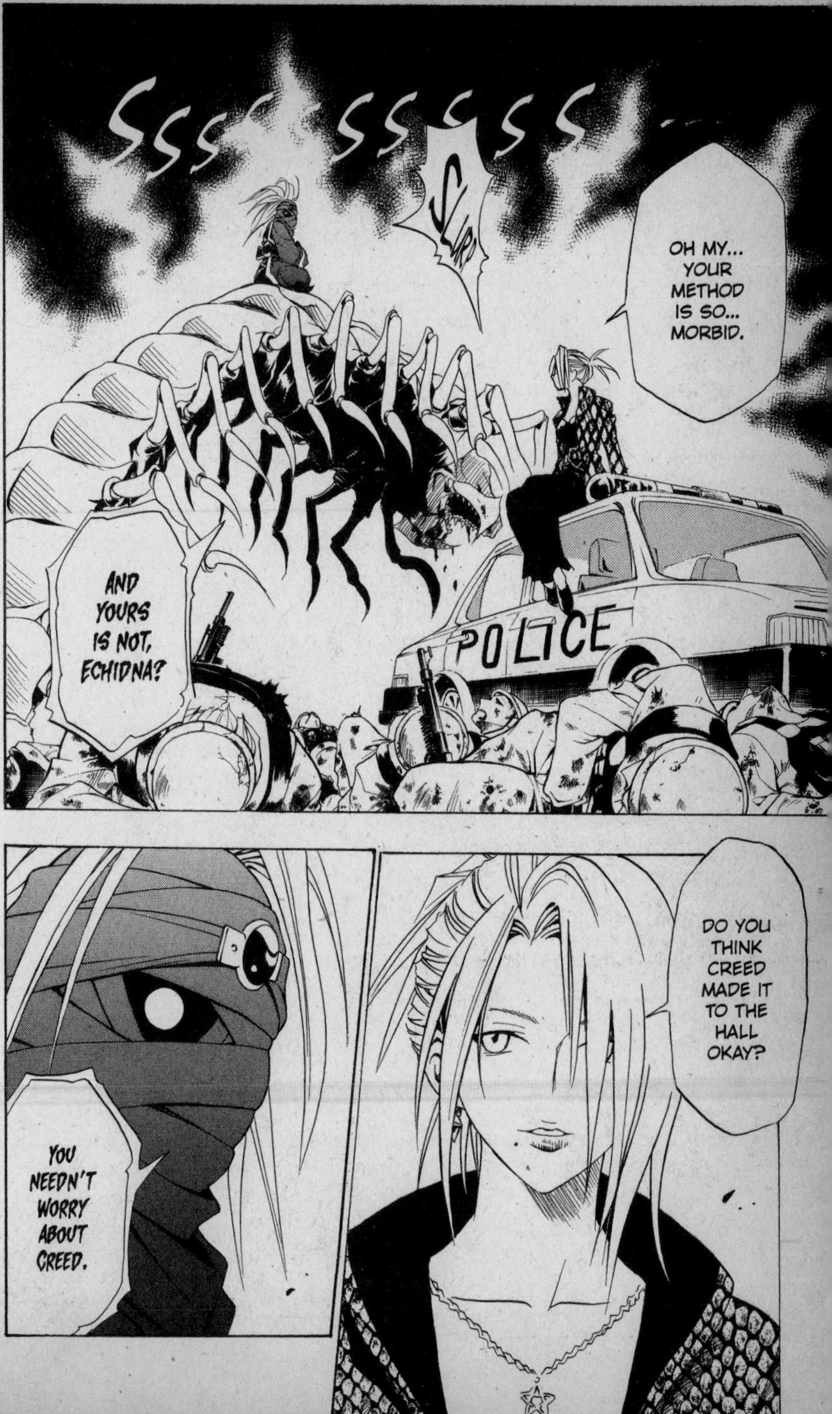
SLURP
OH MY... YOUR METHOD IS SO... MORBID.
AND YOURS IS NOT, ECHIDNA?
DO YOU THINK CREED MADE IT TO THE HALL OKAY?
YOU NEEDN'T WORRY ABOUT CREED.

READ THIS WAY

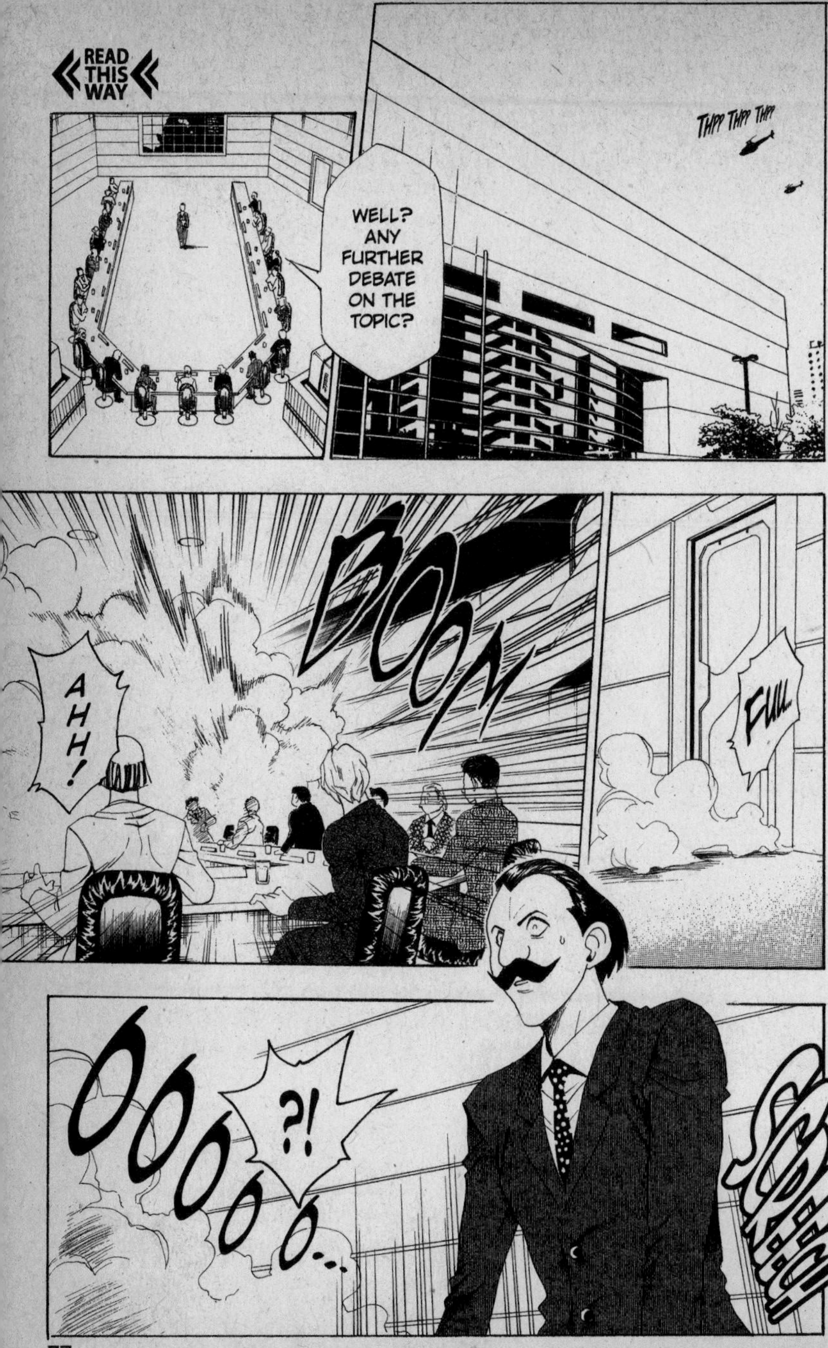
THPP THPP THPP
WELL? ANY FURTHER DEBATE ON THE TOPIC?
FUU
BOOM
AHH!
SCREECH!
?!
OOOOOO...

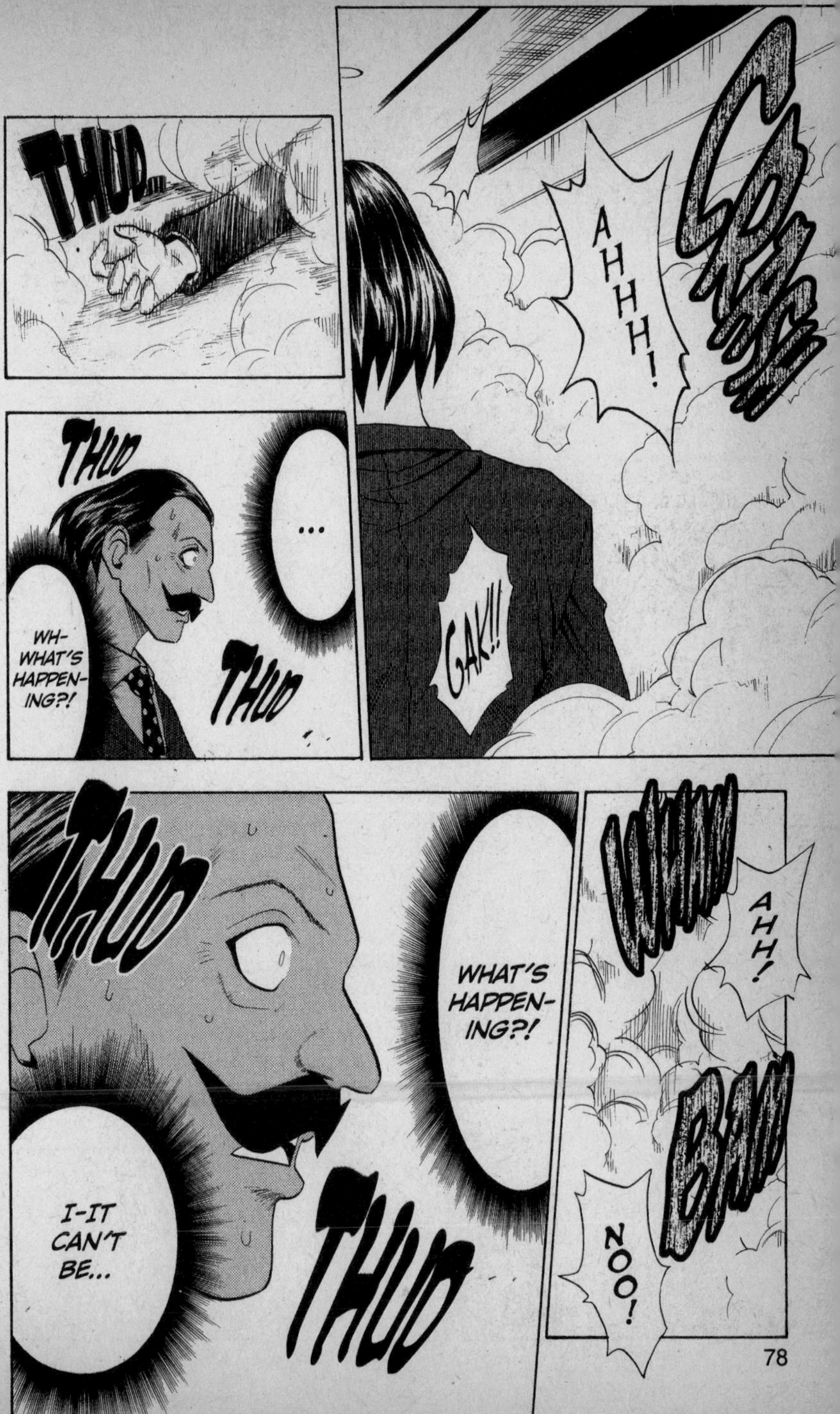
AHHHH!
GAK!!
THUD...
THUD
...
WH-WHAT'S HAPPENING?!
THUD
AHH!
BAM
NOO!
THUD
WHAT'S HAPPENING?!
I-IT CAN'T BE...
THUD

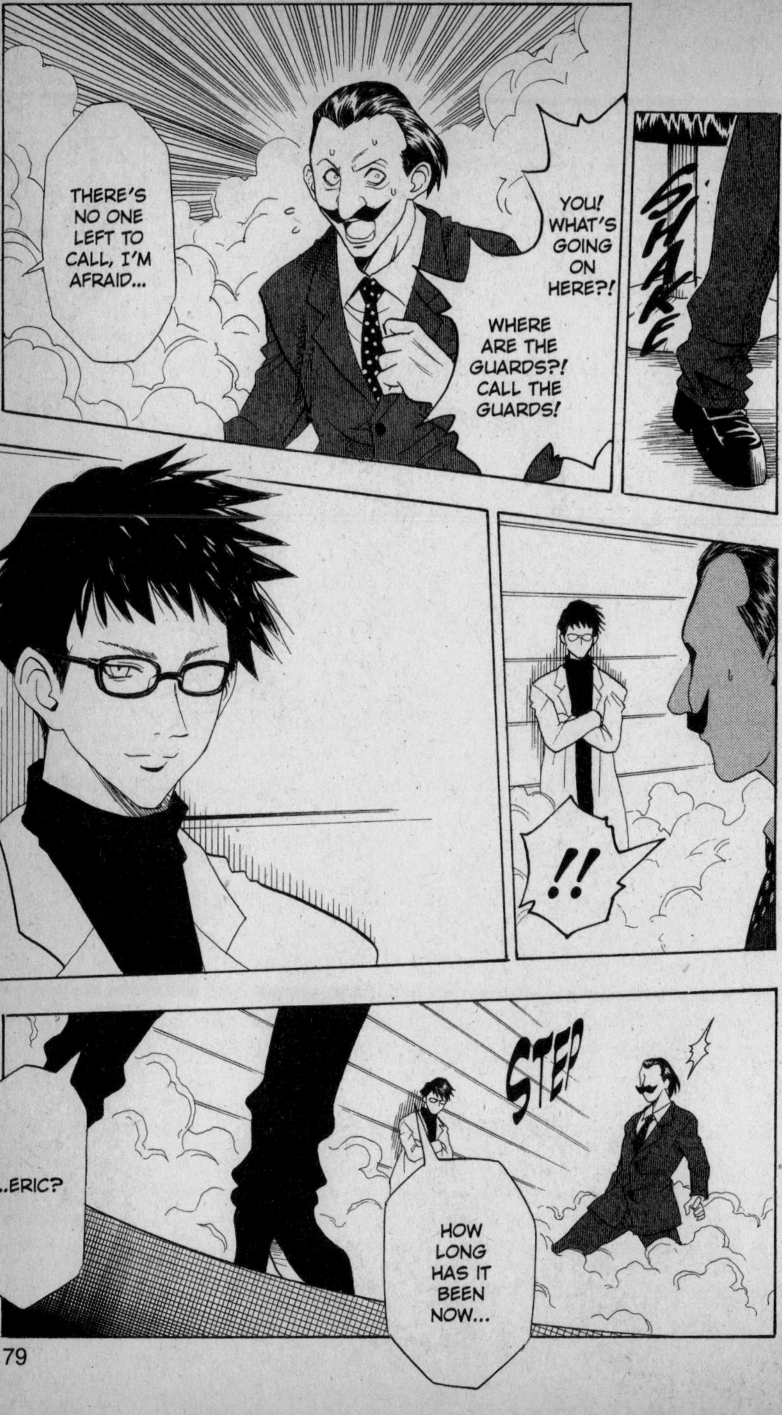
SHAKE
YOU! WHAT'S GOING ON HERE?!
WHERE ARE THE GUARDS?! CALL THE GUARDS!
THERE'S NO ONE LEFT TO CALL, I'M AFRAID...
!!
STEP
HOW LONG HAS IT BEEN NOW...
...ERIC?

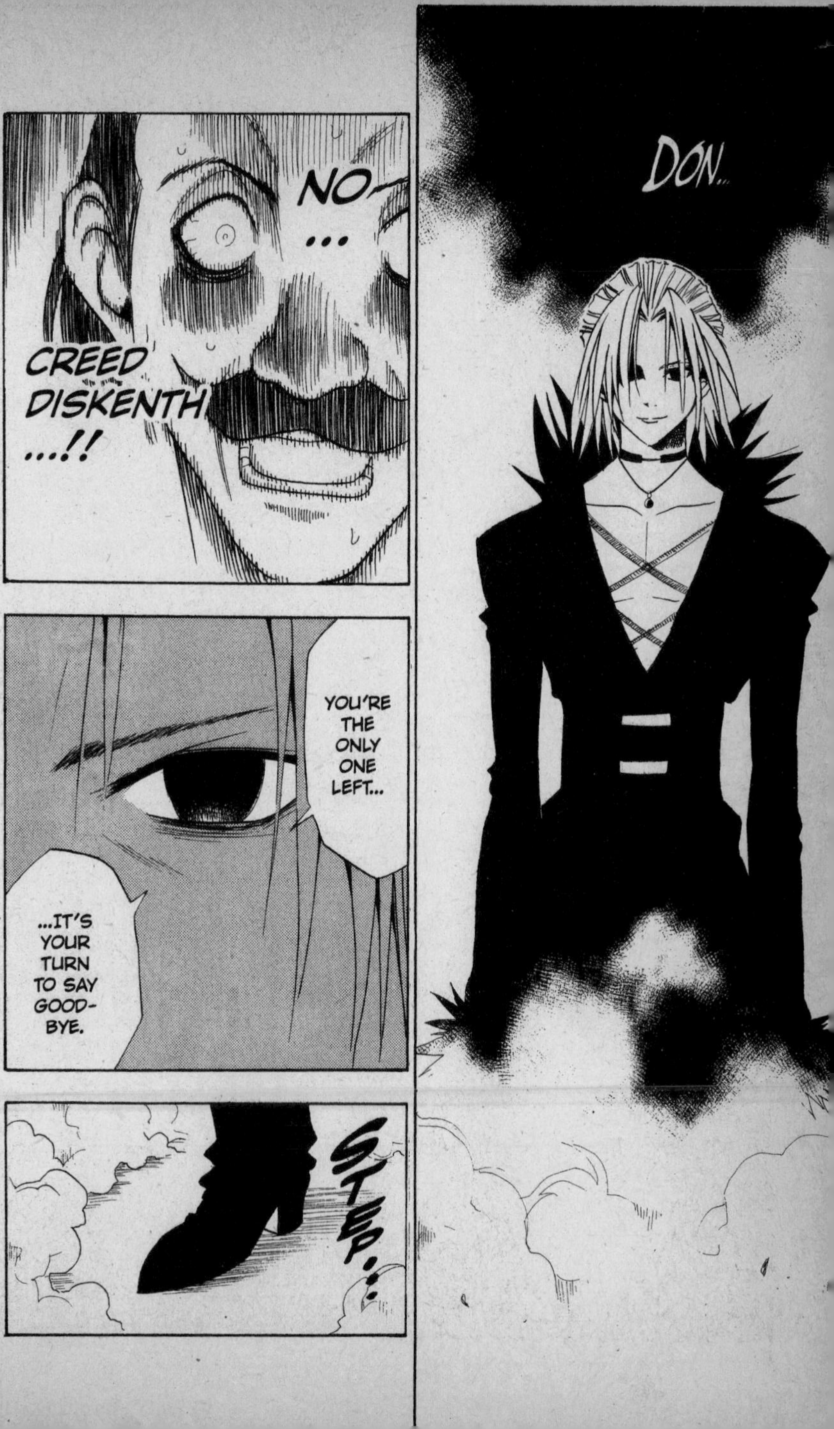
DON...
NO—
...
CREED DISKENTH ...!!
YOU'RE THE ONLY ONE LEFT...
...IT'S YOUR TURN TO SAY GOOD-BYE.
STEP...

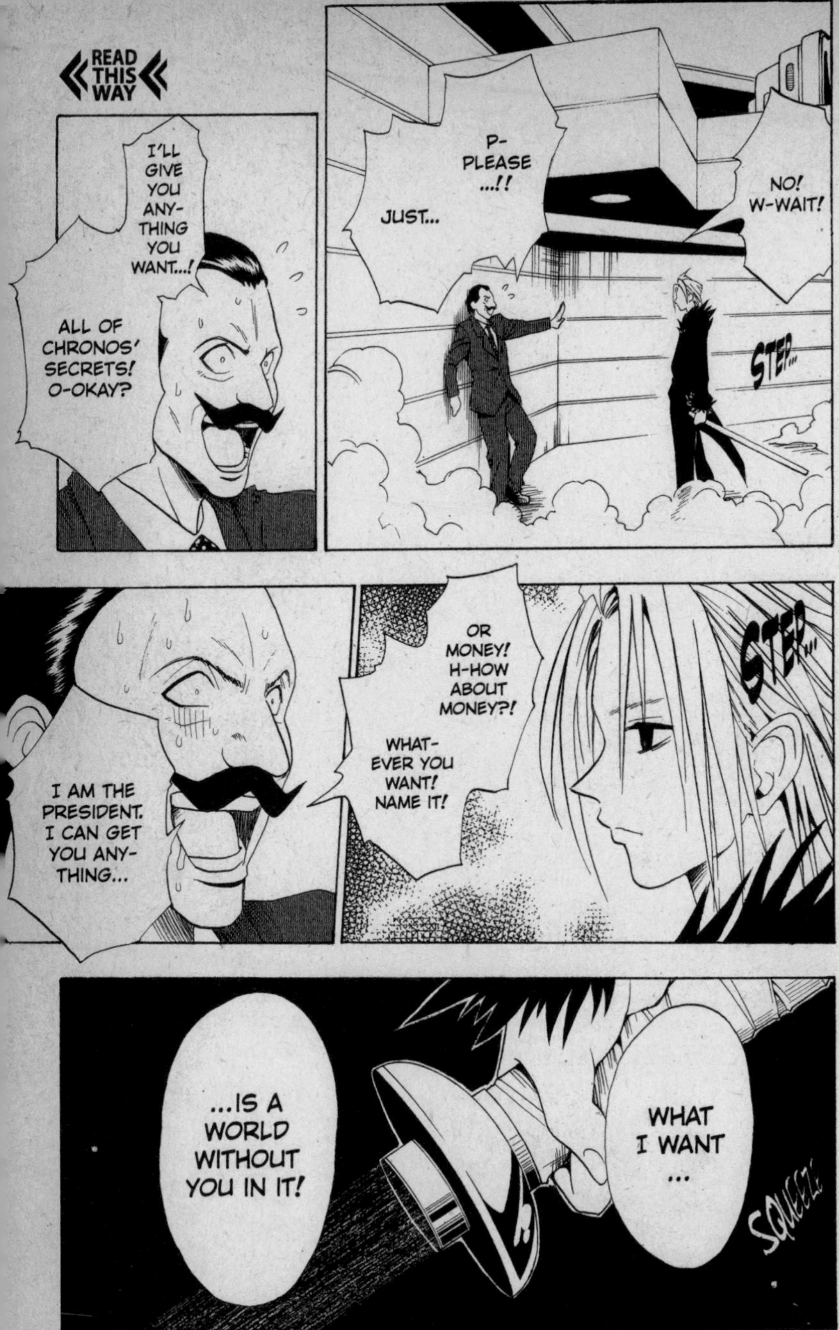
READ THIS WAY
NO! W-WAIT!
P-PLEASE...!!
JUST...
STEP...
I'LL GIVE YOU ANYTHING YOU WANT...!
ALL OF CHRONOS' SECRETS! O-OKAY?
STEP...
OR MONEY! H-HOW ABOUT MONEY?!
WHATEVER YOU WANT! NAME IT!
I AM THE PRESIDENT. I CAN GET YOU ANYTHING...
WHAT I WANT...
...IS A WORLD WITHOUT YOU IN IT!
SQUEEZE

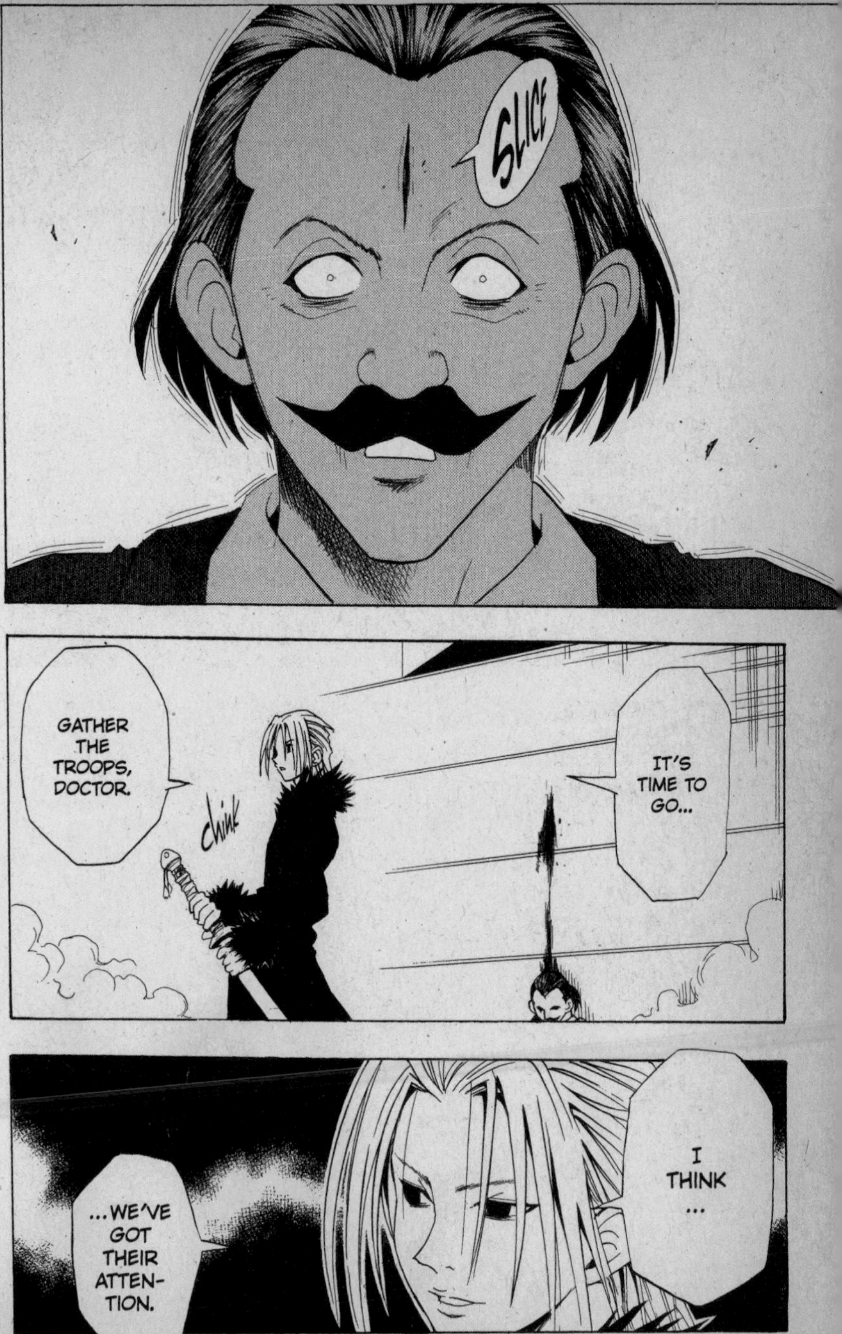
SLICE
IT'S TIME TO GO...
GATHER THE TROOPS, DOCTOR.
CHINK
I THINK...
...WE'VE GOT THEIR ATTEN-TION.

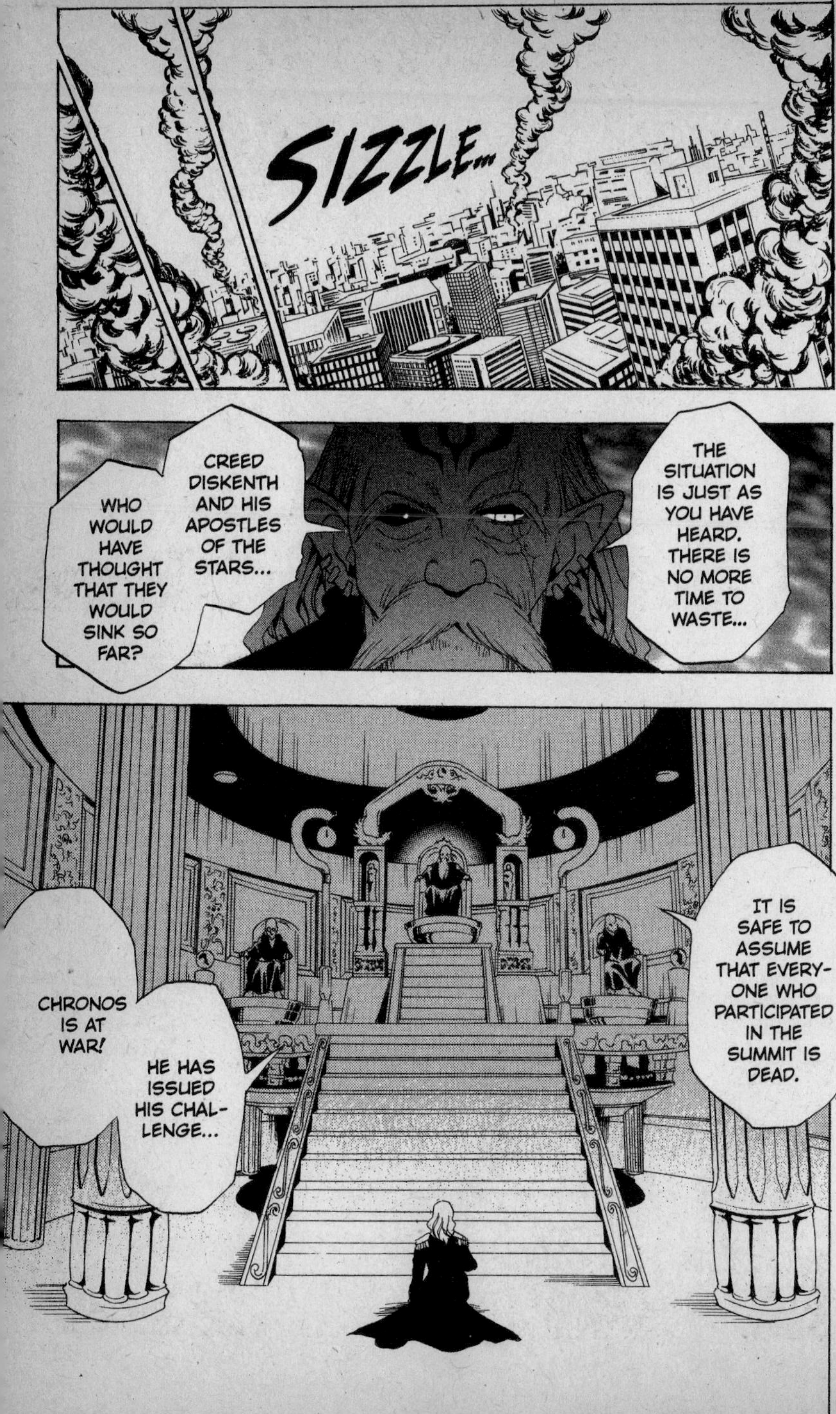
SIZZLE...
THE SITUATION IS JUST AS YOU HAVE HEARD. THERE IS NO MORE TIME TO WASTE...
CREED DISKENTH AND HIS APOSTLES OF THE STARS...
WHO WOULD HAVE THOUGHT THAT THEY WOULD SINK SO FAR?
IT IS SAFE TO ASSUME THAT EVERY-ONE WHO PARTICIPATED IN THE SUMMIT IS DEAD.
CHRONOS IS AT WAR!
HE HAS ISSUED HIS CHAL-LENGE...

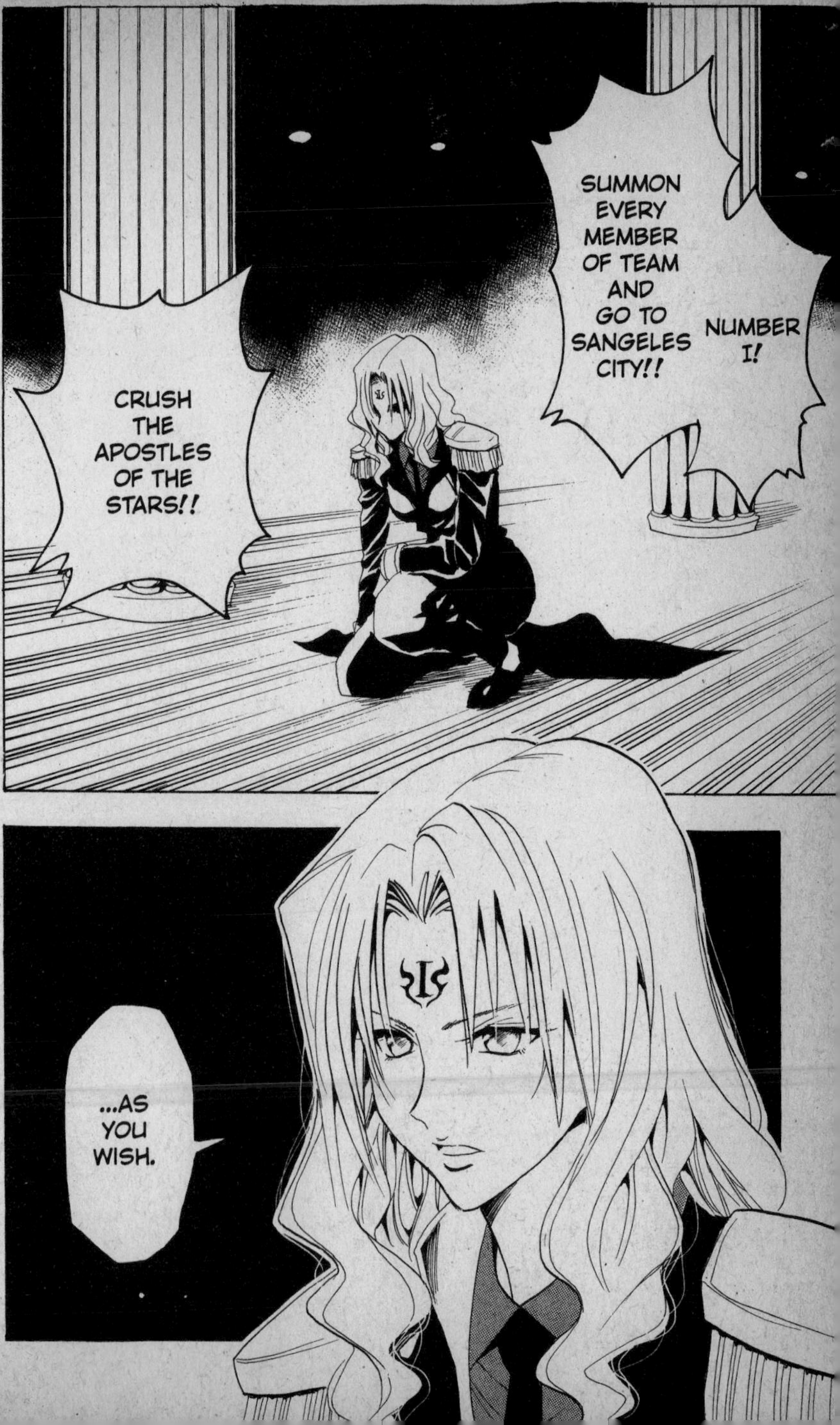
NUMBER I!
SUMMON EVERY MEMBER OF TEAM AND GO TO SANGELES CITY!!
CRUSH THE APOSTLES OF THE STARS!!
...AS YOU WISH.

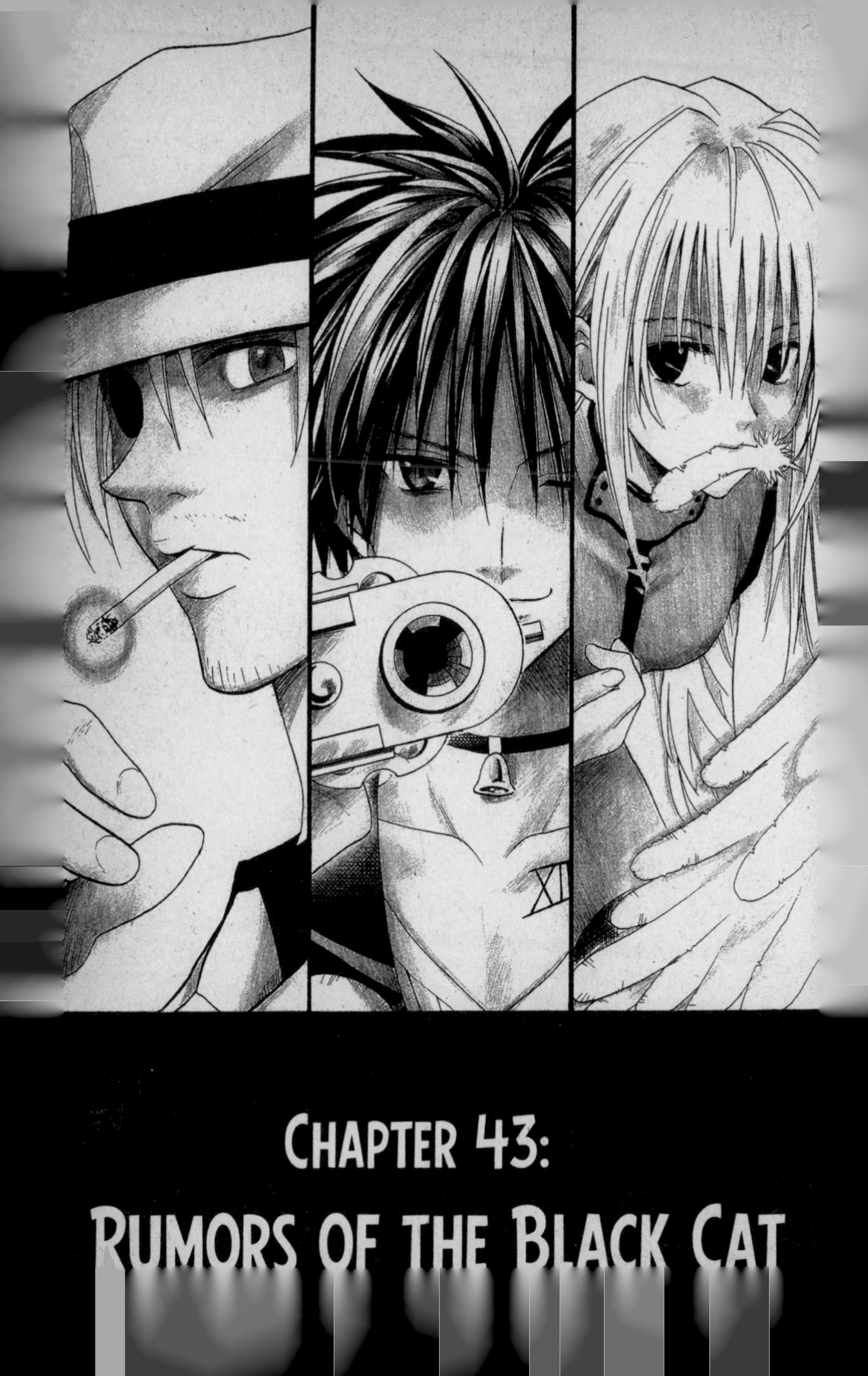
XII

Chapter 43: Rumors of the Black Cat

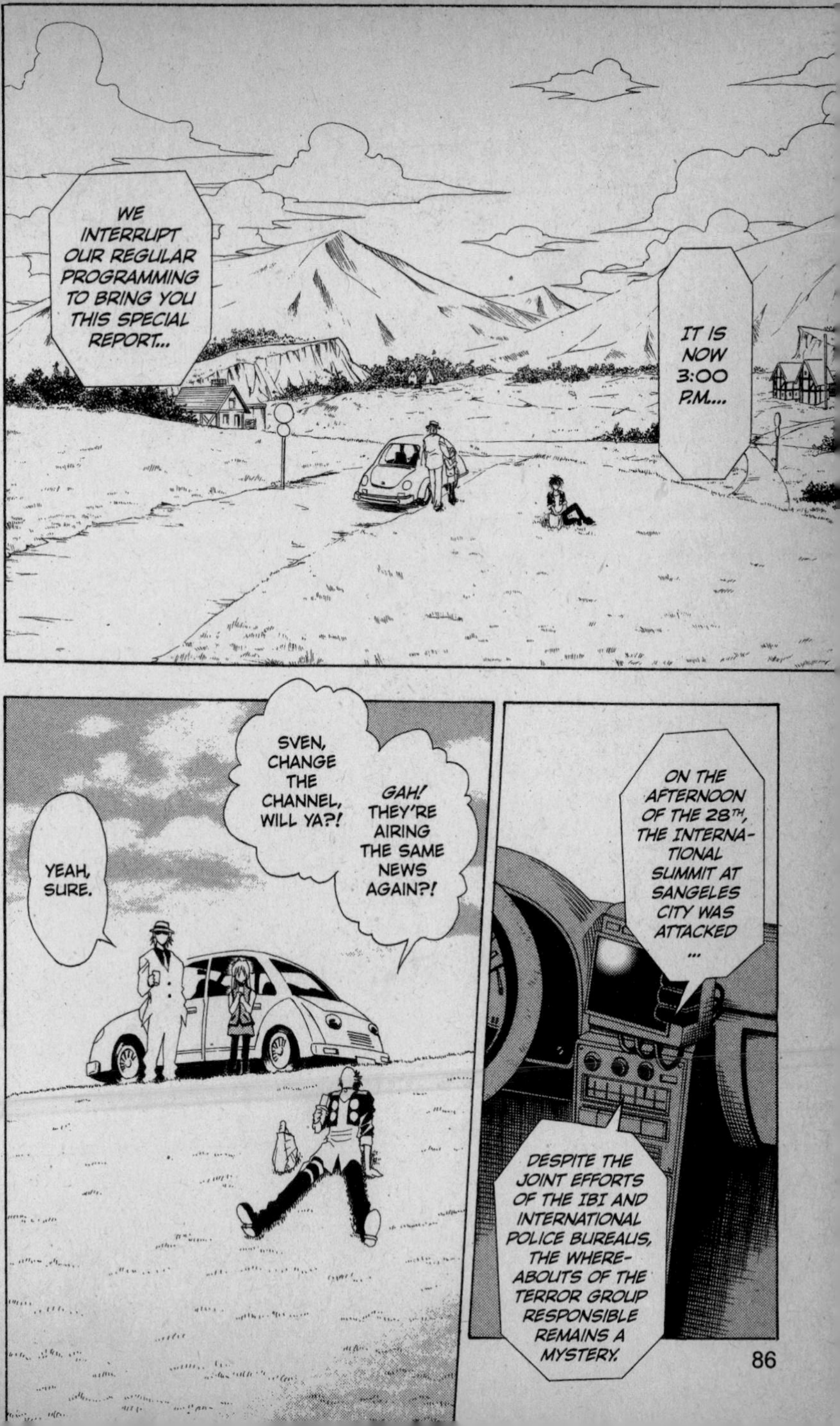
WE INTERRUPT OUR REGULAR PROGRAMMING TO BRING YOU THIS SPECIAL REPORT...
IT IS NOW 3:00 P.M...
ON THE AFTERNOON OF THE 28TH, THE INTERNATIONAL SUMMIT AT SANGELES CITY WAS ATTACKED...
DESPITE THE JOINT EFFORTS OF THE IBI AND INTERNATIONAL POLICE BUREAUS, THE WHEREABOUTS OF THE TERROR GROUP RESPONSIBLE REMAINS A MYSTERY.
GAH! THEY'RE AIRING THE SAME NEWS AGAIN?!
SVEN, CHANGE THE CHANNEL, WILL YA?!
YEAH, SURE.

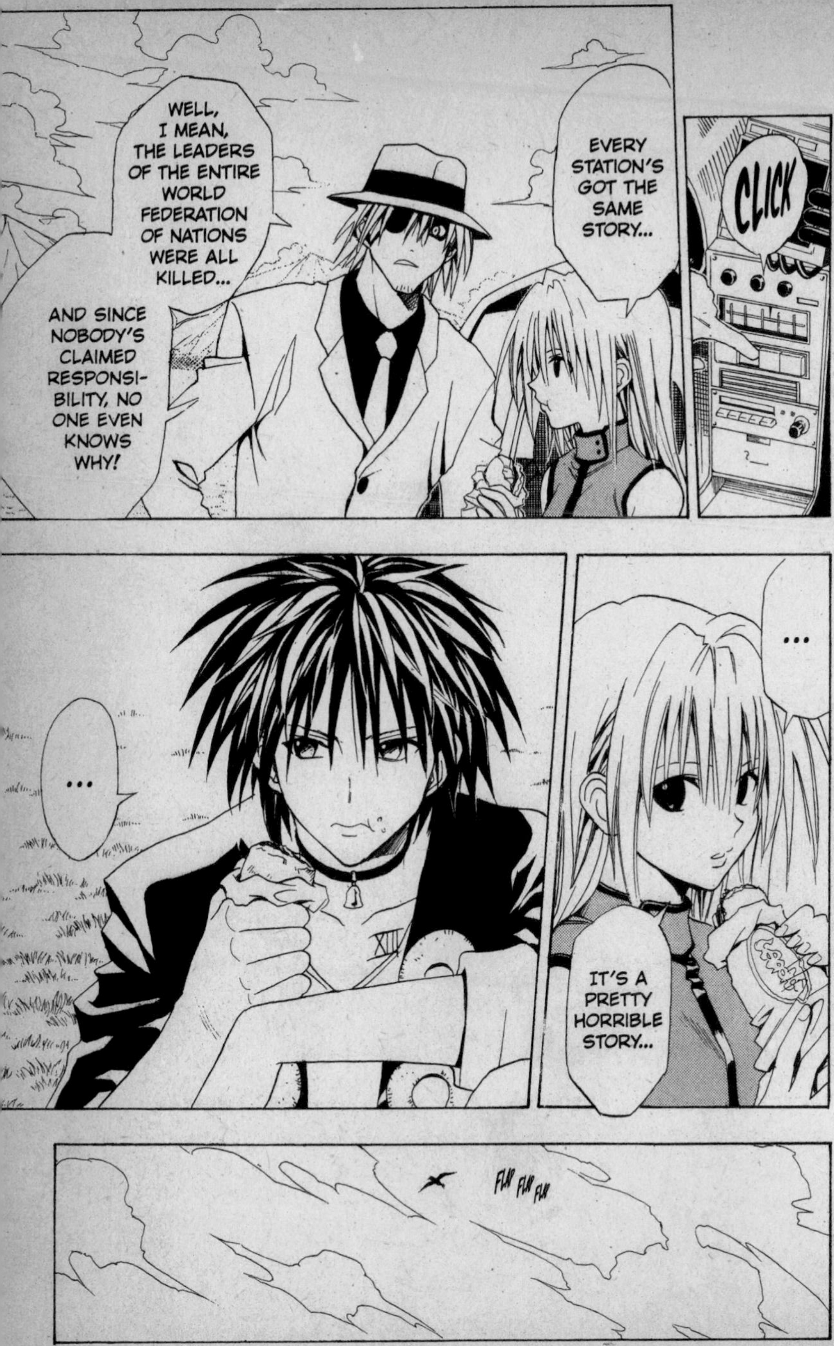
CLICK
EVERY STATION'S GOT THE SAME STORY...
WELL, I MEAN, THE LEADERS OF THE ENTIRE WORLD FEDERATION OF NATIONS WERE ALL KILLED...
AND SINCE NOBODY'S CLAIMED RESPONSIBILITY, NO ONE EVEN KNOWS WHY!
...
IT'S A PRETTY HORRIBLE STORY...
...
FLAP FLAP FLAP

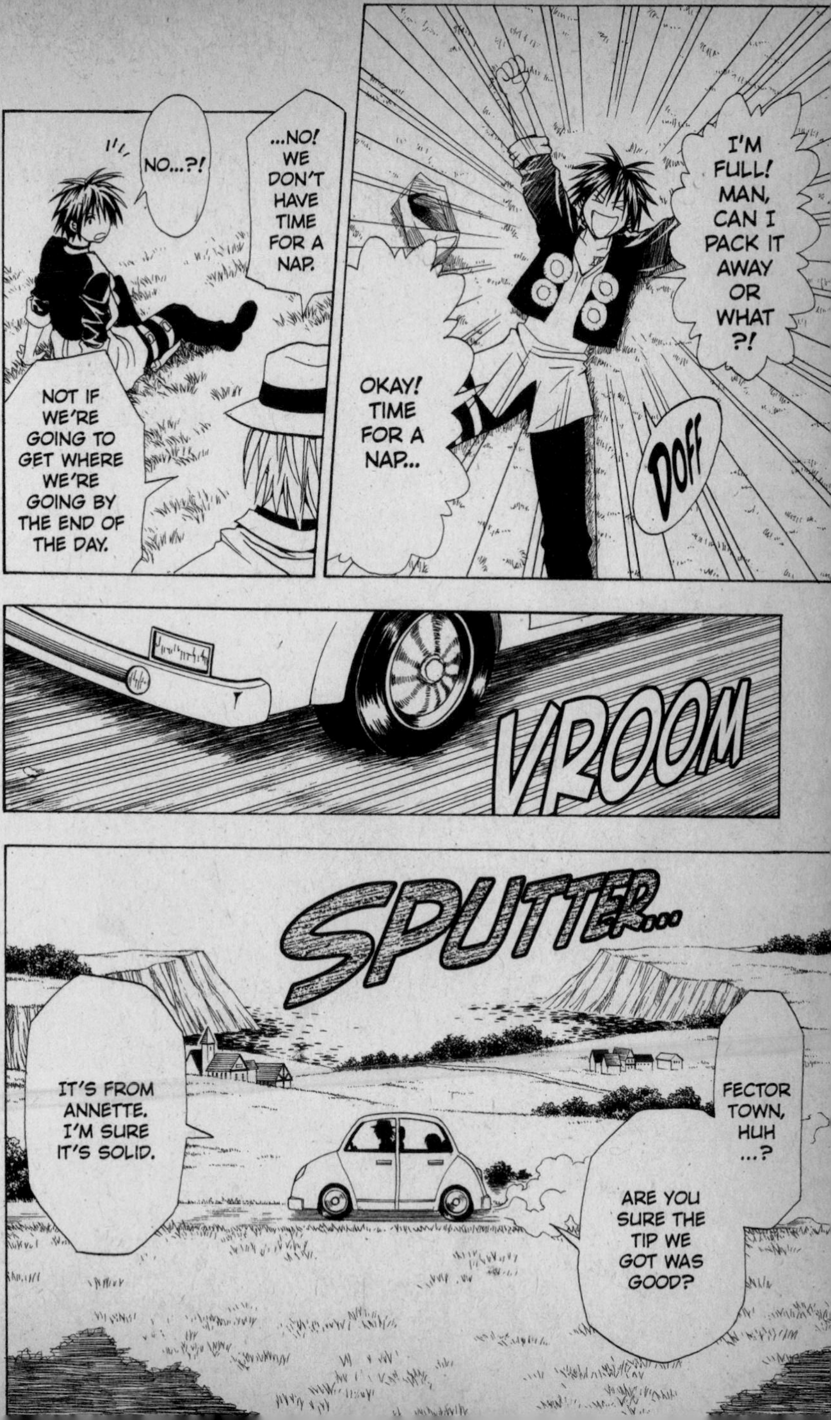
I'M FULL! MAN, CAN I PACK IT AWAY OR WHAT?!
DOFF
OKAY! TIME FOR A NAP...
...NO! WE DON'T HAVE TIME FOR A NAP.
NO...?!
NOT IF WE'RE GOING TO GET WHERE WE'RE GOING BY THE END OF THE DAY.
VROOM
SPUTTER...
FECTOR TOWN, HUH...?
ARE YOU SURE THE TIP WE GOT WAS GOOD?
IT'S FROM ANNETTE. I'M SURE IT'S SOLID.

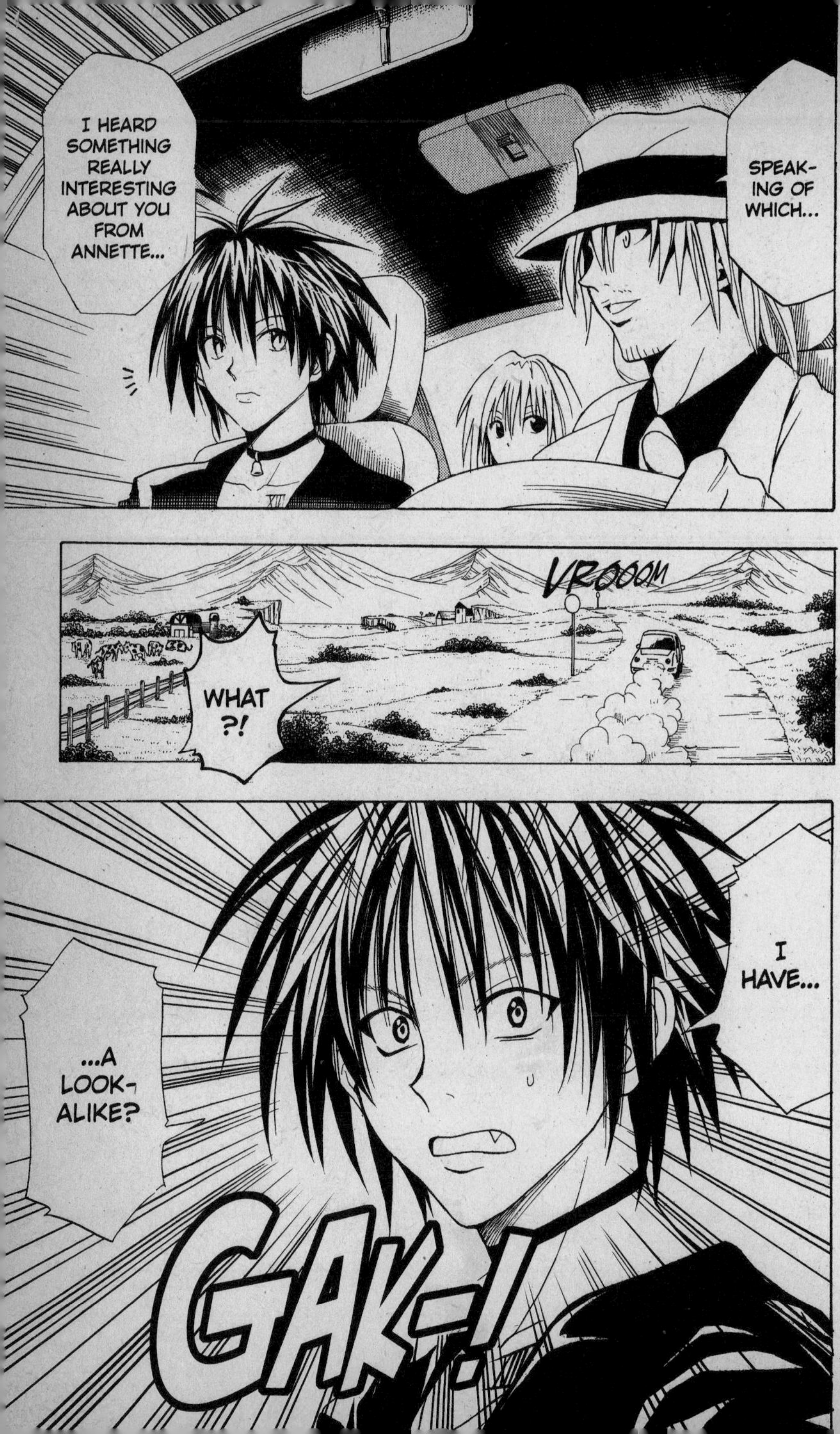
SPEAK-ING OF WHICH...
I HEARD SOMETHING REALLY INTERESTING ABOUT YOU FROM ANNETTE...
VROOOM
WHAT?!
I HAVE...
...A LOOK-ALIKE?
GAK-!

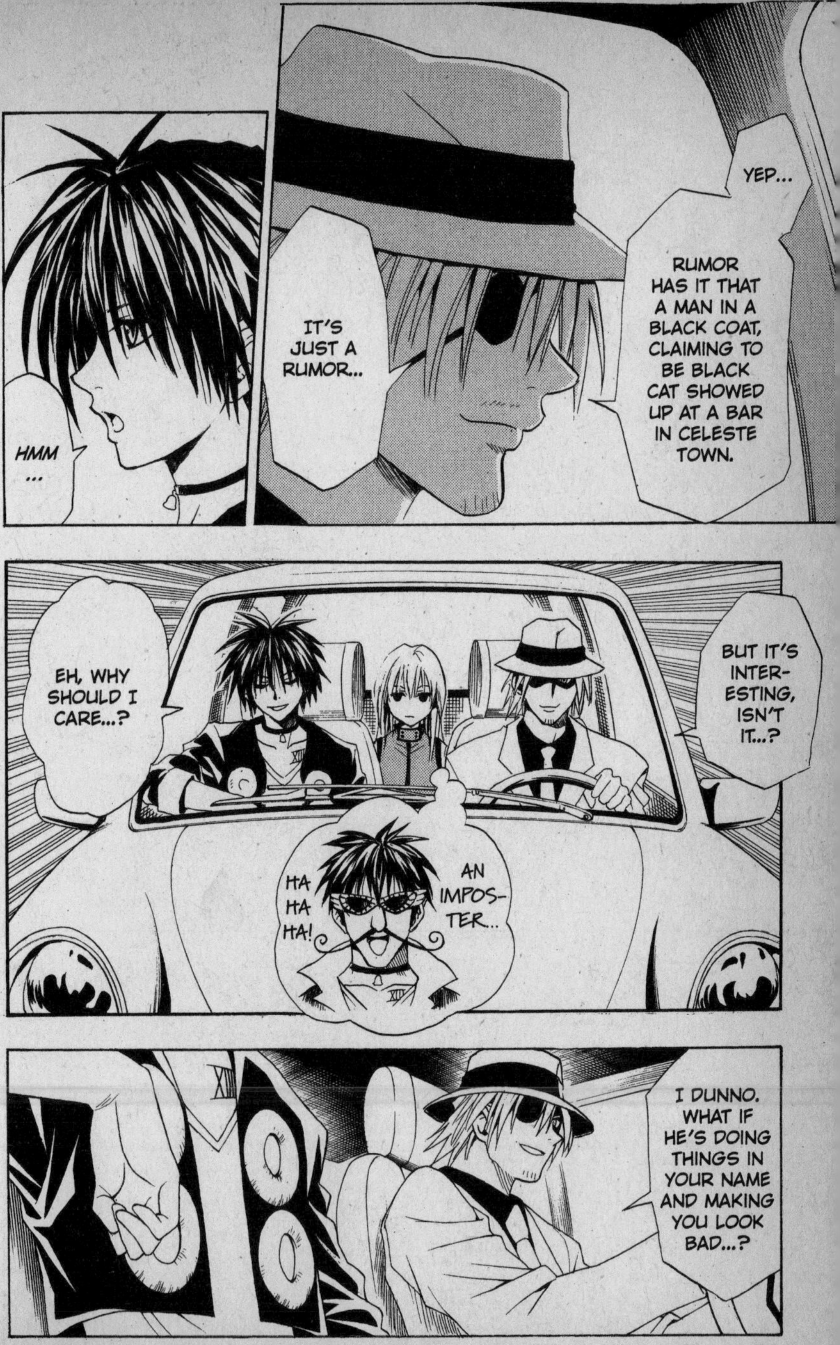
YEP...
RUMOR HAS IT THAT A MAN IN A BLACK COAT, CLAIMING TO BE BLACK CAT SHOWED UP AT A BAR IN CELESTE TOWN.
IT'S JUST A RUMOR...
HMM...
BUT IT'S INTER-ESTING, ISN'T IT...?
EH, WHY SHOULD I CARE...?
AN IMPOS-TER...
HA HA HA!
I DUNNO. WHAT IF HE'S DOING THINGS IN YOUR NAME AND MAKING YOU LOOK BAD...?

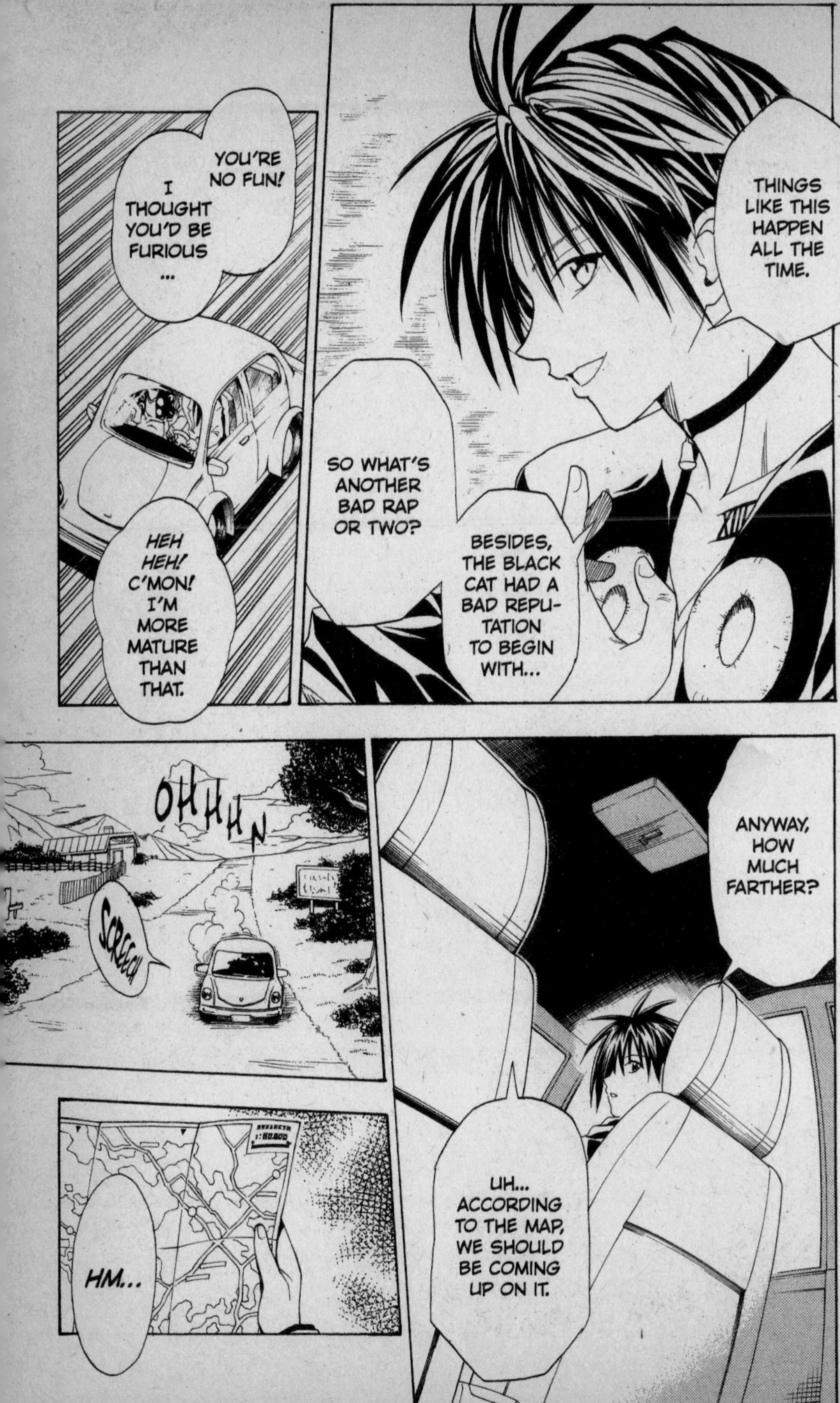
THINGS LIKE THIS HAPPEN ALL THE TIME.
BESIDES, THE BLACK CAT HAD A BAD REPUTATION TO BEGIN WITH...
SO WHAT'S ANOTHER BAD RAP OR TWO?
YOU'RE NO FUN!
I THOUGHT YOU'D BE FURIOUS...
HEH HEH! C'MON! I'M MORE MATURE THAN THAT.
ANYWAY, HOW MUCH FARTHER?
UH... ACCORDING TO THE MAP, WE SHOULD BE COMING UP ON IT.
OHHHN
SCREECH
HM...

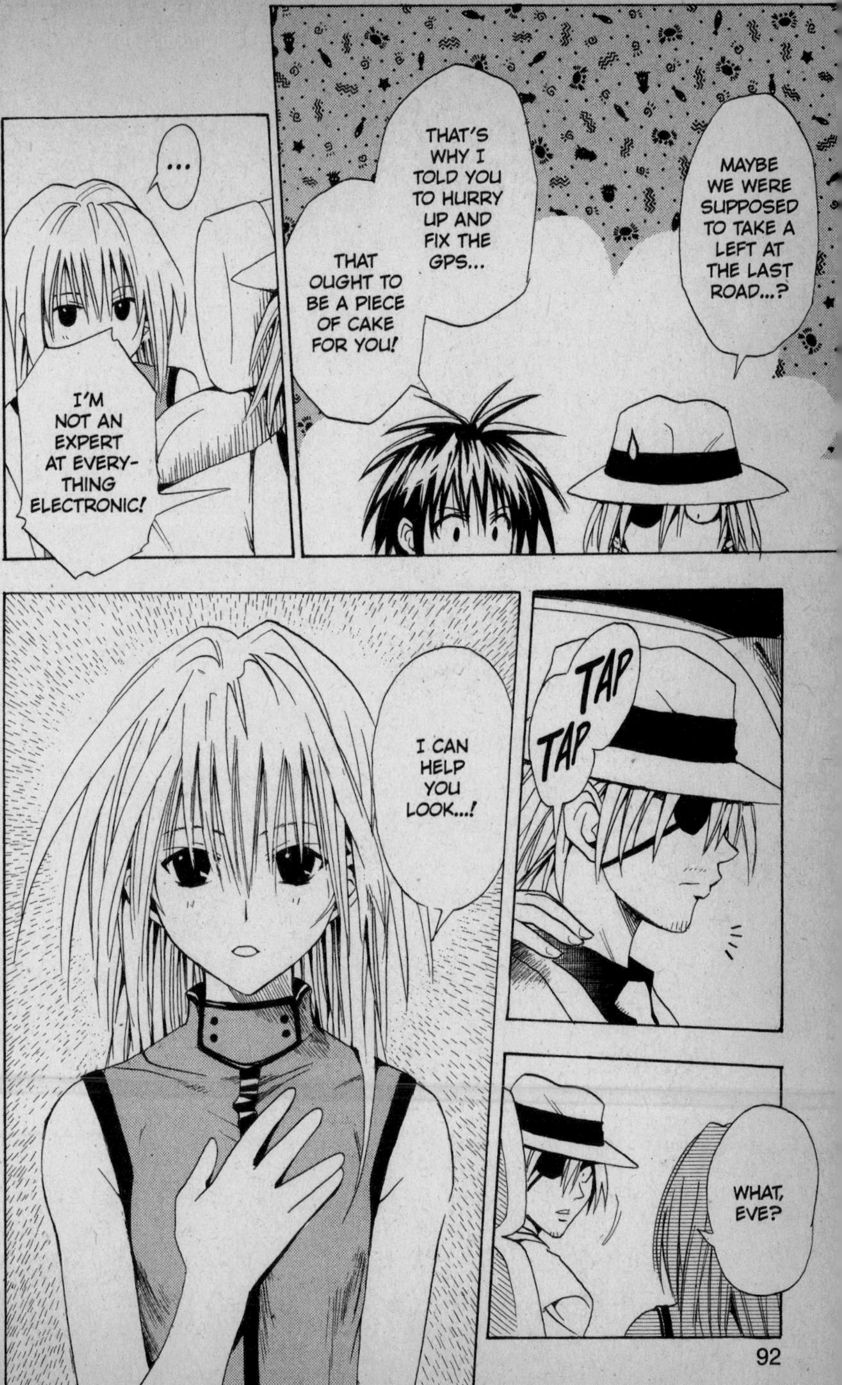
MAYBE WE WERE SUPPOSED TO TAKE A LEFT AT THE LAST ROAD...?
THAT'S WHY I TOLD YOU TO HURRY UP AND FIX THE GPS...
THAT OUGHT TO BE A PIECE OF CAKE FOR YOU!
...
I'M NOT AN EXPERT AT EVERY-THING ELECTRONIC!
TAP TAP
WHAT, EVE?
I CAN HELP YOU LOOK...!

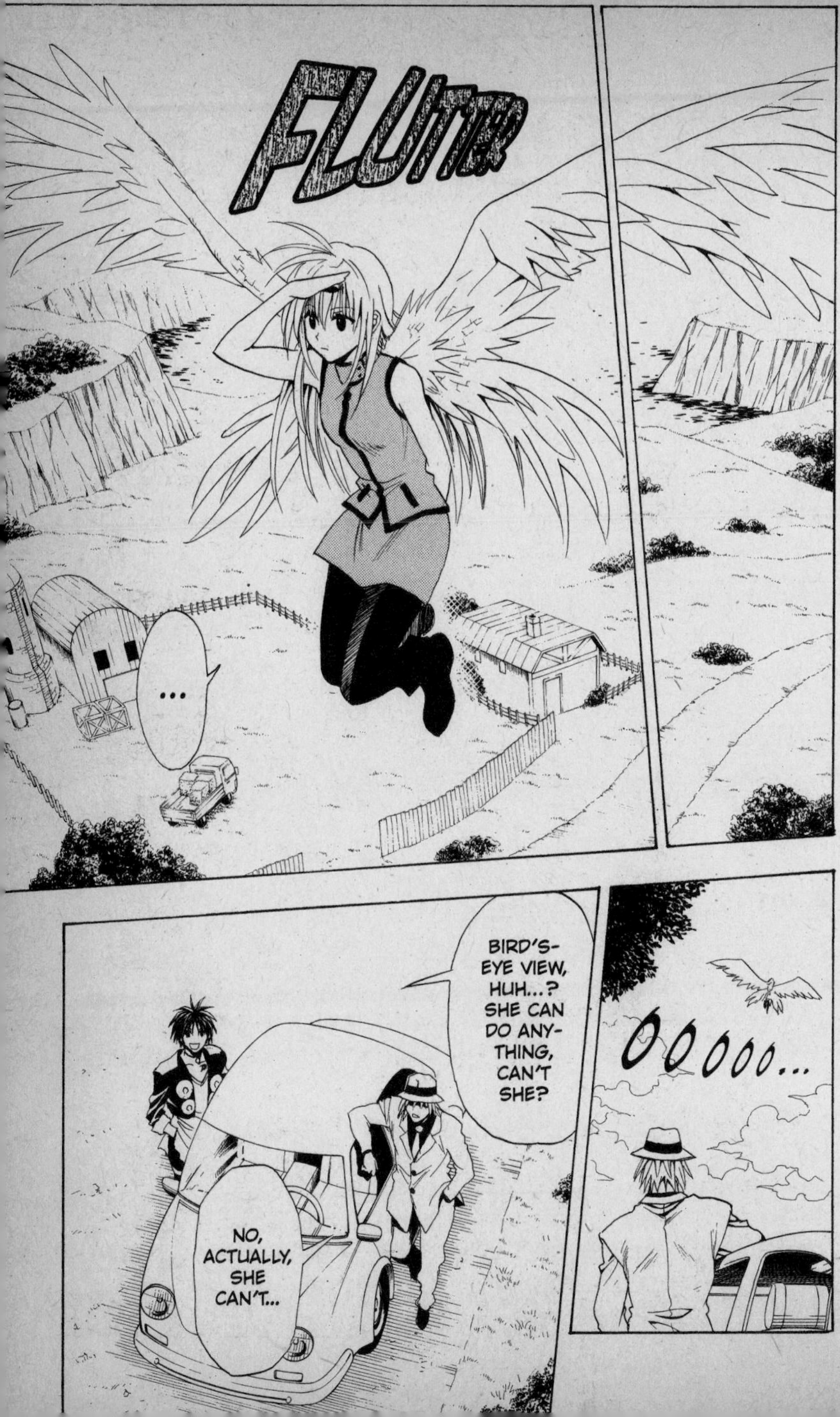
FLUTTER
...
OOOOO...
BIRD'S-EYE VIEW, HUH...? SHE CAN DO ANYTHING, CAN'T SHE?
NO, ACTUALLY, SHE CAN'T...

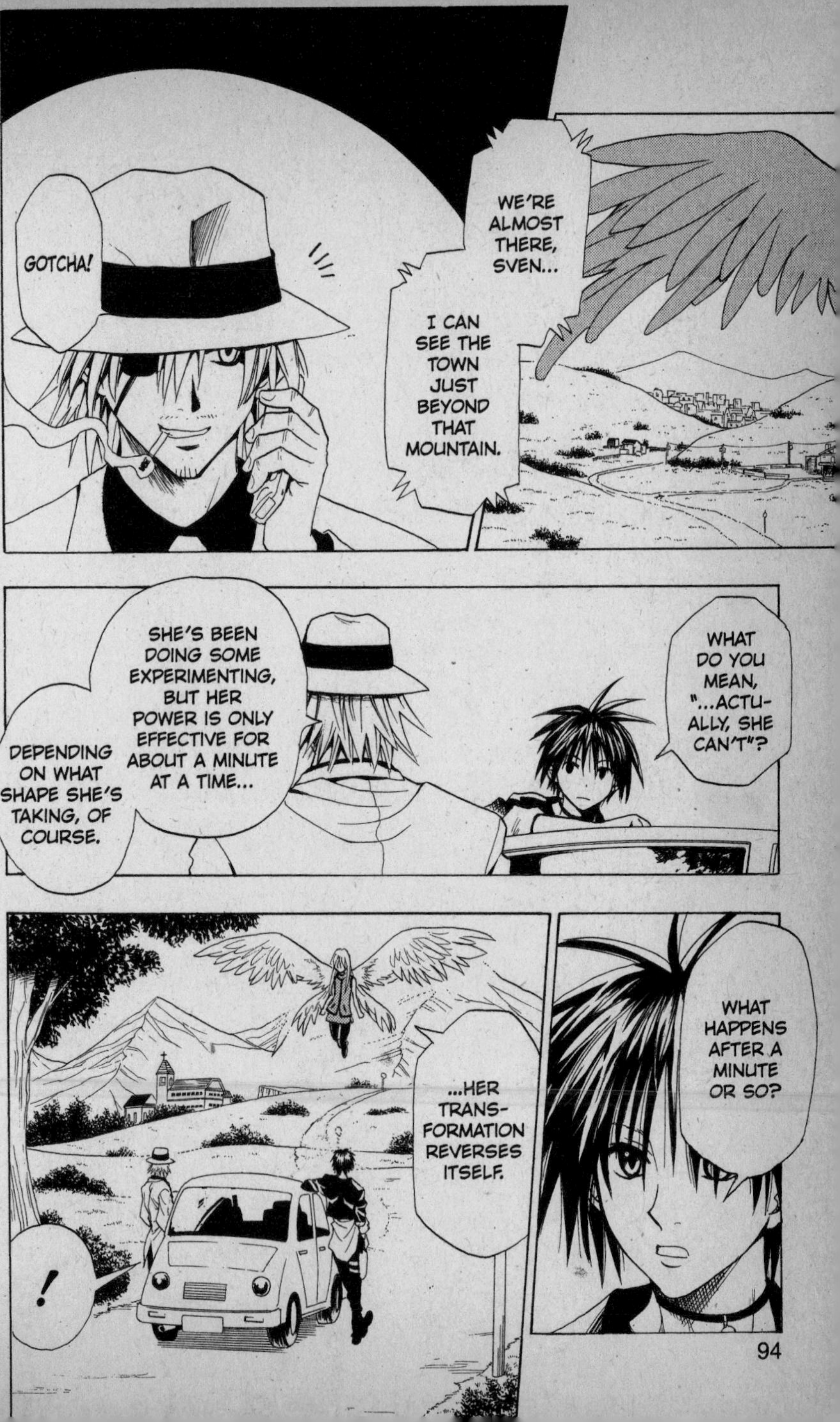
WE'RE ALMOST THERE, SVEN...
I CAN SEE THE TOWN JUST BEYOND THAT MOUNTAIN.
GOTCHA!
WHAT DO YOU MEAN, "...ACTUALLY, SHE CAN'T"?
SHE'S BEEN DOING SOME EXPERIMENTING, BUT HER POWER IS ONLY EFFECTIVE FOR ABOUT A MINUTE AT A TIME...
DEPENDING ON WHAT SHAPE SHE'S TAKING, OF COURSE.
WHAT HAPPENS AFTER A MINUTE OR SO?
...HER TRANSFORMATION REVERSES ITSELF.
!

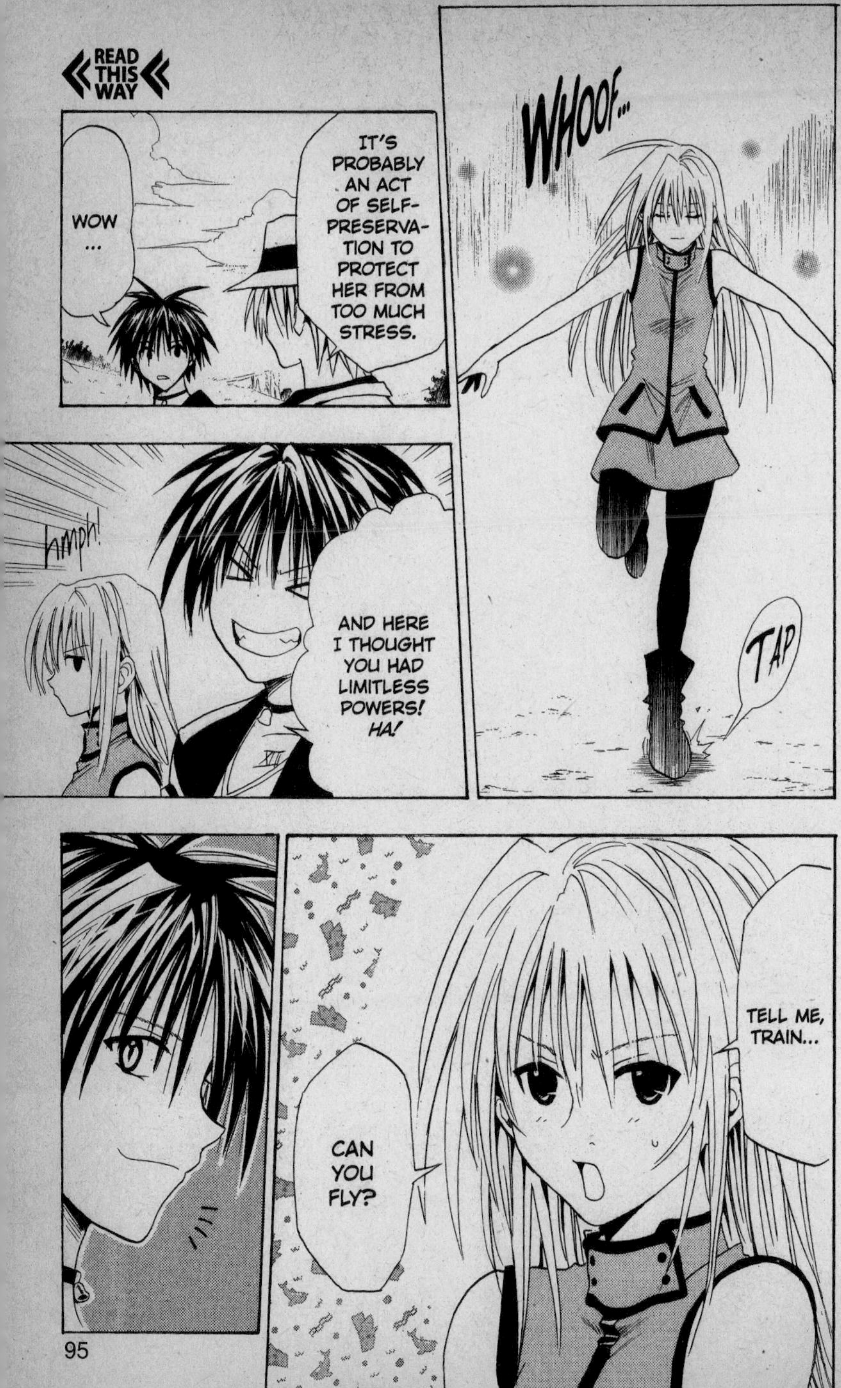
READ THIS WAY
WHOOF...
TAP
IT'S PROBABLY AN ACT OF SELF-PRESERVATION TO PROTECT HER FROM TOO MUCH STRESS.
WOW ...
hmph!
AND HERE I THOUGHT YOU HAD LIMITLESS POWERS! HA!
TELL ME, TRAIN...
CAN YOU FLY?

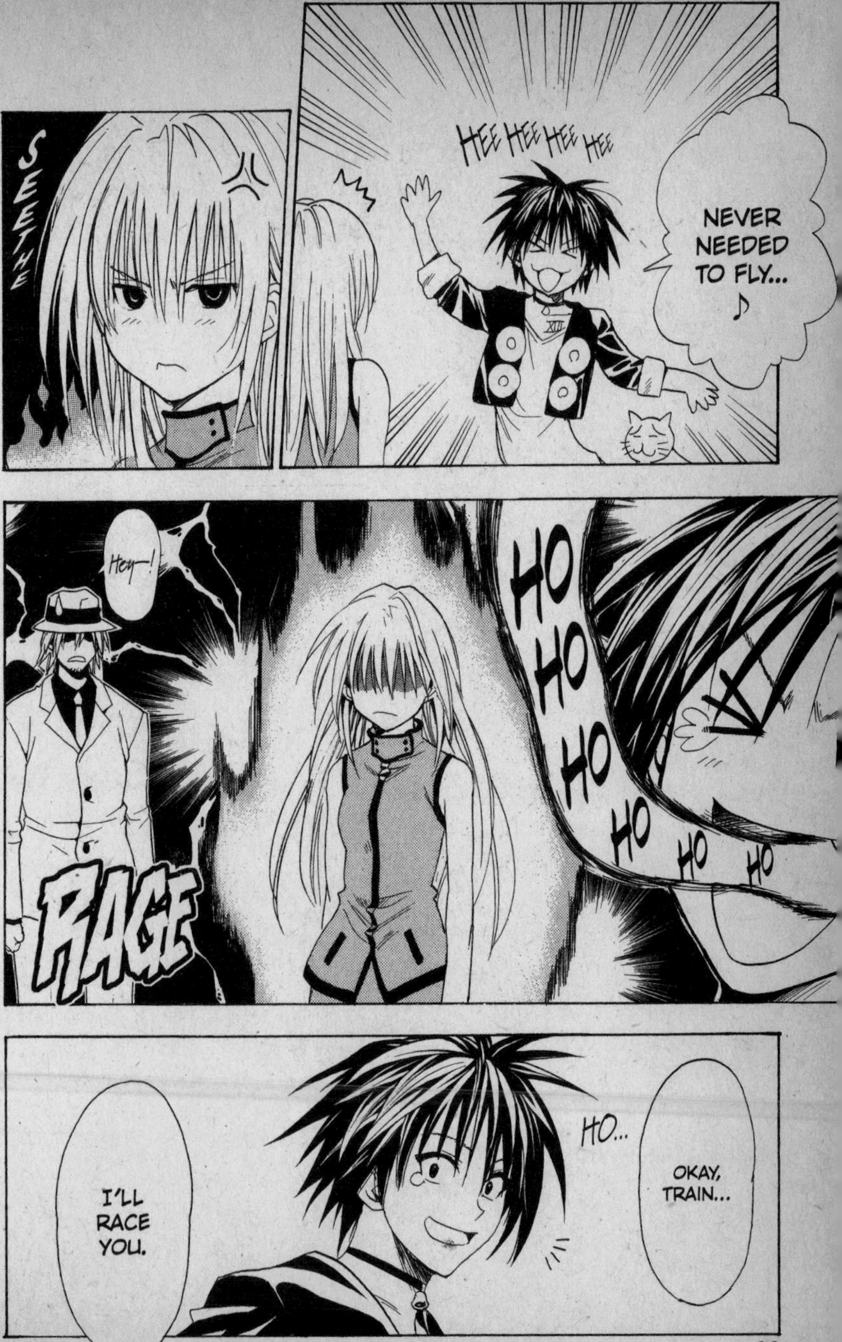
NEVER NEEDED TO FLY... ♪
HEE HEE HEE HEE
SEETHE
HO HO HO HO HO HO HO HO
Hey—!
RAGE
OKAY, TRAIN...
HO...
I'LL RACE YOU.

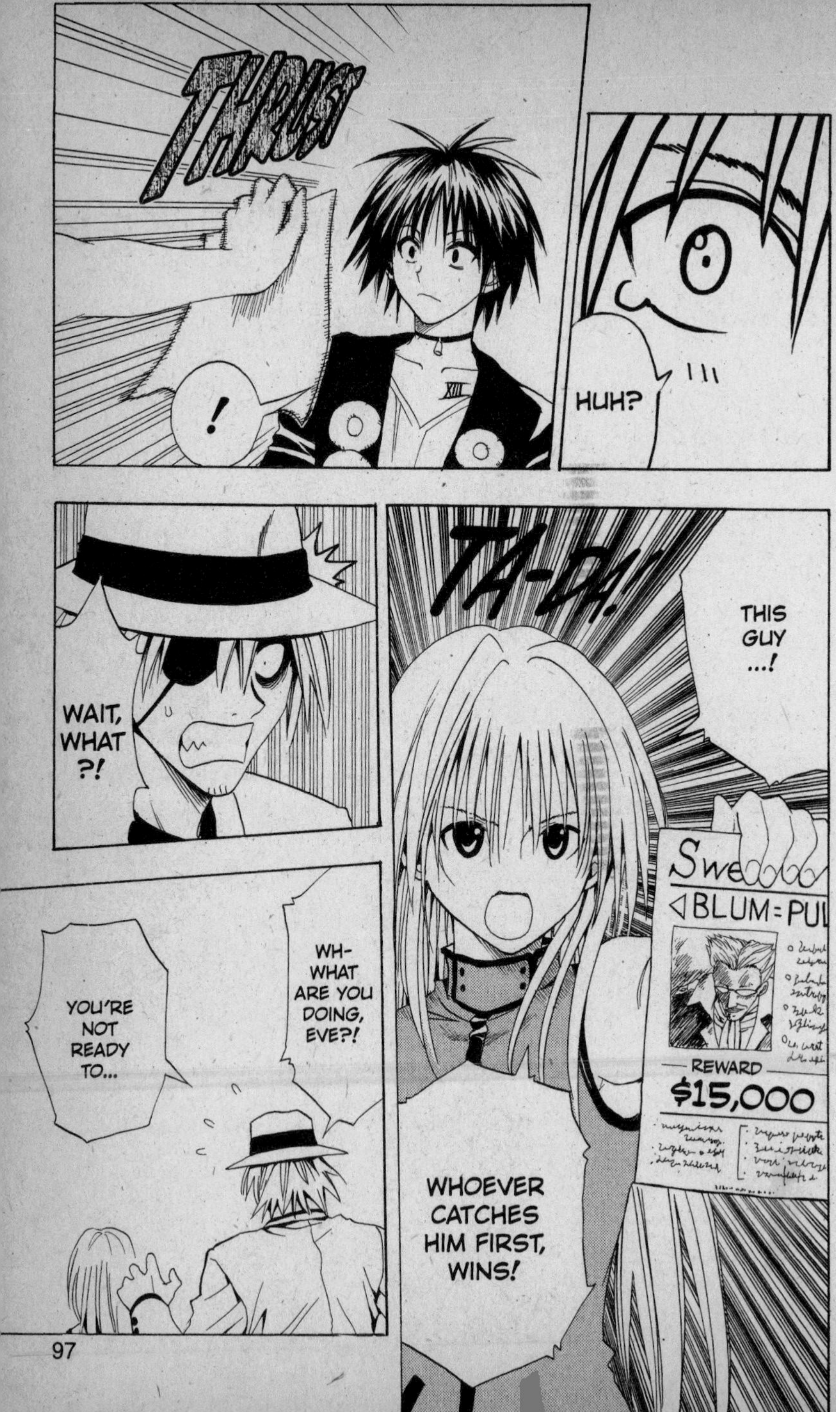
HUH?
THRUST
!
TA-DA!!
THIS GUY ...!
REWARD
$15,000
WHOEVER CATCHES HIM FIRST, WINS!
WAIT, WHAT ?!
WH- WHAT ARE YOU DOING, EVE?!
YOU'RE NOT READY TO...

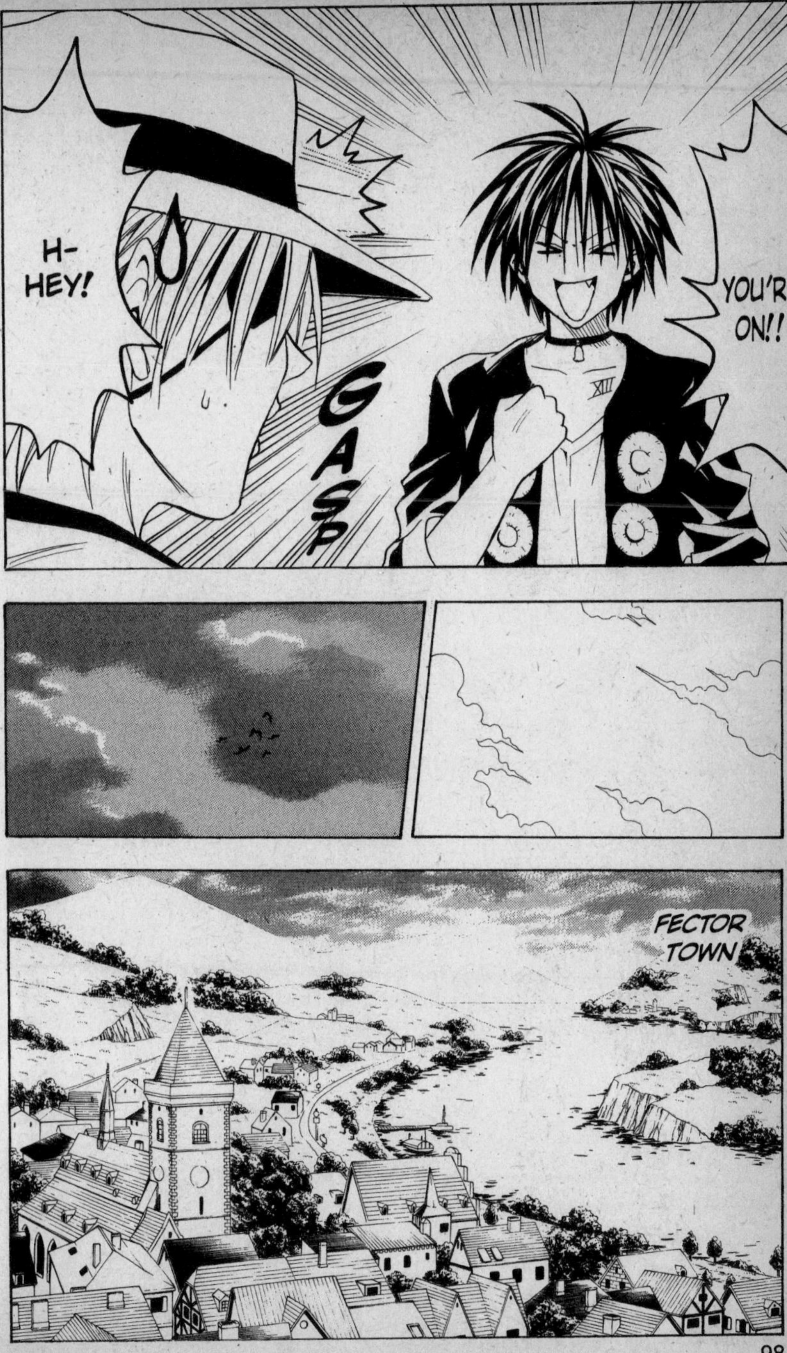
YOU'RE ON!!
H- HEY!
GASP
FECTOR TOWN

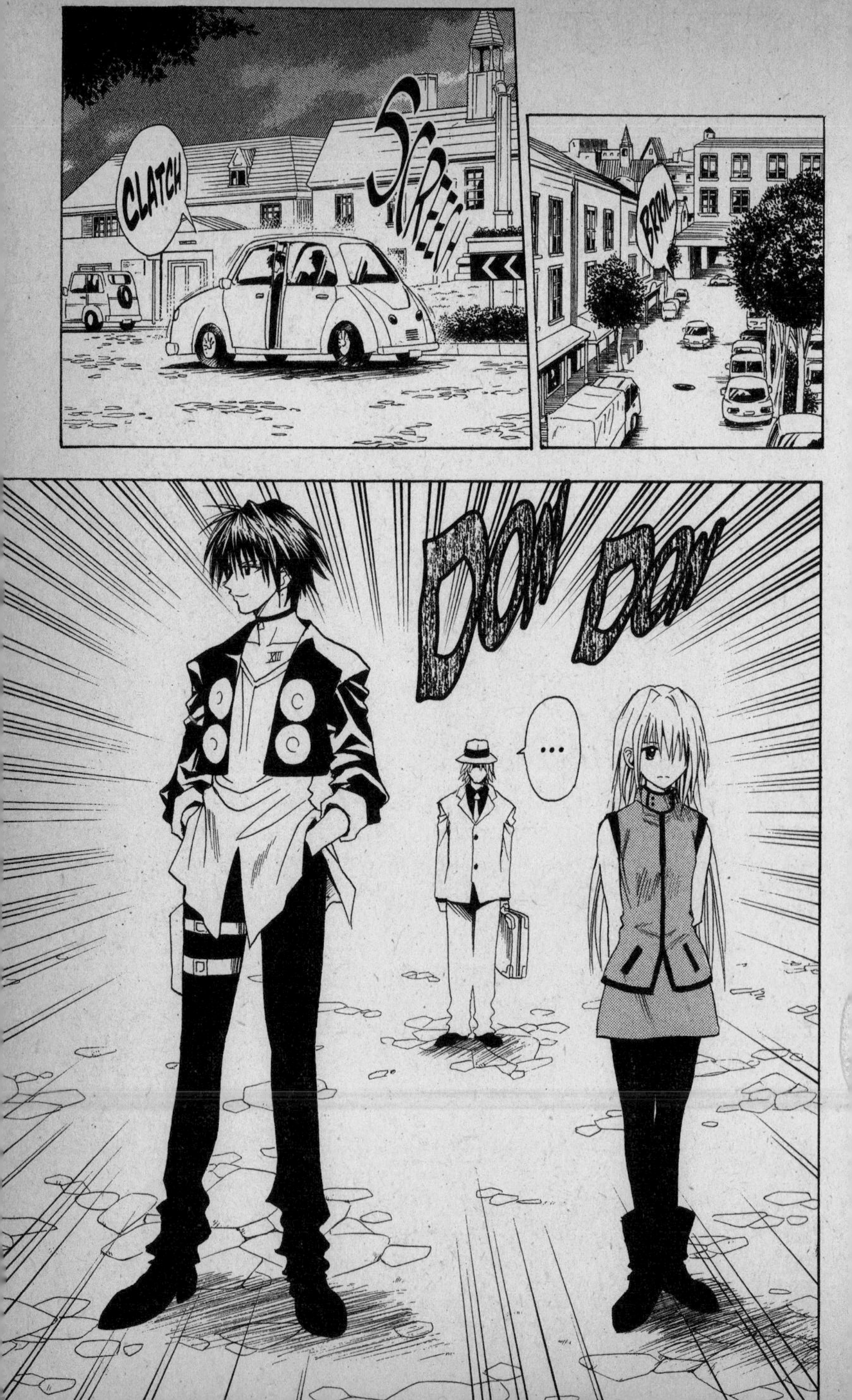
BRRM...
SCREECH
CLATCH
DON DON
...

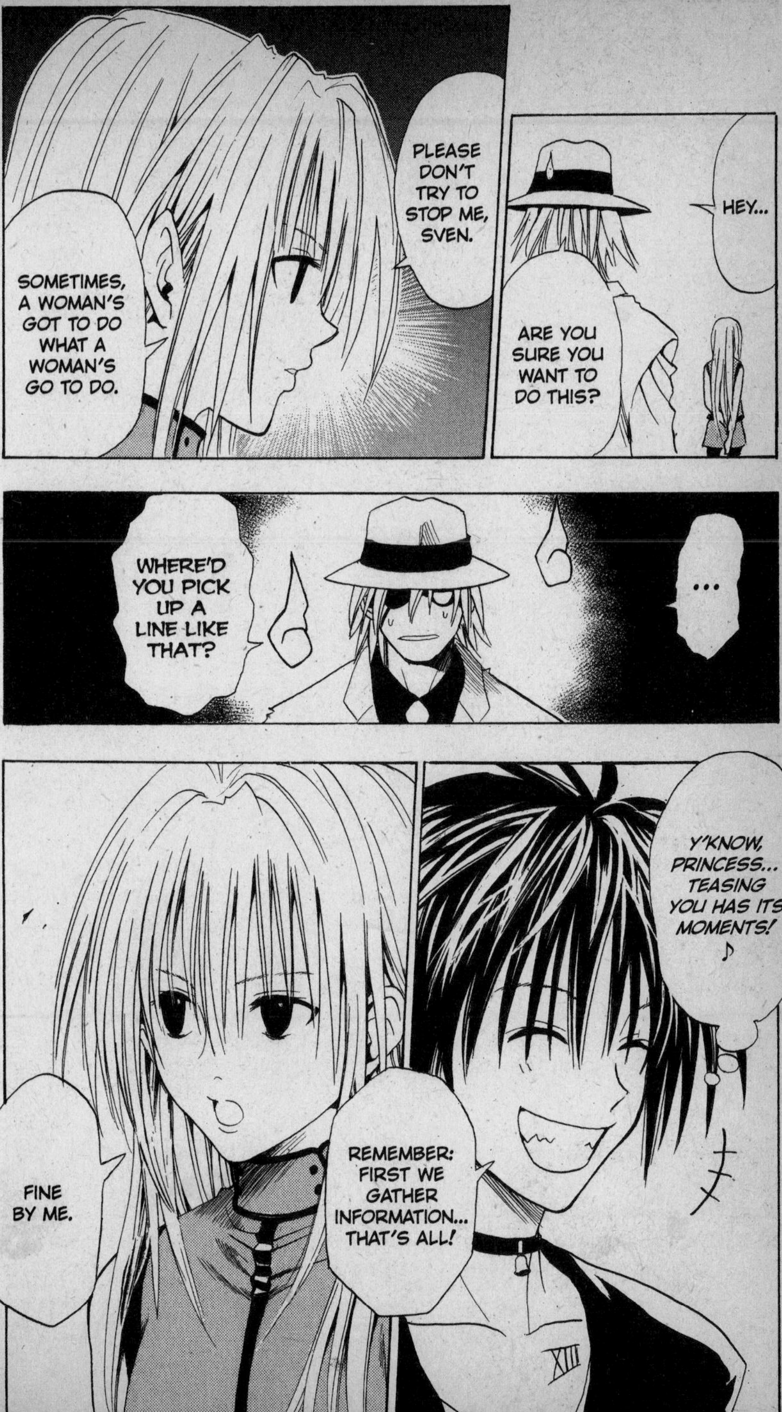
HEY...
ARE YOU SURE YOU WANT TO DO THIS?
PLEASE DON'T TRY TO STOP ME, SVEN.
SOMETIMES, A WOMAN'S GOT TO DO WHAT A WOMAN'S GO TO DO.
...
WHERE'D YOU PICK UP A LINE LIKE THAT?
Y'KNOW, PRINCESS... TEASING YOU HAS ITS MOMENTS! ♪
REMEMBER: FIRST WE GATHER INFORMATION... THAT'S ALL!
FINE BY ME.

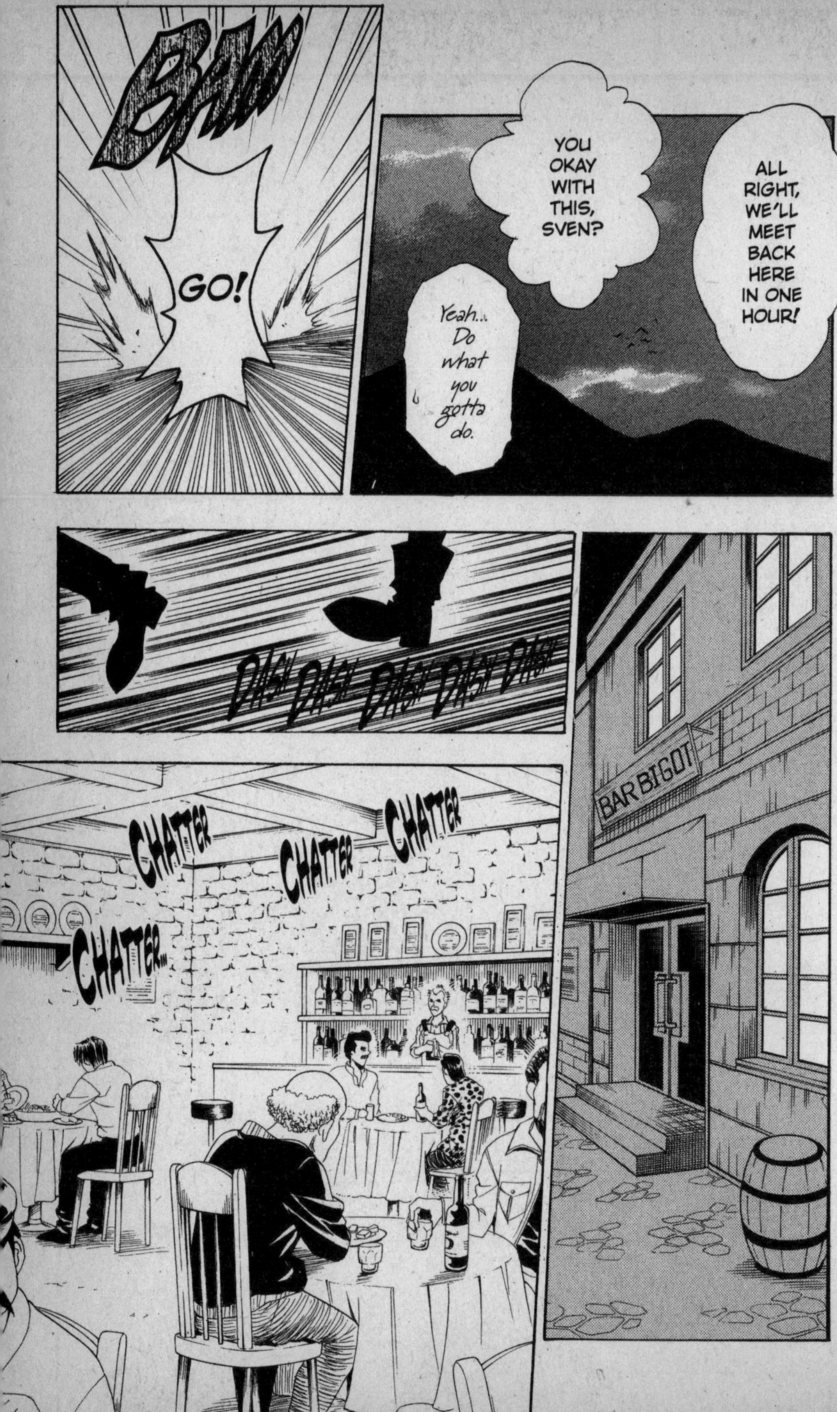
ALL RIGHT, WE'LL MEET BACK HERE IN ONE HOUR!
YOU OKAY WITH THIS, SVEN?
Yeah... Do what you gotta do.
BAM
GO!
BAR BIGOT
DASH DASH DASH DASH DASH
CHATTER
CHATTER
CHATTER
CHATTER...

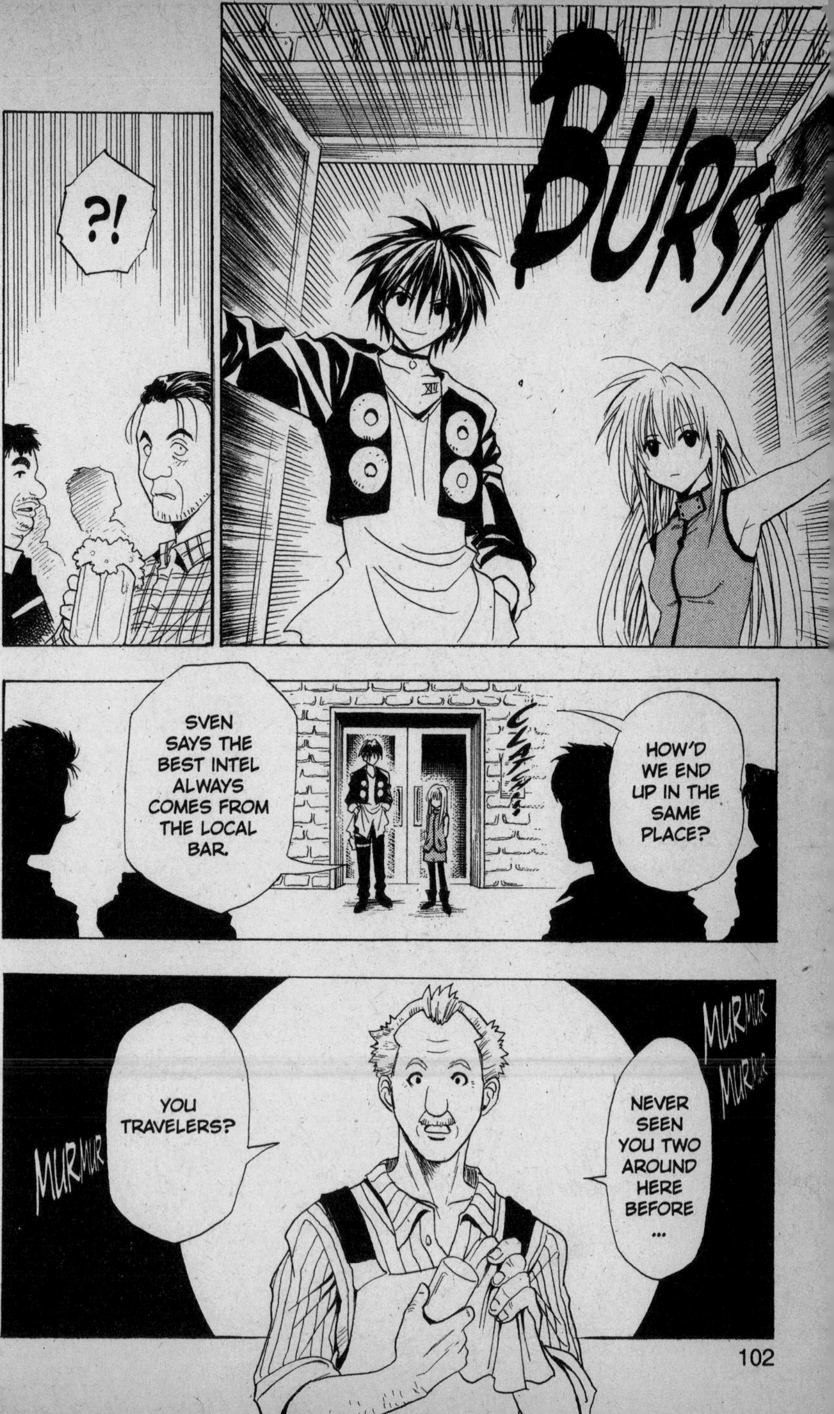
BURST
?!
HOW'D WE END UP IN THE SAME PLACE?
SVEN SAYS THE BEST INTEL ALWAYS COMES FROM THE LOCAL BAR.
MURMUR MURMUR
NEVER SEEN YOU TWO AROUND HERE BEFORE ...
YOU TRAVELERS?
MURMUR

READ THIS WAY

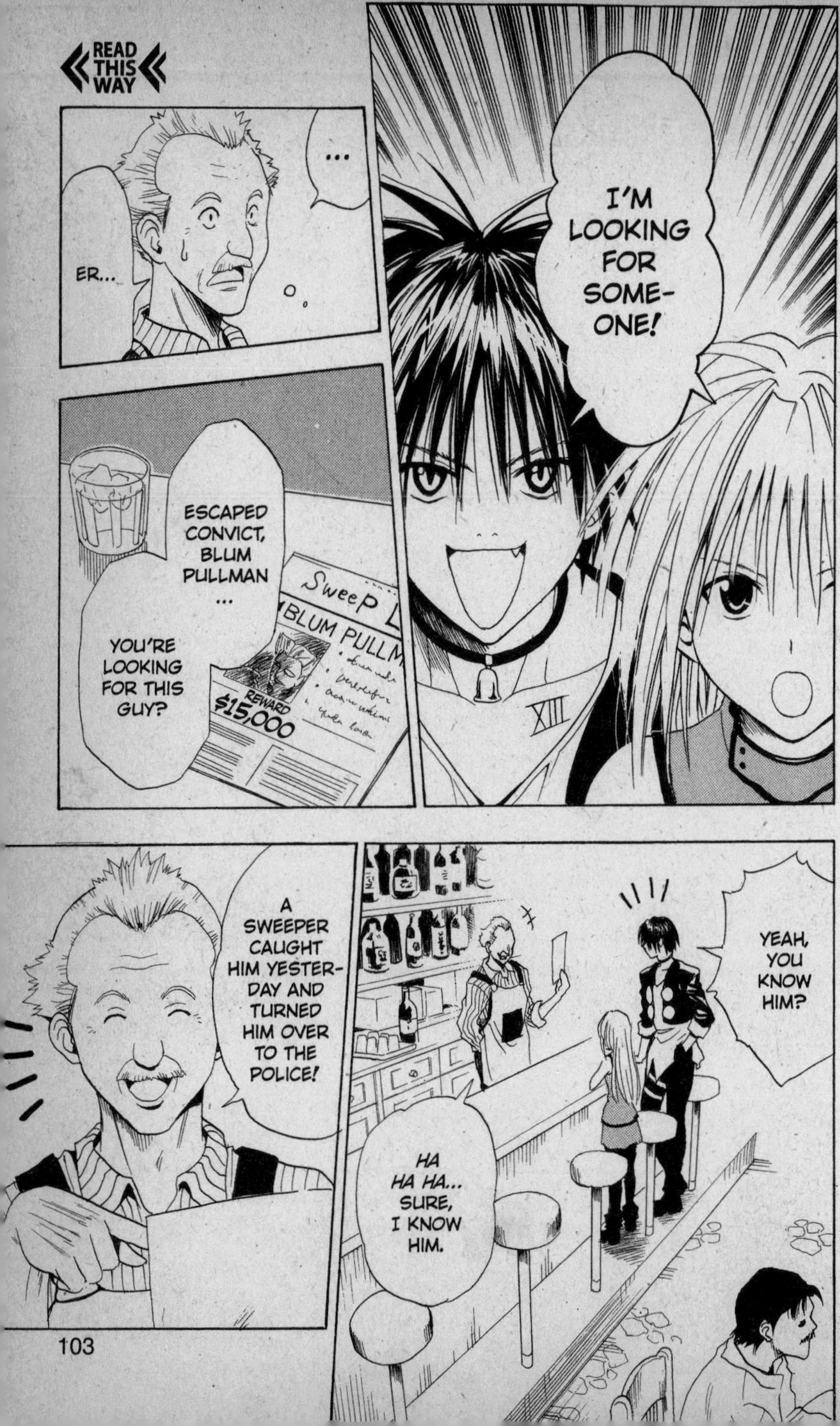

I'M LOOKING FOR SOME-ONE!
...
ER...
ESCAPED CONVICT, BLUM PULLMAN ...
YOU'RE LOOKING FOR THIS GUY?
Sweep
BLUM PULLM
REWARD $15,000
YEAH, YOU KNOW HIM?
HA HA HA... SURE, I KNOW HIM.
A SWEEPER CAUGHT HIM YESTER-DAY AND TURNED HIM OVER TO THE POLICE!

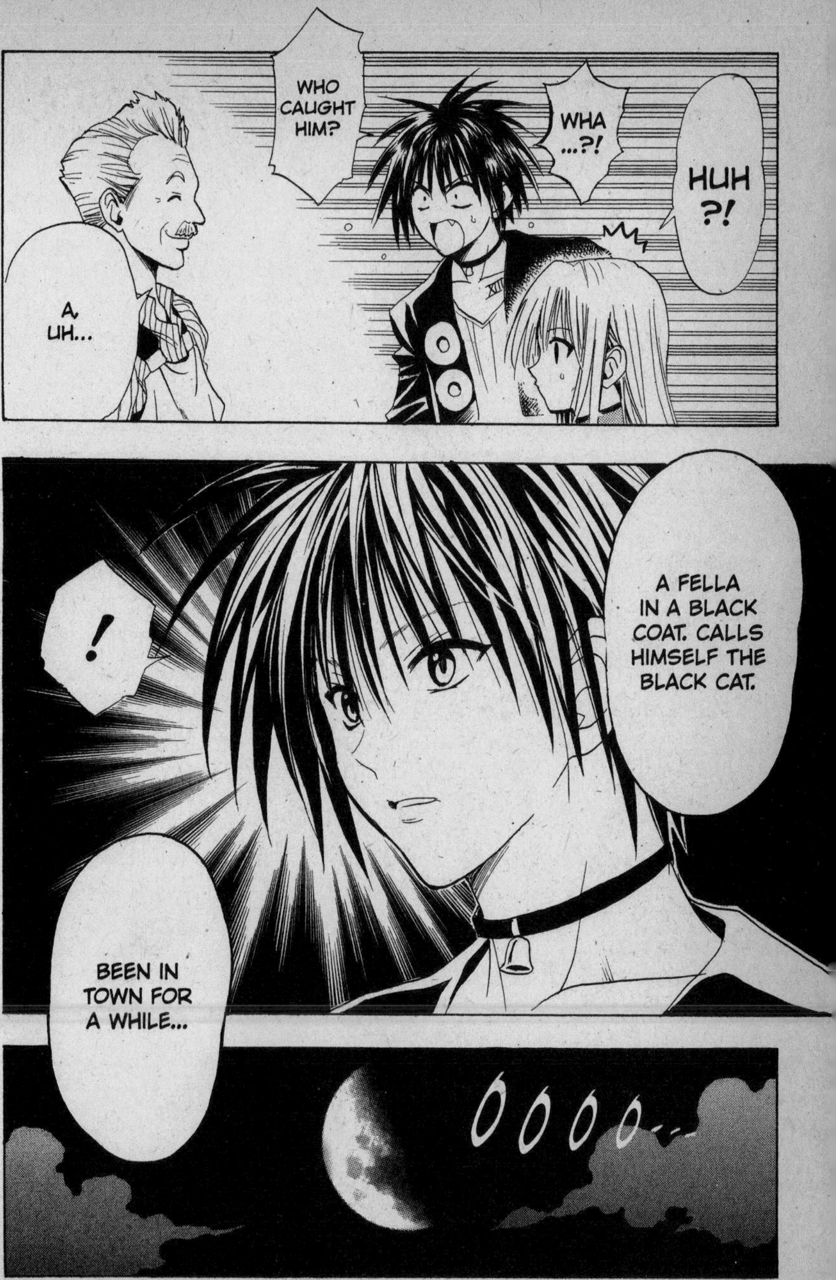
HUH ?!
WHA ...?!
WHO CAUGHT HIM?
A, UH...
A FELLA IN A BLACK COAT. CALLS HIMSELF THE BLACK CAT.
!
BEEN IN TOWN FOR A WHILE...
OOOO-

Chapter 44: The 13th Man

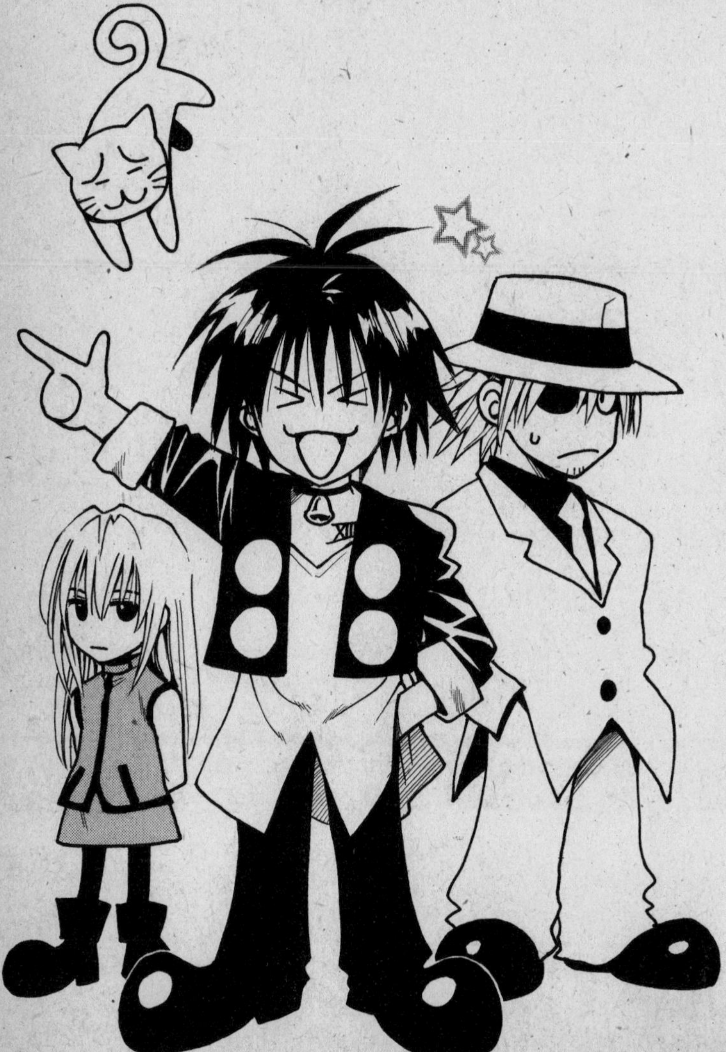

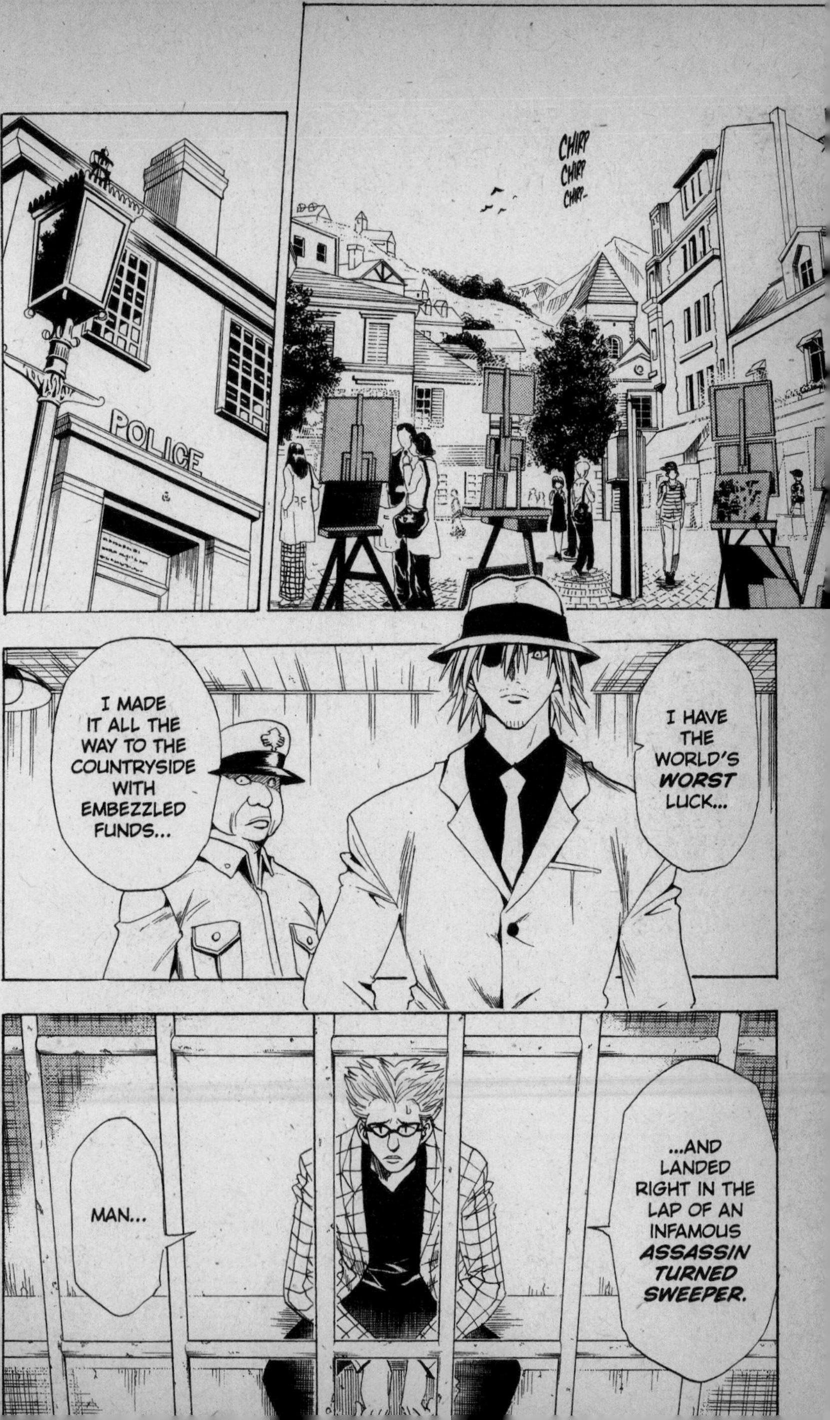
CHIRP CHIRP CHIRP...
POLICE
I HAVE THE WORLD'S *WORST* LUCK...
I MADE IT ALL THE WAY TO THE COUNTRYSIDE WITH EMBEZZLED FUNDS...
...AND LANDED RIGHT IN THE LAP OF AN INFAMOUS ***ASSASSIN TURNED SWEEPER.***
MAN...

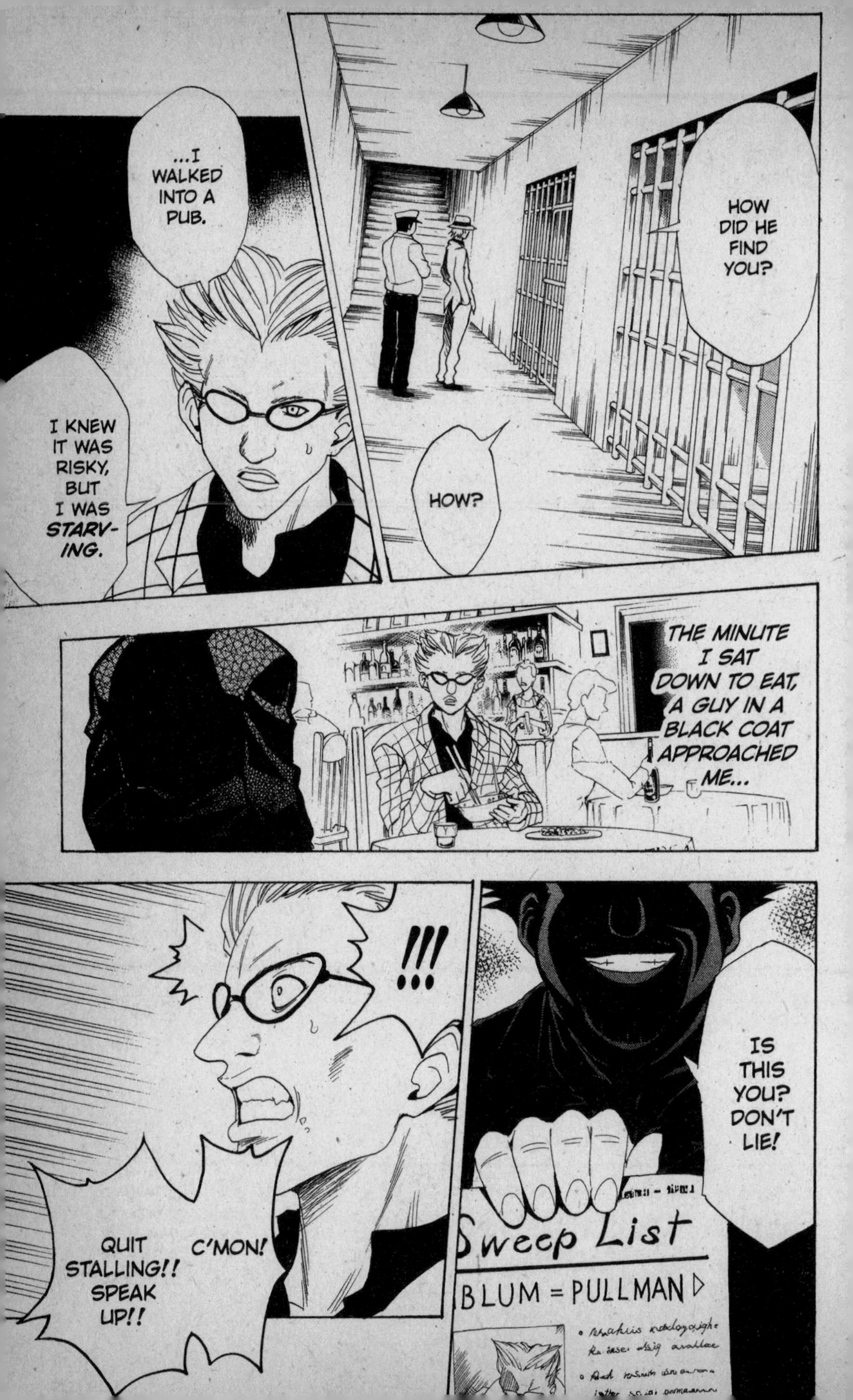
HOW DID HE FIND YOU?
HOW?
...I WALKED INTO A PUB.
I KNEW IT WAS RISKY, BUT I WAS *STARVING.*
THE MINUTE I SAT DOWN TO EAT, A GUY IN A BLACK COAT APPROACHED ME...
IS THIS YOU? DON'T LIE!
Sweep List
BLUM = PULLMAN
!!!
C'MON!
QUIT STALLING!! SPEAK UP!!

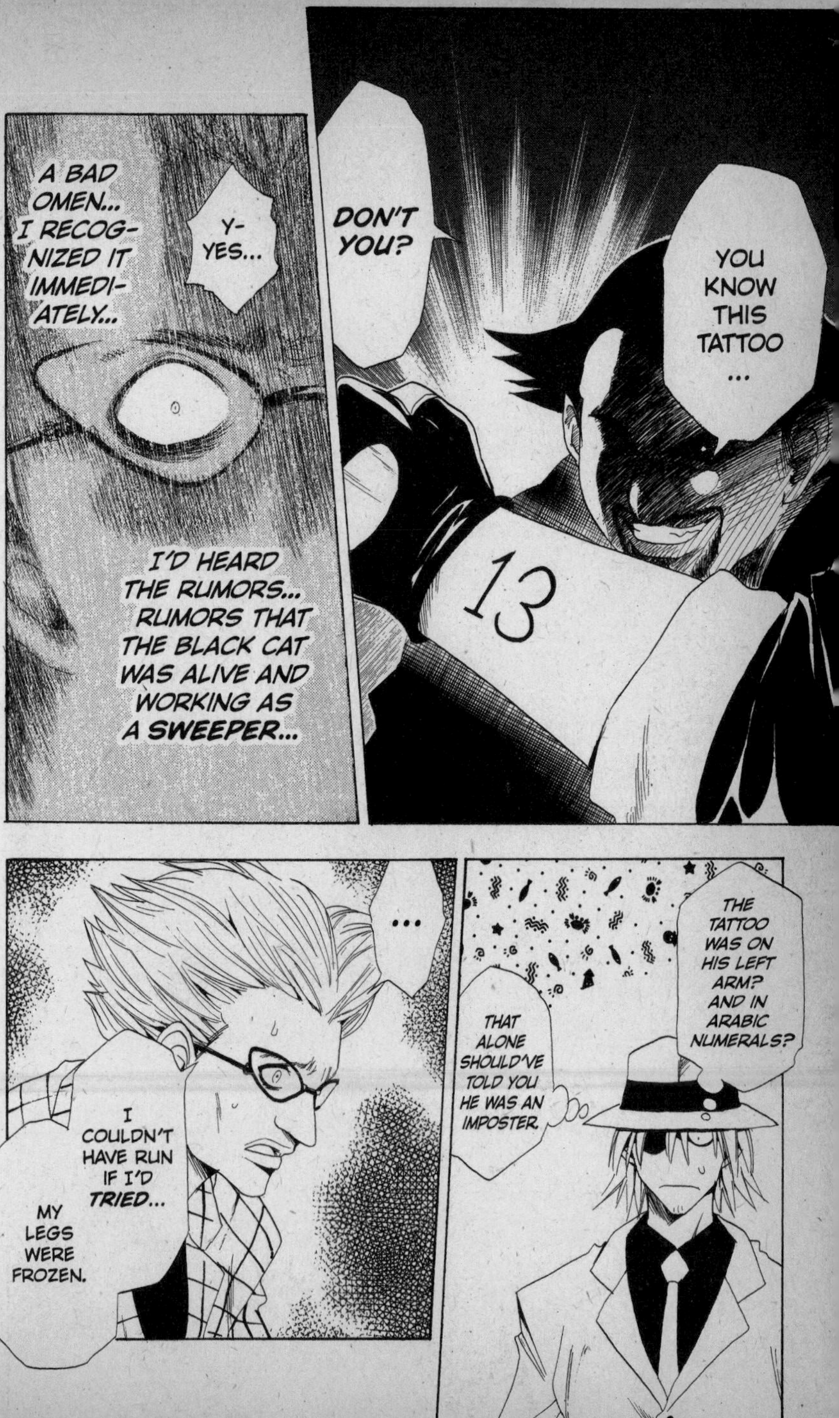
YOU KNOW THIS TATTOO...
DON'T YOU?
Y-YES...
A BAD OMEN... I RECOG-NIZED IT IMMEDI-ATELY...
I'D HEARD THE RUMORS... RUMORS THAT THE BLACK CAT WAS ALIVE AND WORKING AS A SWEEPER...
THE TATTOO WAS ON HIS LEFT ARM? AND IN ARABIC NUMERALS?
THAT ALONE SHOULD'VE TOLD YOU HE WAS AN IMPOSTER.
...
I COULDN'T HAVE RUN IF I'D TRIED...
MY LEGS WERE FROZEN.

READ THIS WAY

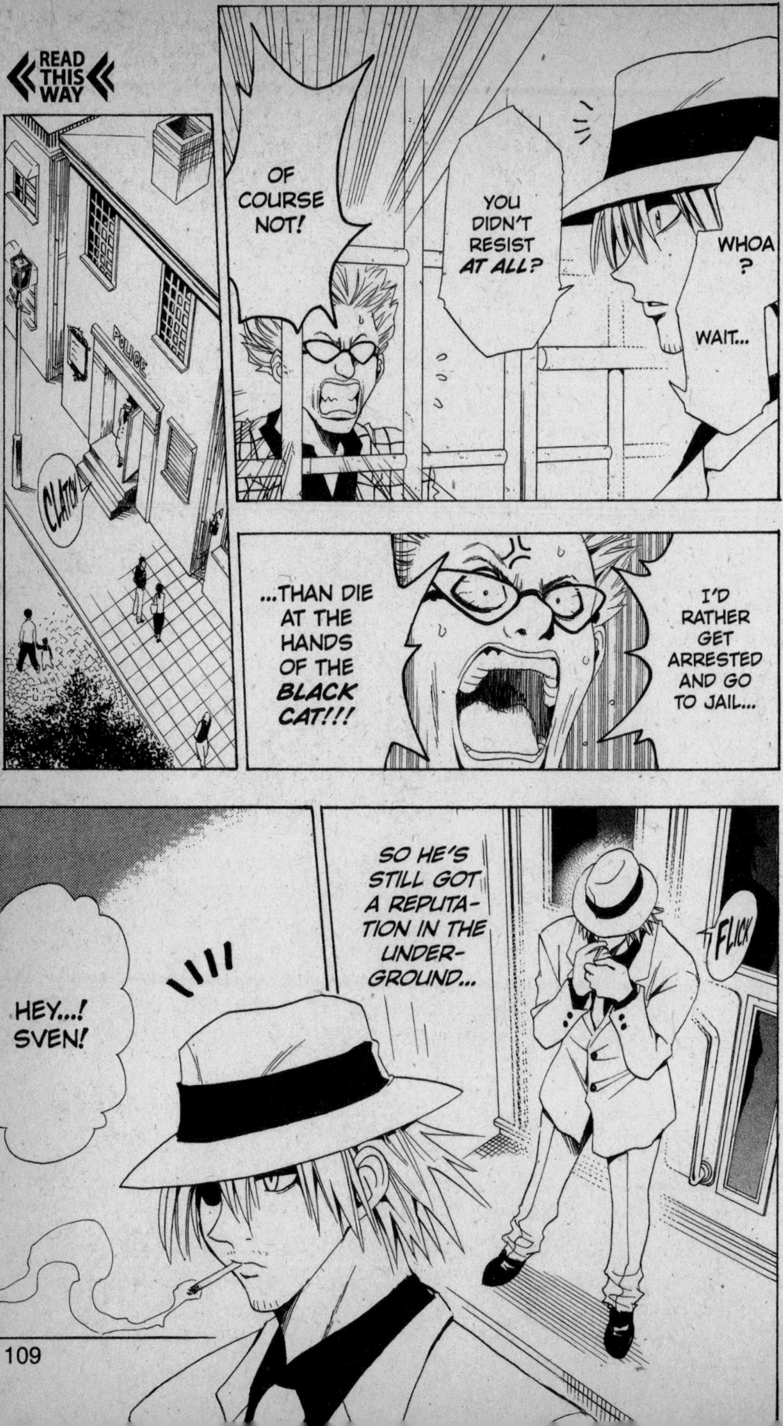

WHOA ?
WAIT...
YOU DIDN'T RESIST AT ALL?
OF COURSE NOT!
I'D RATHER GET ARRESTED AND GO TO JAIL...
...THAN DIE AT THE HANDS OF THE BLACK CAT!!!
CLATCH
FLICK
SO HE'S STILL GOT A REPUTATION IN THE UNDERGROUND...
HEY...! SVEN!

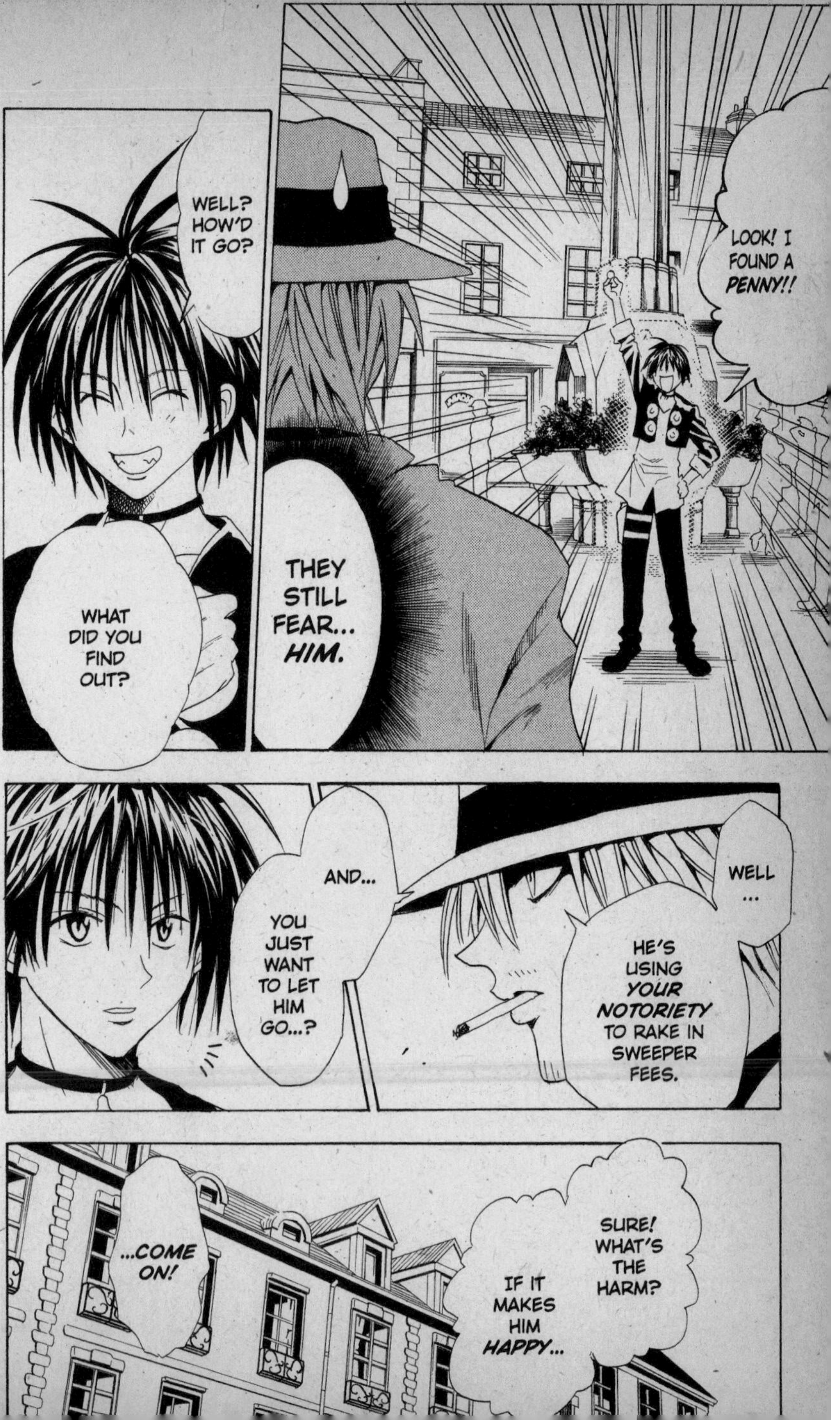
LOOK! I FOUND A PENNY!!
THEY STILL FEAR... HIM.
WELL? HOW'D IT GO?
WHAT DID YOU FIND OUT?
WELL ...
HE'S USING YOUR NOTORIETY TO RAKE IN SWEEPER FEES.
AND...
YOU JUST WANT TO LET HIM GO...?
SURE! WHAT'S THE HARM?
IF IT MAKES HIM HAPPY...
...COME ON!

READ THIS WAY

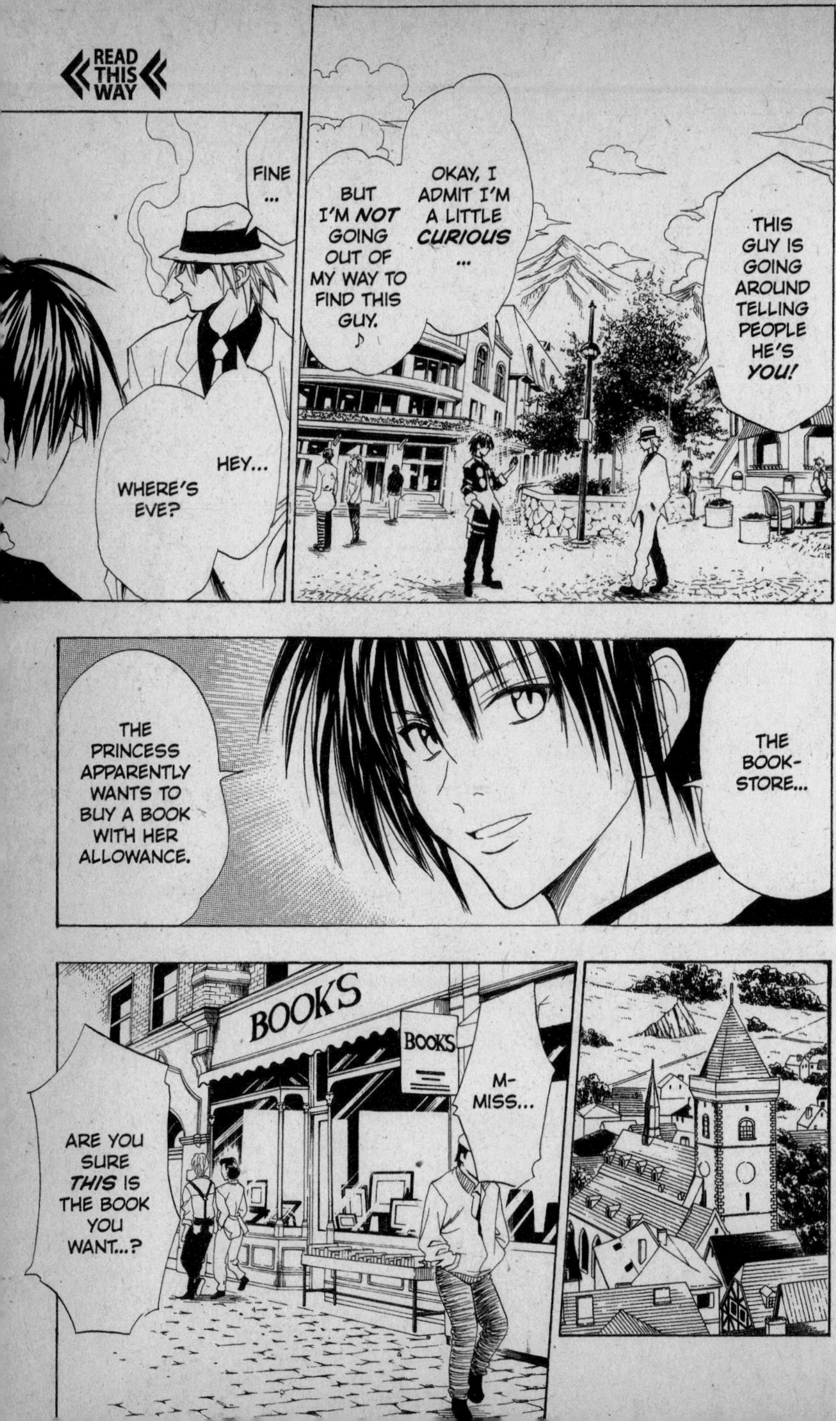

THIS GUY IS GOING AROUND TELLING PEOPLE HE'S *YOU!*
OKAY, I ADMIT I'M A LITTLE *CURIOUS*...
BUT I'M *NOT* GOING OUT OF MY WAY TO FIND THIS GUY. ♪
FINE...
HEY...
WHERE'S EVE?
THE BOOK-STORE...
THE PRINCESS APPARENTLY WANTS TO BUY A BOOK WITH HER ALLOWANCE.
BOOKS
BOOKS
M-MISS...
ARE YOU SURE *THIS* IS THE BOOK YOU WANT...?

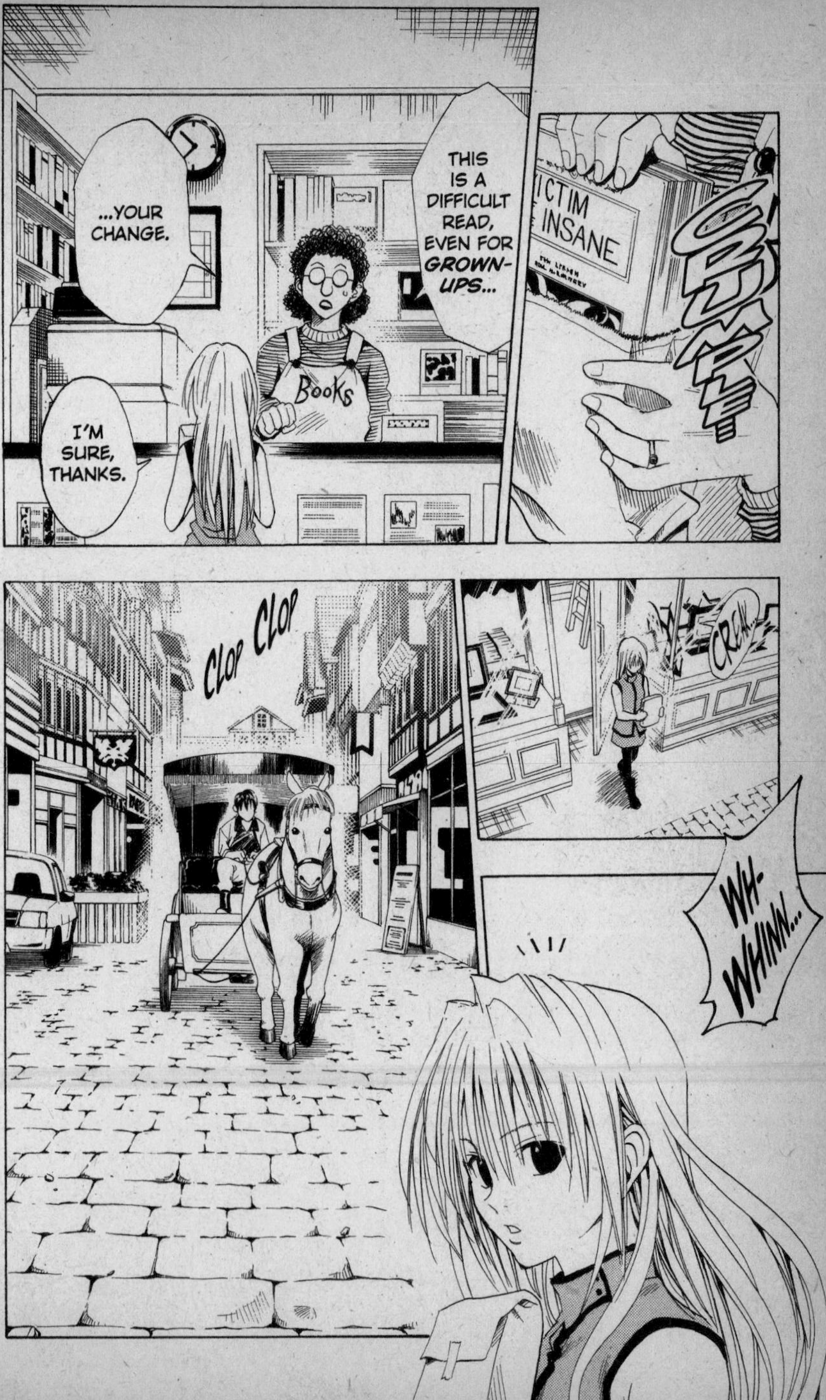
VICTIM
INSANE
THIS IS A DIFFICULT READ, EVEN FOR GROWN-UPS...
...YOUR CHANGE.
I'M SURE, THANKS.
CREA...
WH-WHINN...
CLOP CLOP

READ THIS WAY

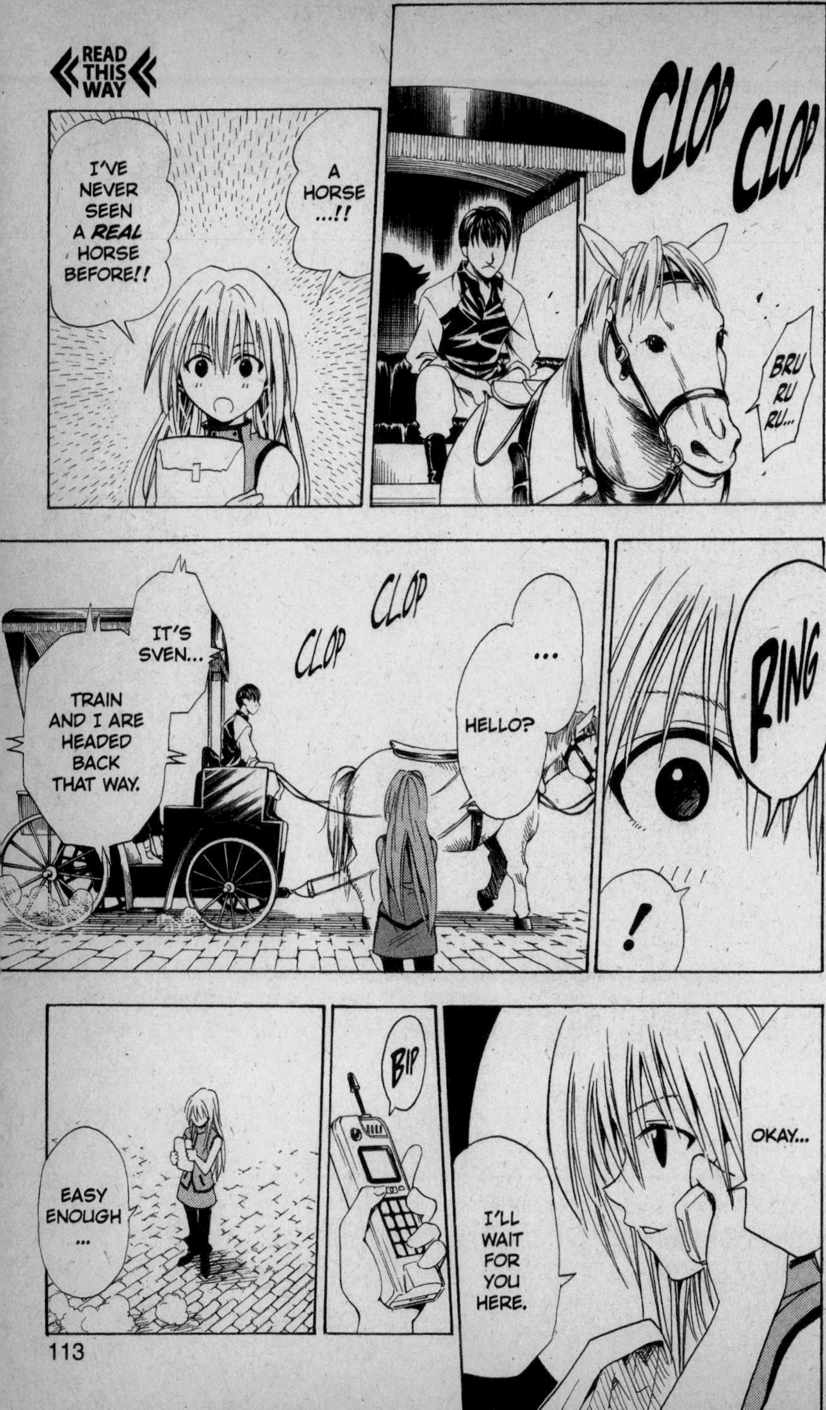

CLOP CLOP
BRU RU RU...
A HORSE ...!!
I'VE NEVER SEEN A *REAL* HORSE BEFORE!!
RING
!
... HELLO?
CLOP CLOP
IT'S SVEN...
TRAIN AND I ARE HEADED BACK THAT WAY.
OKAY...
I'LL WAIT FOR YOU HERE.
BIP
EASY ENOUGH ...

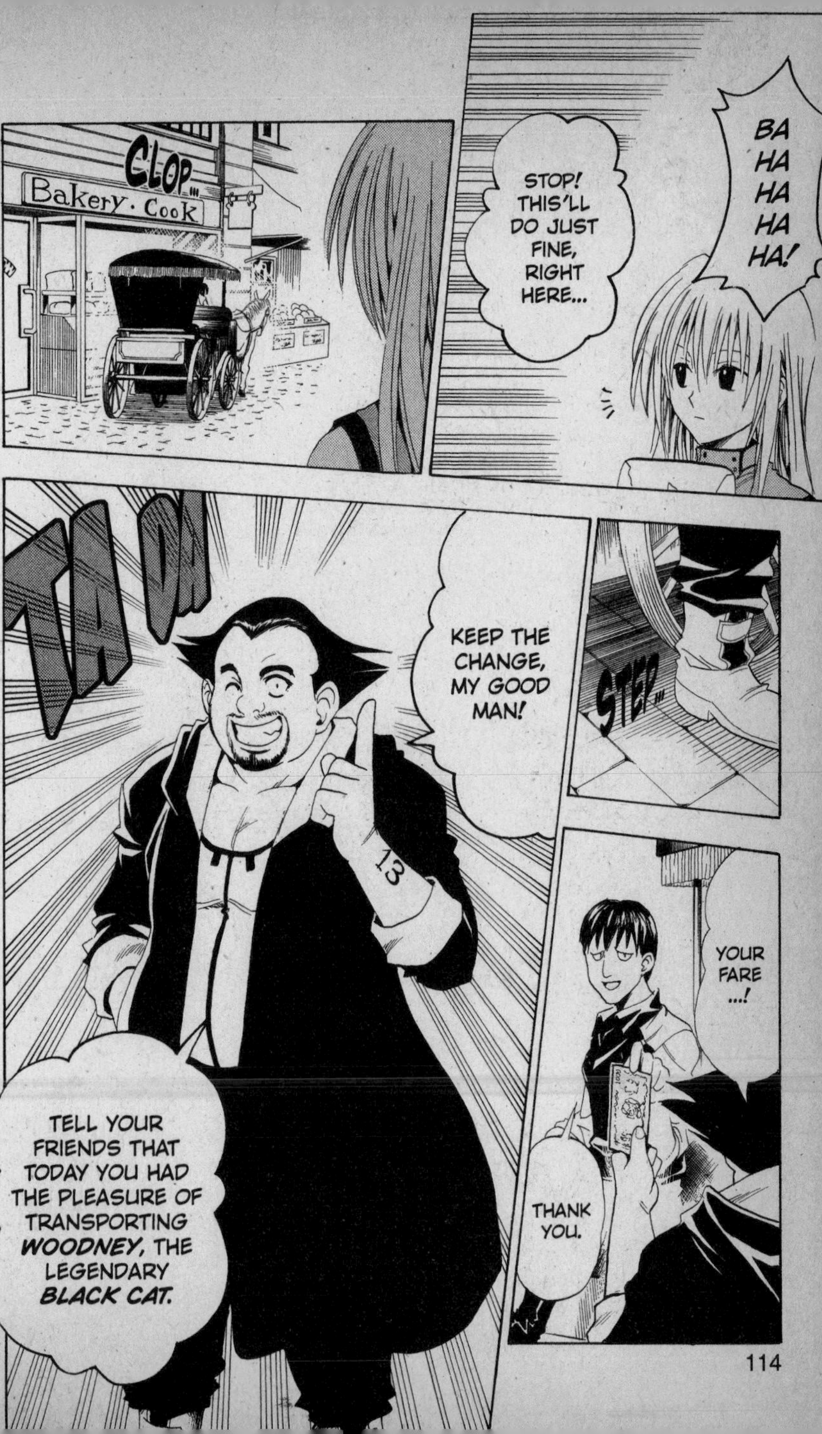
BA HA HA HA HA!
STOP! THIS'LL DO JUST FINE, RIGHT HERE...
CLOP...
Bakery · Cook
STEP...
YOUR FARE ...!
THANK YOU.
TA DA
KEEP THE CHANGE, MY GOOD MAN!
TELL YOUR FRIENDS THAT TODAY YOU HAD THE PLEASURE OF TRANSPORTING WOODNEY, THE LEGENDARY BLACK CAT.

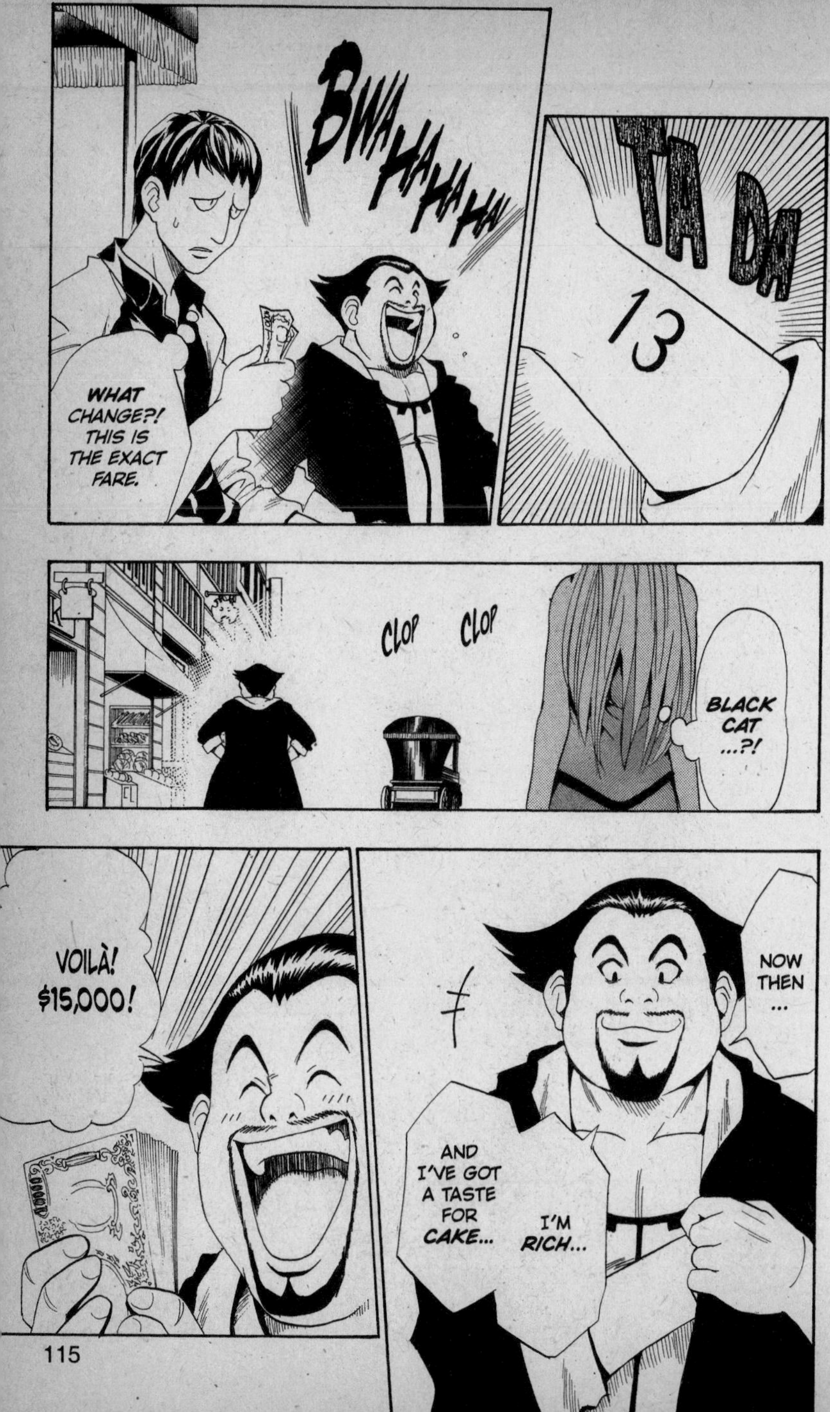
TA DA
13
BWAHAHAHAHA
WHAT CHANGE?! THIS IS THE EXACT FARE.
BLACK CAT ...?!
CLOP CLOP
NOW THEN ...
I'M RICH...
AND I'VE GOT A TASTE FOR CAKE...
VOILÀ! $15,000!

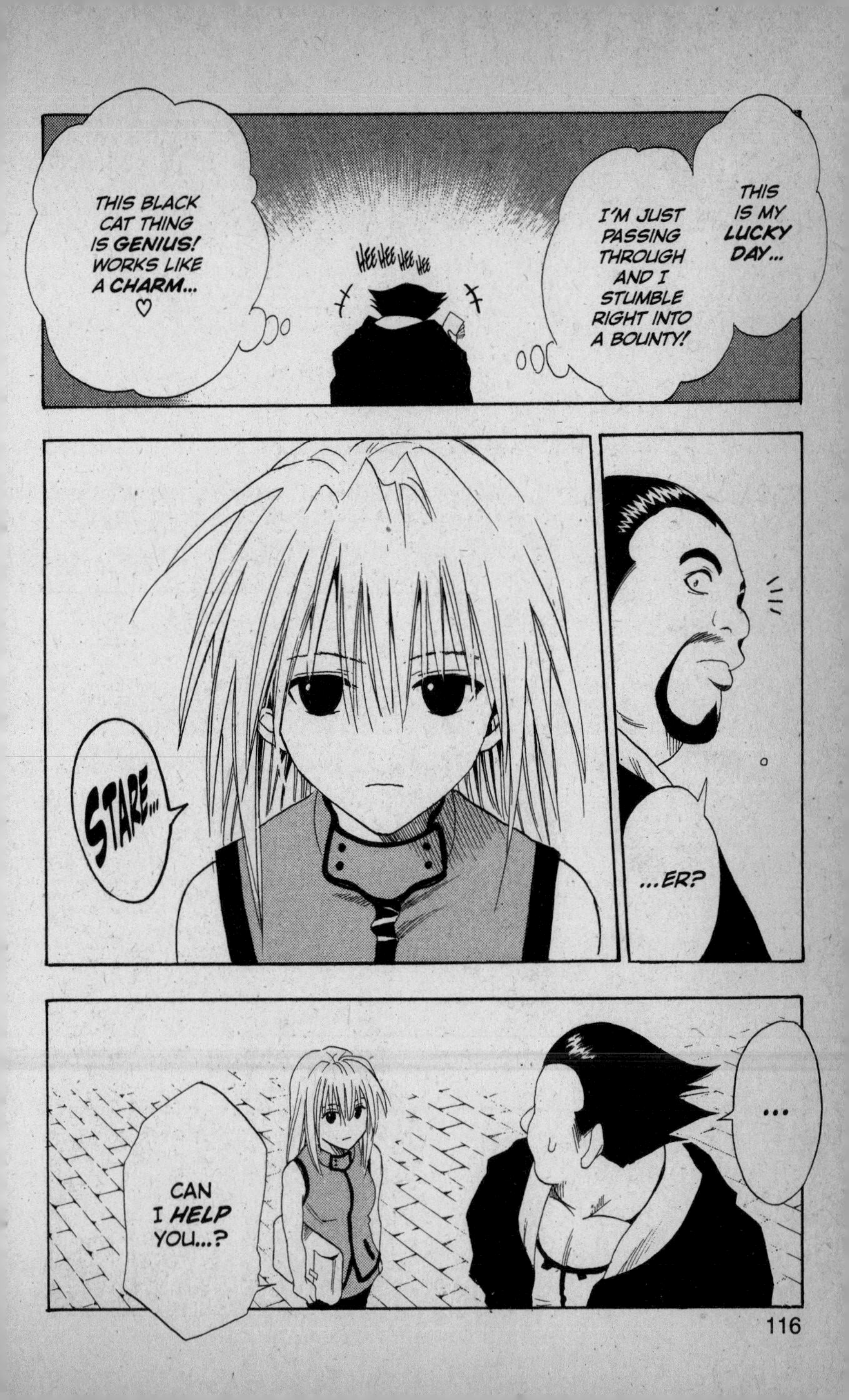
THIS IS MY LUCKY DAY...
I'M JUST PASSING THROUGH AND I STUMBLE RIGHT INTO A BOUNTY!
HEE HEE HEE HEE
THIS BLACK CAT THING IS GENIUS! WORKS LIKE A CHARM... ♡
...ER?
STARE...
...
CAN I HELP YOU...?

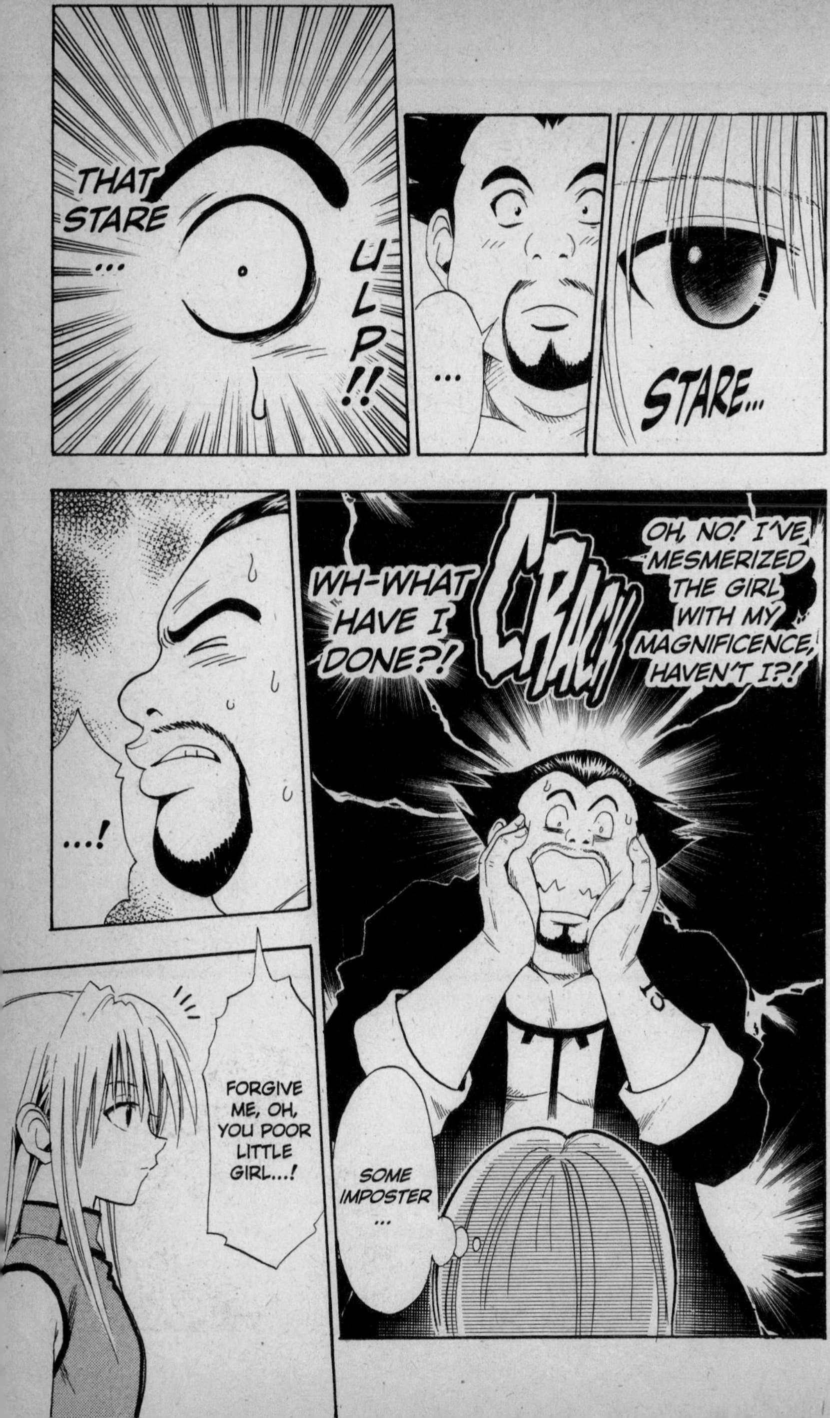
STARE...
...
THAT STARE ...
ULP!!
OH, NO! I'VE MESMERIZED THE GIRL WITH MY MAGNIFICENCE, HAVEN'T I?!
CRACK
WH-WHAT HAVE I DONE?!
SOME IMPOSTER ...
...!
FORGIVE ME, OH, YOU POOR LITTLE GIRL...!

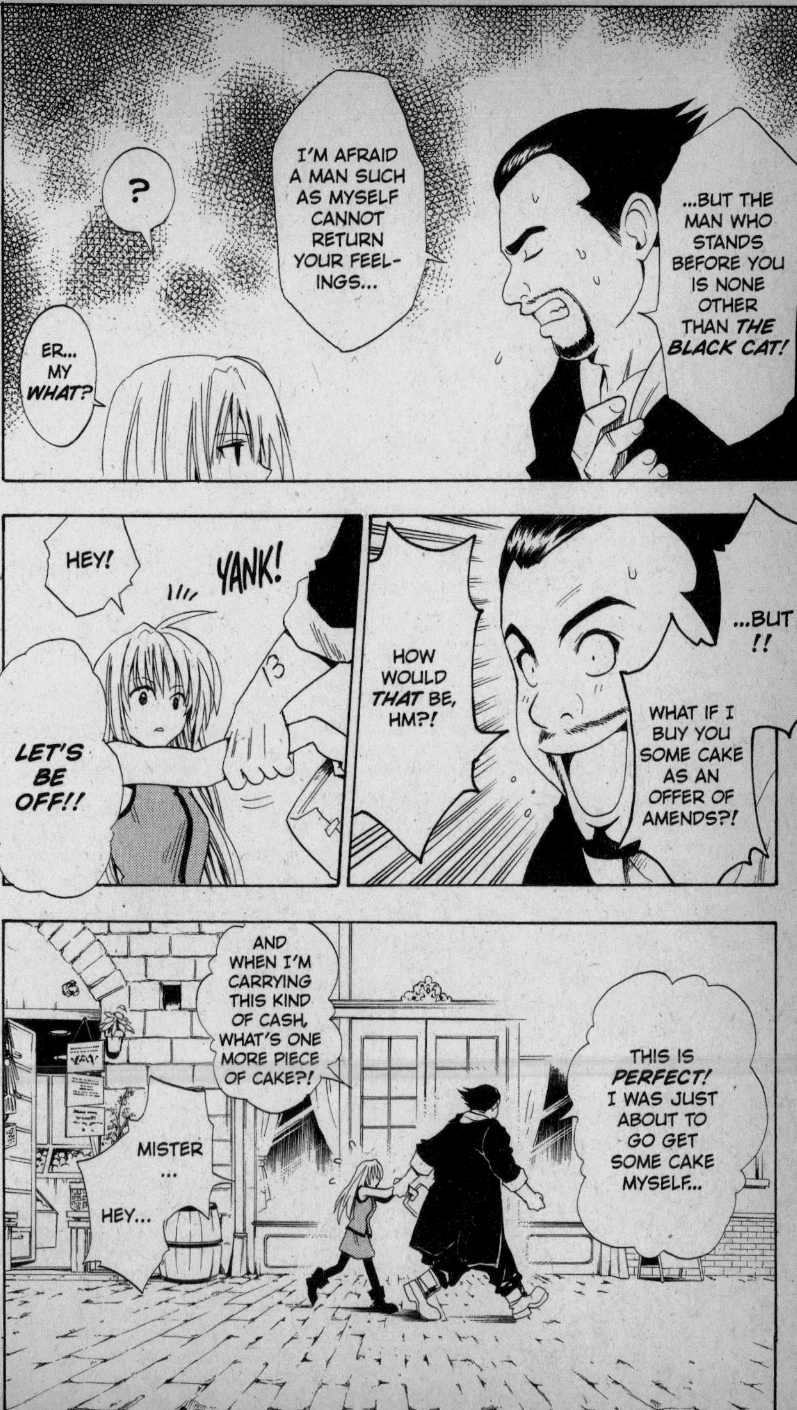
...BUT THE MAN WHO STANDS BEFORE YOU IS NONE OTHER THAN THE BLACK CAT!
I'M AFRAID A MAN SUCH AS MYSELF CANNOT RETURN YOUR FEEL- INGS...
?
ER... MY WHAT?
...BUT !!
WHAT IF I BUY YOU SOME CAKE AS AN OFFER OF AMENDS?!
HOW WOULD THAT BE, HM?!
HEY!
YANK!
LET'S BE OFF!!
THIS IS PERFECT! I WAS JUST ABOUT TO GO GET SOME CAKE MYSELF...
AND WHEN I'M CARRYING THIS KIND OF CASH, WHAT'S ONE MORE PIECE OF CAKE?!
MISTER ...
HEY...

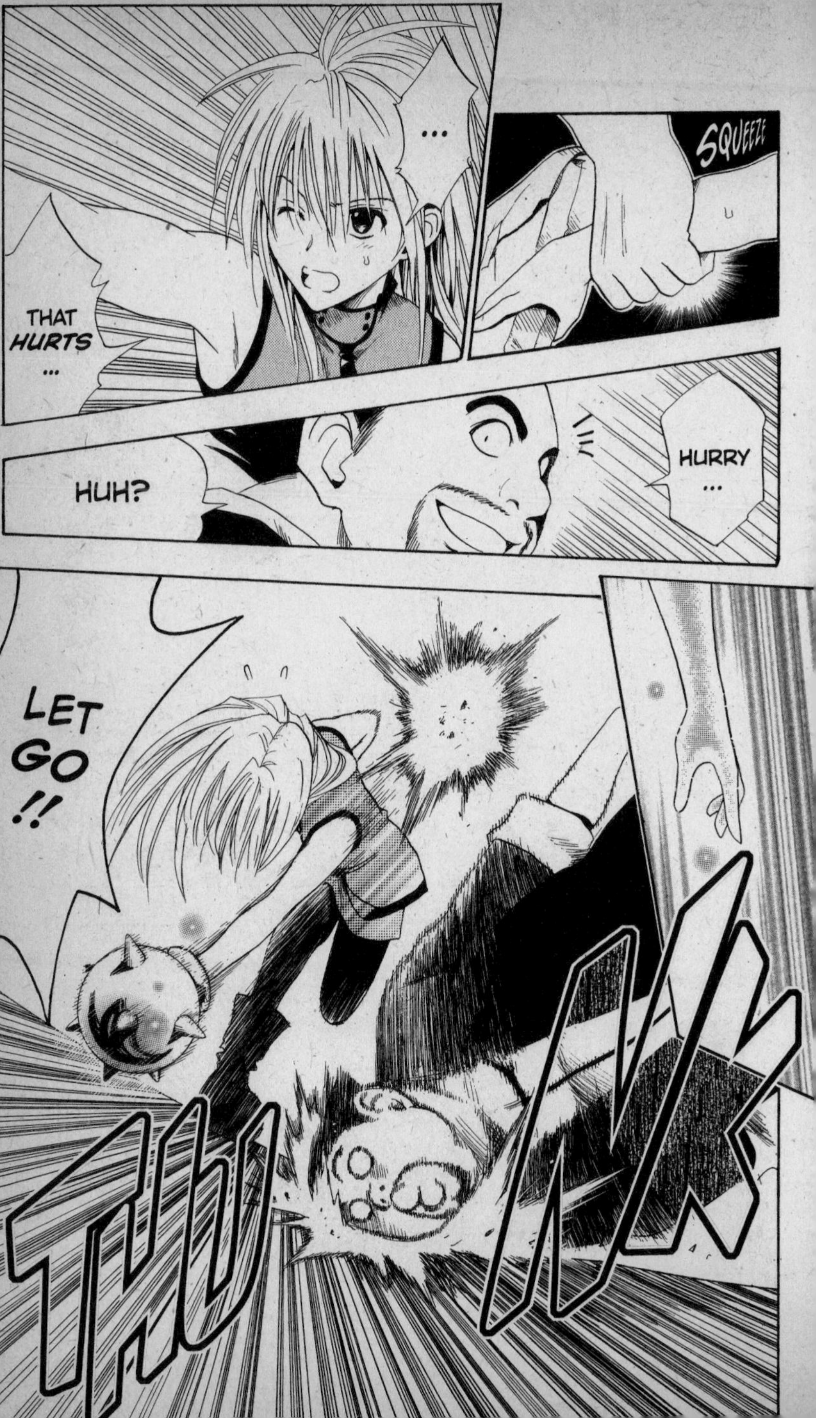
SQUEEZE
...
THAT HURTS ...
HURRY ...
HUH?
LET GO !!
THUNK

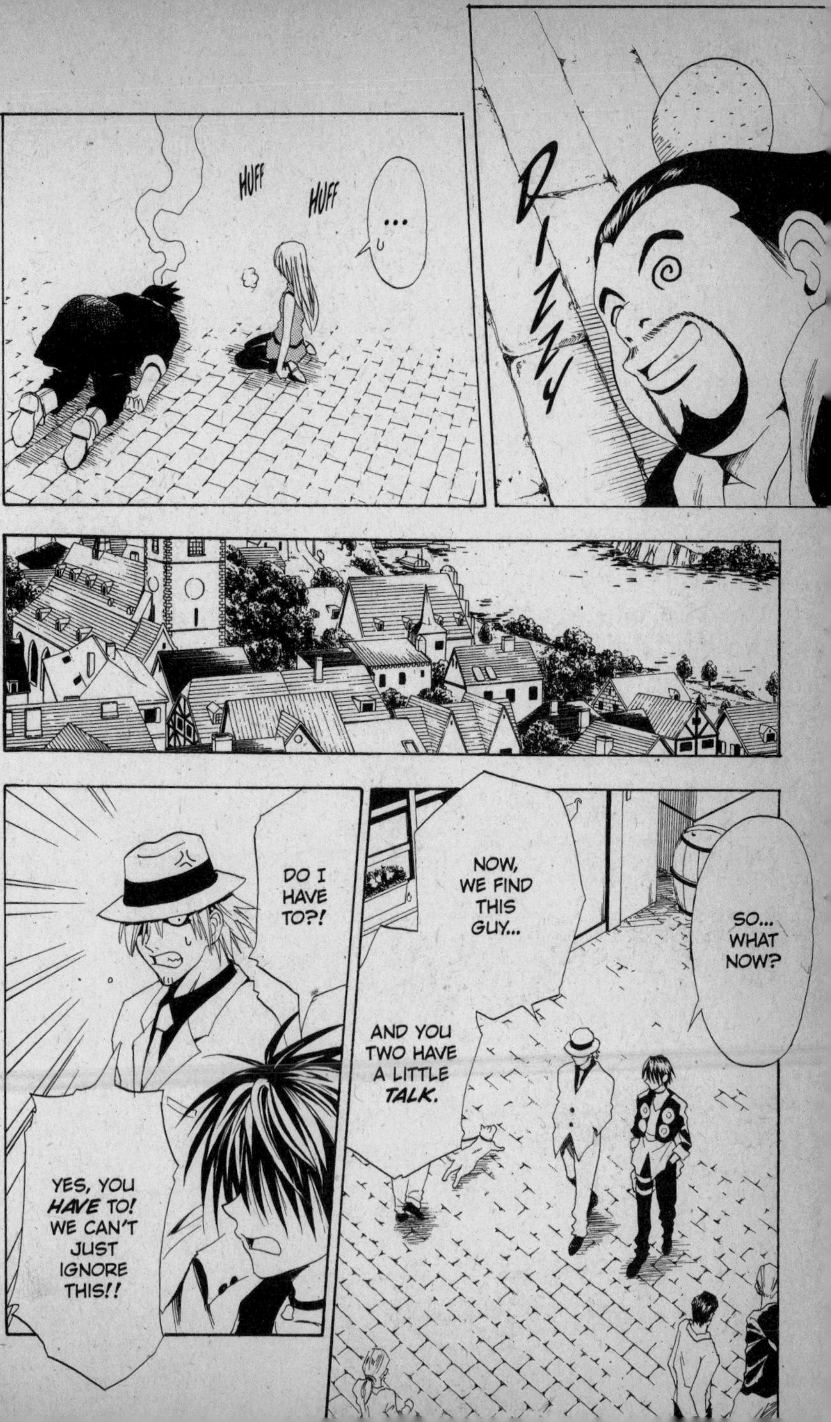
DIZZY
HUFF
HUFF
...
SO... WHAT NOW?
NOW, WE FIND THIS GUY...
AND YOU TWO HAVE A LITTLE *TALK*.
DO I HAVE TO?!
YES, YOU *HAVE* TO! WE CAN'T JUST IGNORE THIS!!

READ THIS WAY

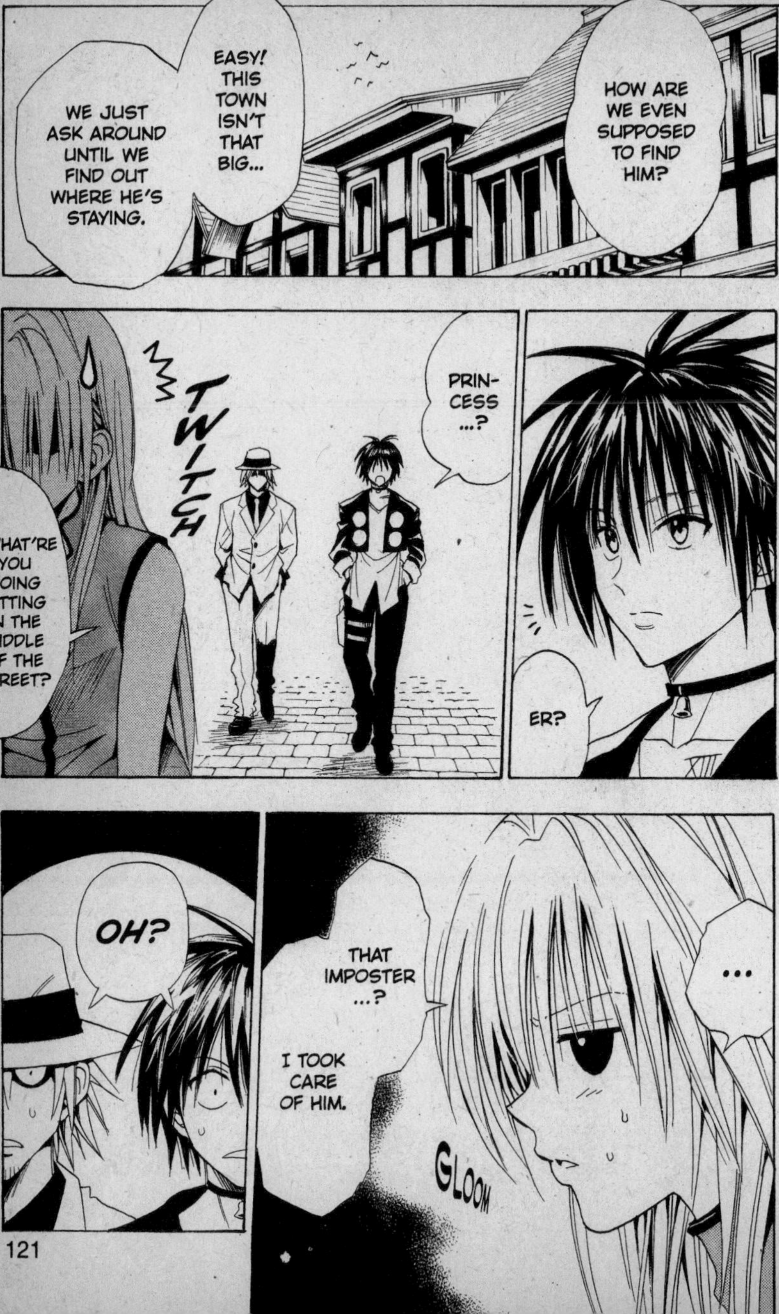

HOW ARE WE EVEN SUPPOSED TO FIND HIM?
EASY! THIS TOWN ISN'T THAT BIG...
WE JUST ASK AROUND UNTIL WE FIND OUT WHERE HE'S STAYING.
ER?
PRIN-CESS ...?
TWITCH
...WHAT'RE YOU DOING SITTING IN THE MIDDLE OF THE STREET?
...
THAT IMPOSTER ...?
I TOOK CARE OF HIM.
GLOOM
OH?

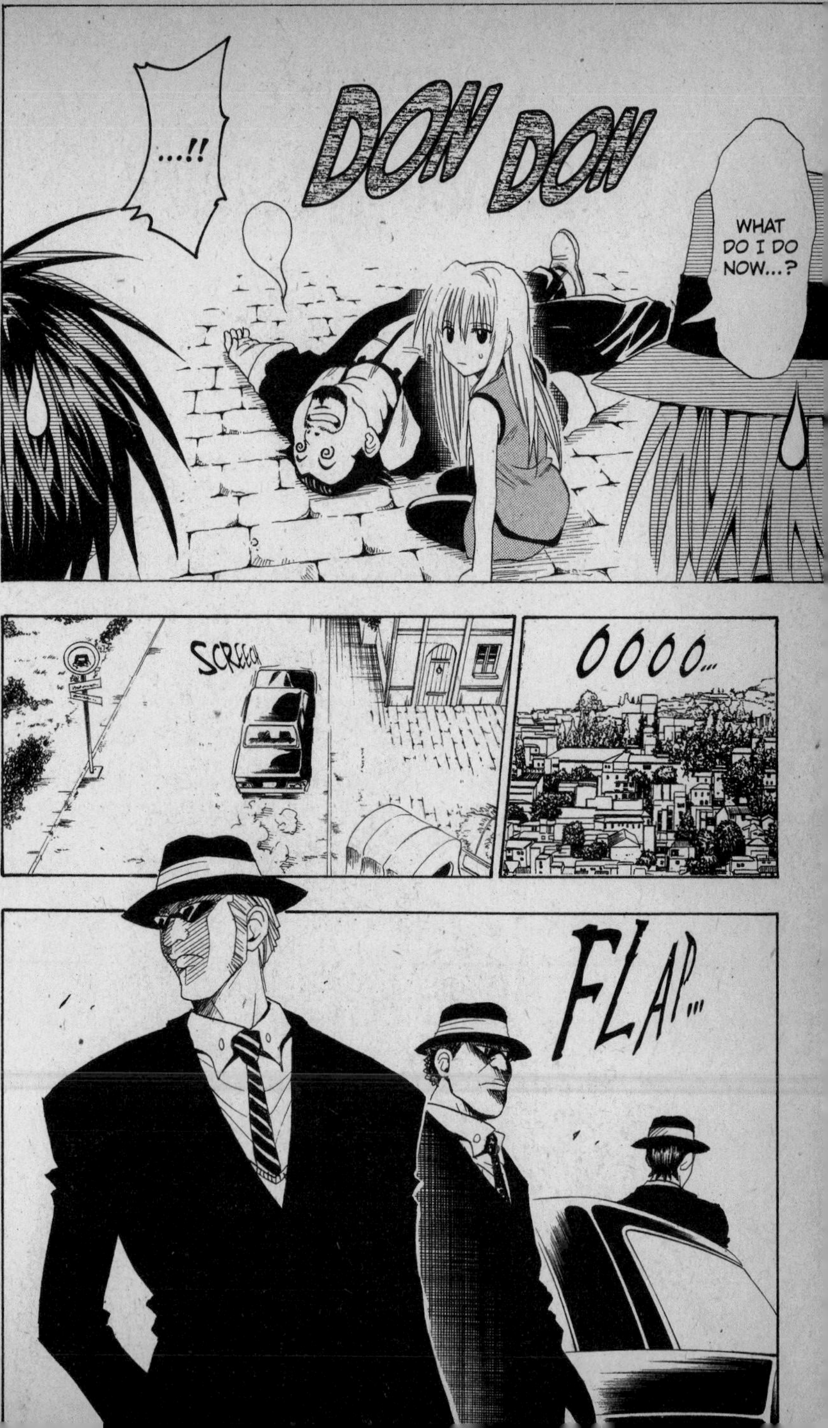
WHAT DO I DO NOW...?
DON DON
...!!
OOOO...
SCREECH
FLAP...

Chapter 45: Train and Woodney

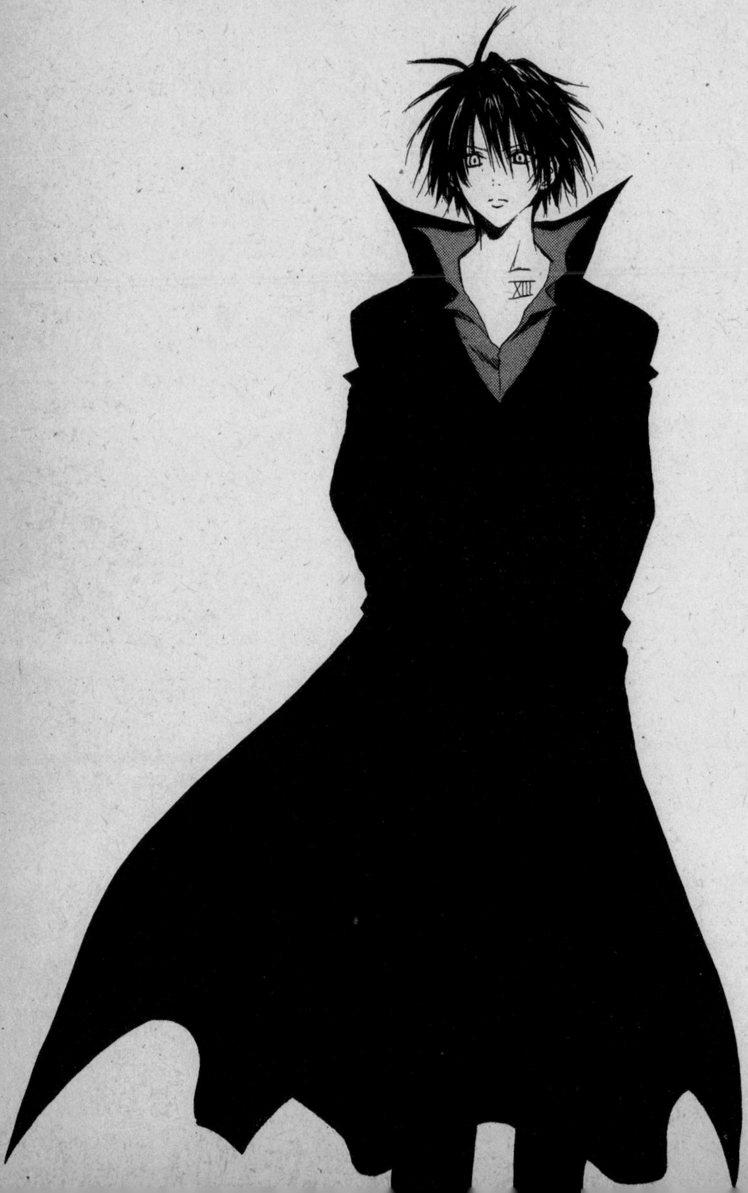
XIII

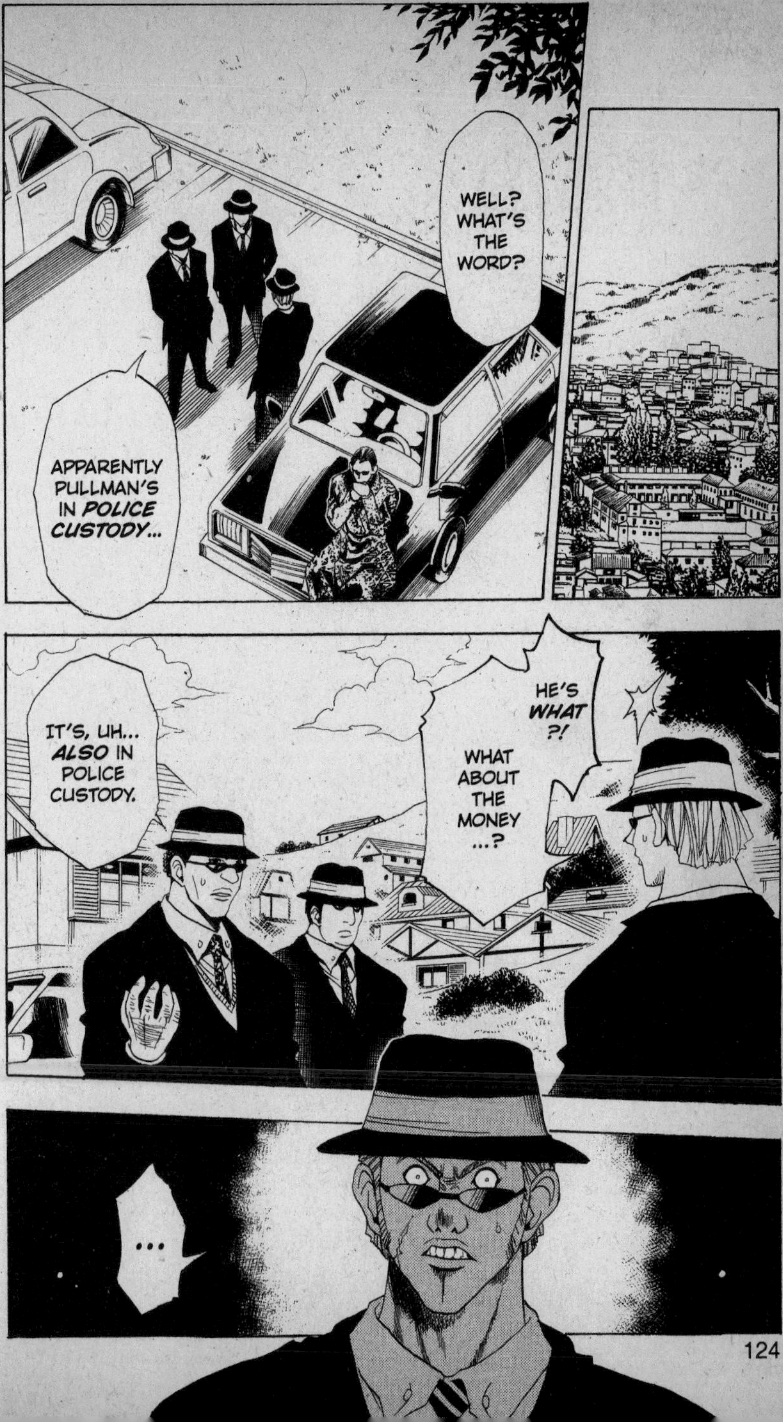
WELL? WHAT'S THE WORD?
APPARENTLY PULLMAN'S IN *POLICE CUSTODY*...
HE'S *WHAT*?!
WHAT ABOUT THE MONEY ...?
IT'S, UH... *ALSO* IN POLICE CUSTODY.
...

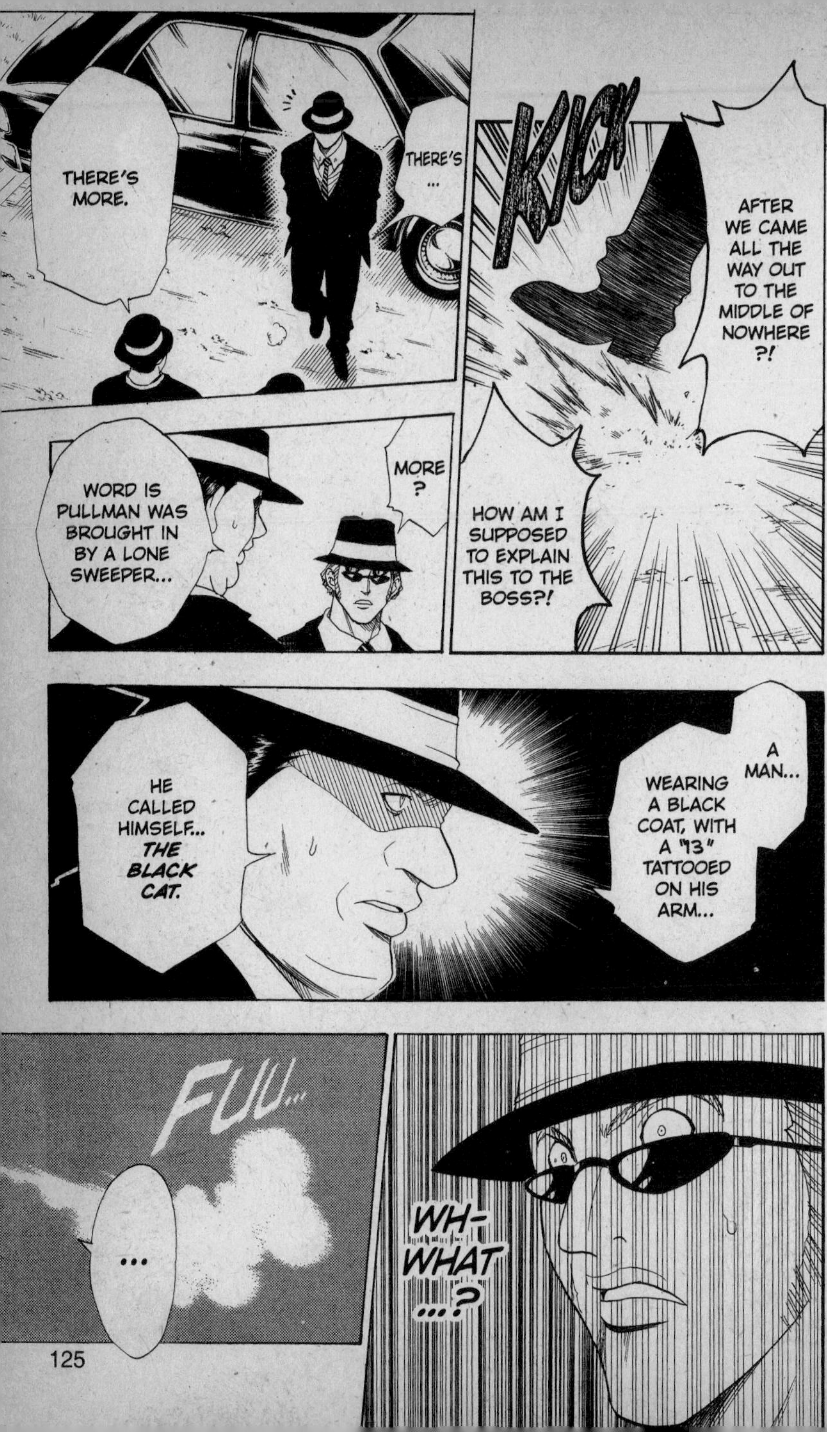
KICK
AFTER WE CAME ALL THE WAY OUT TO THE MIDDLE OF NOWHERE ?!
HOW AM I SUPPOSED TO EXPLAIN THIS TO THE BOSS?!
THERE'S ...
THERE'S MORE.
MORE ?
WORD IS PULLMAN WAS BROUGHT IN BY A LONE SWEEPER...
A MAN...
WEARING A BLACK COAT, WITH A "13" TATTOOED ON HIS ARM...
HE CALLED HIMSELF... *THE BLACK CAT.*
WH- WHAT ...?
FUU...
...

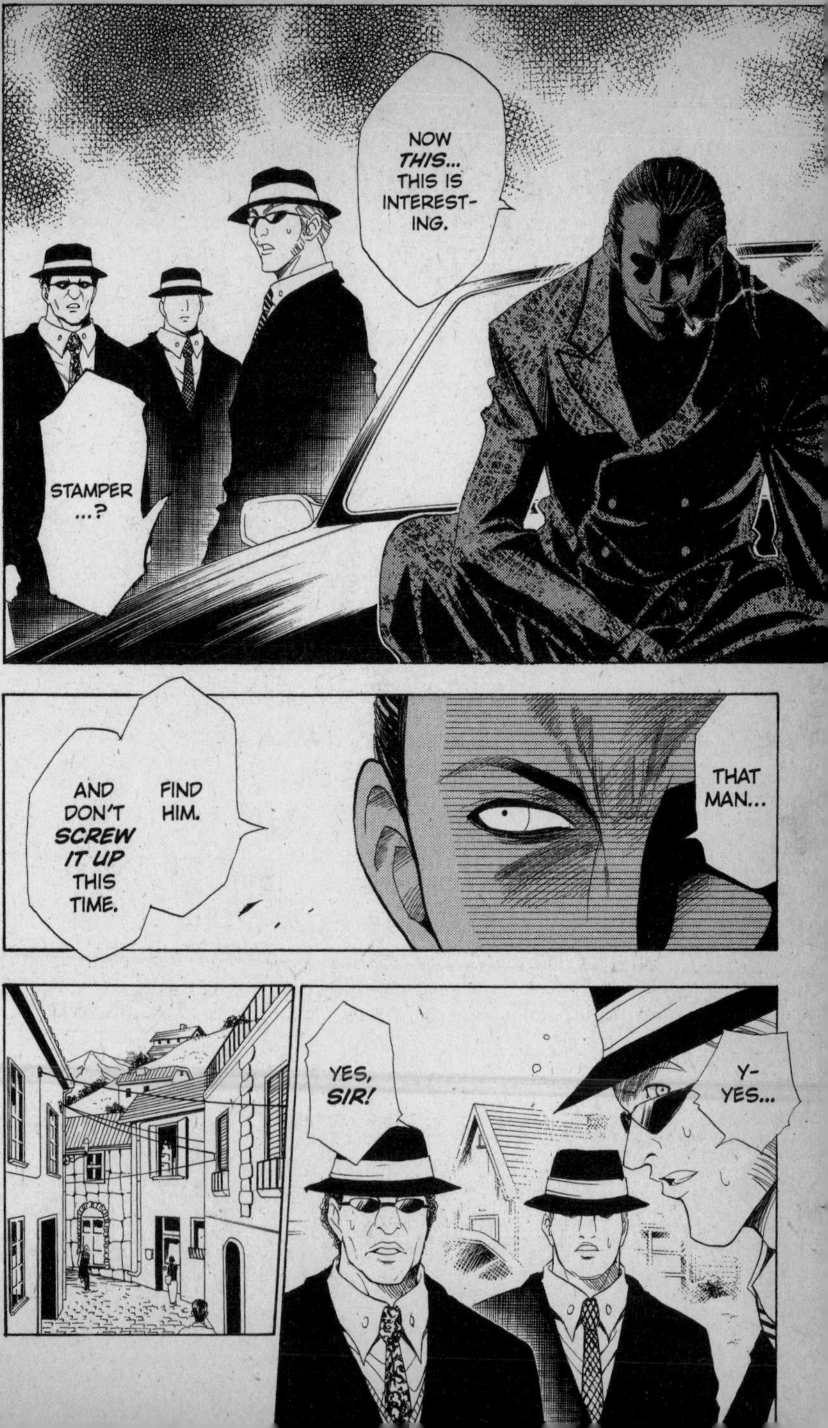
NOW *THIS*... THIS IS INTEREST-ING.
STAMPER ...?
THAT MAN...
FIND HIM.
AND DON'T ***SCREW IT UP*** THIS TIME.
Y-YES...
YES, ***SIR!***

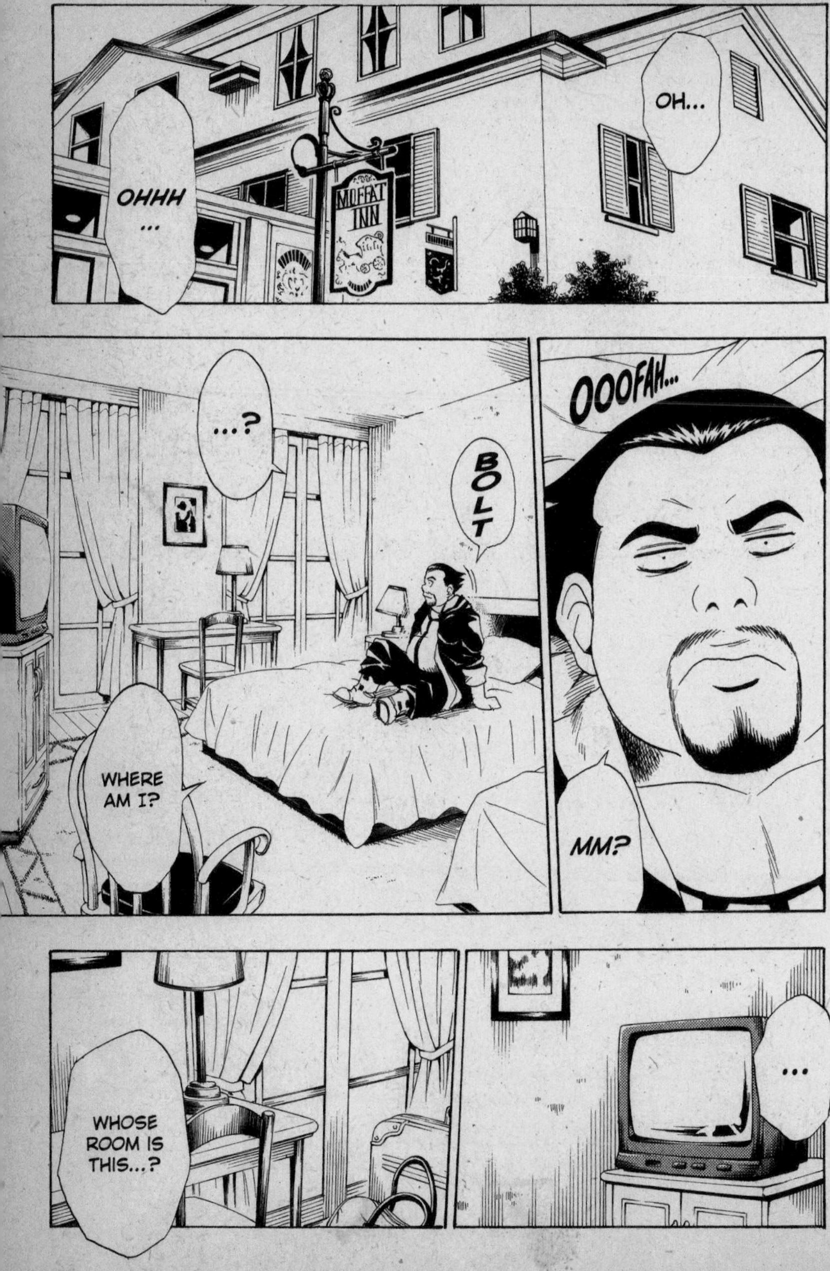
OH...
MOFFAT INN
OHHH ...
OOOFAH...
MM?
BOLT
...?
WHERE AM I?
...
WHOSE ROOM IS THIS...?

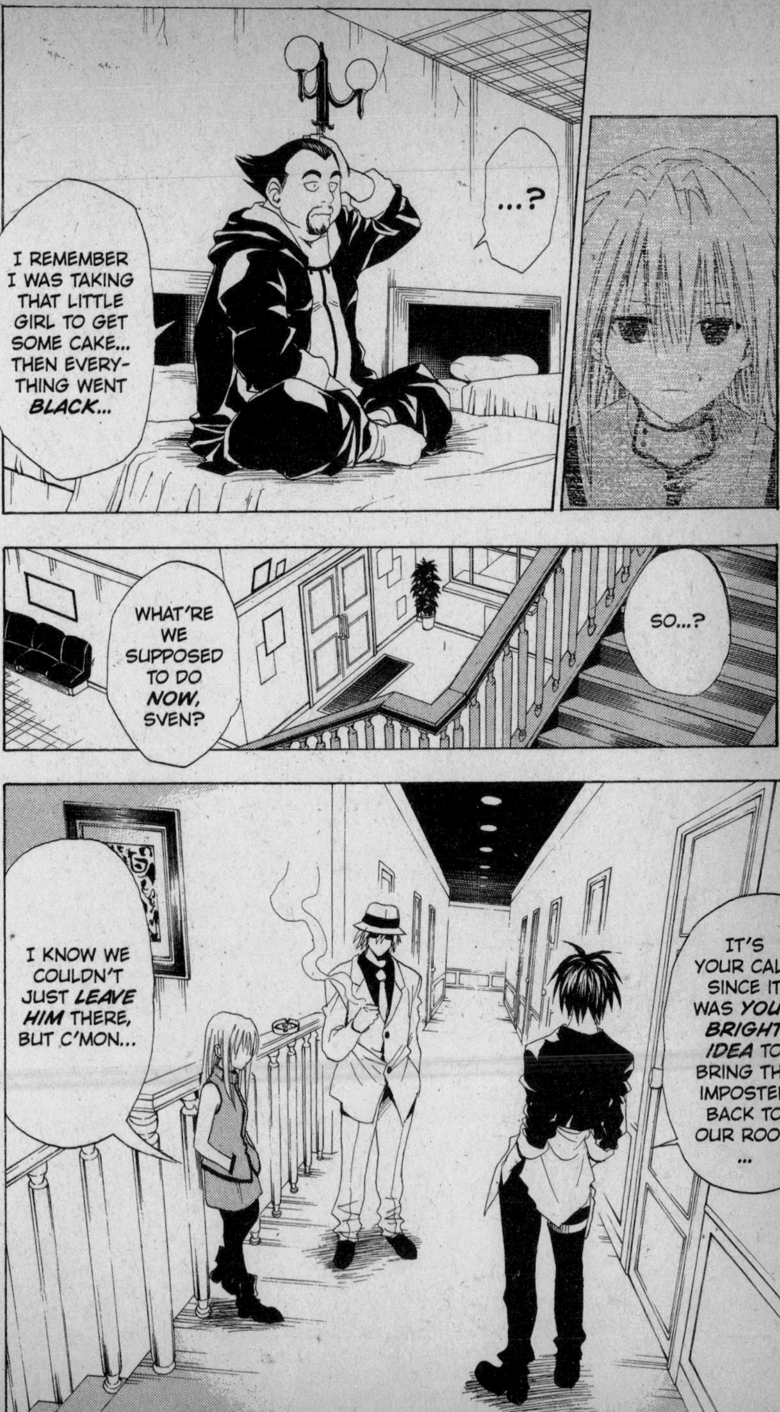
...?
I REMEMBER I WAS TAKING THAT LITTLE GIRL TO GET SOME CAKE... THEN EVERY-THING WENT BLACK...
SO...?
WHAT'RE WE SUPPOSED TO DO NOW, SVEN?
IT'S YOUR CALL SINCE IT WAS YOUR BRIGHT IDEA TO BRING THE IMPOSTER BACK TO OUR ROOM ...
I KNOW WE COULDN'T JUST LEAVE HIM THERE, BUT C'MON...

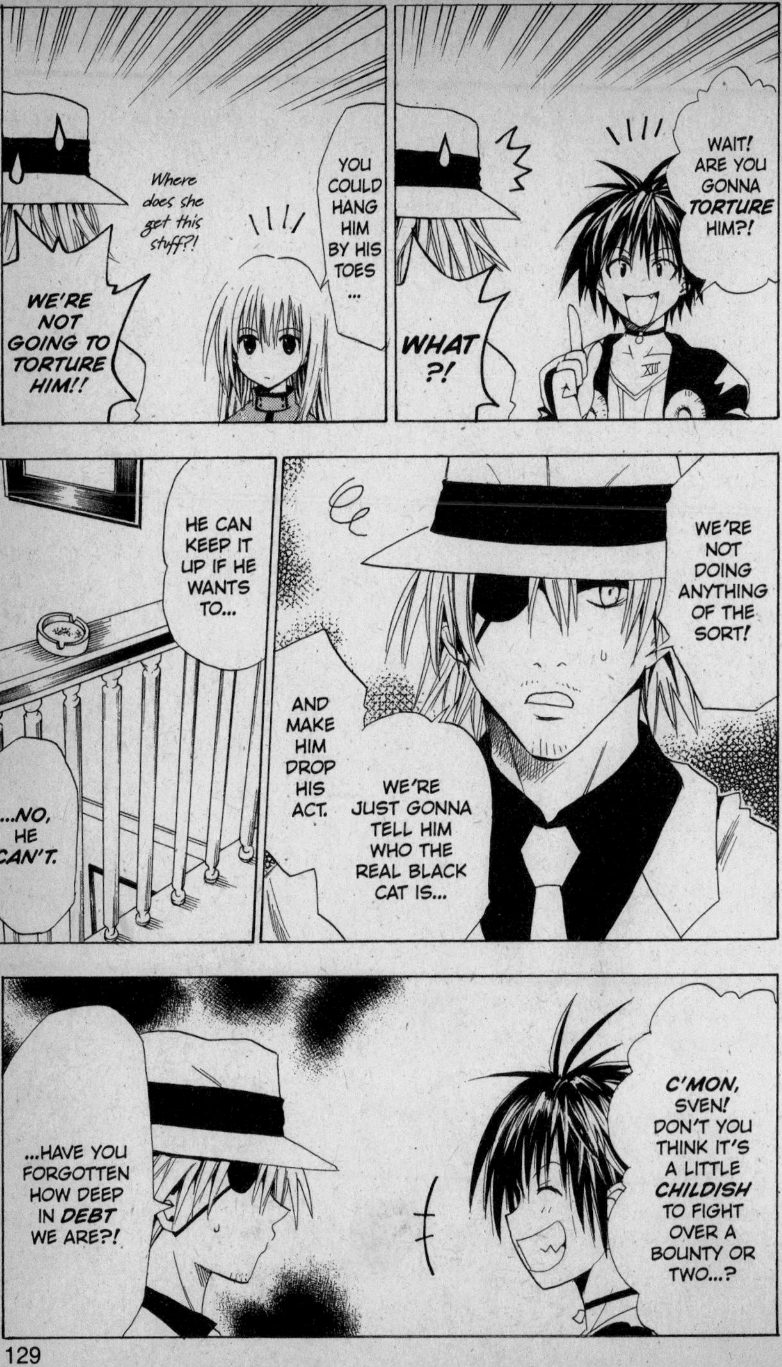
WAIT! ARE YOU GONNA TORTURE HIM?!
WHAT?!
YOU COULD HANG HIM BY HIS TOES ...
Where does she get this stuff?!
WE'RE NOT GOING TO TORTURE HIM!!
WE'RE NOT DOING ANYTHING OF THE SORT!
WE'RE JUST GONNA TELL HIM WHO THE REAL BLACK CAT IS...
AND MAKE HIM DROP HIS ACT.
HE CAN KEEP IT UP IF HE WANTS TO...
...NO, HE CAN'T.
C'MON, SVEN! DON'T YOU THINK IT'S A LITTLE CHILDISH TO FIGHT OVER A BOUNTY OR TWO...?
...HAVE YOU FORGOTTEN HOW DEEP IN DEBT WE ARE?!

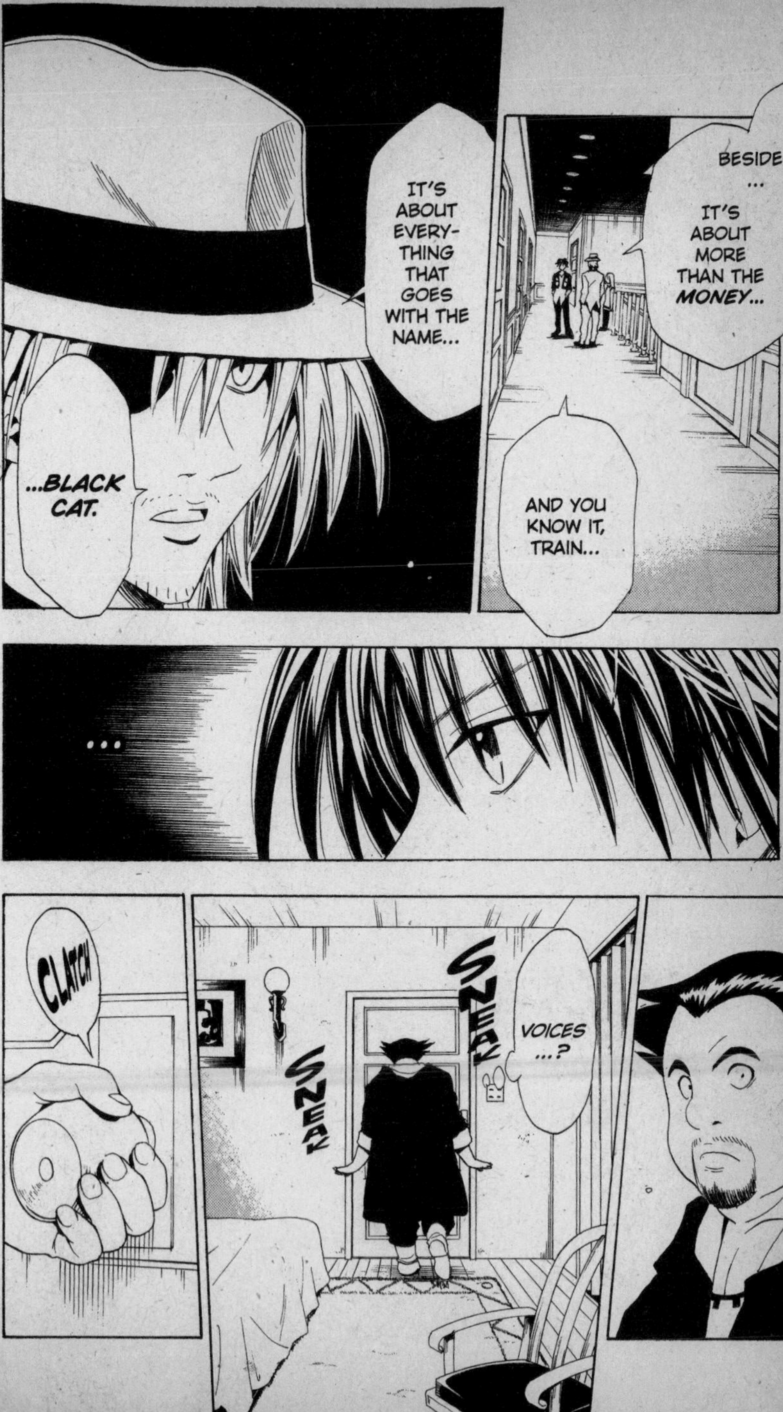
BESIDES ... IT'S ABOUT MORE THAN THE *MONEY*...
AND YOU KNOW IT, TRAIN...
IT'S ABOUT EVERY-THING THAT GOES WITH THE NAME...
...BLACK CAT.
...
SNEAK
VOICES ...?
SNEAK
CLATCH

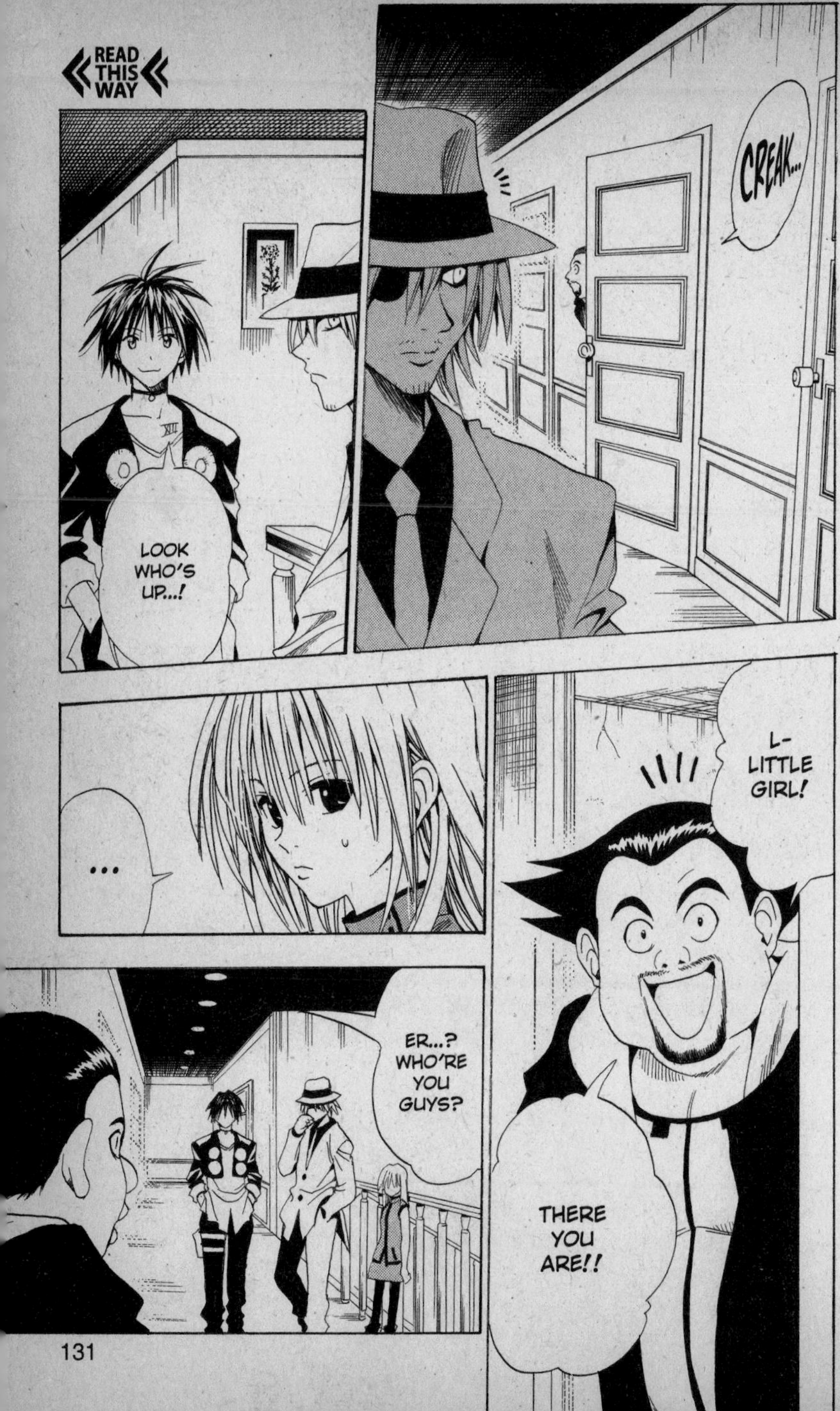
READ THIS WAY
CREAK...
LOOK WHO'S UP...!
L- LITTLE GIRL!
THERE YOU ARE!!
...
ER...? WHO'RE YOU GUYS?

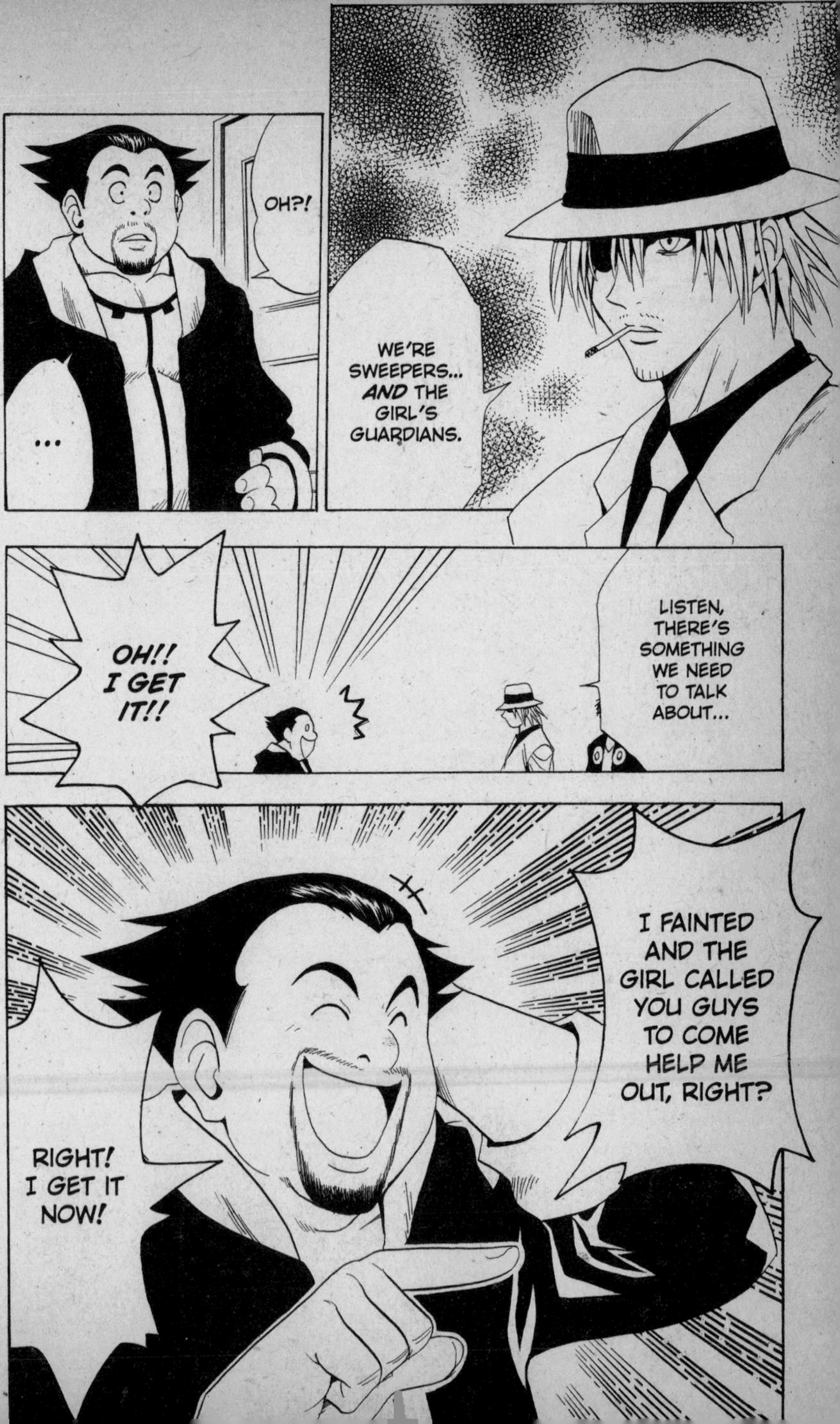
WE'RE SWEEPERS... AND THE GIRL'S GUARDIANS.
OH?!
...
LISTEN, THERE'S SOMETHING WE NEED TO TALK ABOUT...
OH!! I GET IT!!
I FAINTED AND THE GIRL CALLED YOU GUYS TO COME HELP ME OUT, RIGHT?
RIGHT! I GET IT NOW!

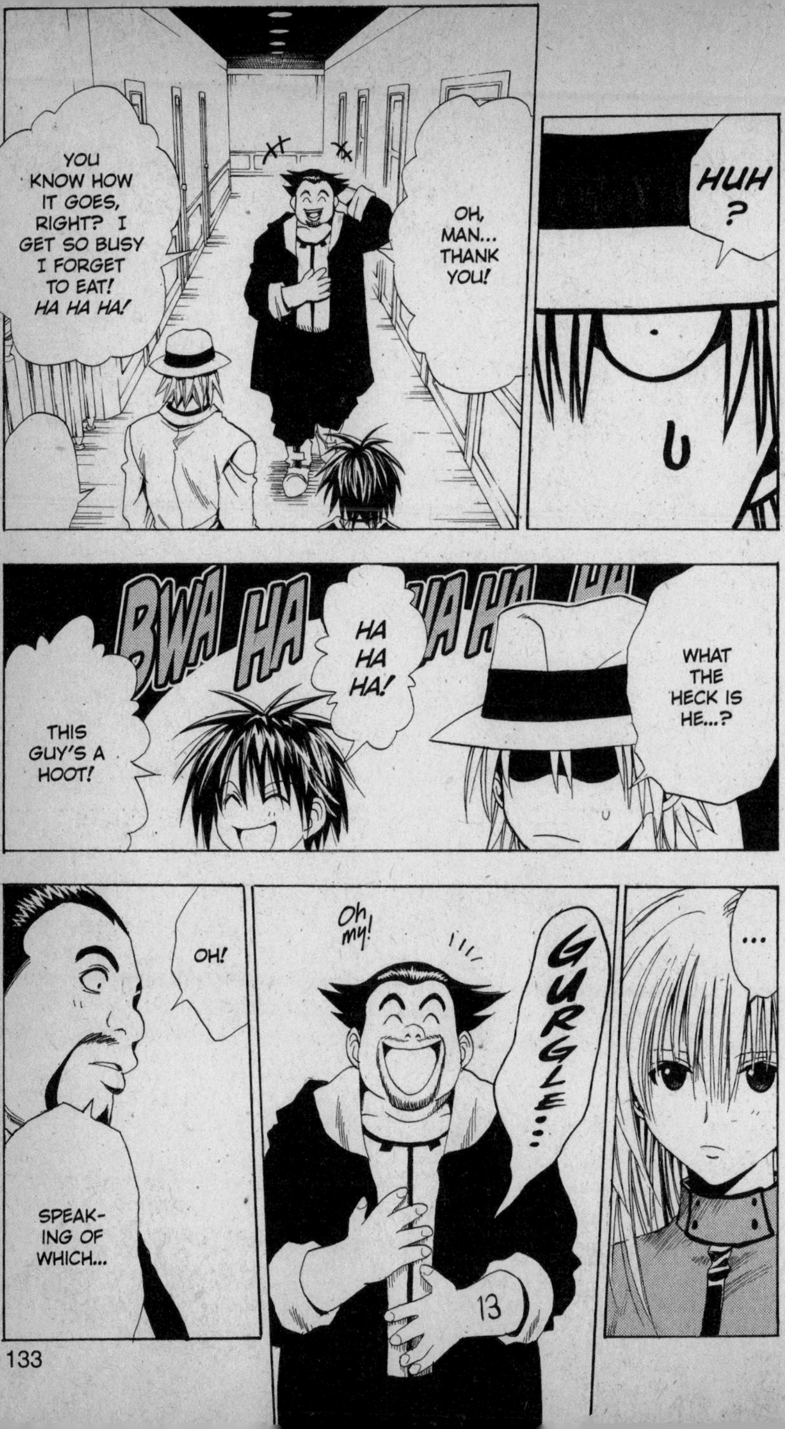
HUH?
OH, MAN... THANK YOU!
YOU KNOW HOW IT GOES, RIGHT? I GET SO BUSY I FORGET TO EAT! HA HA HA!
WHAT THE HECK IS HE...?
BWA HA HA HA HA
HA HA HA!
THIS GUY'S A HOOT!
...
GURGLE...
Oh my!
OH!
SPEAK-ING OF WHICH...

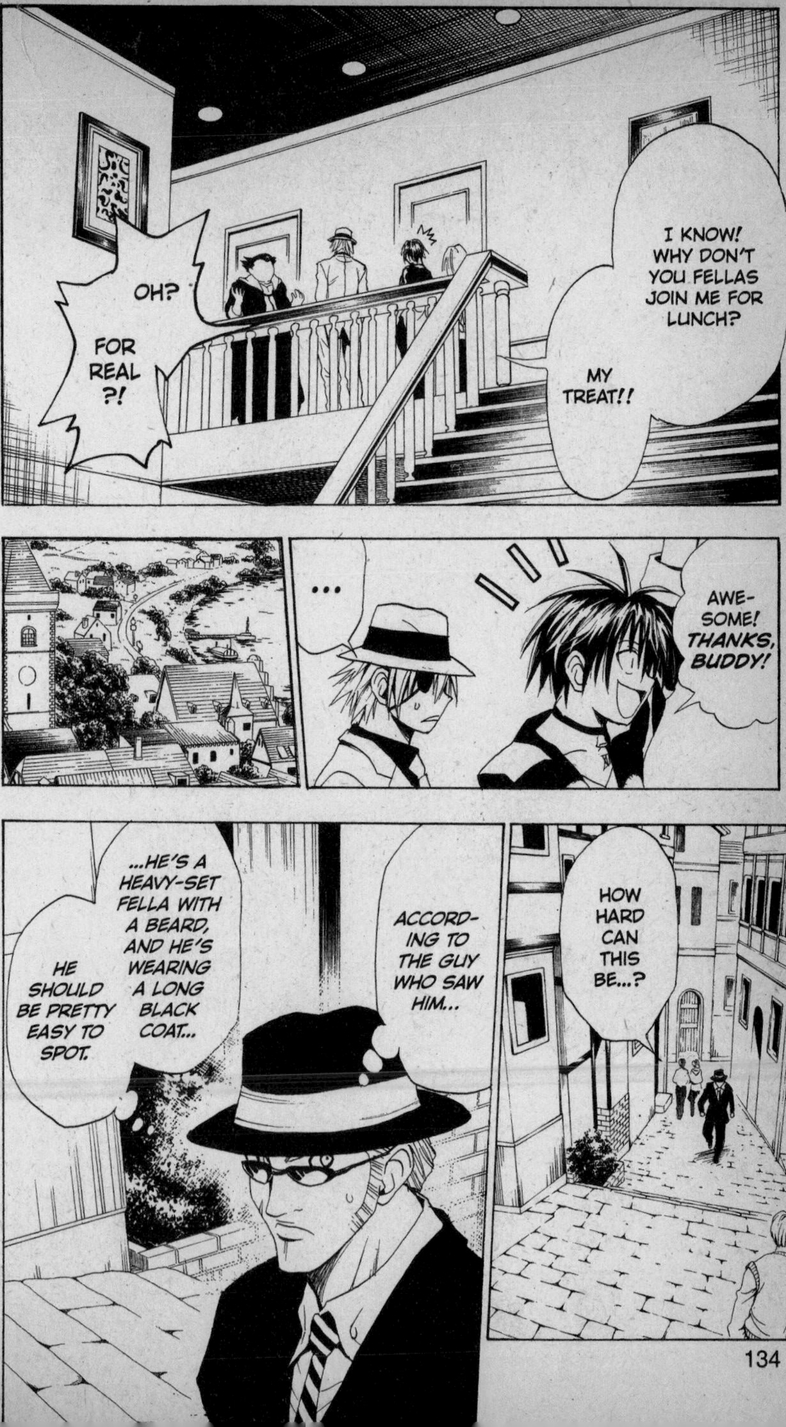
I KNOW! WHY DON'T YOU FELLAS JOIN ME FOR LUNCH?
MY TREAT!!
OH?
FOR REAL?!
AWE-SOME! THANKS, BUDDY!
...
HOW HARD CAN THIS BE...?
ACCORD-ING TO THE GUY WHO SAW HIM...
...HE'S A HEAVY-SET FELLA WITH A BEARD, AND HE'S WEARING A LONG BLACK COAT...
HE SHOULD BE PRETTY EASY TO SPOT.

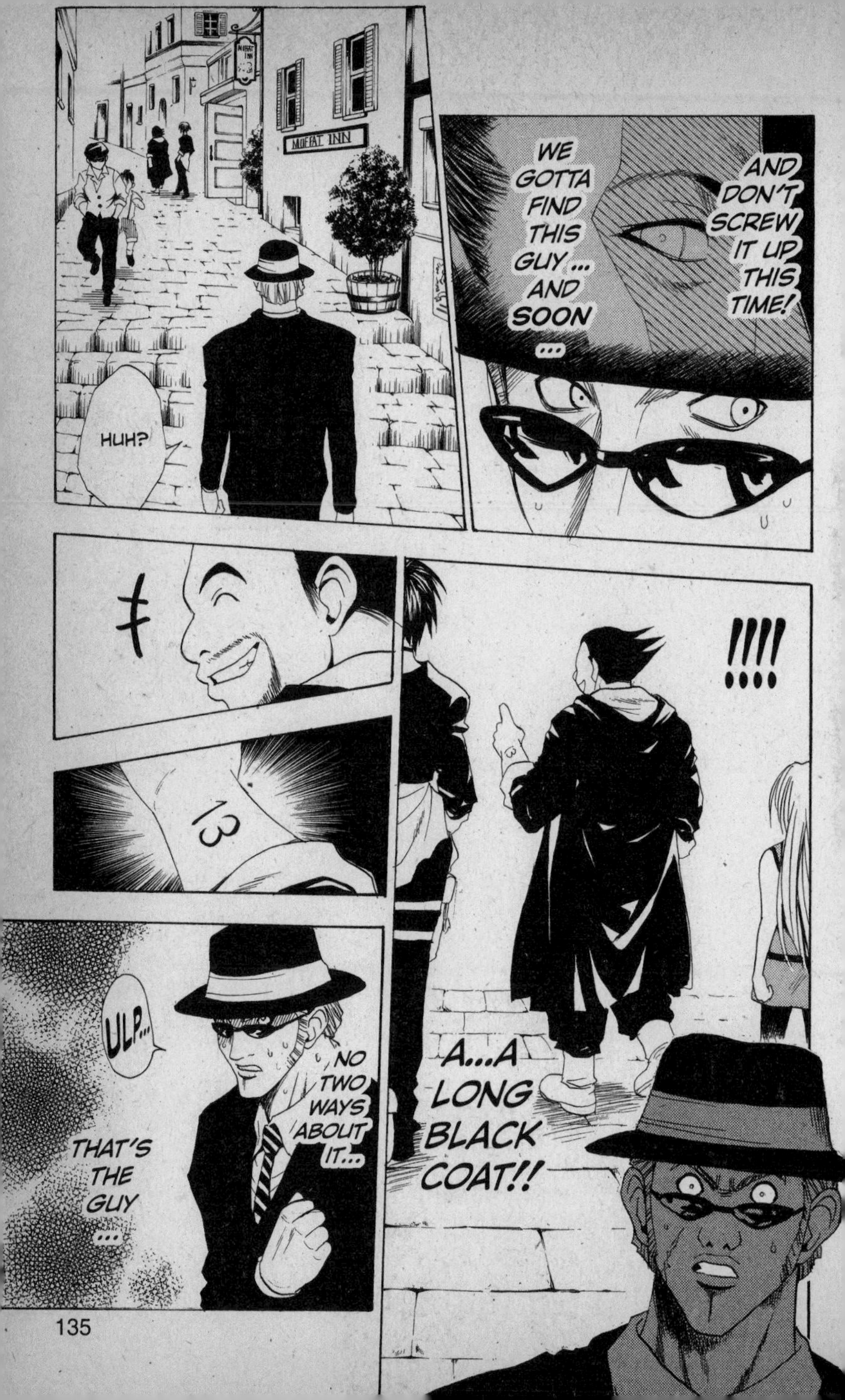
WE GOTTA FIND THIS GUY ... AND SOON ...
AND DON'T SCREW IT UP THIS TIME!
MOFFAT INN
HUH?
!!!!
A...A LONG BLACK COAT!!
13
ULP...
NO TWO WAYS ABOUT IT...
THAT'S THE GUY ...

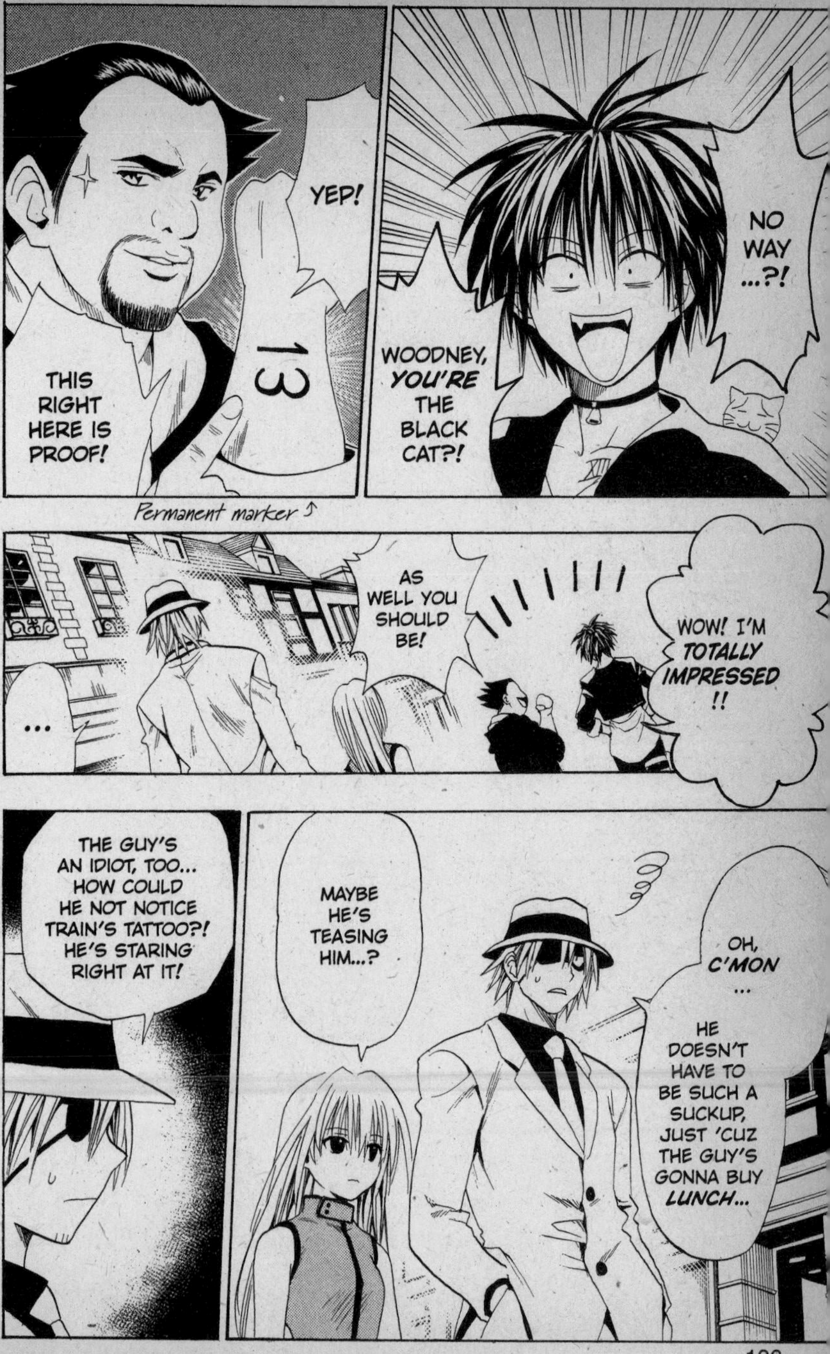
NO WAY ...?!
WOODNEY, *YOU'RE* THE BLACK CAT?!
YEP!
13
THIS RIGHT HERE IS PROOF!
Permanent marker
WOW! I'M *TOTALLY IMPRESSED* !!
AS WELL YOU SHOULD BE!
...
OH, *C'MON* ...
HE DOESN'T HAVE TO BE SUCH A SUCKUP, JUST 'CUZ THE GUY'S GONNA BUY *LUNCH*...
MAYBE HE'S TEASING HIM...?
THE GUY'S AN IDIOT, TOO... HOW COULD HE NOT NOTICE TRAIN'S TATTOO?! HE'S STARING RIGHT AT IT!

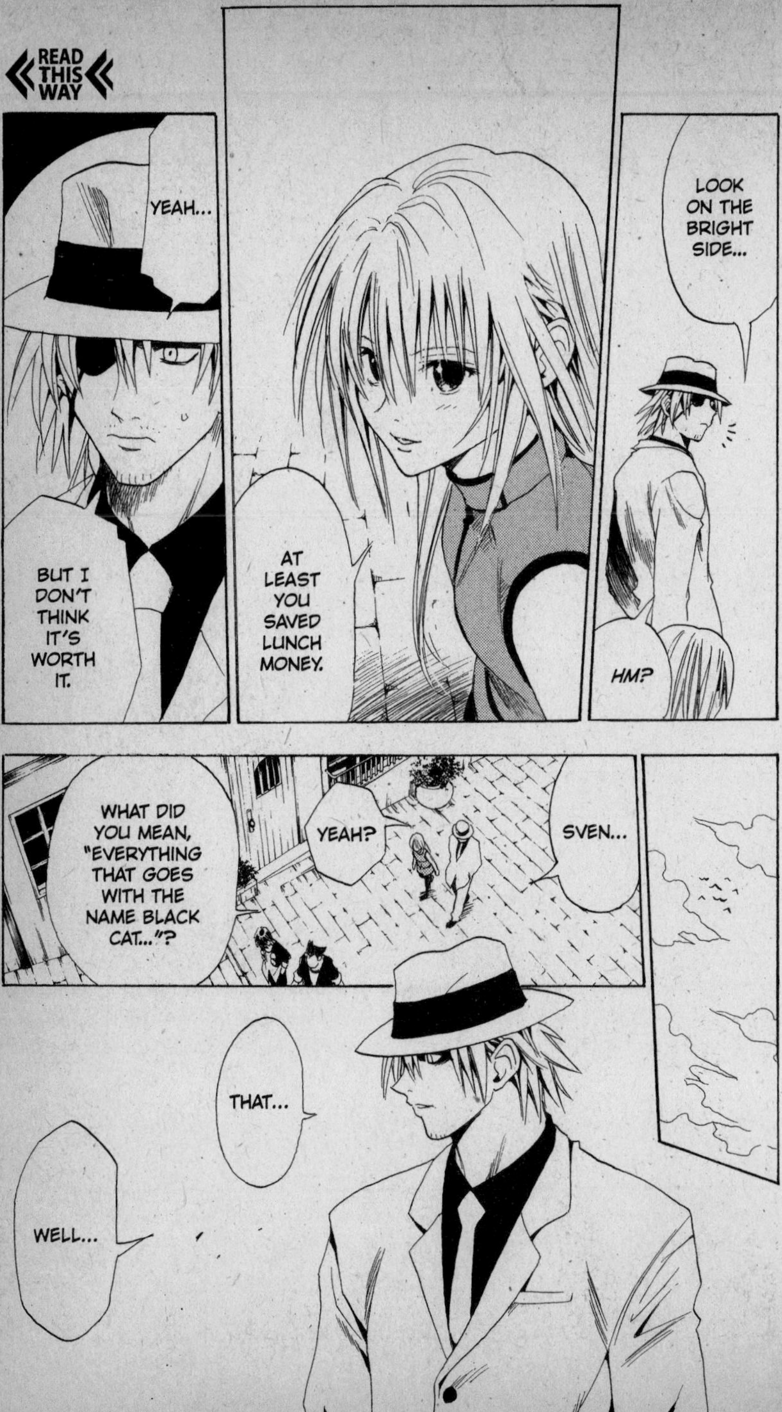
READ THIS WAY
LOOK ON THE BRIGHT SIDE...
HM?
AT LEAST YOU SAVED LUNCH MONEY.
YEAH...
BUT I DON'T THINK IT'S WORTH IT.
SVEN...
YEAH?
WHAT DID YOU MEAN, "EVERYTHING THAT GOES WITH THE NAME BLACK CAT..."?
THAT...
WELL...

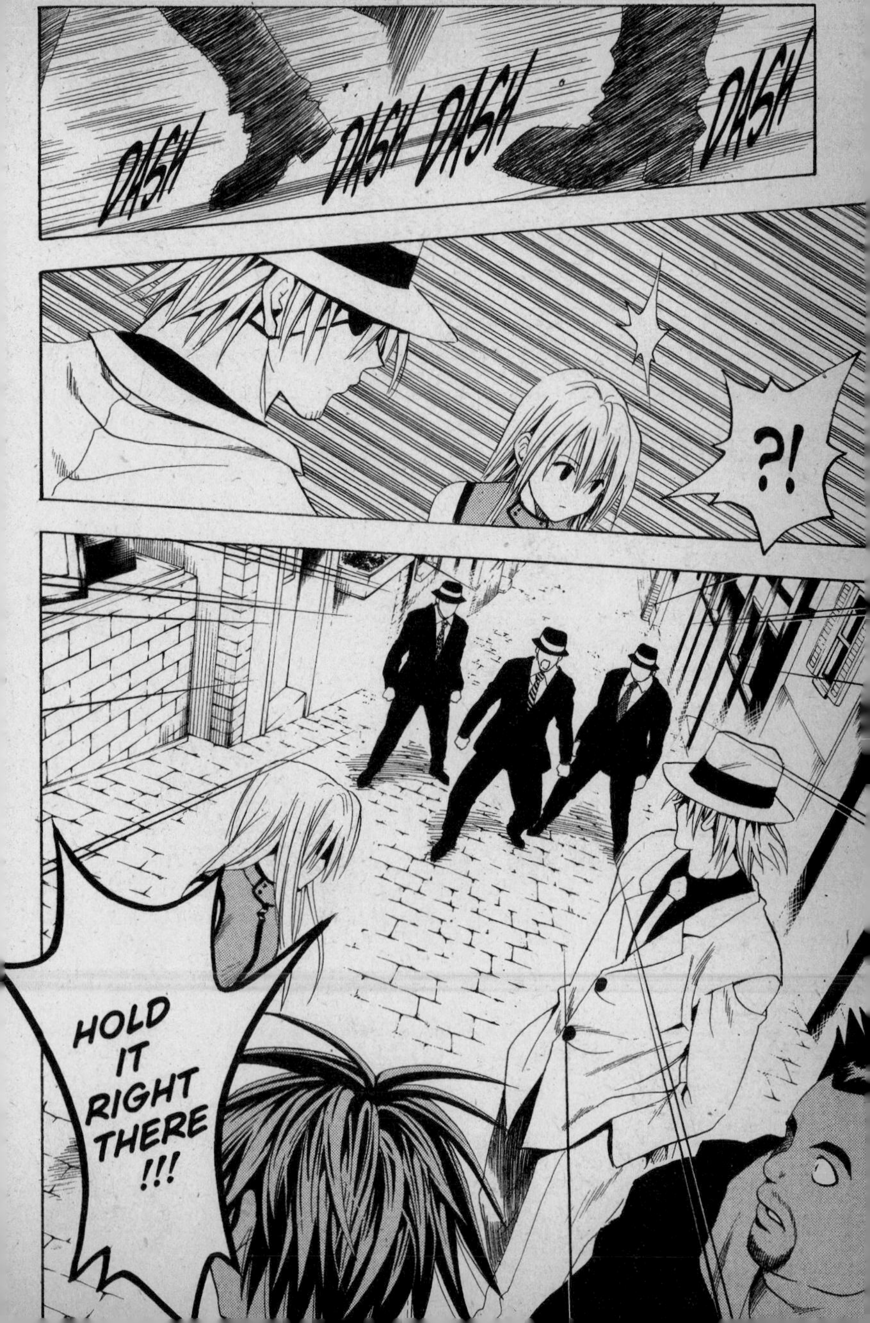
DASH
DASH DASH
DASH
?!
HOLD IT RIGHT THERE !!!

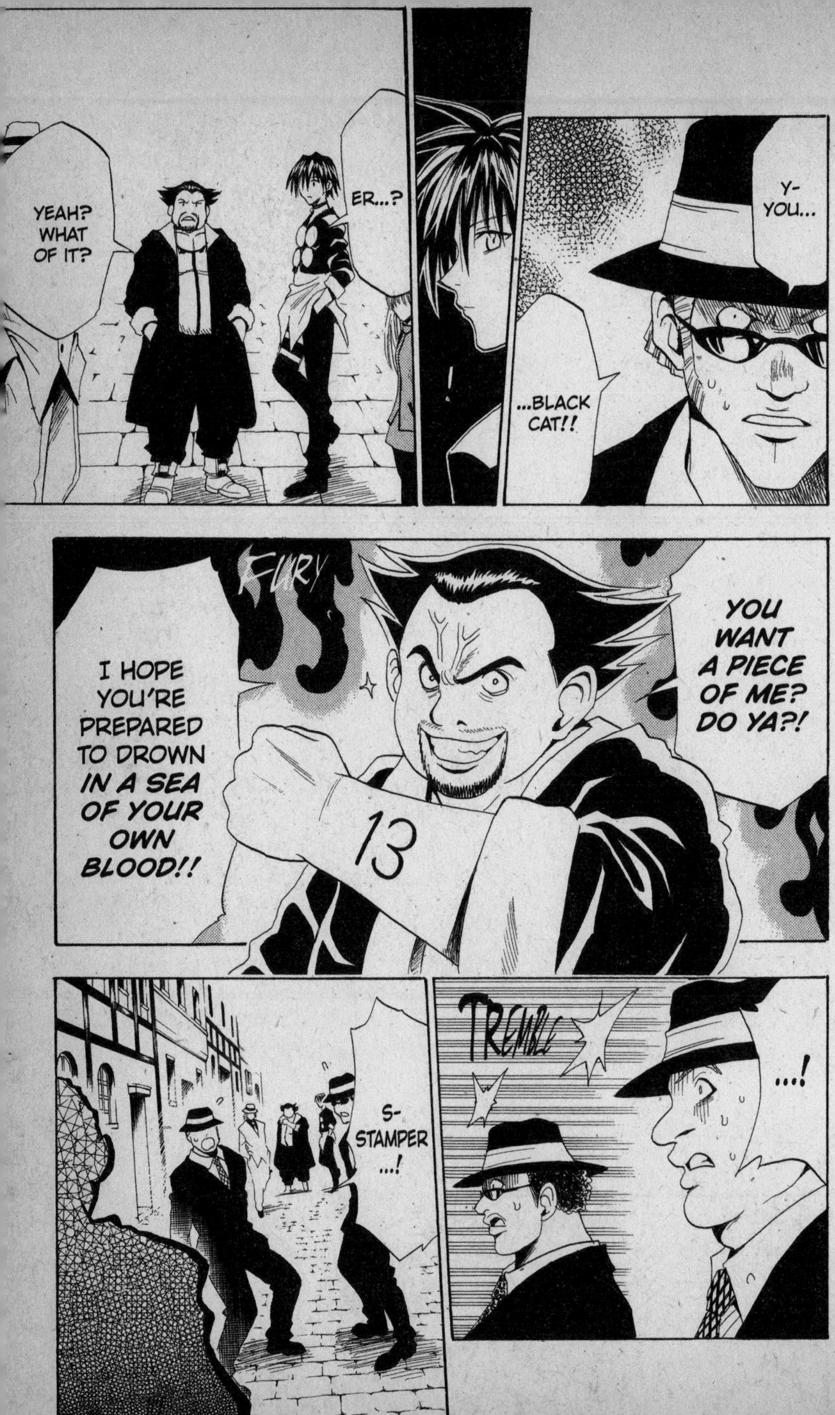
Y- YOU...
...BLACK CAT!!
ER...?
YEAH? WHAT OF IT?
YOU WANT A PIECE OF ME? DO YA?!
FURY
I HOPE YOU'RE PREPARED TO DROWN IN A SEA OF YOUR OWN BLOOD!!
13
...!
TREMBLE
S-STAMPER ...!

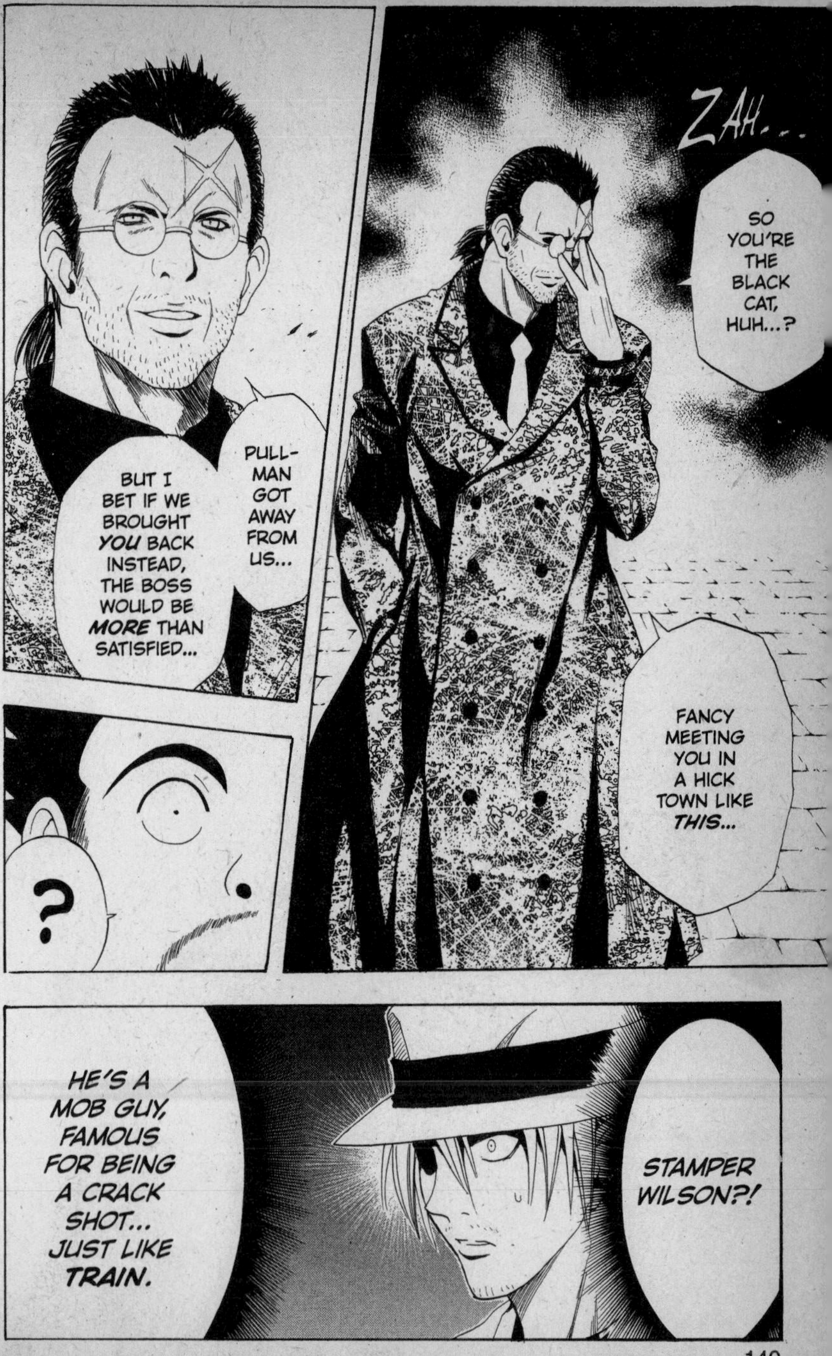
ZAH...
SO YOU'RE THE BLACK CAT, HUH...?
FANCY MEETING YOU IN A HICK TOWN LIKE THIS...
PULLMAN GOT AWAY FROM US...
BUT I BET IF WE BROUGHT YOU BACK INSTEAD, THE BOSS WOULD BE MORE THAN SATISFIED...
?
STAMPER WILSON?!
HE'S A MOB GUY, FAMOUS FOR BEING A CRACK SHOT... JUST LIKE TRAIN.

READ THIS WAY

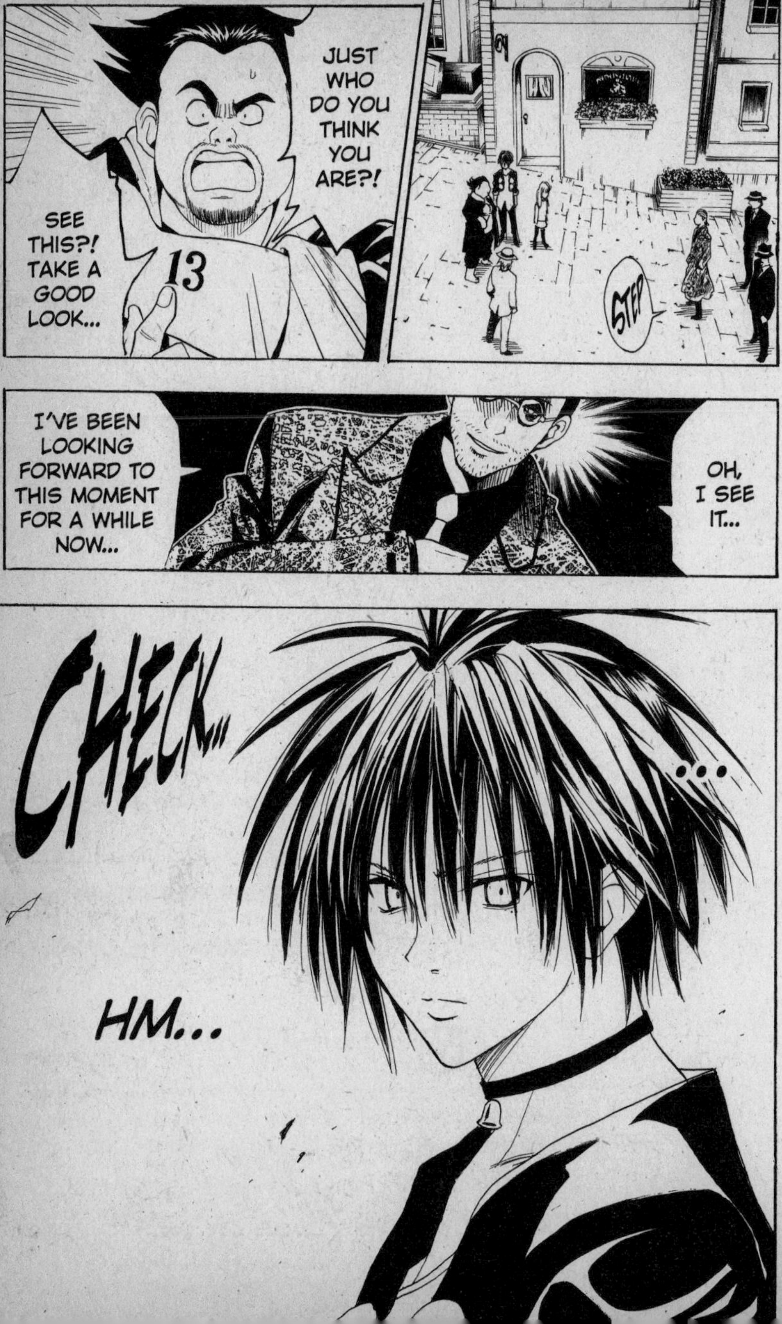
STEP
JUST WHO DO YOU THINK YOU ARE?!
13
SEE THIS?! TAKE A GOOD LOOK...
OH, I SEE IT...
I'VE BEEN LOOKING FORWARD TO THIS MOMENT FOR A WHILE NOW...
...
CHECK...
HM...

BLACK CAT

profile

MARO

DATA	
BIRTHDAY:	?
AGE:	33 YEARS OLD
BLOOD TYPE:	O
HEIGHT:	215 CM
WEIGHT:	301 KG
PRIDE AND JOY:	A BODY COVERED WITH FLESH SO DENSE NOT EVEN A BULLET CAN PENETRATE IT.
STRENGTH:	GRAVITY
NOTES:	A TAOIST WHO IS ABLE TO CHANGE THE FLOW OF THE EARTH'S ENERGY AND ELEVATE THE GRAVITATIONAL FORCE AROUND HIMSELF. LIKE SHIKI, MARO HAILS FROM THE BIRTHPLACE OF THE TAO.

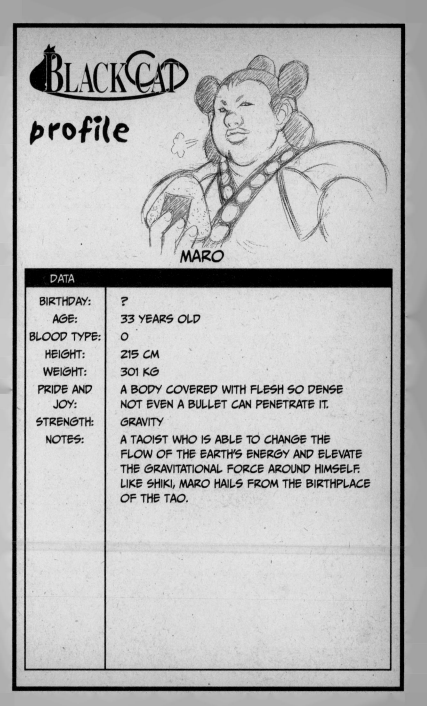

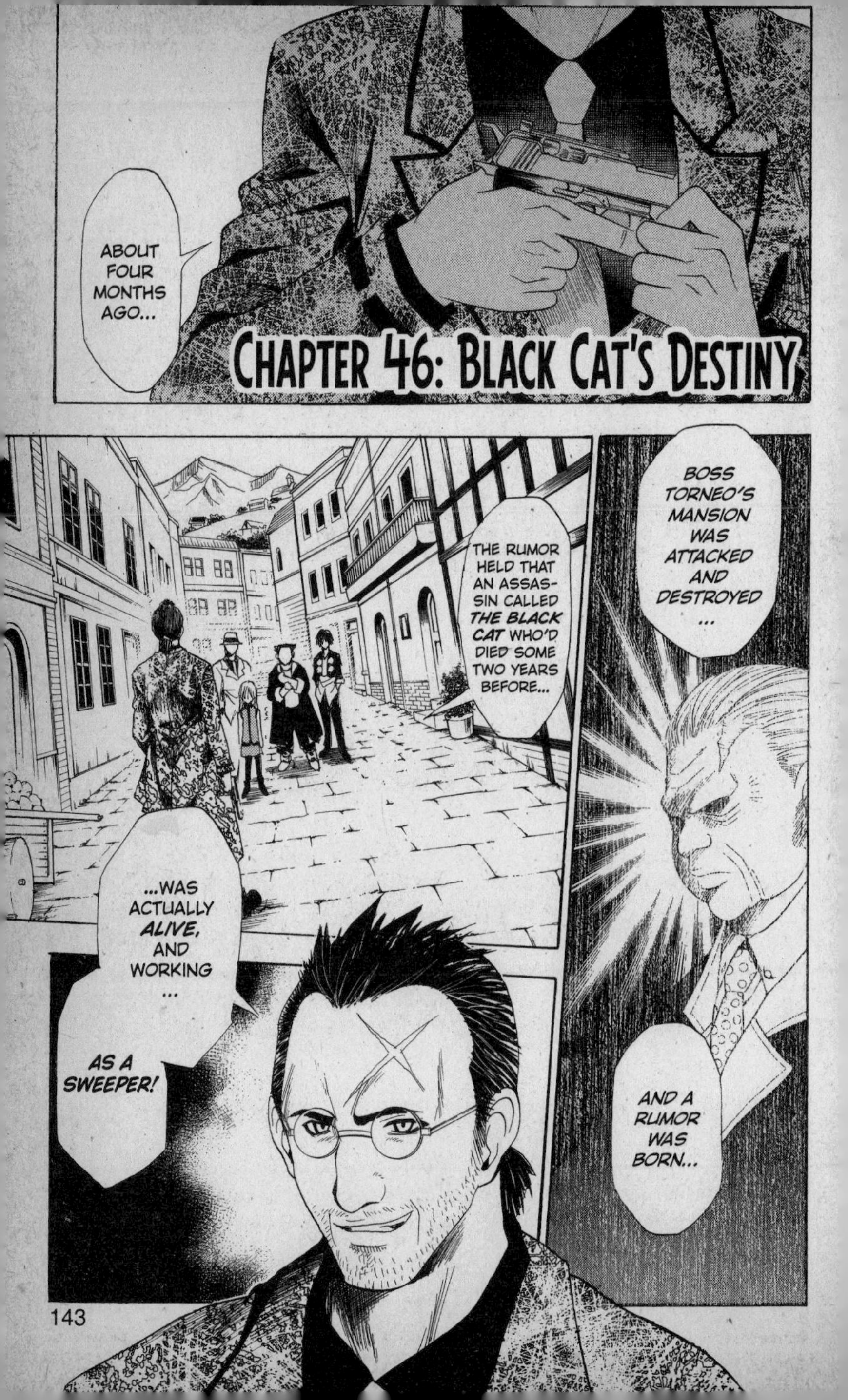
ABOUT FOUR MONTHS AGO...
CHAPTER 46: BLACK CAT'S DESTINY
BOSS TORNEO'S MANSION WAS ATTACKED AND DESTROYED...
AND A RUMOR WAS BORN...
THE RUMOR HELD THAT AN ASSAS-SIN CALLED THE BLACK CAT WHO'D DIED SOME TWO YEARS BEFORE...
...WAS ACTUALLY ALIVE, AND WORKING...
AS A SWEEPER!

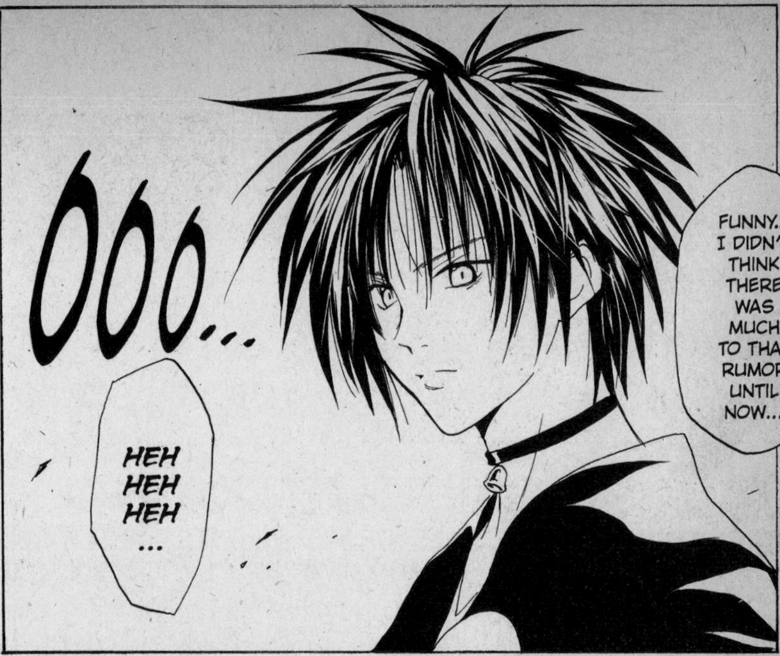
FUNNY... I DIDN'T THINK THERE WAS MUCH TO THAT RUMOR UNTIL NOW...
HEH HEH HEH ...
OOO...

Chapter 46: Black Cat's Destiny

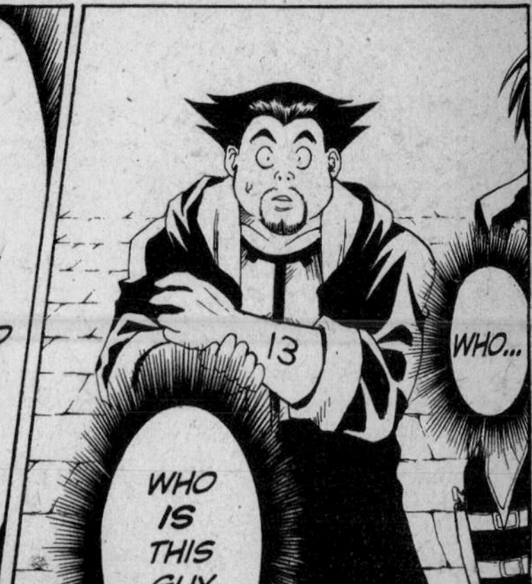
WHO...
WHO IS THIS GUY ...?

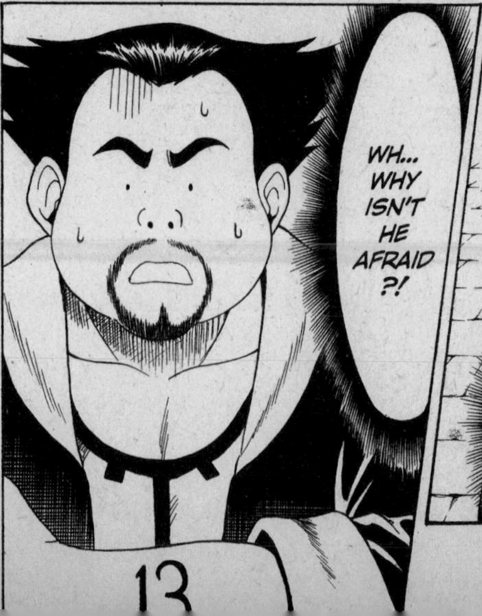
WH... WHY ISN'T HE AFRAID ?!

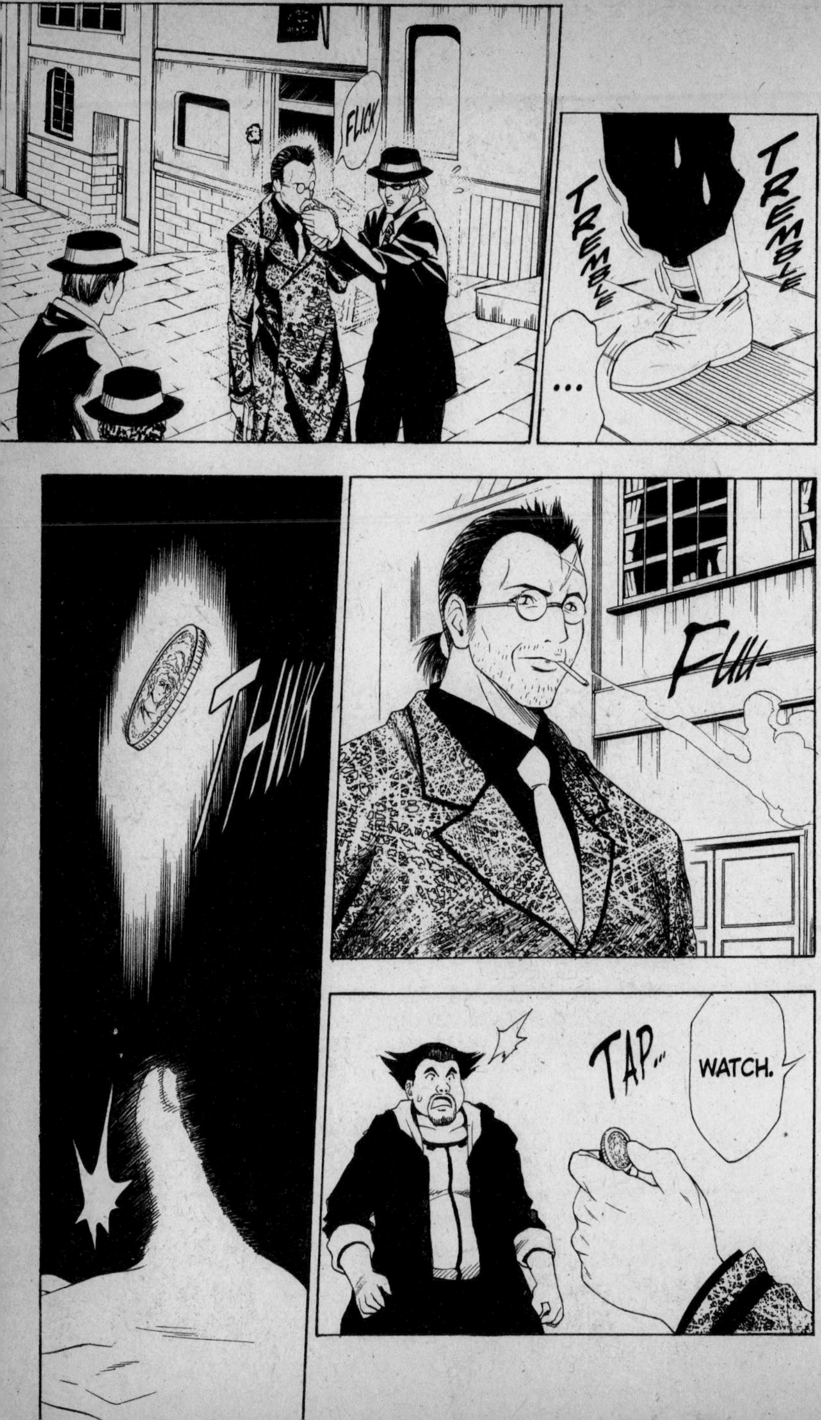
TREMBLE
TREMBLE
...
FLICK
FUU-
TAP...
WATCH.

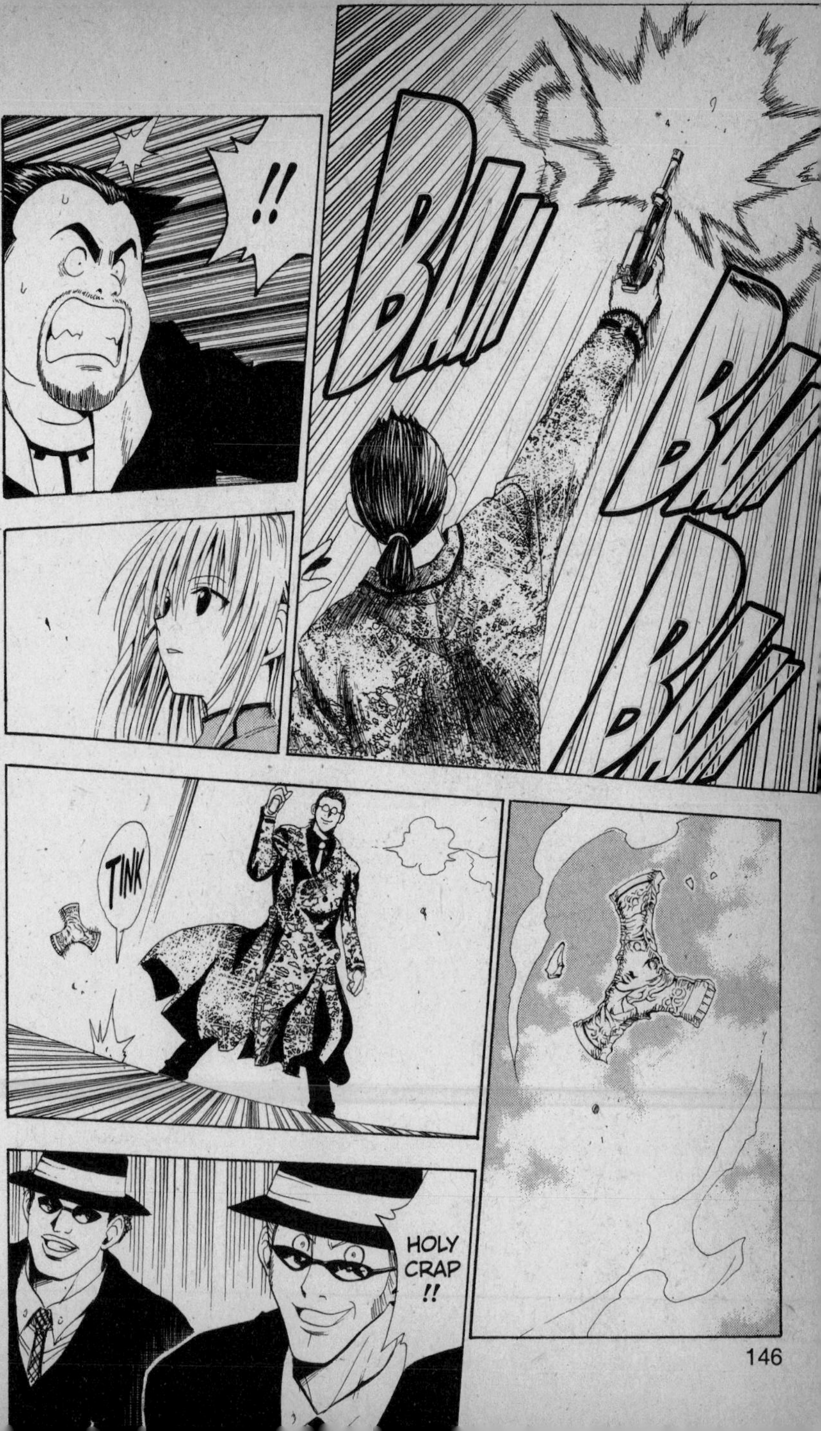
BAM
BAM
BAM
!!
TINK
HOLY CRAP!!

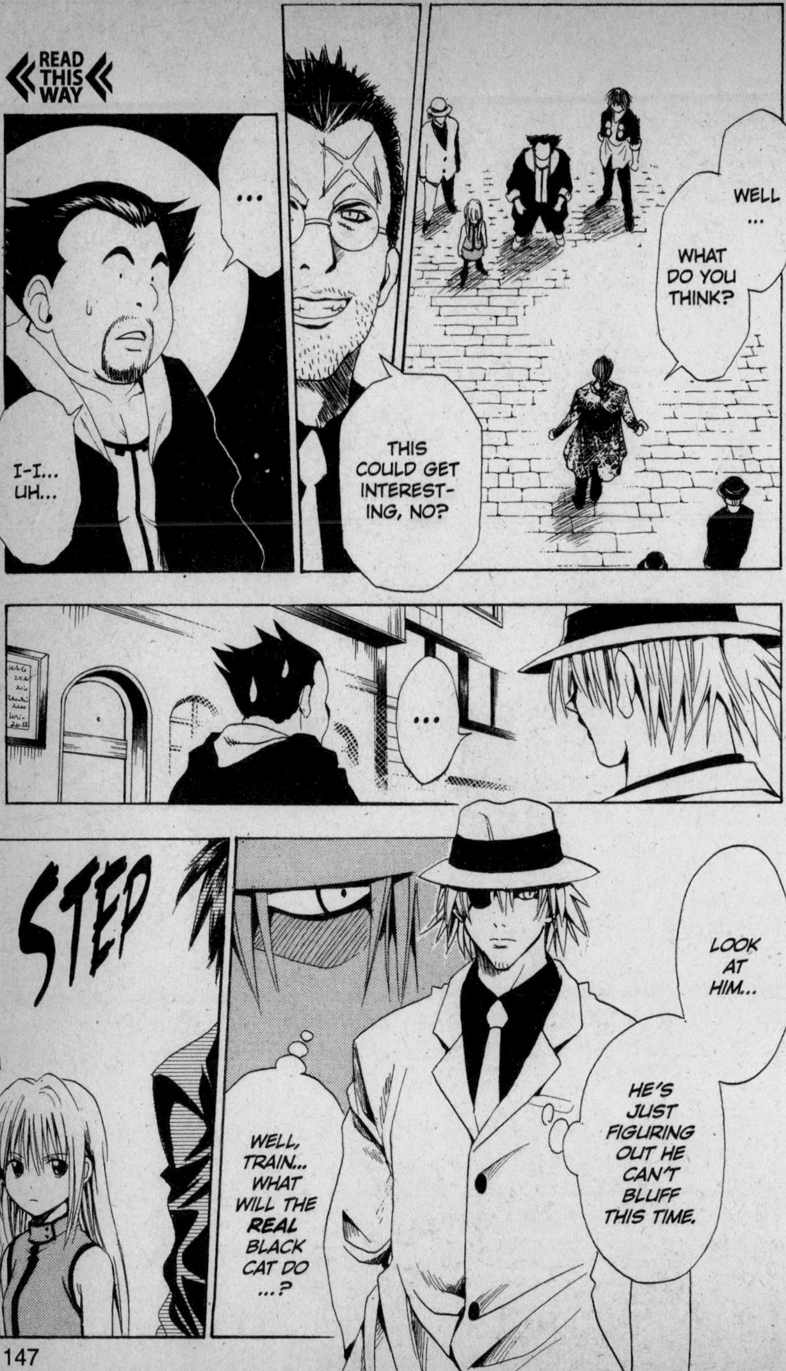
READ THIS WAY
WELL ... WHAT DO YOU THINK?
...
THIS COULD GET INTEREST-ING, NO?
I-I... UH...
...
LOOK AT HIM...
HE'S JUST FIGURING OUT HE CAN'T BLUFF THIS TIME.
WELL, TRAIN... WHAT WILL THE **REAL** BLACK CAT DO ...?
STEP

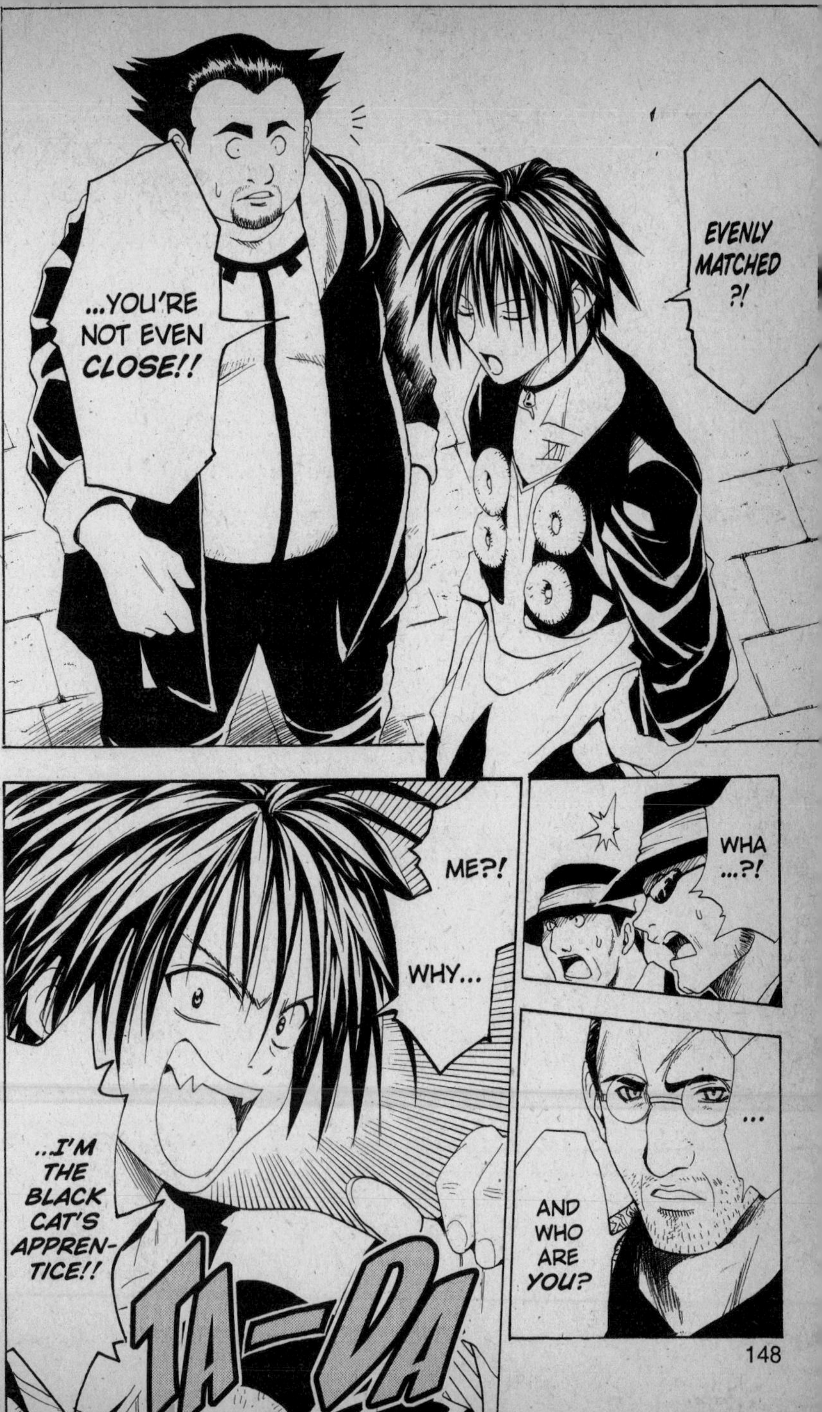
EVENLY MATCHED ?!
...YOU'RE NOT EVEN CLOSE!!
WHA ...?!
...
AND WHO ARE YOU?
ME?!
WHY...
...I'M THE BLACK CAT'S APPREN-TICE!!
TA-DA

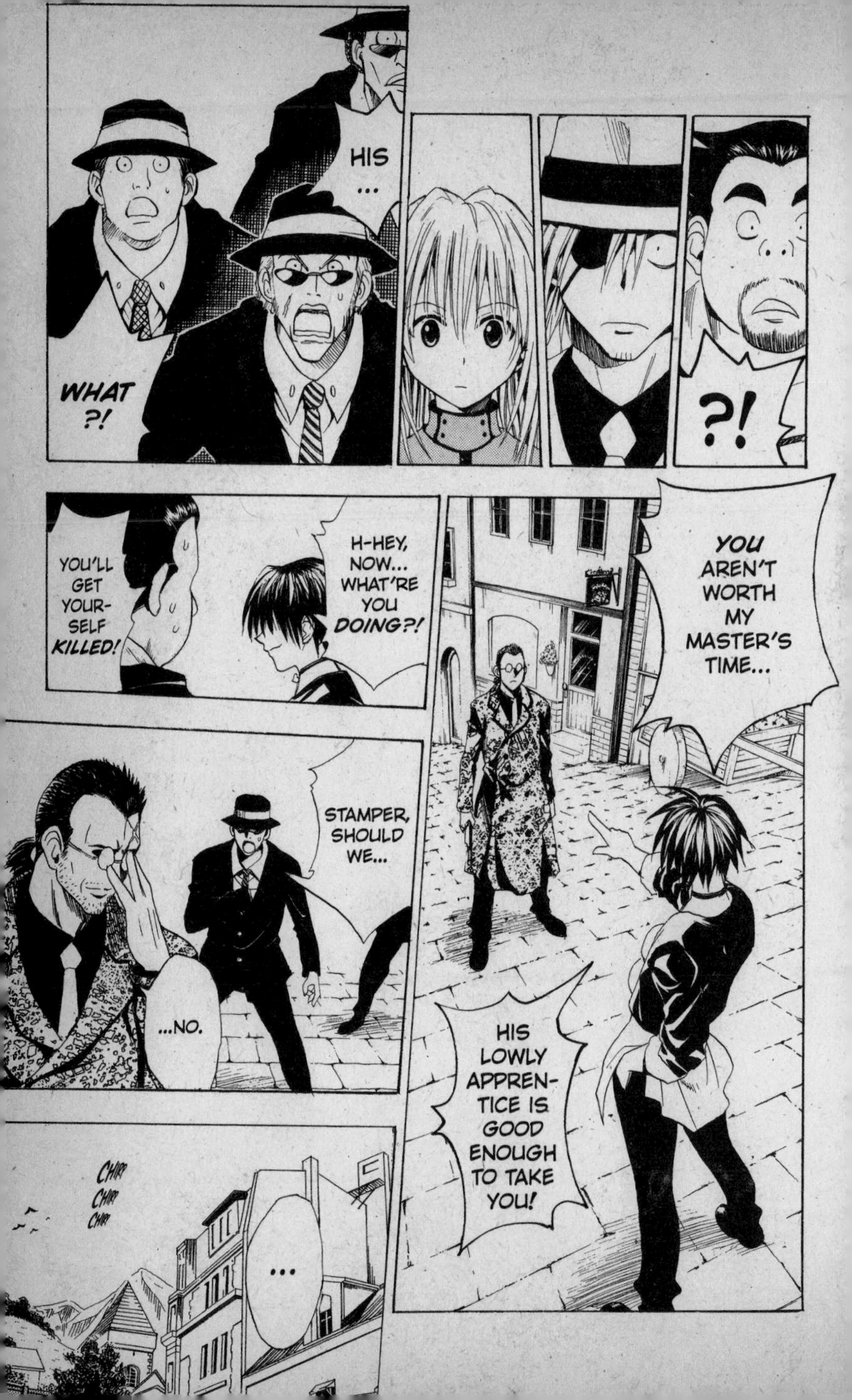
?!
HIS ...
WHAT ?!
YOU AREN'T WORTH MY MASTER'S TIME...
HIS LOWLY APPREN-TICE IS GOOD ENOUGH TO TAKE YOU!
H-HEY, NOW... WHAT'RE YOU DOING?!
YOU'LL GET YOUR-SELF KILLED!
STAMPER, SHOULD WE...
...NO.
CHIRP CHIRP CHIRP
...

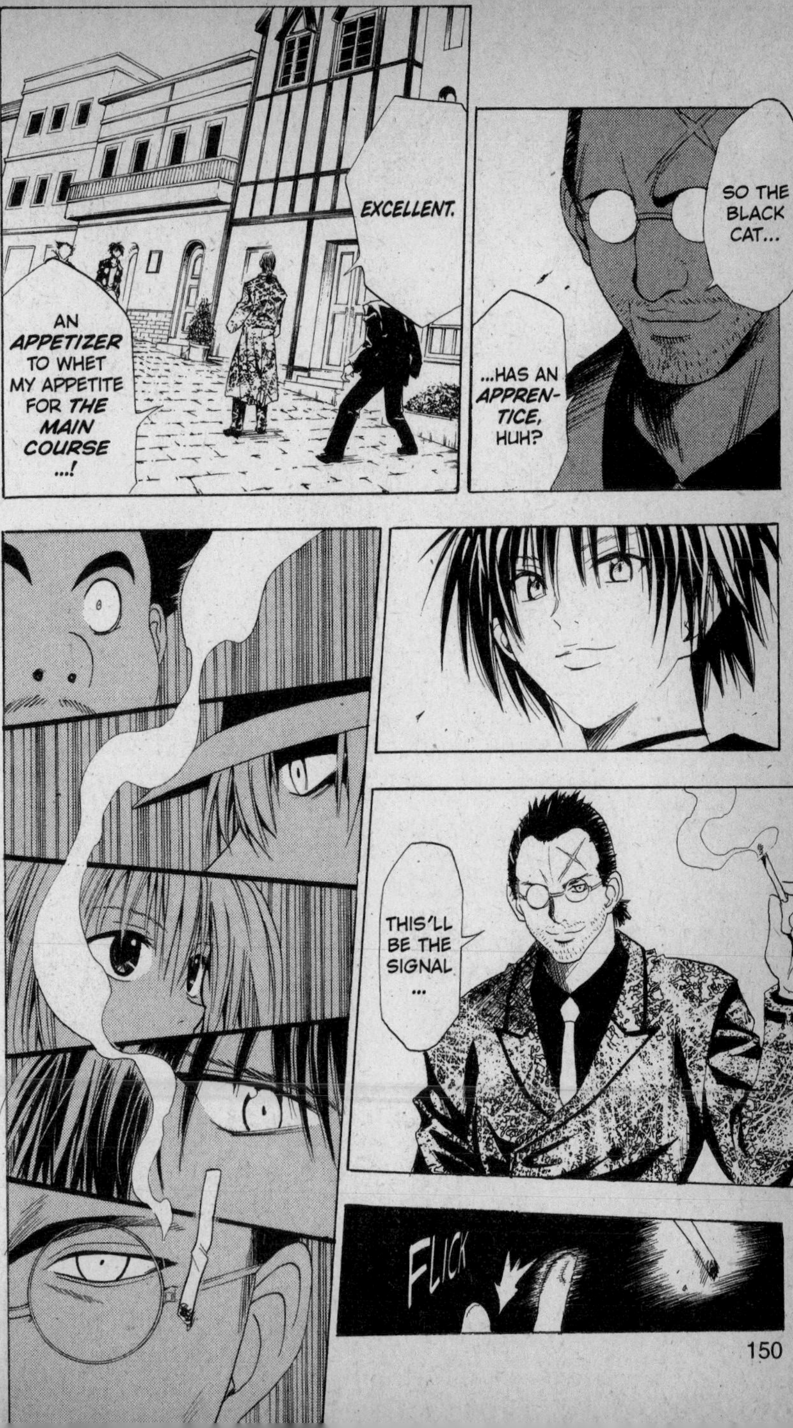
SO THE BLACK CAT...
...HAS AN APPREN-TICE, HUH?
EXCELLENT.
AN APPETIZER TO WHET MY APPETITE FOR THE MAIN COURSE ...!
THIS'LL BE THE SIGNAL ...
FLICK

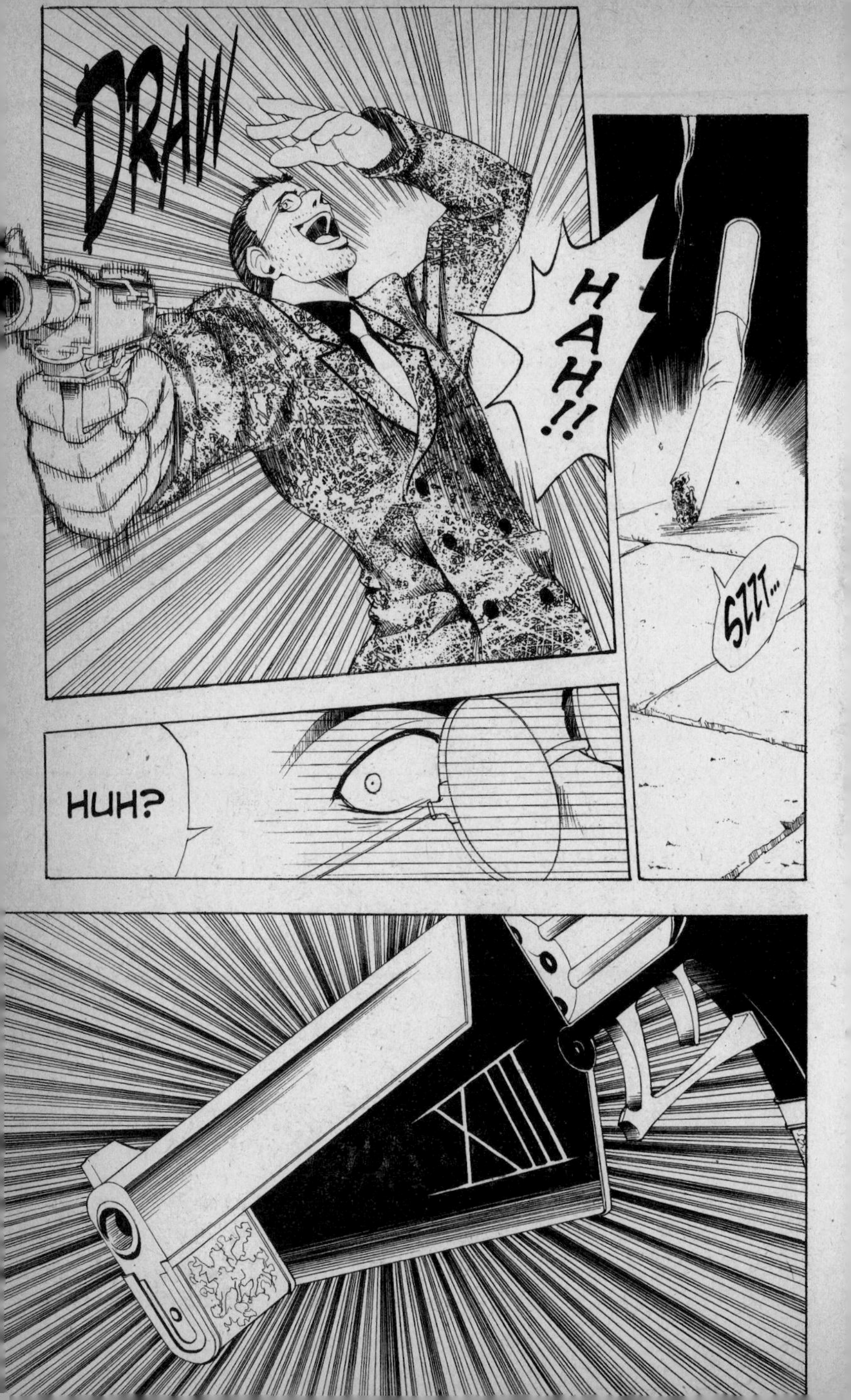
DRAW
HAH!!
SZZT...
HUH?

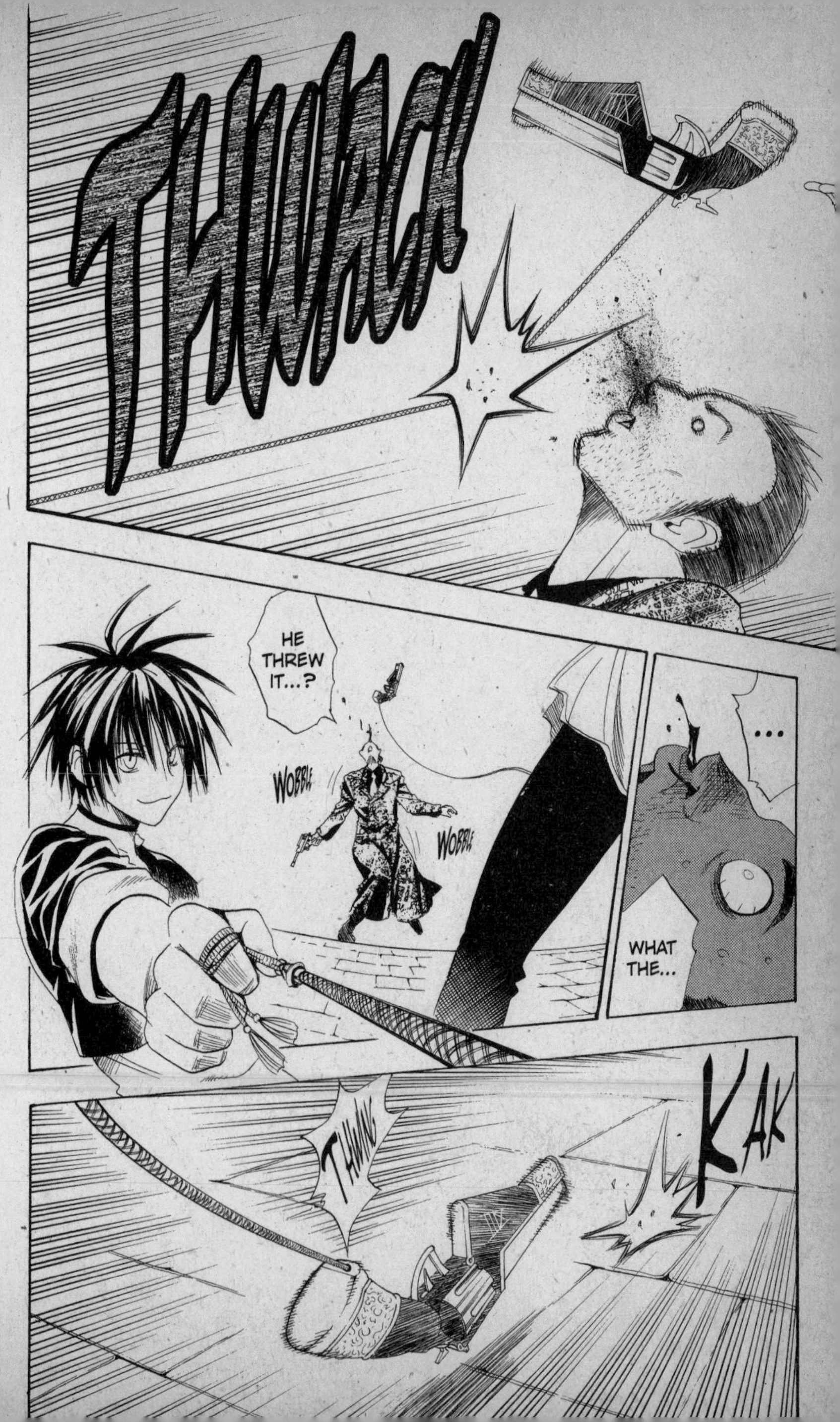
THWACK!
...
WHAT THE...
HE THREW IT...?
WOBBLE
WOBBLE
KAK
THWING

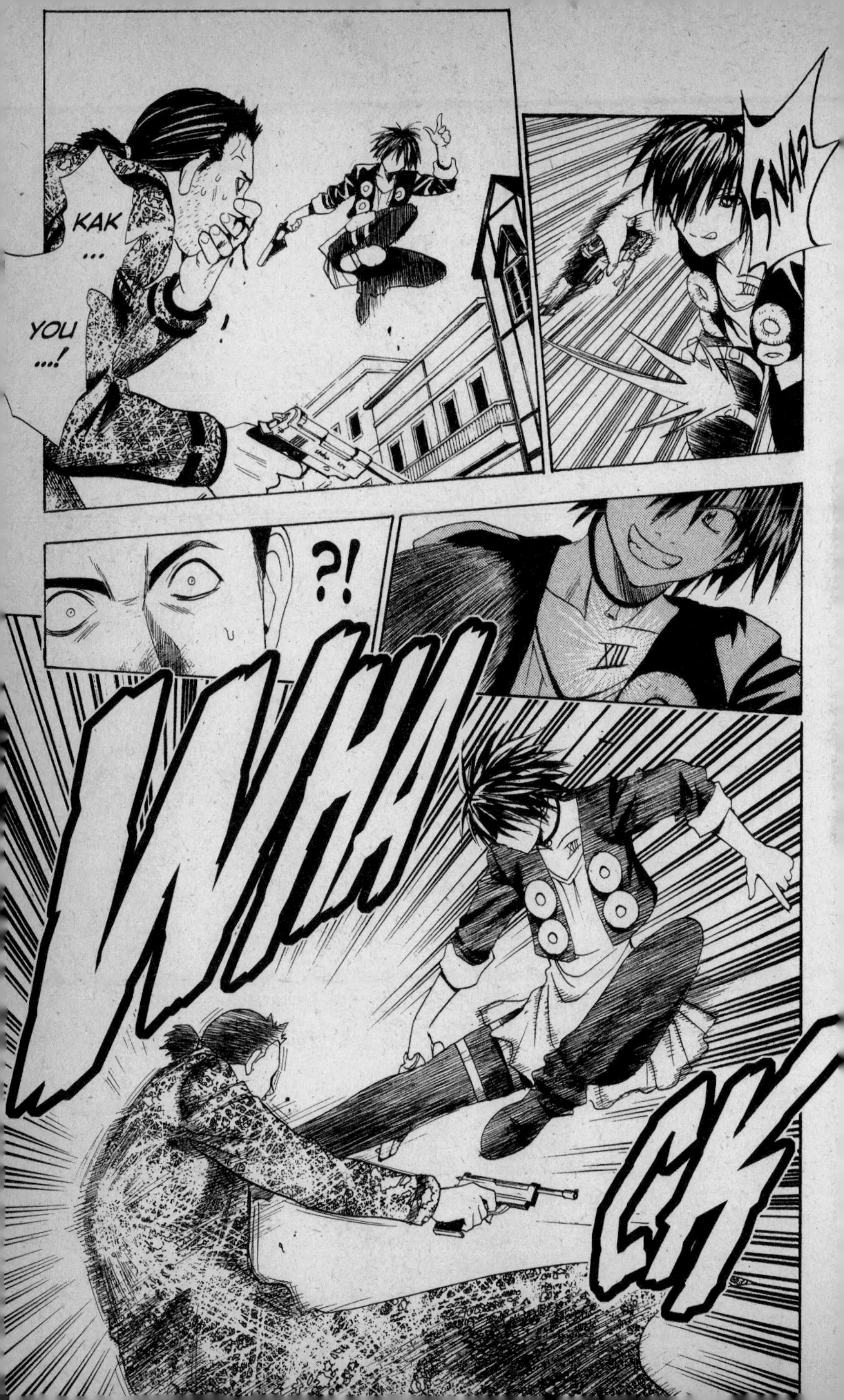
SNAP
KAK ...
YOU ...!
?!
WHACK

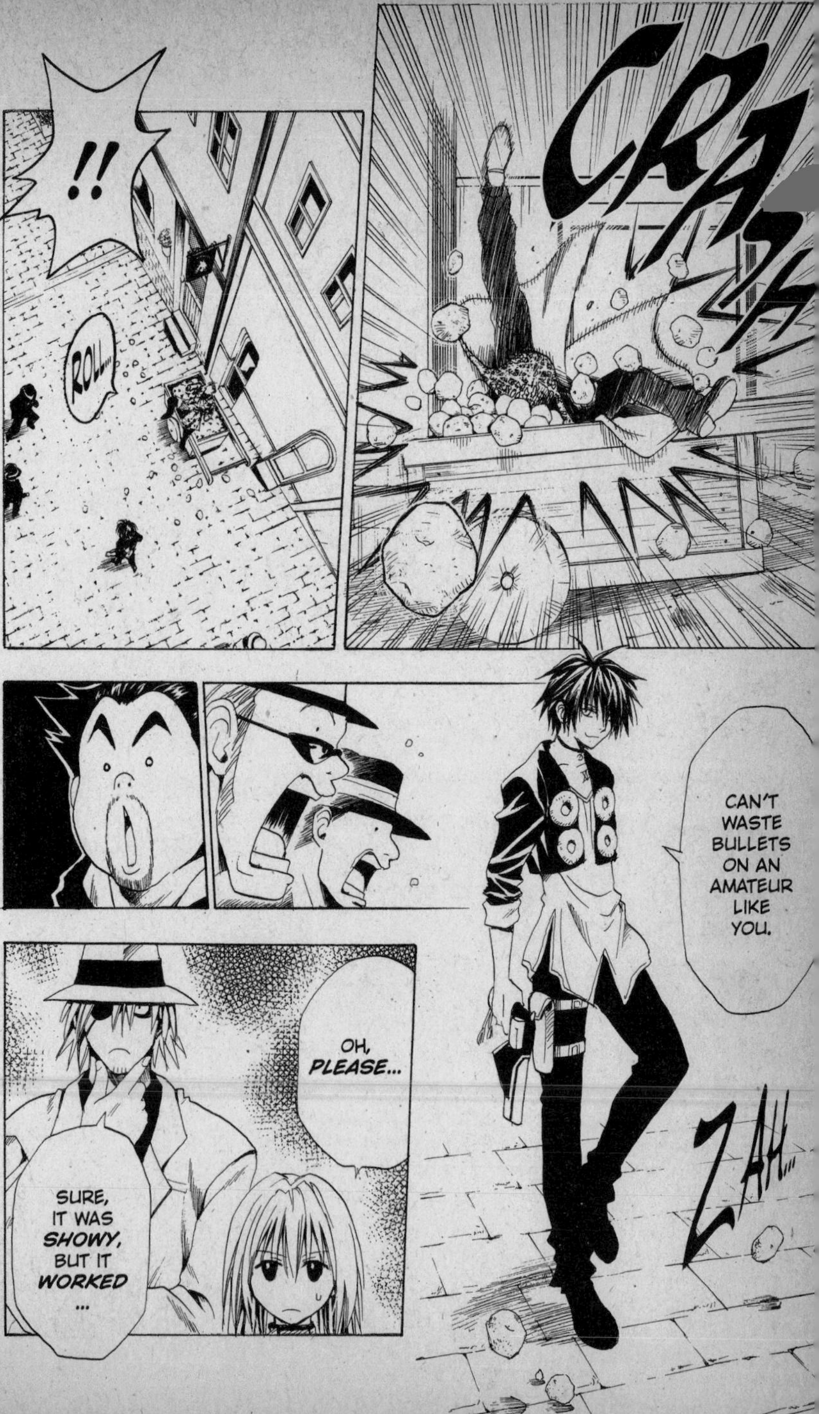
CRASH
!!
ROLL...
CAN'T WASTE BULLETS ON AN AMATEUR LIKE YOU.
ZAH...
OH, PLEASE...
SURE, IT WAS SHOWY, BUT IT WORKED ...

READ THIS WAY

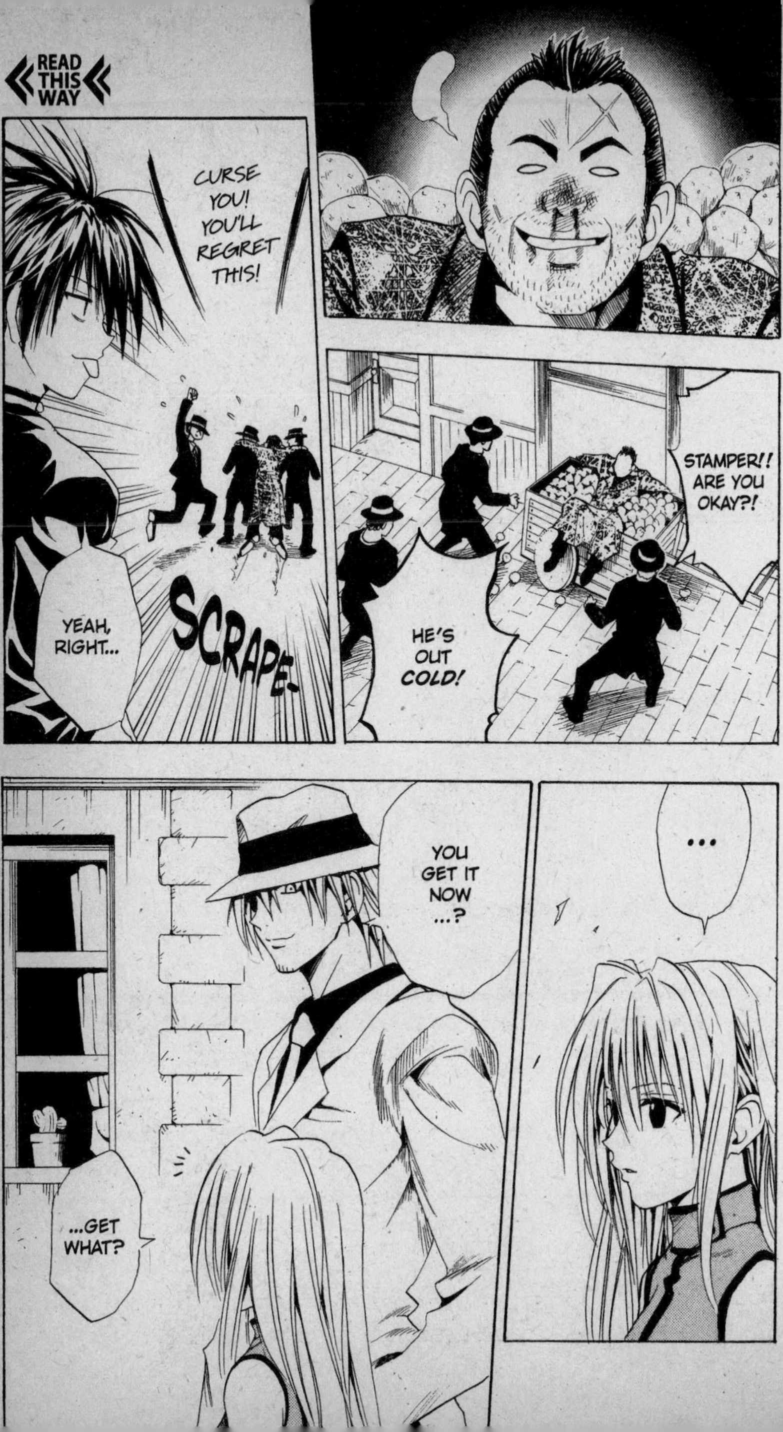

STAMPER!! ARE YOU OKAY?!
HE'S OUT COLD!
CURSE YOU! YOU'LL REGRET THIS!
SCRAPE-
YEAH, RIGHT...
...
YOU GET IT NOW ...?
...GET WHAT?

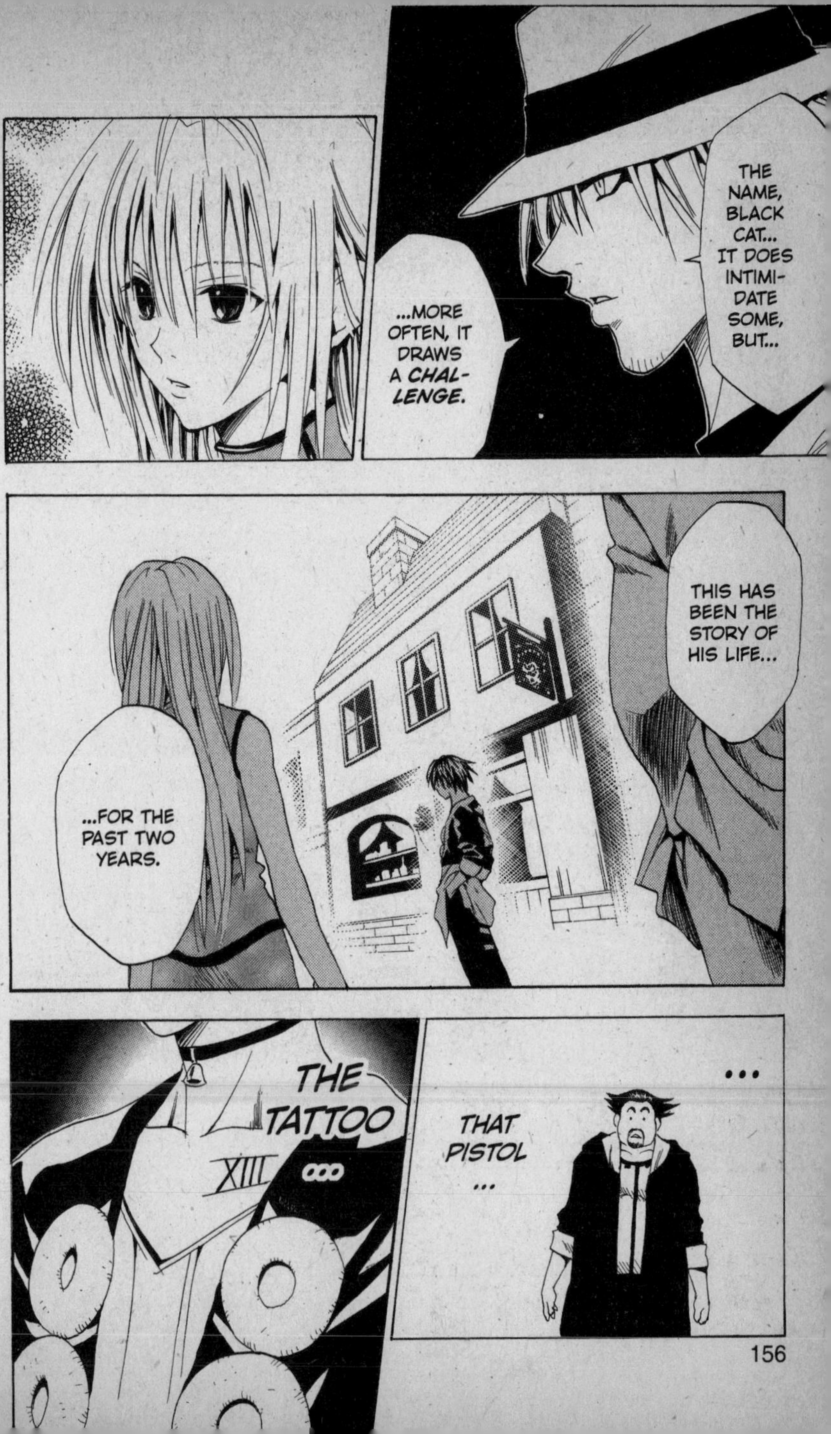
THE NAME, BLACK CAT... IT DOES INTIMIDATE SOME, BUT...
...MORE OFTEN, IT DRAWS A *CHALLENGE.*
THIS HAS BEEN THE STORY OF HIS LIFE...
...FOR THE PAST TWO YEARS.
...
THAT PISTOL ...
THE TATTOO ...

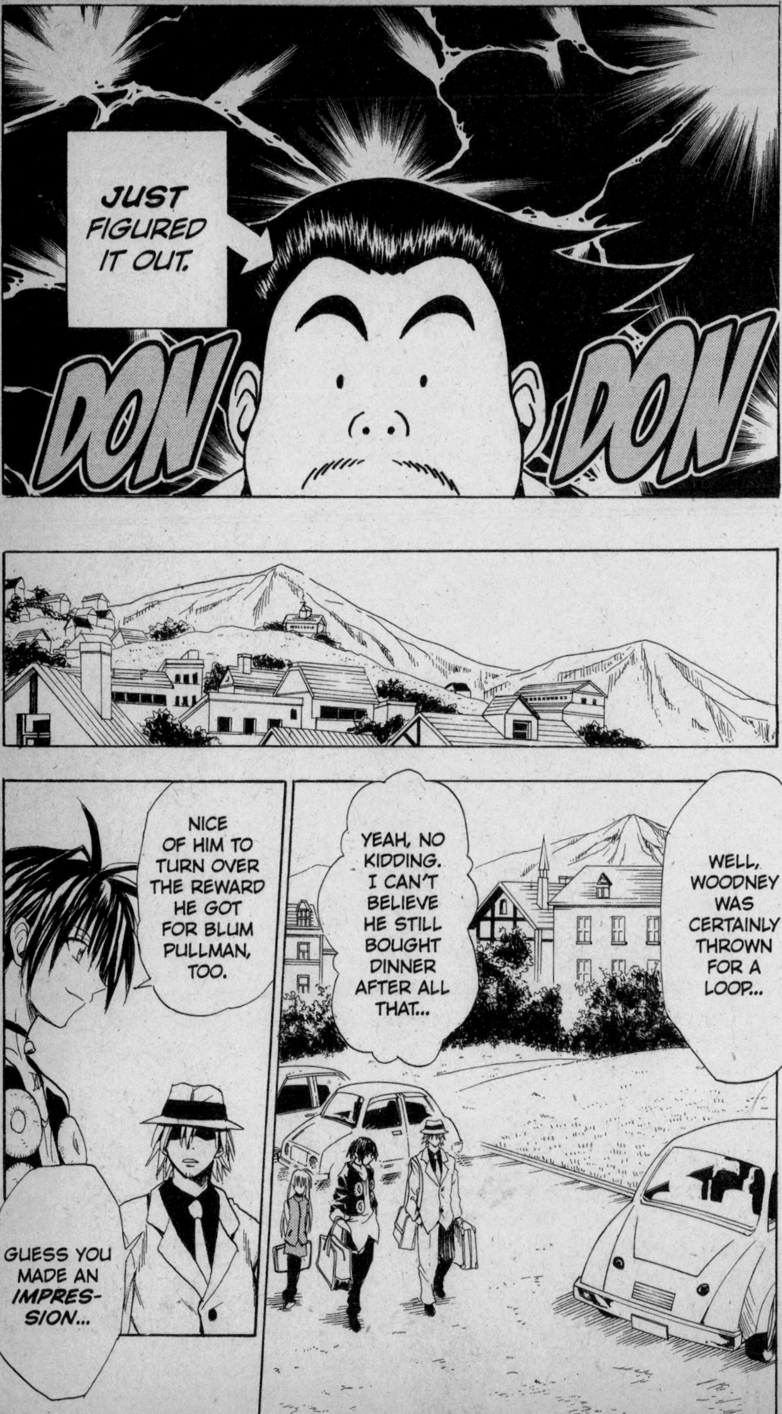
JUST FIGURED IT OUT.
DON DON
WELL, WOODNEY WAS CERTAINLY THROWN FOR A LOOP...
YEAH, NO KIDDING. I CAN'T BELIEVE HE STILL BOUGHT DINNER AFTER ALL THAT...
NICE OF HIM TO TURN OVER THE REWARD HE GOT FOR BLUM PULLMAN, TOO.
GUESS YOU MADE AN *IMPRES-SION*...

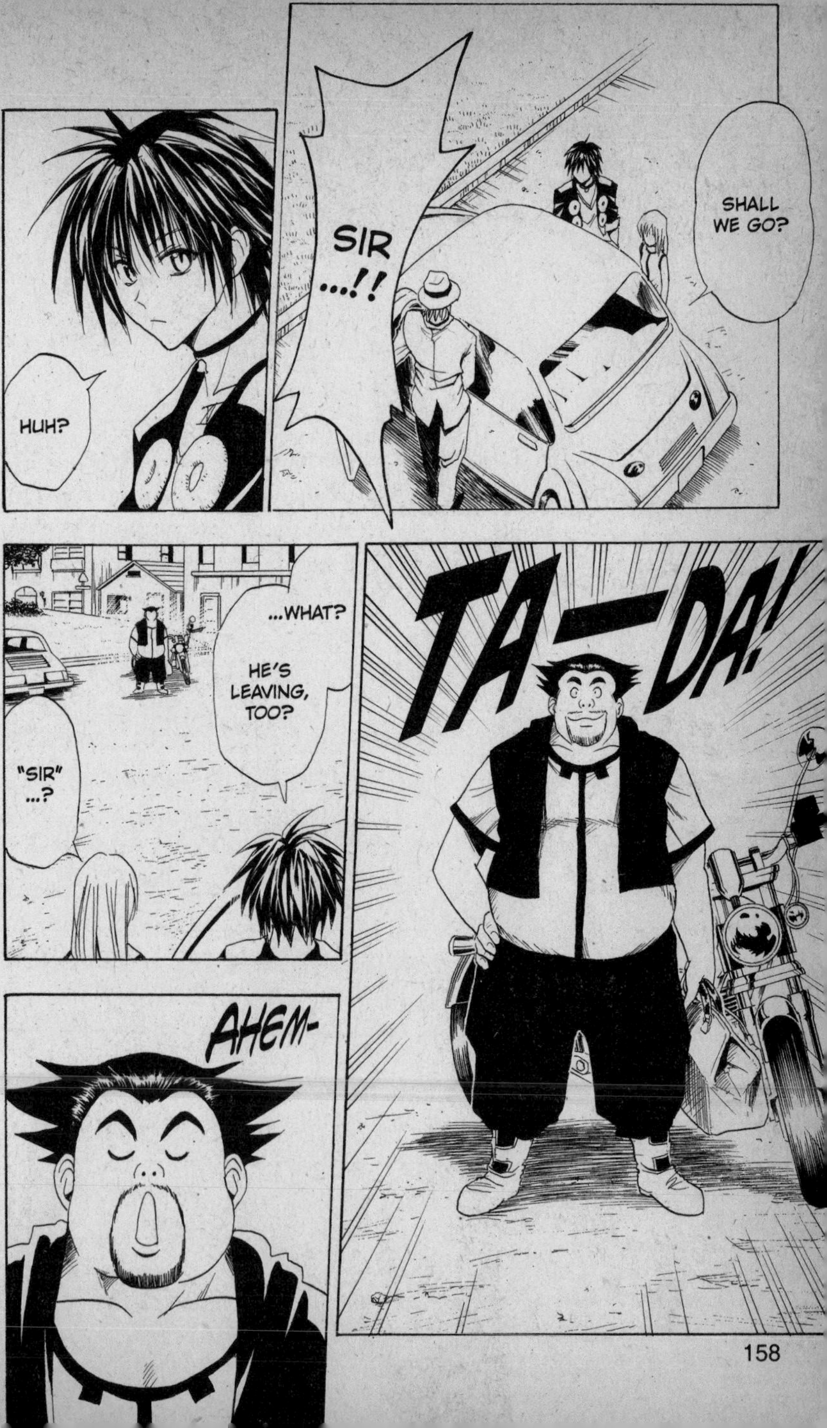
SHALL WE GO?
SIR ...!!
HUH?
TA-DA!
...WHAT?
HE'S LEAVING, TOO?
"SIR" ...?
AHEM-

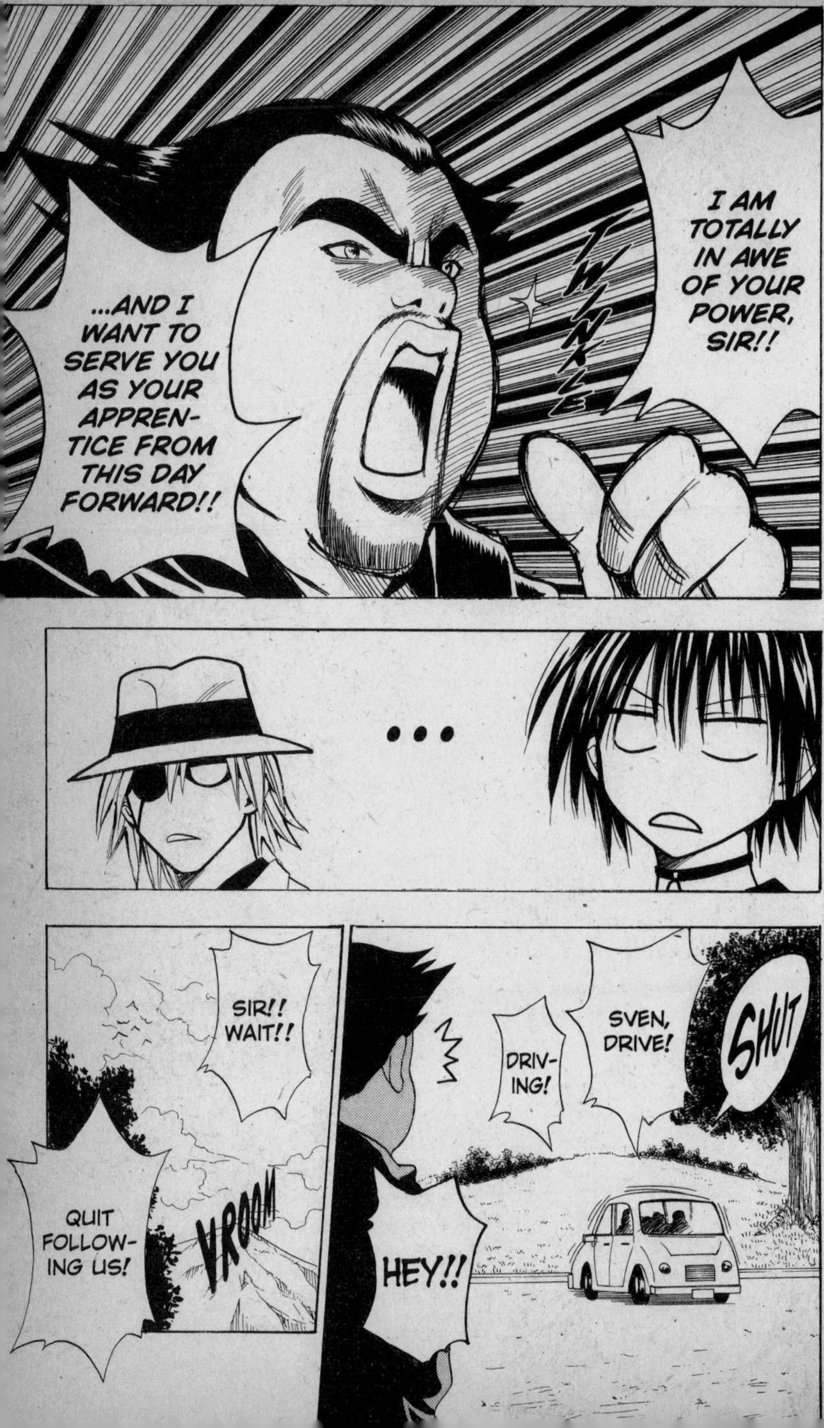

I AM TOTALLY IN AWE OF YOUR POWER, SIR!!
...AND I WANT TO SERVE YOU AS YOUR APPREN-TICE FROM THIS DAY FORWARD!!
TWINKLE
...
SVEN, DRIVE!
SHUT
DRIV-ING!
HEY!!
SIR!! WAIT!!
VROOM
QUIT FOLLOW-ING US!

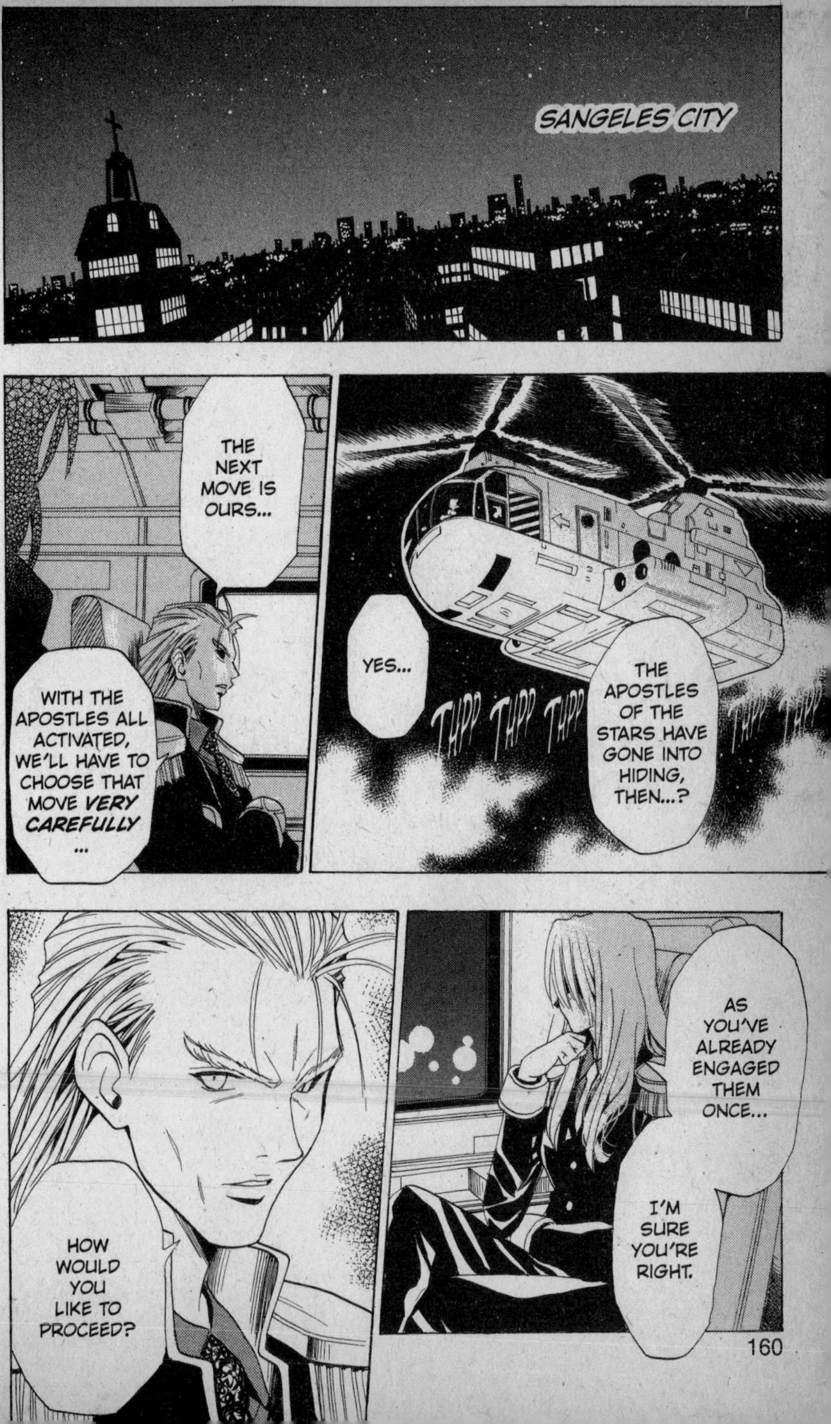

SANGELES CITY
THE APOSTLES OF THE STARS HAVE GONE INTO HIDING, THEN...?
YES...
THPP THPP THPP
THPP THPP
THE NEXT MOVE IS OURS...
WITH THE APOSTLES ALL ACTIVATED, WE'LL HAVE TO CHOOSE THAT MOVE ***VERY CAREFULLY***...
AS YOU'VE ALREADY ENGAGED THEM ONCE...
I'M SURE YOU'RE RIGHT.
HOW WOULD YOU LIKE TO PROCEED?

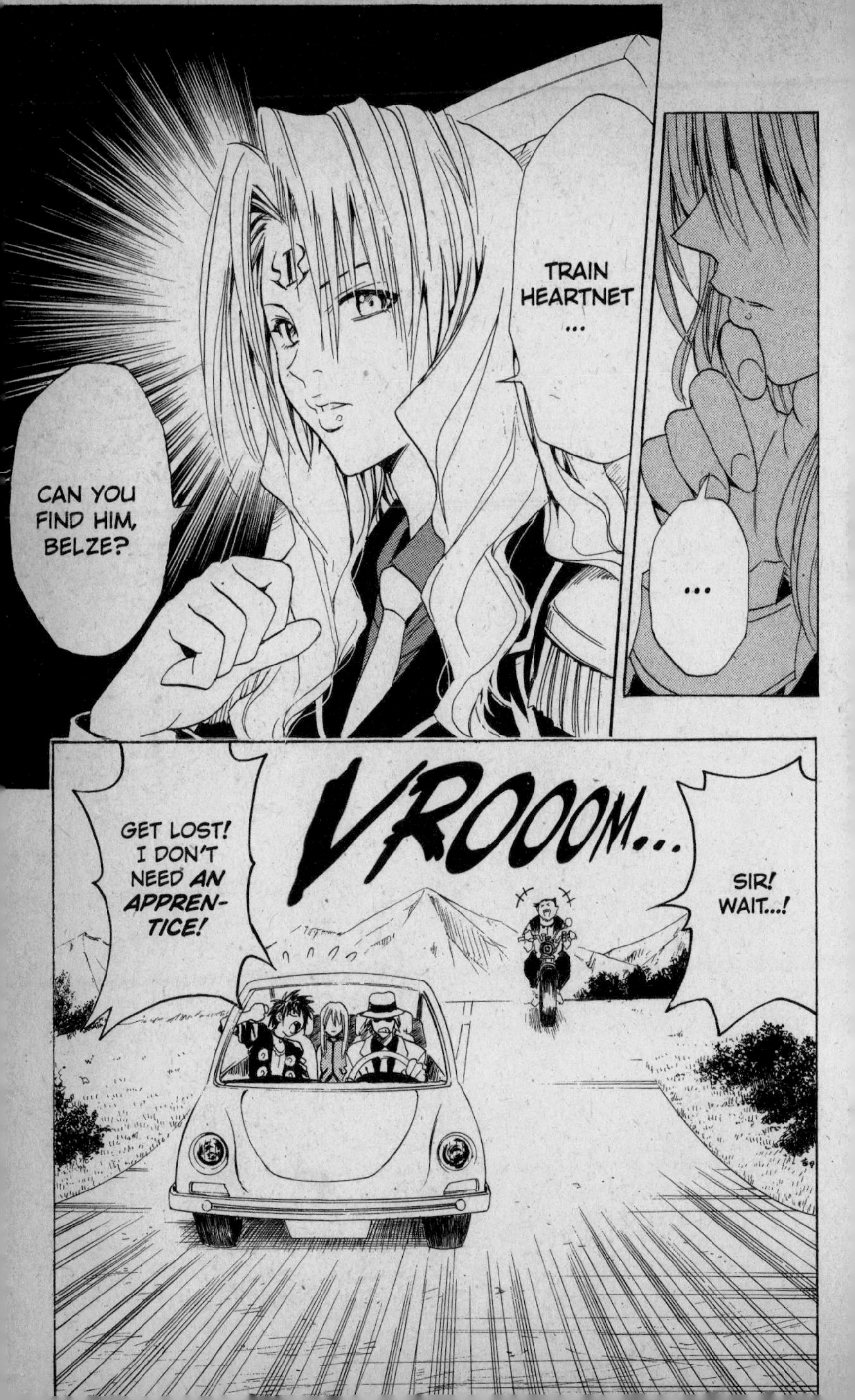
...
TRAIN HEARTNET ...
CAN YOU FIND HIM, BELZE?
SIR! WAIT...!
VROOOM...
GET LOST! I DON'T NEED AN APPREN-TICE!

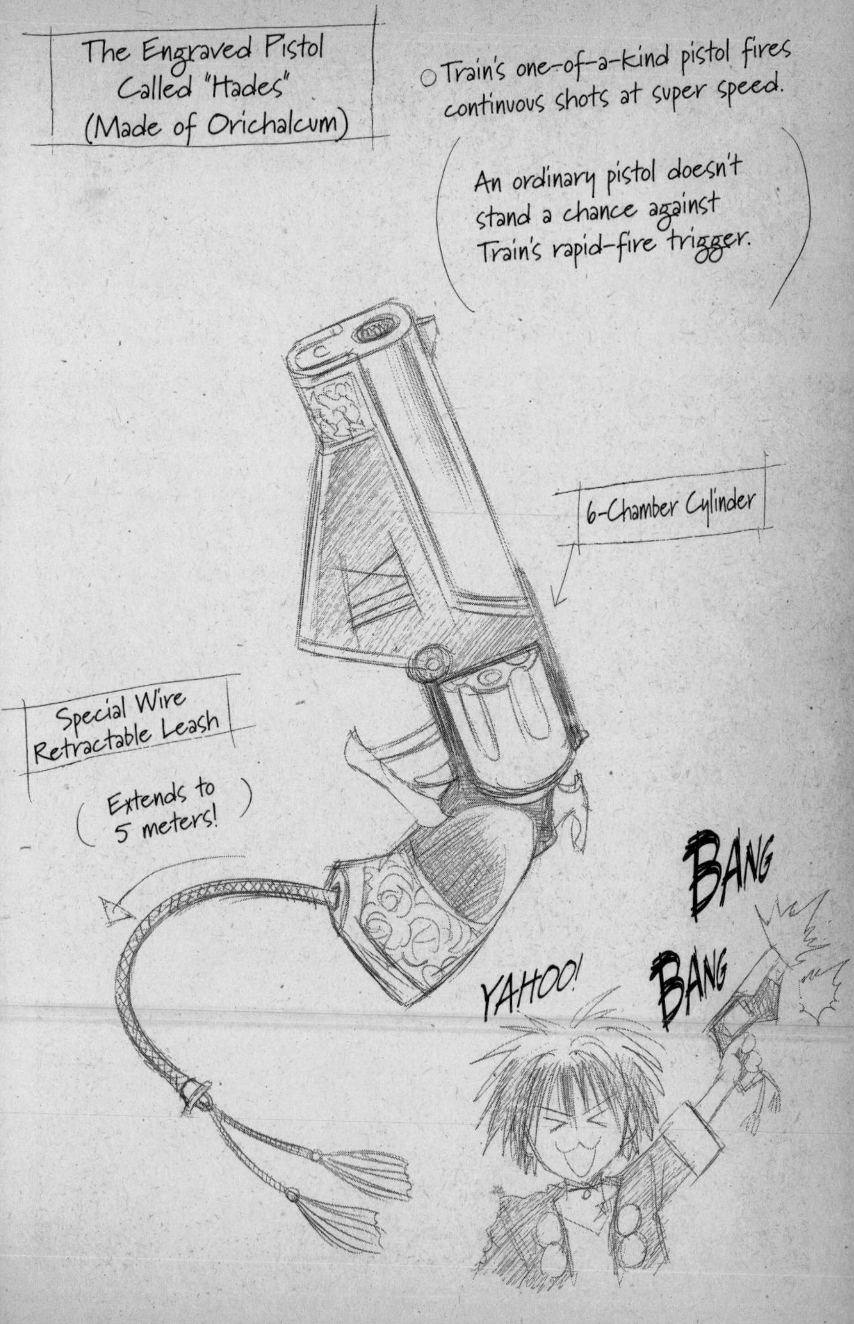
The Engraved Pistol Called "Hades" (Made of Orichalcum)
Train's one-of-a-kind pistol fires continuous shots at super speed.
An ordinary pistol doesn't stand a chance against Train's rapid-fire trigger.
6-Chamber Cylinder
Special Wire Retractable Leash
(Extends to 5 meters!)
BANG
BANG
YAHOO!

Chapter 47: Number I Pays a Call

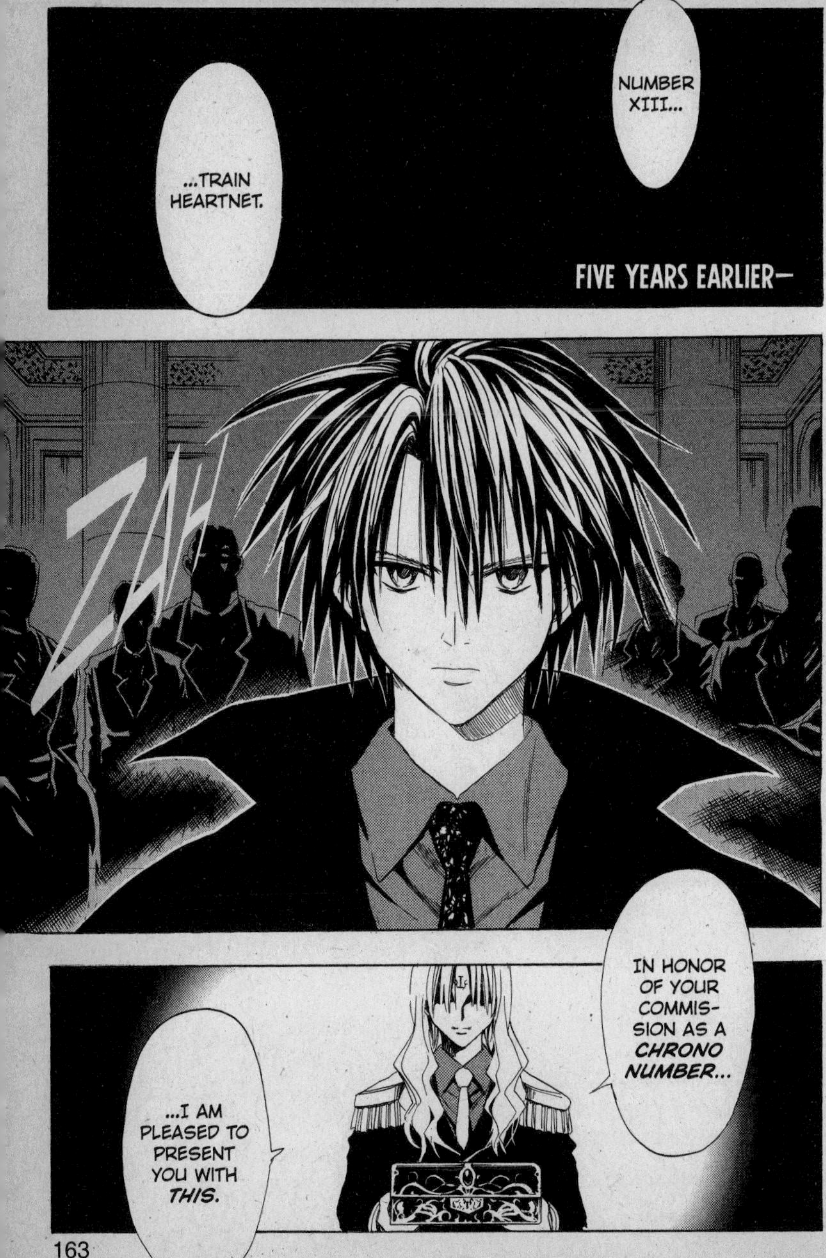
NUMBER XIII...
...TRAIN HEARTNET.
FIVE YEARS EARLIER—
ZAH
IN HONOR OF YOUR COMMISSION AS A *CHRONO NUMBER...*
...I AM PLEASED TO PRESENT YOU WITH *THIS.*

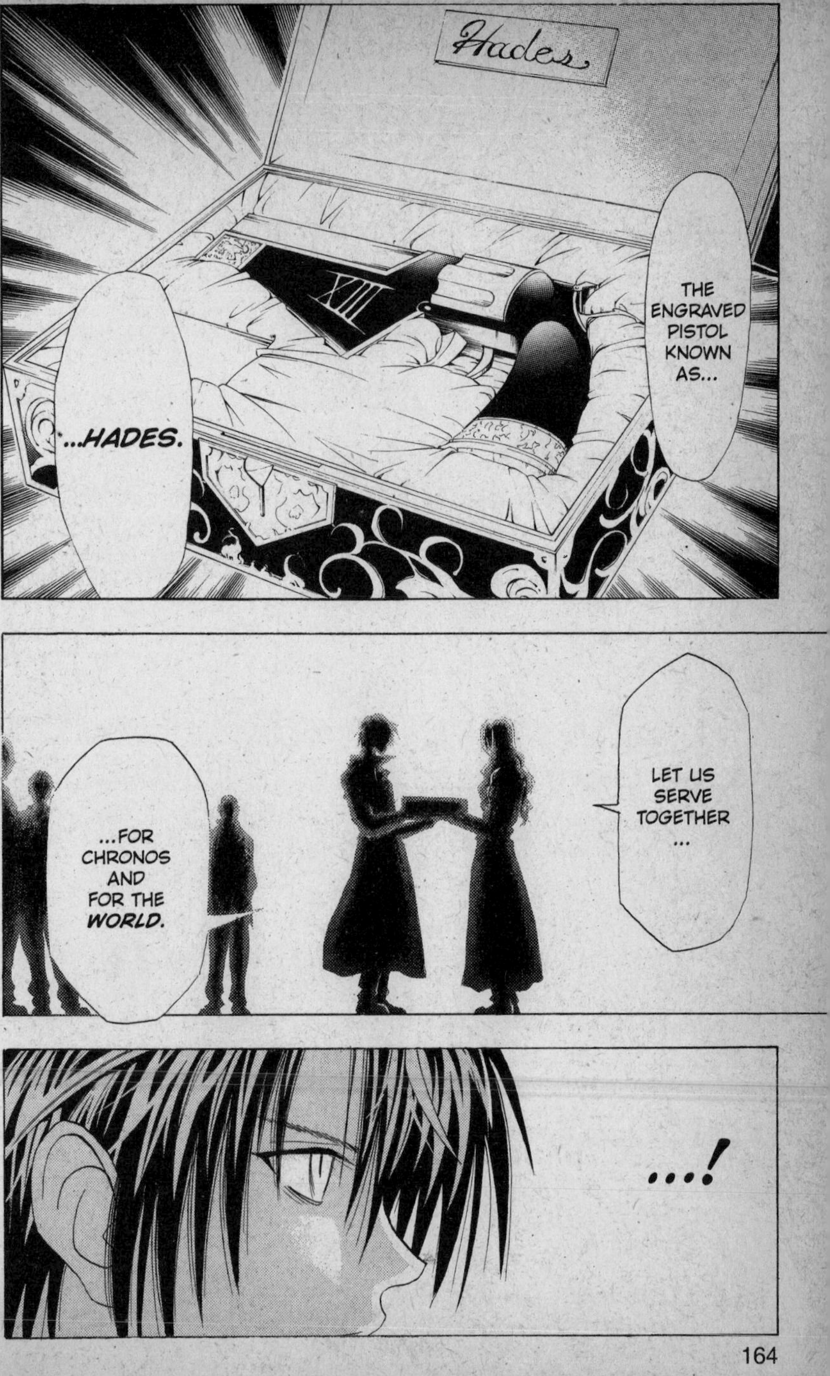
Hades
THE ENGRAVED PISTOL KNOWN AS...
...HADES.
LET US SERVE TOGETHER ...
...FOR CHRONOS AND FOR THE WORLD.
...!

Chapter 47: Number I Pays a Call

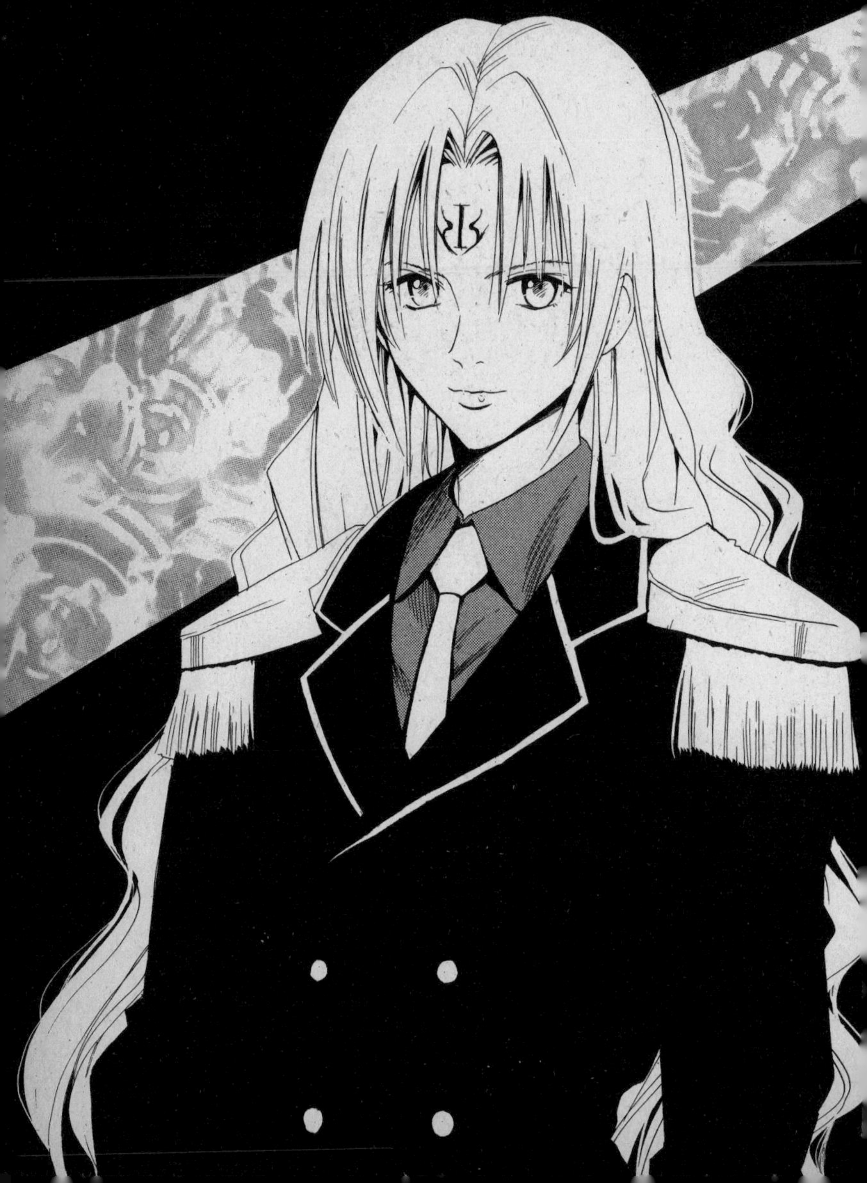

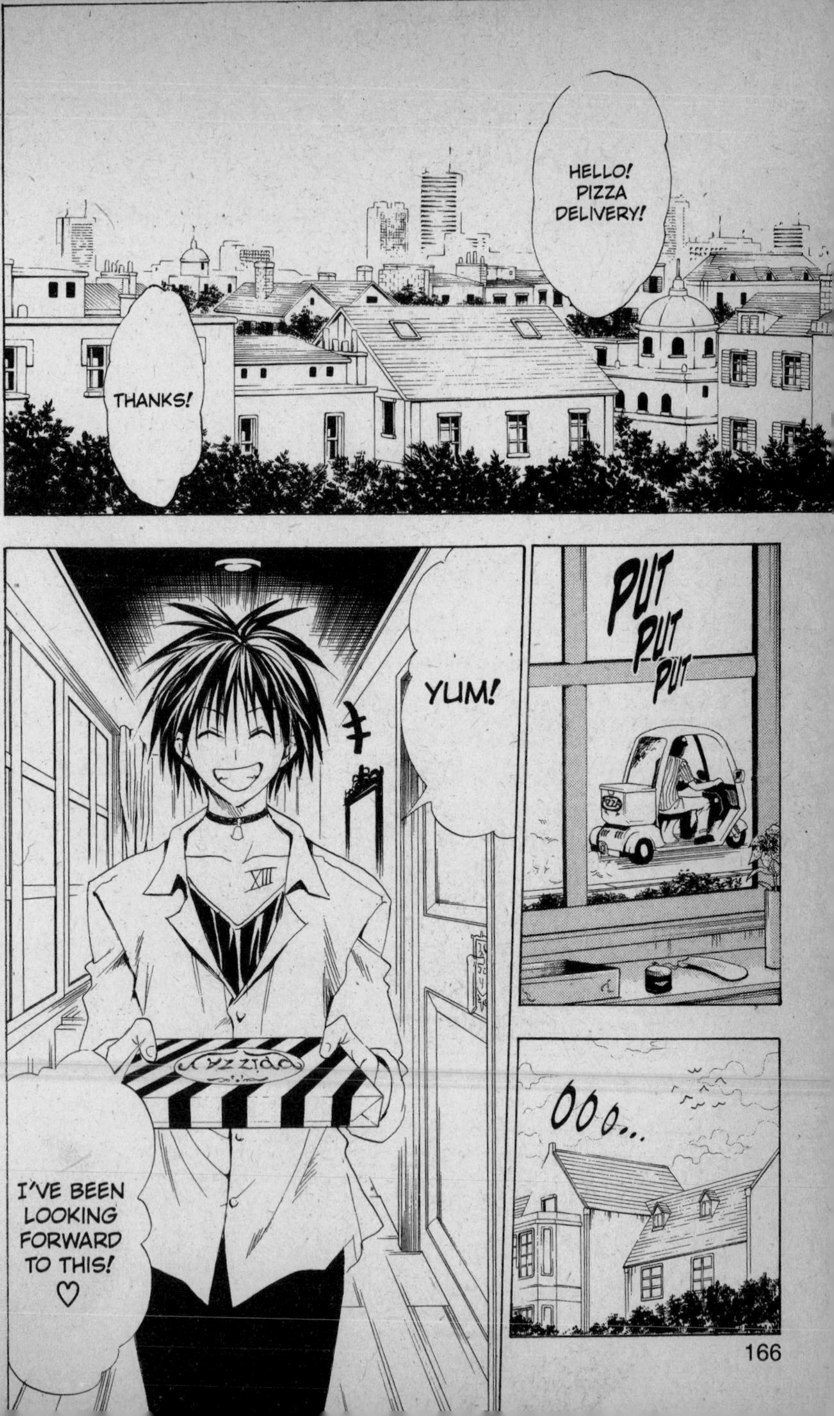
HELLO! PIZZA DELIVERY!
THANKS!
PUT PUT PUT
OOO...
YUM!
I'VE BEEN LOOKING FORWARD TO THIS! ♡

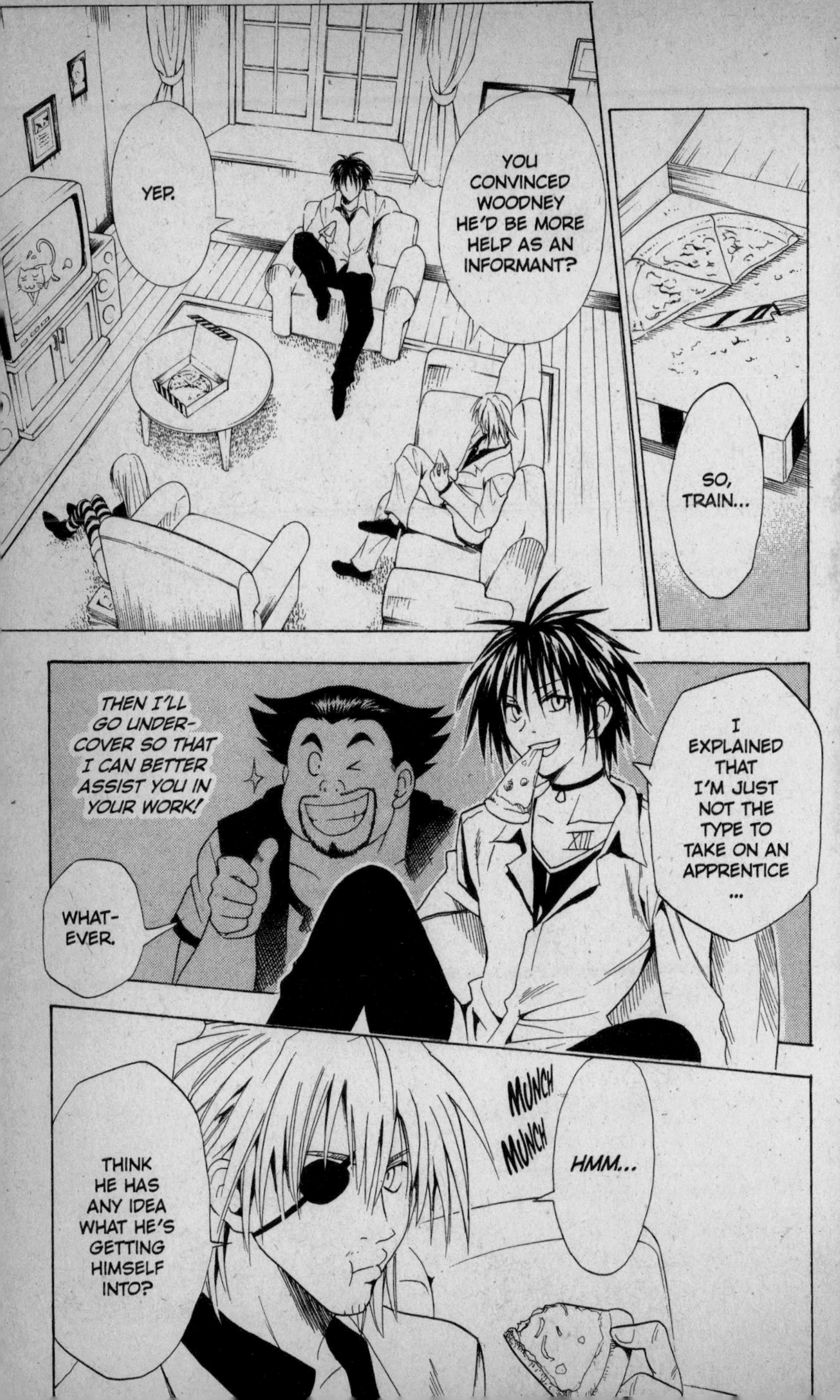
SO, TRAIN...
YOU CONVINCED WOODNEY HE'D BE MORE HELP AS AN INFORMANT?
YEP.
I EXPLAINED THAT I'M JUST NOT THE TYPE TO TAKE ON AN APPRENTICE ...
THEN I'LL GO UNDER-COVER SO THAT I CAN BETTER ASSIST YOU IN YOUR WORK!
WHAT-EVER.
HMM...
MUNCH MUNCH
THINK HE HAS ANY IDEA WHAT HE'S GETTING HIMSELF INTO?

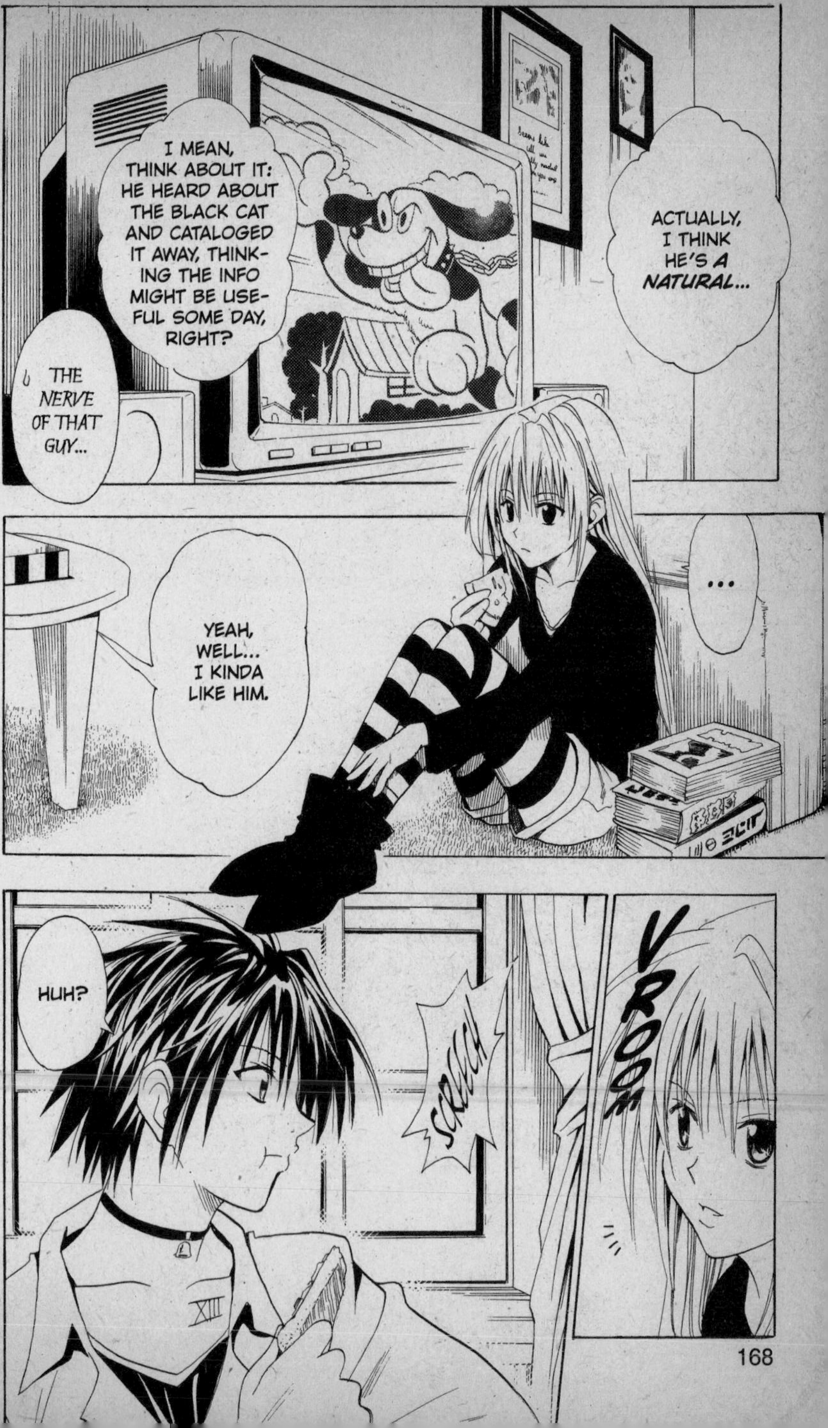

ACTUALLY, I THINK HE'S *A NATURAL*...
I MEAN, THINK ABOUT IT: HE HEARD ABOUT THE BLACK CAT AND CATALOGED IT AWAY, THINKING THE INFO MIGHT BE USEFUL SOME DAY, RIGHT?
THE *NERVE* OF THAT GUY...
...
YEAH, WELL... I KINDA LIKE HIM.
VROOM
SCREECH
HUH?

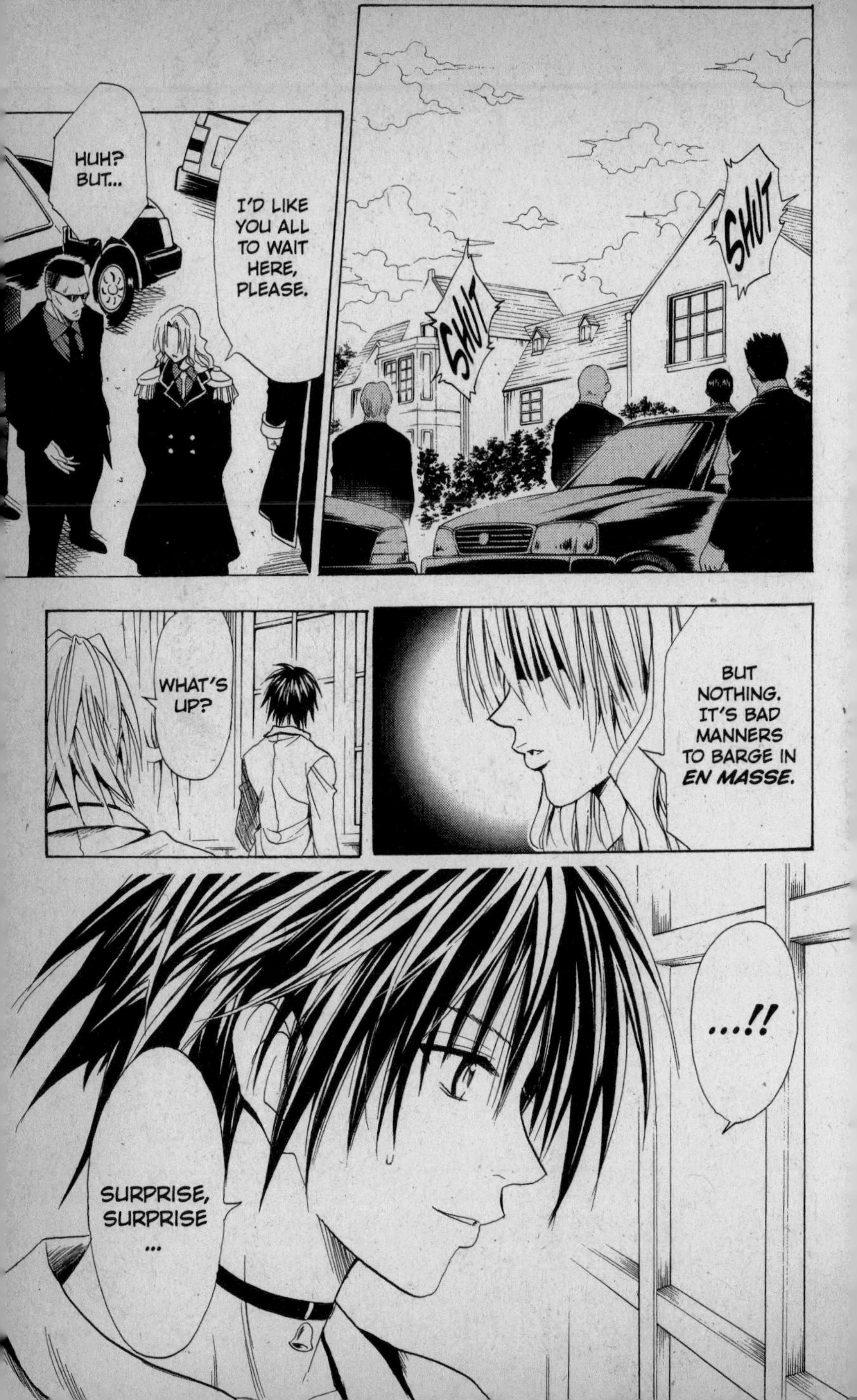
SHUT
SHUT
I'D LIKE YOU ALL TO WAIT HERE, PLEASE.
HUH? BUT...
BUT NOTHING. IT'S BAD MANNERS TO BARGE IN *EN MASSE.*
WHAT'S UP?
...!!
SURPRISE, SURPRISE ...

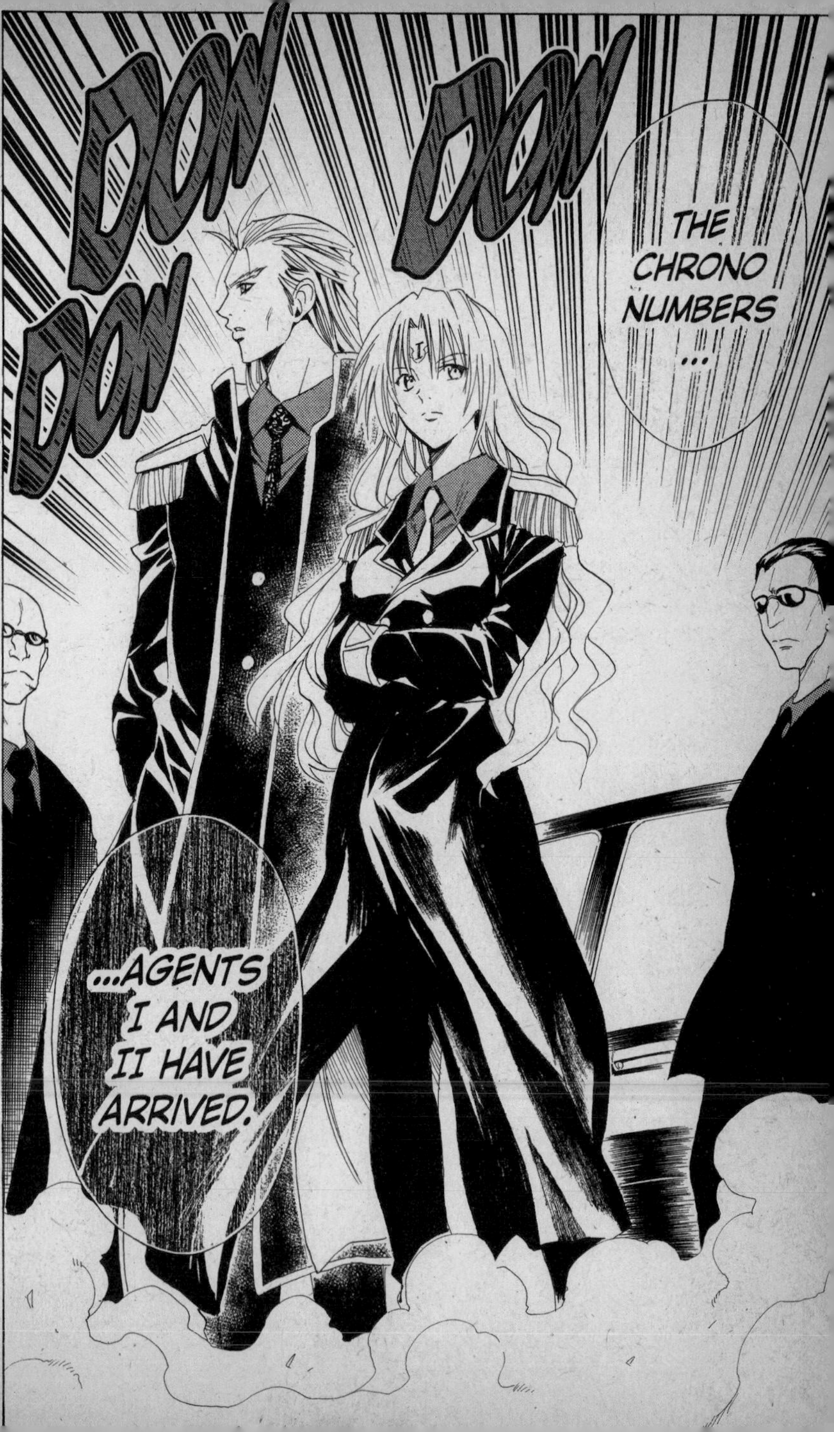
DON DON
DON DON
THE CHRONO NUMBERS ...
...AGENTS I AND II HAVE ARRIVED.

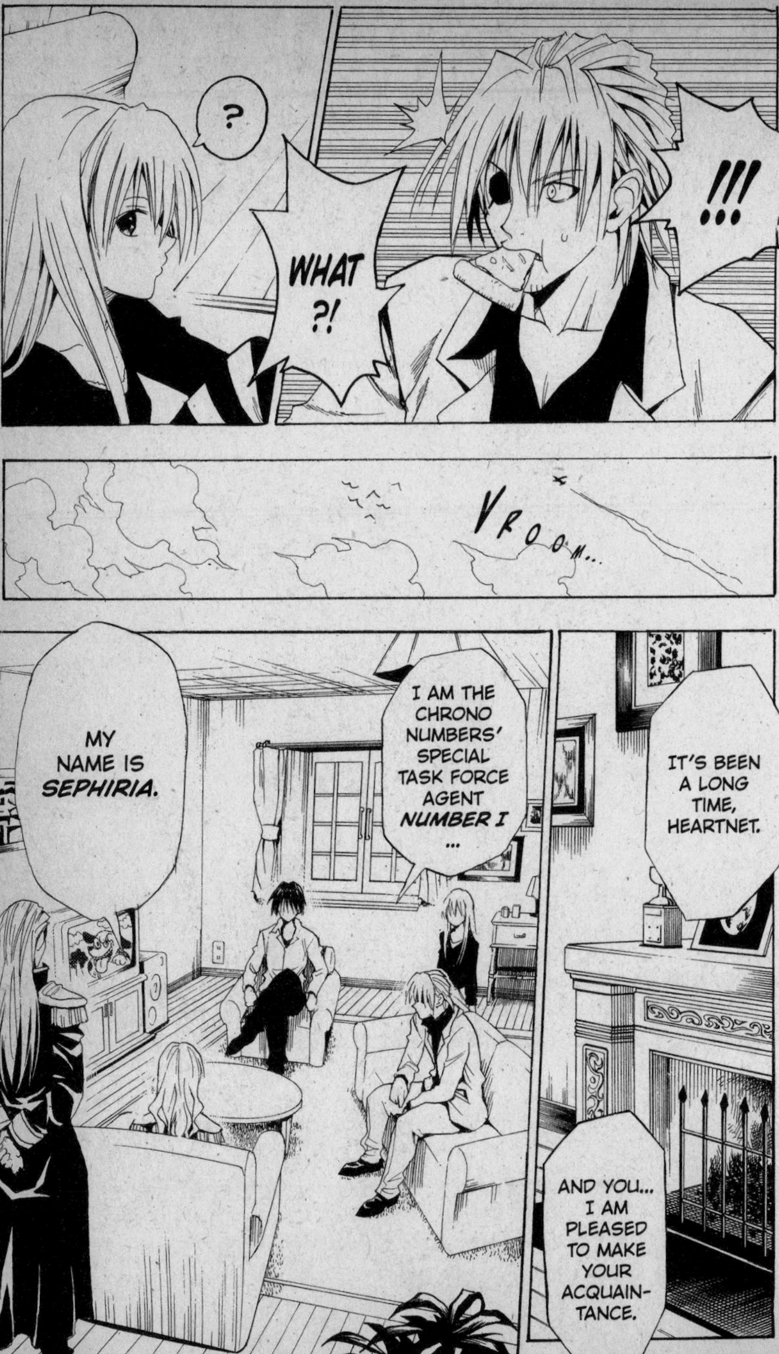
!!!
WHAT ?!
?
VROOM...
IT'S BEEN A LONG TIME, HEARTNET.
AND YOU... I AM PLEASED TO MAKE YOUR ACQUAIN-TANCE.
I AM THE CHRONO NUMBERS' SPECIAL TASK FORCE AGENT NUMBER I ...
MY NAME IS SEPHIRIA.

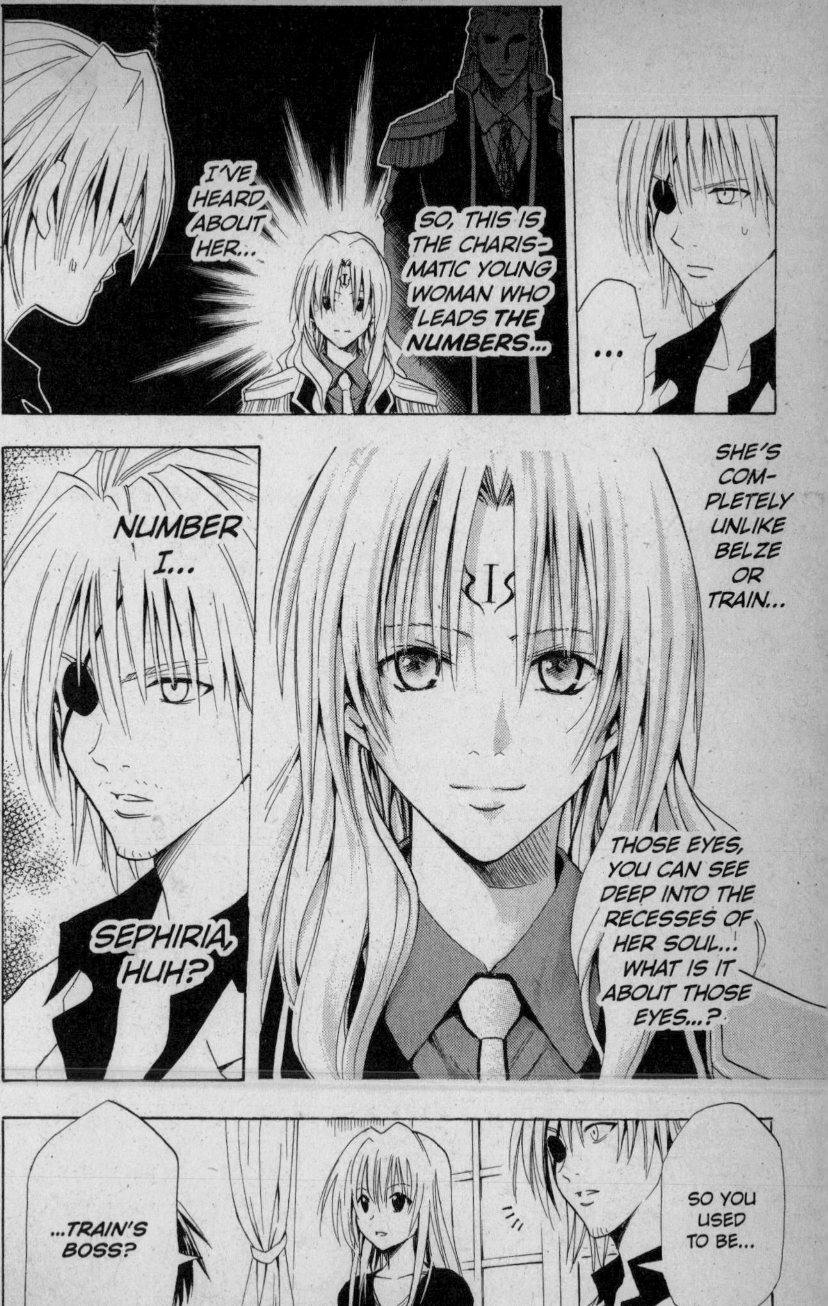
...
I'VE HEARD ABOUT HER...
SO, THIS IS THE CHARIS-MATIC YOUNG WOMAN WHO LEADS THE NUMBERS...
SHE'S COM-PLETELY UNLIKE BELZE OR TRAIN...
THOSE EYES, YOU CAN SEE DEEP INTO THE RECESSES OF HER SOUL... WHAT IS IT ABOUT THOSE EYES...?
NUMBER I...
SEPHIRIA, HUH?
SO YOU USED TO BE...
...TRAIN'S BOSS?

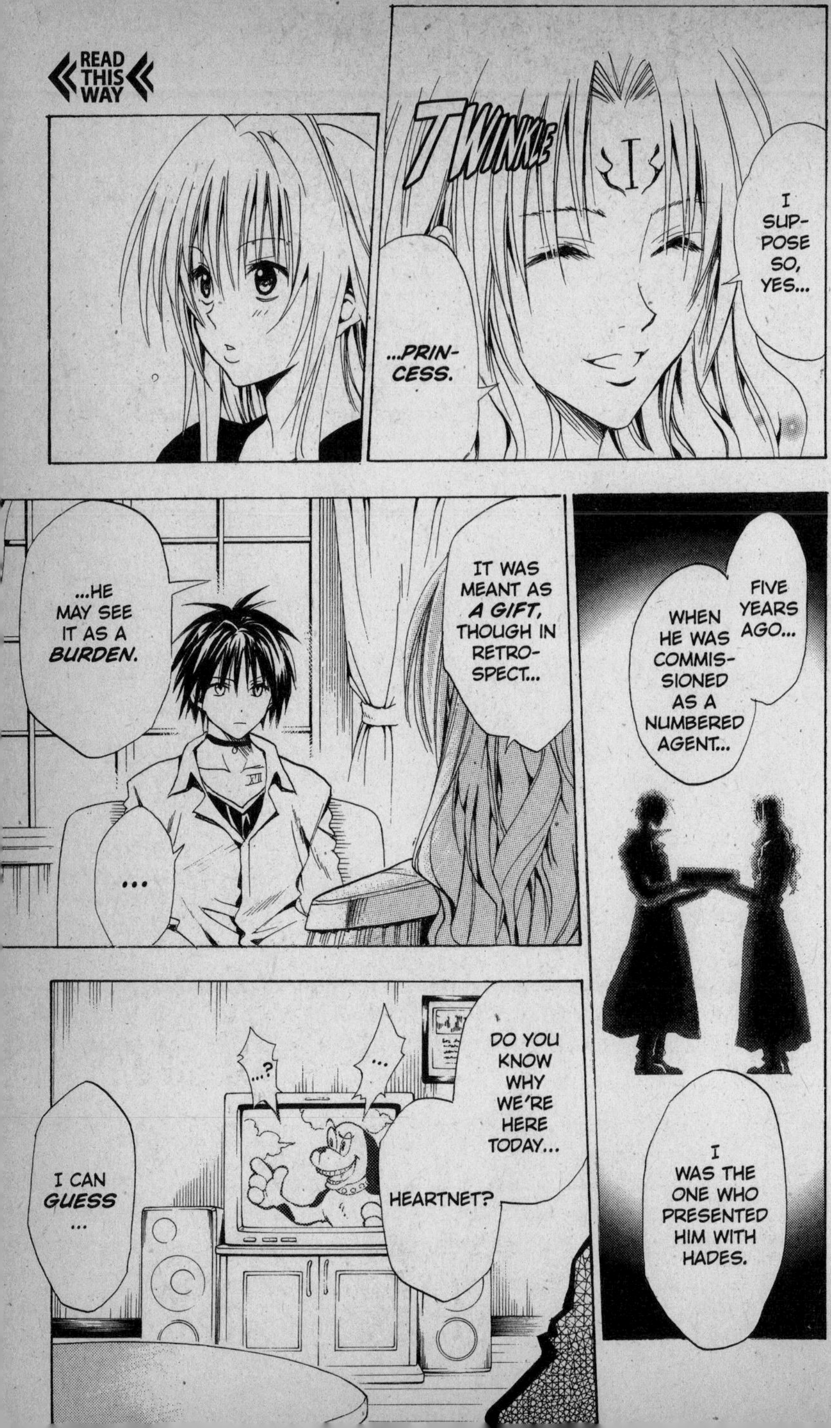
READ THIS WAY
TWINKLE
I SUP-POSE SO, YES...
...PRIN-CESS.
FIVE YEARS AGO...
WHEN HE WAS COMMIS-SIONED AS A NUMBERED AGENT...
I WAS THE ONE WHO PRESENTED HIM WITH HADES.
IT WAS MEANT AS *A GIFT,* THOUGH IN RETRO-SPECT...
...HE MAY SEE IT AS A *BURDEN.*
...
DO YOU KNOW WHY WE'RE HERE TODAY...
HEARTNET?
...
...?
I CAN *GUESS* ...

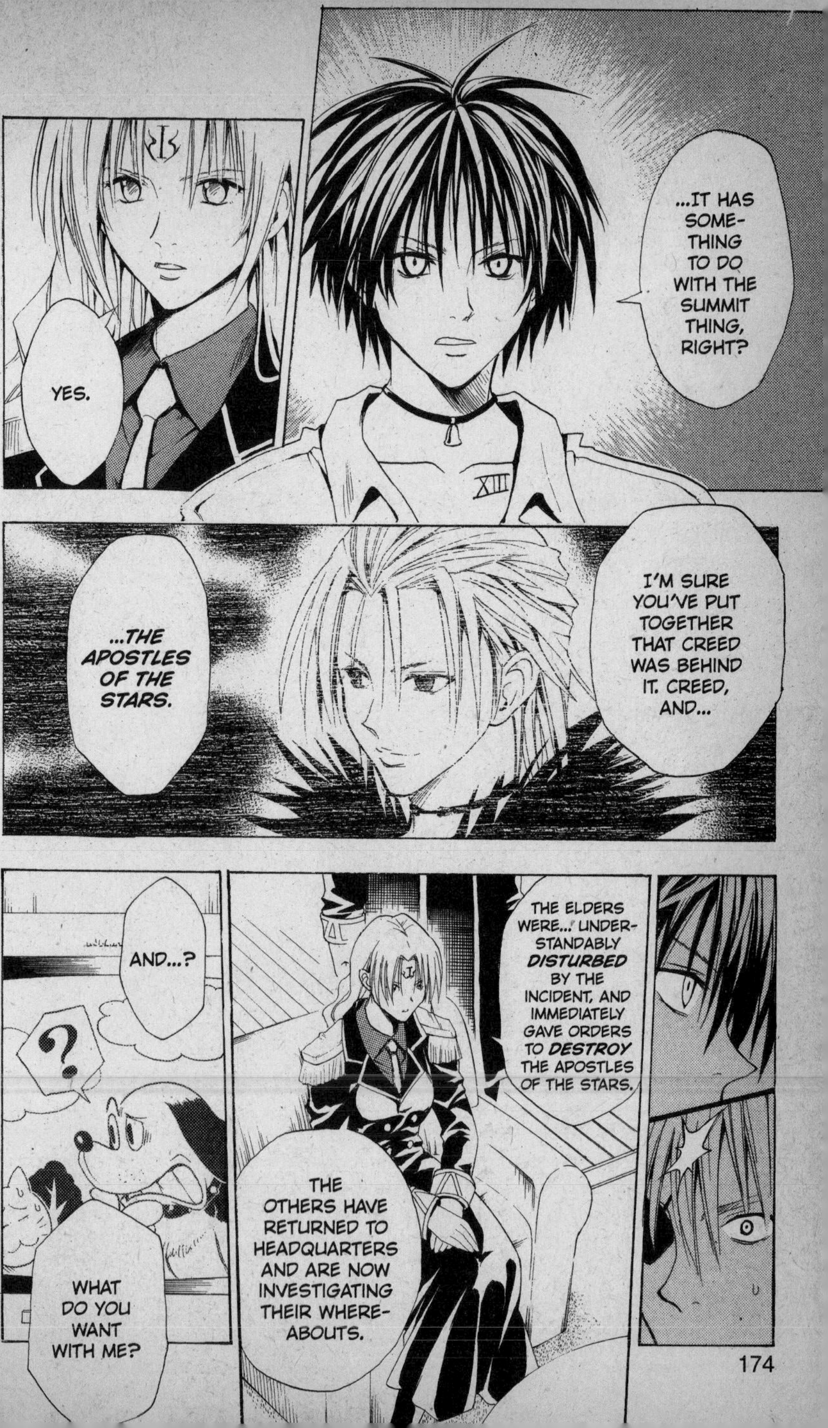
...IT HAS SOMETHING TO DO WITH THE SUMMIT THING, RIGHT?
YES.
I'M SURE YOU'VE PUT TOGETHER THAT CREED WAS BEHIND IT. CREED, AND...
...THE APOSTLES OF THE STARS.
THE ELDERS WERE... UNDERSTANDABLY ***DISTURBED*** BY THE INCIDENT, AND IMMEDIATELY GAVE ORDERS TO ***DESTROY*** THE APOSTLES OF THE STARS.
THE OTHERS HAVE RETURNED TO HEADQUARTERS AND ARE NOW INVESTIGATING THEIR WHEREABOUTS.
AND...?
?
WHAT DO YOU WANT WITH ME?

READ THIS WAY

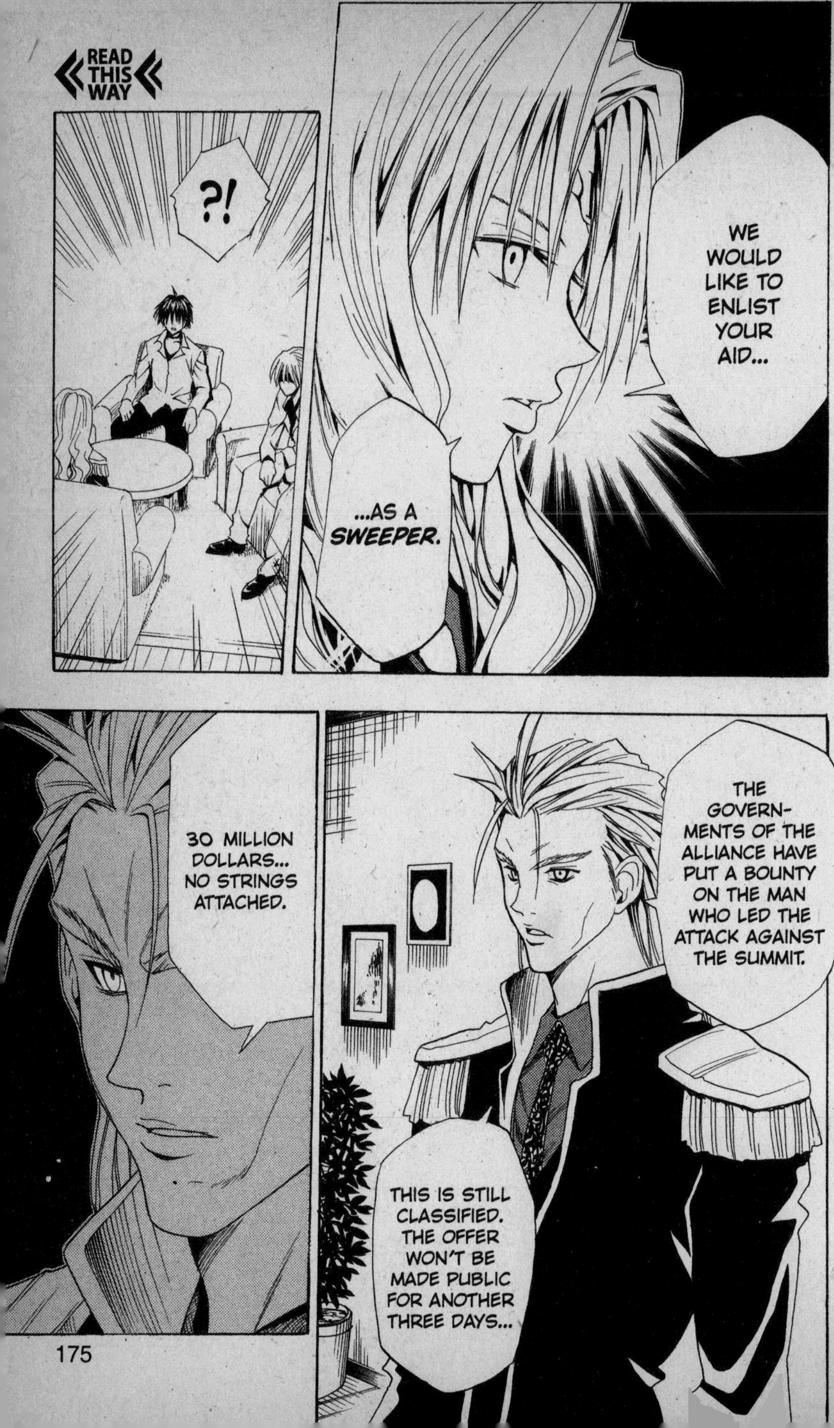
WE WOULD LIKE TO ENLIST YOUR AID...
...AS A SWEEPER.
?!
THE GOVERN-MENTS OF THE ALLIANCE HAVE PUT A BOUNTY ON THE MAN WHO LED THE ATTACK AGAINST THE SUMMIT.
THIS IS STILL CLASSIFIED. THE OFFER WON'T BE MADE PUBLIC FOR ANOTHER THREE DAYS...
30 MILLION DOLLARS... NO STRINGS ATTACHED.

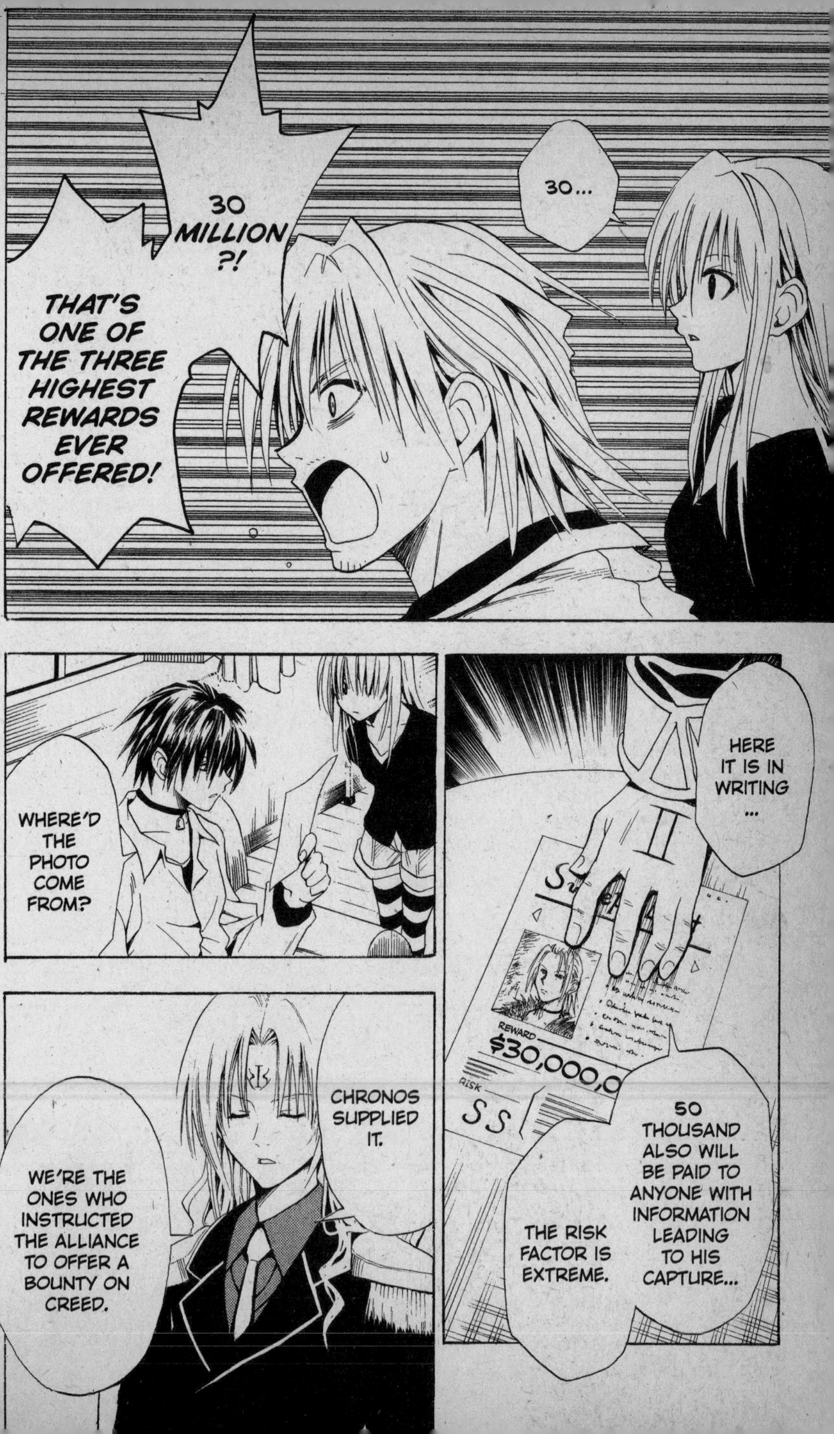
30...
30 MILLION ?!
THAT'S ONE OF THE THREE HIGHEST REWARDS EVER OFFERED!
HERE IT IS IN WRITING...
REWARD
$30,000,0
RISK
SS
50 THOUSAND ALSO WILL BE PAID TO ANYONE WITH INFORMATION LEADING TO HIS CAPTURE...
THE RISK FACTOR IS EXTREME.
WHERE'D THE PHOTO COME FROM?
CHRONOS SUPPLIED IT.
WE'RE THE ONES WHO INSTRUCTED THE ALLIANCE TO OFFER A BOUNTY ON CREED.

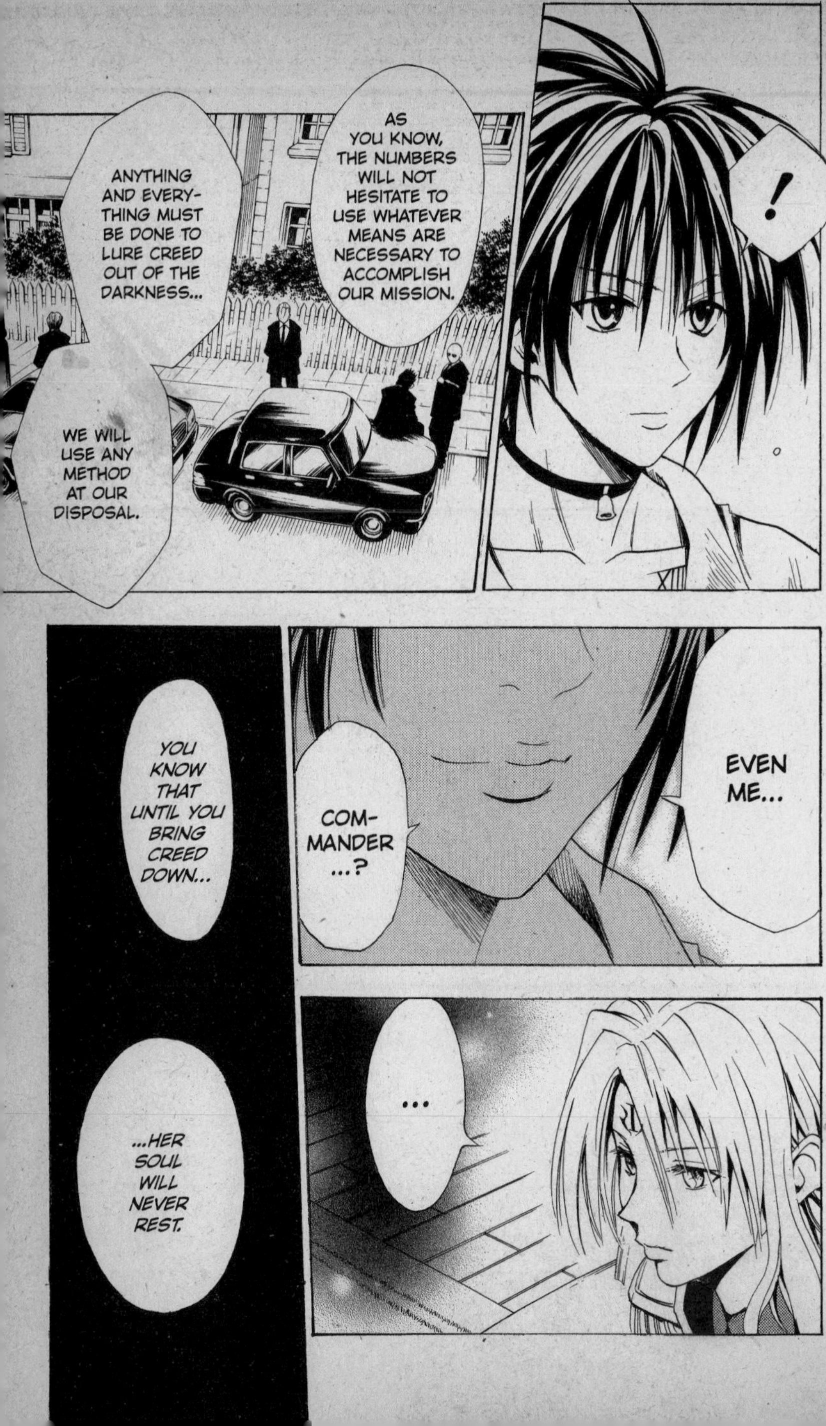
!
AS YOU KNOW, THE NUMBERS WILL NOT HESITATE TO USE WHATEVER MEANS ARE NECESSARY TO ACCOMPLISH OUR MISSION.
ANYTHING AND EVERY-THING MUST BE DONE TO LURE CREED OUT OF THE DARKNESS...
WE WILL USE ANY METHOD AT OUR DISPOSAL.
EVEN ME...
COM-MANDER ...?
...
YOU KNOW THAT UNTIL YOU BRING CREED DOWN...
...HER SOUL WILL NEVER REST.

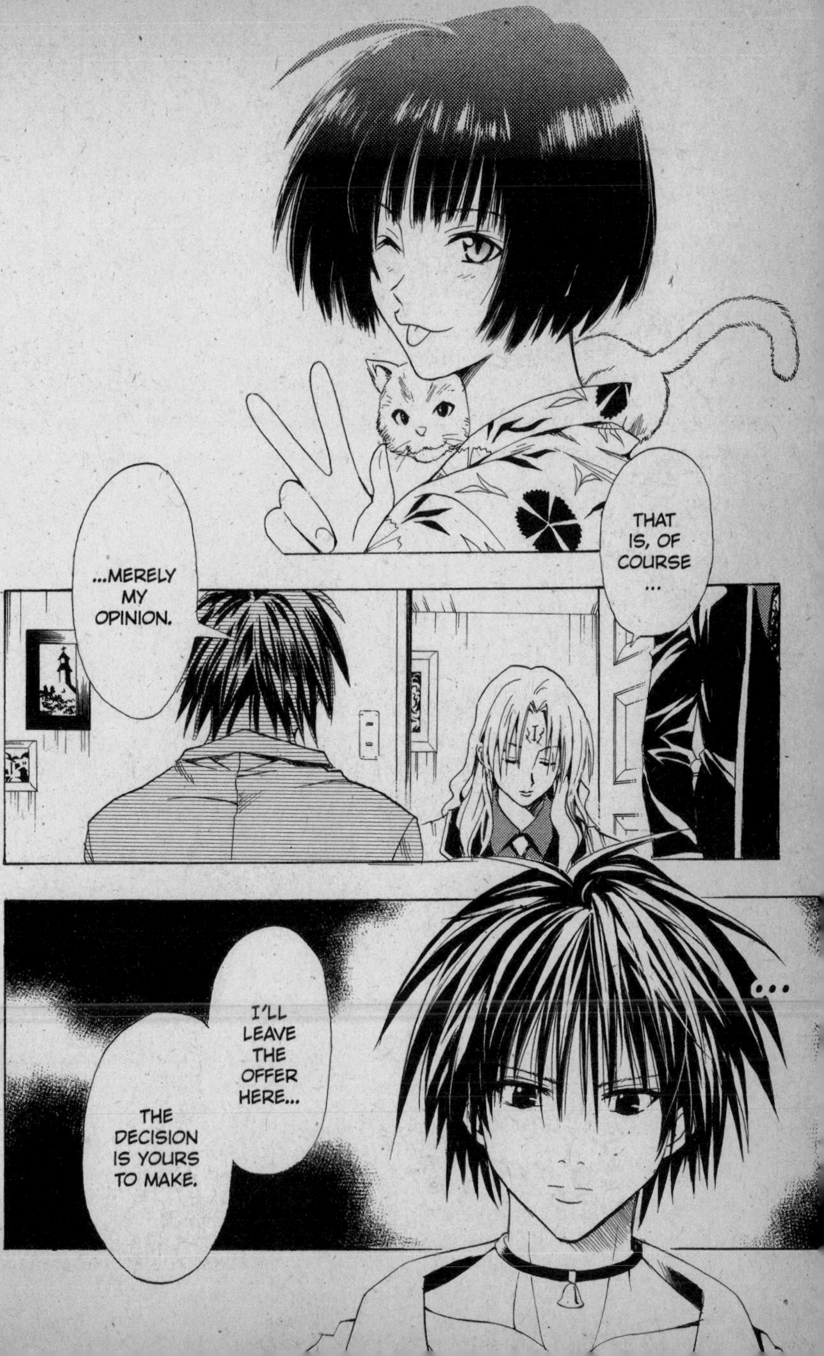
THAT IS, OF COURSE ...
...MERELY MY OPINION.
...
I'LL LEAVE THE OFFER HERE...
THE DECISION IS YOURS TO MAKE.

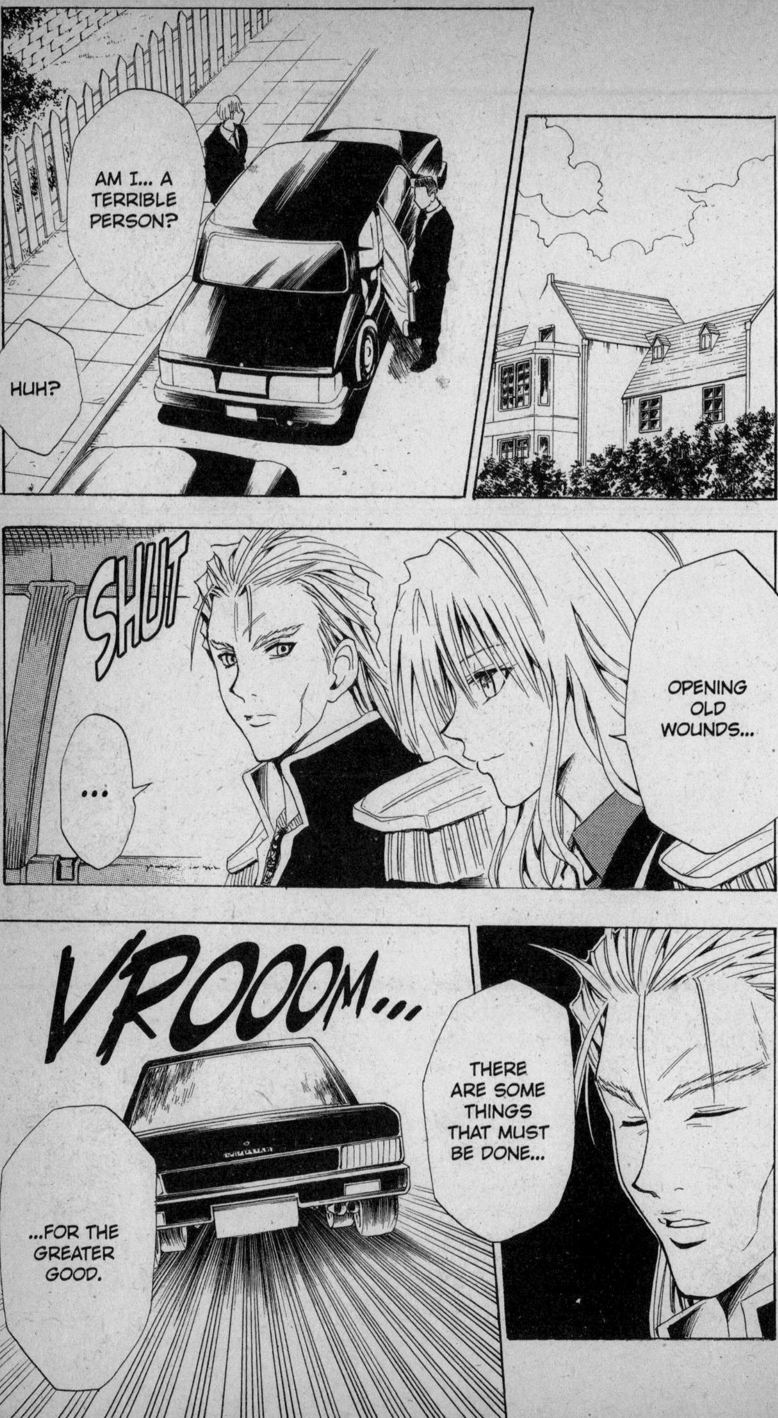
AM I... A TERRIBLE PERSON?
HUH?
OPENING OLD WOUNDS...
SHUT
...
THERE ARE SOME THINGS THAT MUST BE DONE...
VROOOM...
...FOR THE GREATER GOOD.

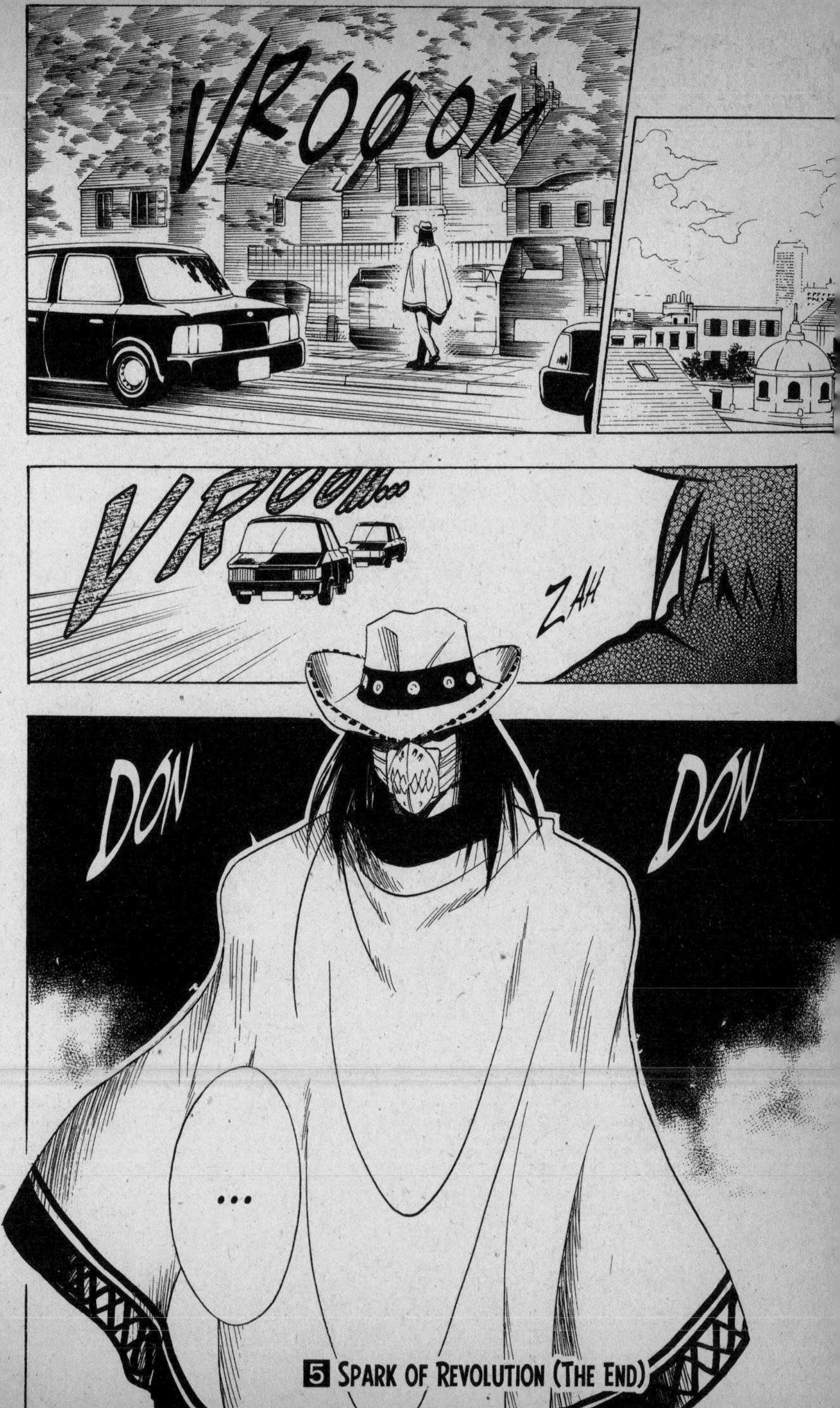
VROOOM
VROOOM...
ZAH
DON
DON
...
5 Spark of Revolution (The End)

SKETCHES PART 2

◎ MARO'S HAIR IS LONG AND STRAIGHT.
I LIKE GODA SENSEI. I WONDER IF HE'LL APPEAR AGAIN...

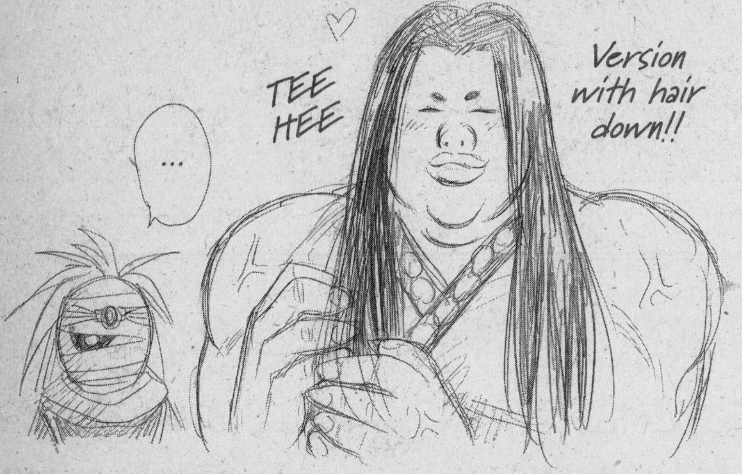
Version with hair down!!
TEE HEE
...

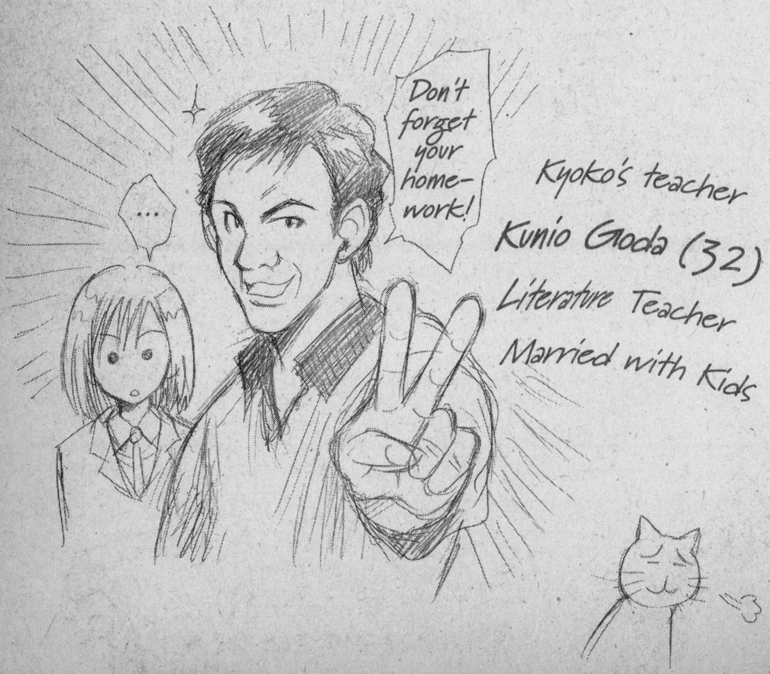
Kyoko's teacher
Kunio Goda (32)
Literature Teacher
Married with Kids
Don't forget your home-work!
...

SKETCHES PART 3

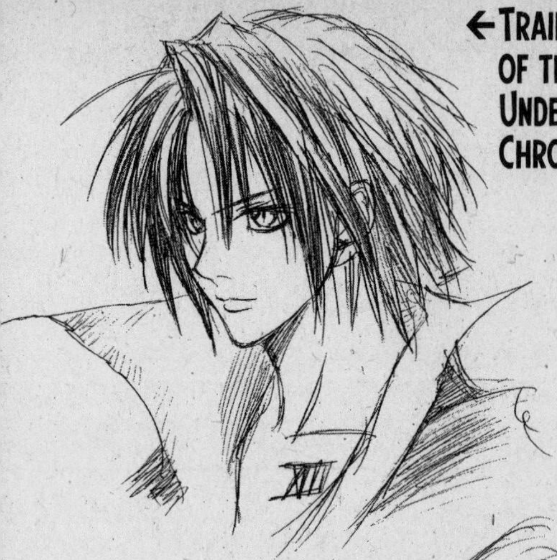

←TRAIN WHEN HE WAS A MEMBER OF THE CHRONO NUMBERS. UNDER HIS COAT, HE WEARS HIS CHRONOS UNIFORM.

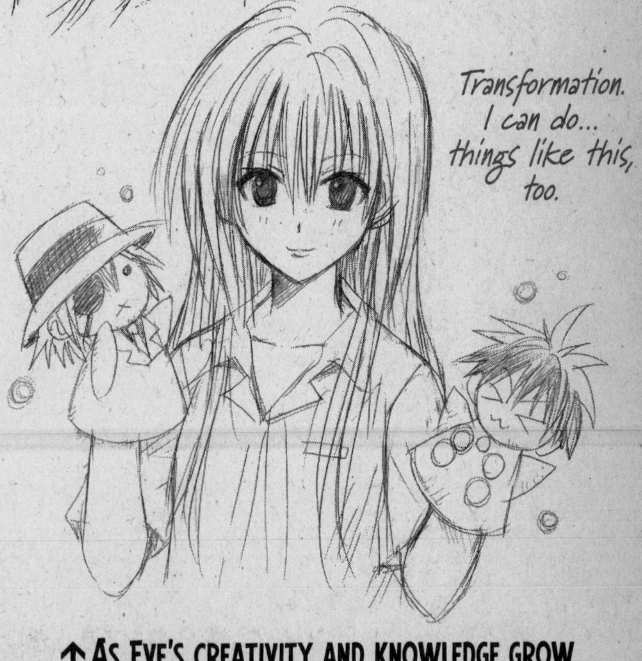
Transformation. I can do... things like this, too.

↑AS EVE'S CREATIVITY AND KNOWLEDGE GROW, THE SCOPE OF HER TRANSFORMATIVE POWER GROWS, TOO.

SKETCHES PART 4

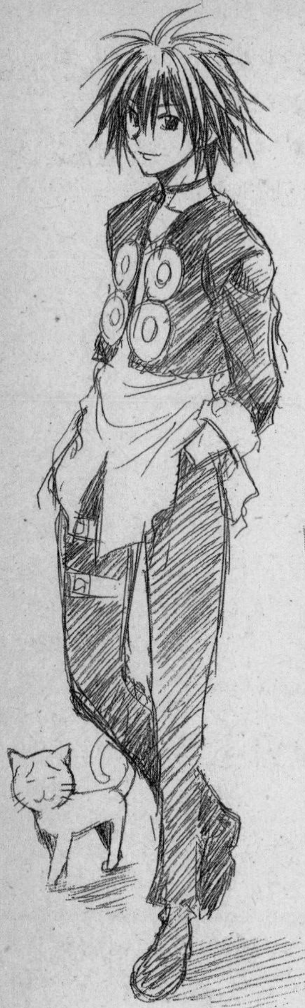

← TRAIN AND CAT.
AS ON THE TABLE OF
CONTENTS PAGE OF VOLUME 1.

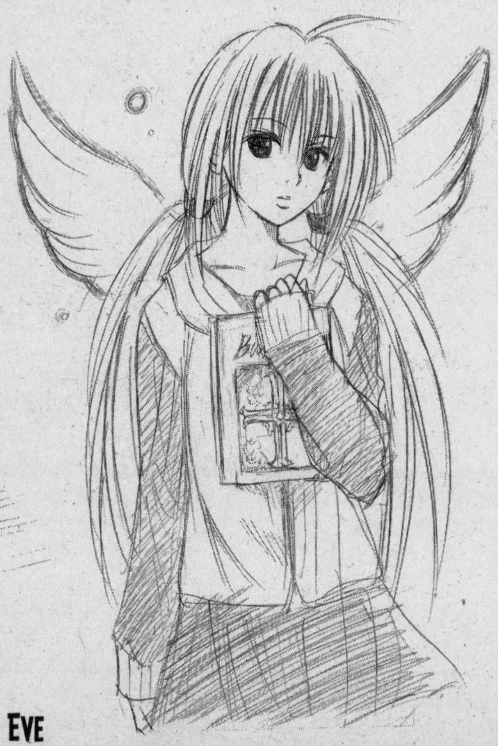

↑ EVE
SHE ALWAYS HAS THE SAME HAIRSTYLE,
SO I TRIED CHANGING IT UP A LITTLE.

IN THE NEXT VOLUME...

After hearing that Black Cat is the "ultimate gunman," metal-mouthed menace Durham Glaster vows to claim that title for himself. Desperate to learn of his rival's whereabouts, Durham beats the information out of Train's friends. When the two finally duel, how far will Train go to exact revenge?

AVAILABLE JANUARY 2007! ◁◁◁◁◁◁

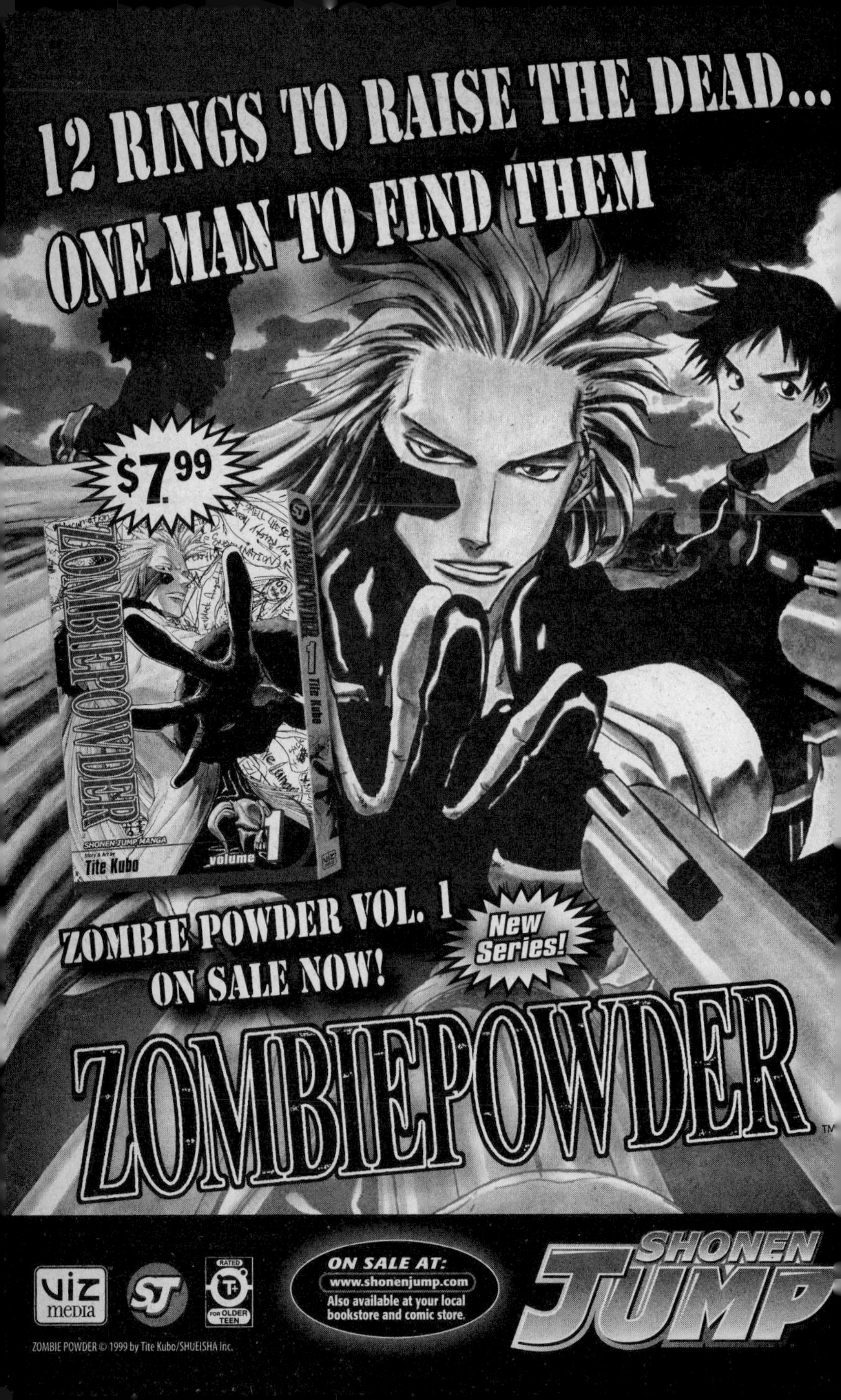
12 RINGS TO RAISE THE DEAD...
ONE MAN TO FIND THEM
$7.99
ZOMBIEPOWDER
SHONEN JUMP MANGA
Story & Art by
Tite Kubo
volume 1
ZOMBIE POWDER VOL. 1
ON SALE NOW!
New Series!
ZOMBIEPOWDER™
viz media
SJ
RATED T+ FOR OLDER TEEN
ON SALE AT:
www.shonenjump.com
Also available at your local bookstore and comic store.
SHONEN JUMP
ZOMBIE POWDER © 1999 by Tite Kubo/SHUEISHA Inc.

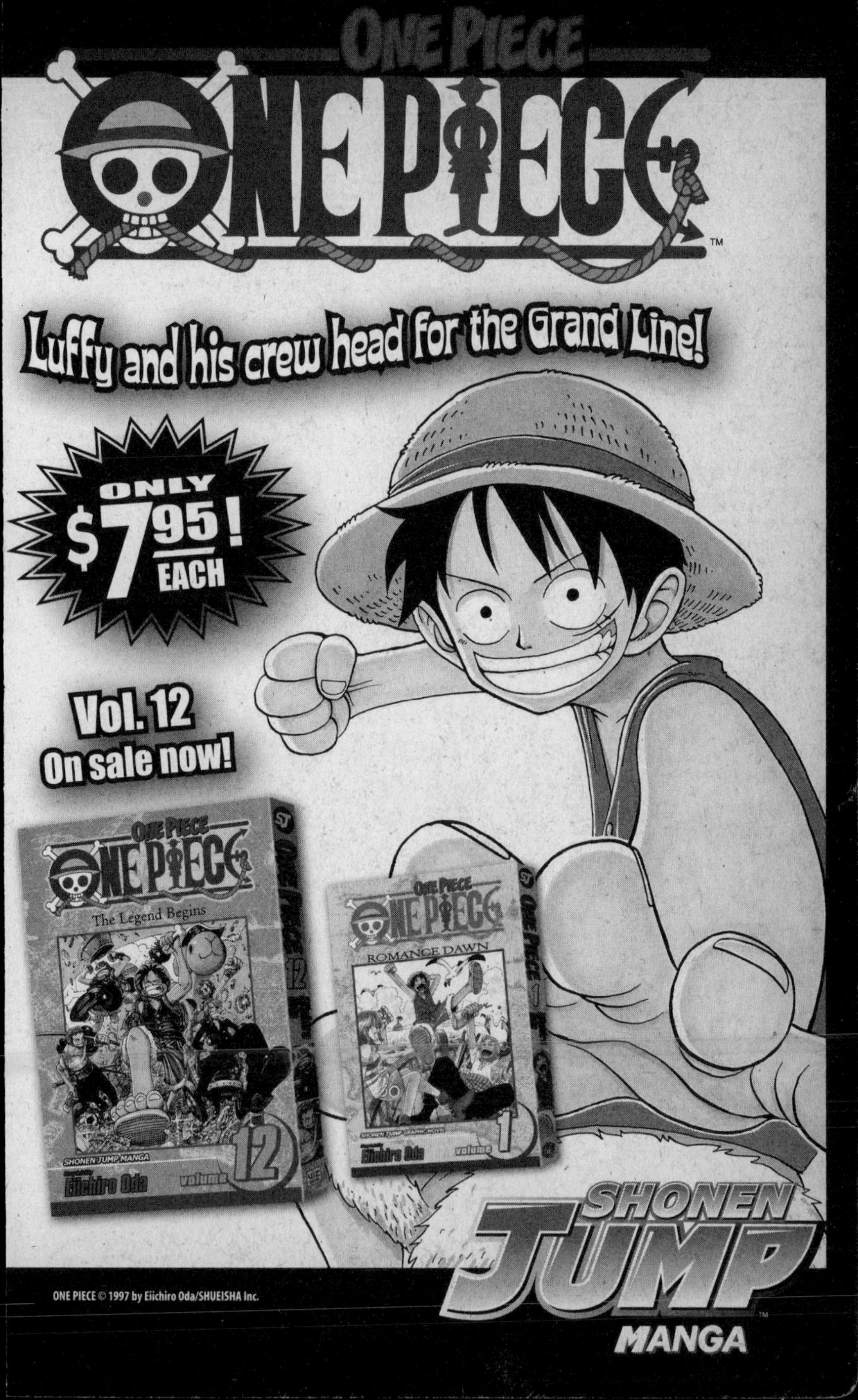

ONE PIECE
ONE PIECE
Luffy and his crew head for the Grand Line!
ONLY $7.95! EACH
Vol. 12
On sale now!
ONE PIECE
ONE PIECE
The Legend Begins
SHONEN JUMP MANGA
Eiichiro Oda
volume 12
ONE PIECE
ONE PIECE
ROMANCE DAWN
Eiichiro Oda
volume 1
ONE PIECE © 1997 by Eiichiro Oda/SHUEISHA Inc.
SHONEN JUMP
MANGA

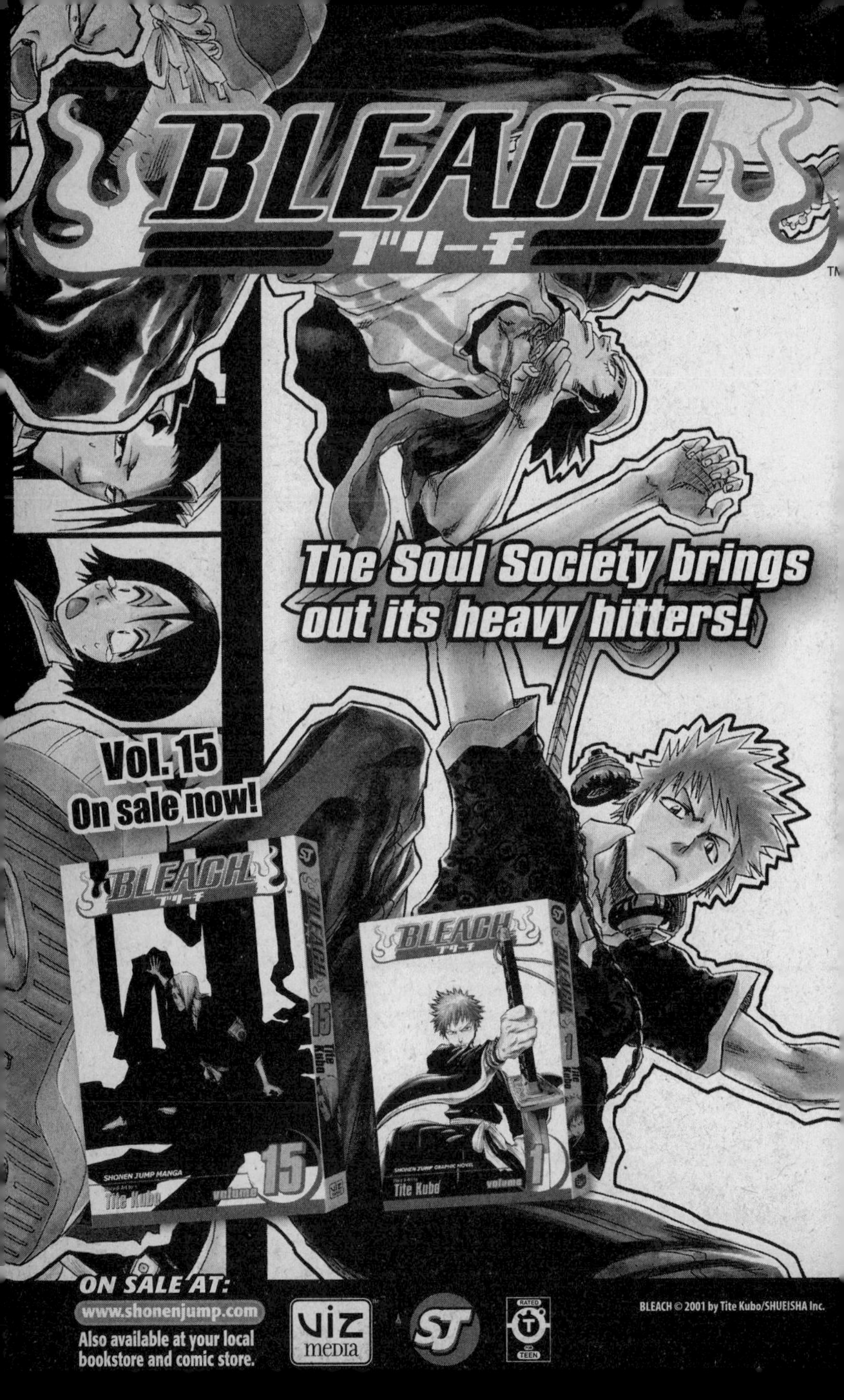
BLEACH
ブリーチ
The Soul Society brings out its heavy hitters!
Vol. 15 On sale now!
ON SALE AT:
www.shonenjump.com
Also available at your local bookstore and comic store.
BLEACH © 2001 by Tite Kubo/SHUEISHA Inc.

Novel $9.99

The popular manga is now available as a novel!

RUROUNI KENSHIN
VOYAGE TO THE MOON WORLD

Original Concept by
Nobuhiro Watsuki

Written by
Kaoru Shizuka

Translated by
Cindy Yamauchi &
Mark Giambruno

SHONEN JUMP FICTION

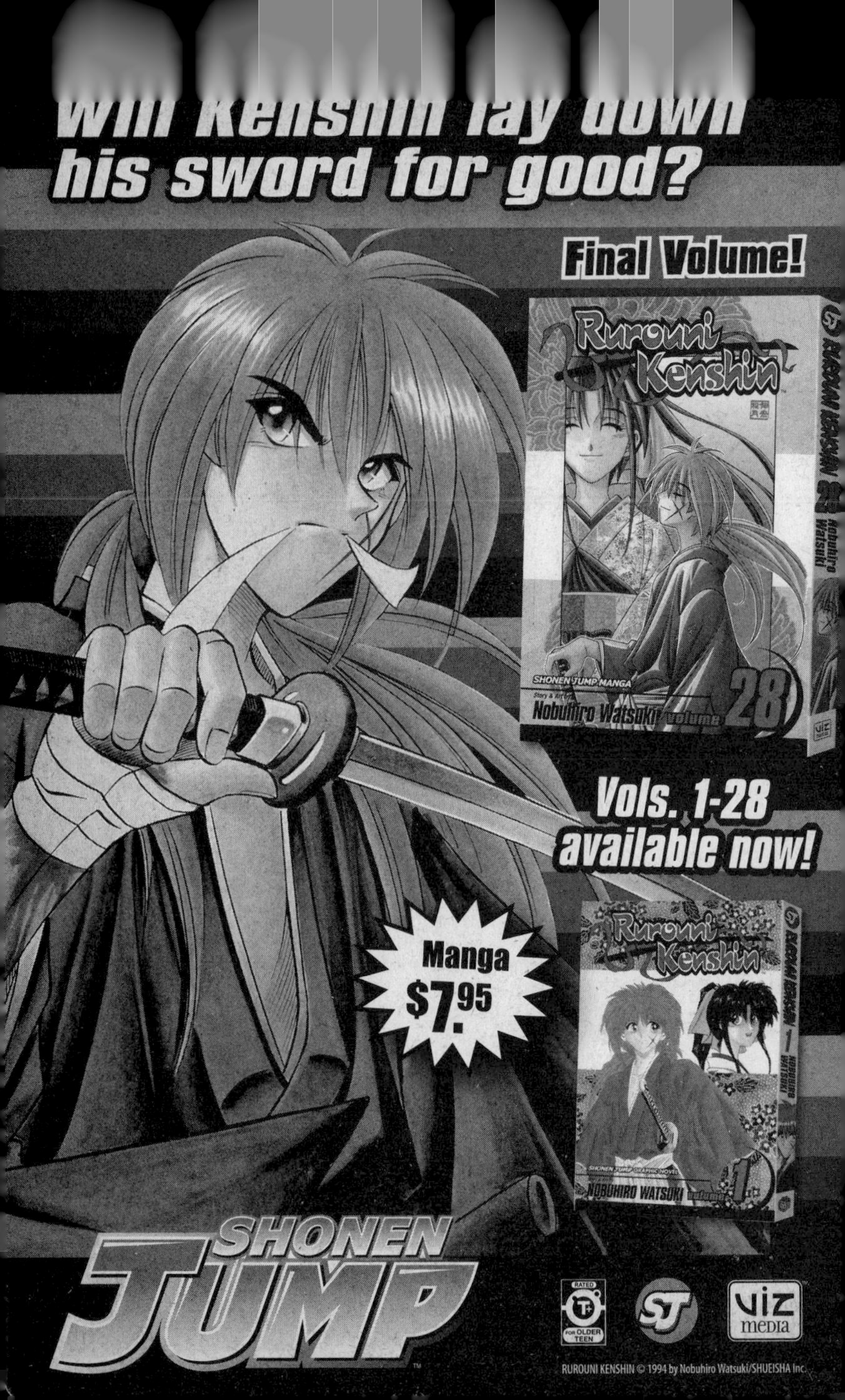
Will Kenshin lay down
his sword for good?
Final Volume!
Rurouni Kenshin
SHONEN JUMP MANGA
Nobuhiro Watsuki volume 28
Vols. 1-28
available now!
Manga
$7.95
Rurouni Kenshin
NOBUHIRO WATSUKI volume 1
SHONEN JUMP
RATED T+ FOR OLDER TEEN
SJ
VIZ media
RUROUNI KENSHIN © 1994 by Nobuhiro Watsuki/SHUEISHA Inc.

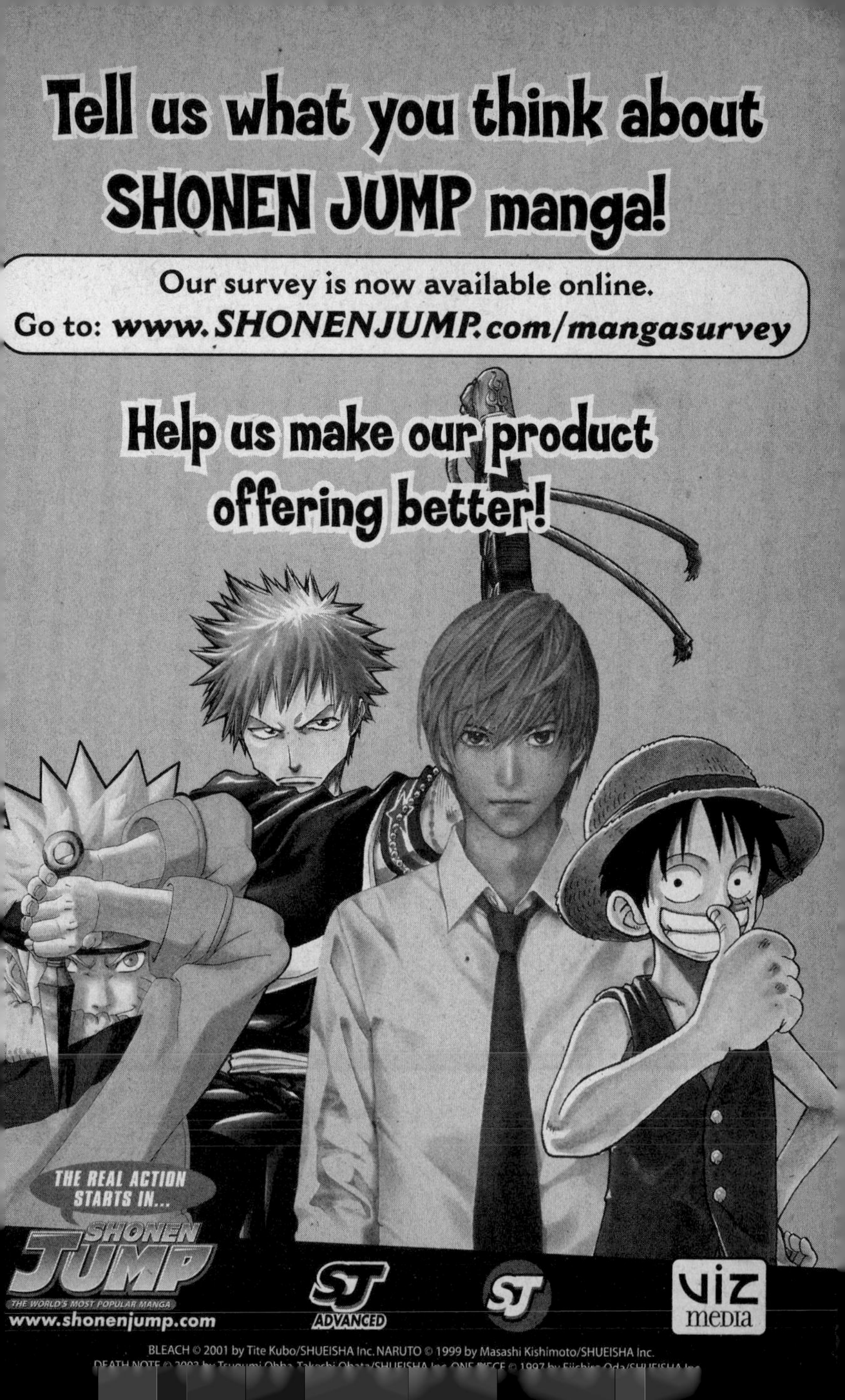

Tell us what you think about
SHONEN JUMP manga!
Our survey is now available online.
Go to: www.SHONENJUMP.com/mangasurvey
Help us make our product
offering better!
THE REAL ACTION STARTS IN...
SHONEN JUMP
THE WORLD'S MOST POPULAR MANGA
www.shonenjump.com
SJ ADVANCED
SJ
VIZ media
BLEACH © 2001 by Tite Kubo/SHUEISHA Inc. NARUTO © 1999 by Masashi Kishimoto/SHUEISHA Inc.
DEATH NOTE © 2003 by Tsugumi Ohba, Takeshi Obata/SHUEISHA Inc. ONE PIECE © 1997 by Eiichiro Oda/SHUEISHA Inc.

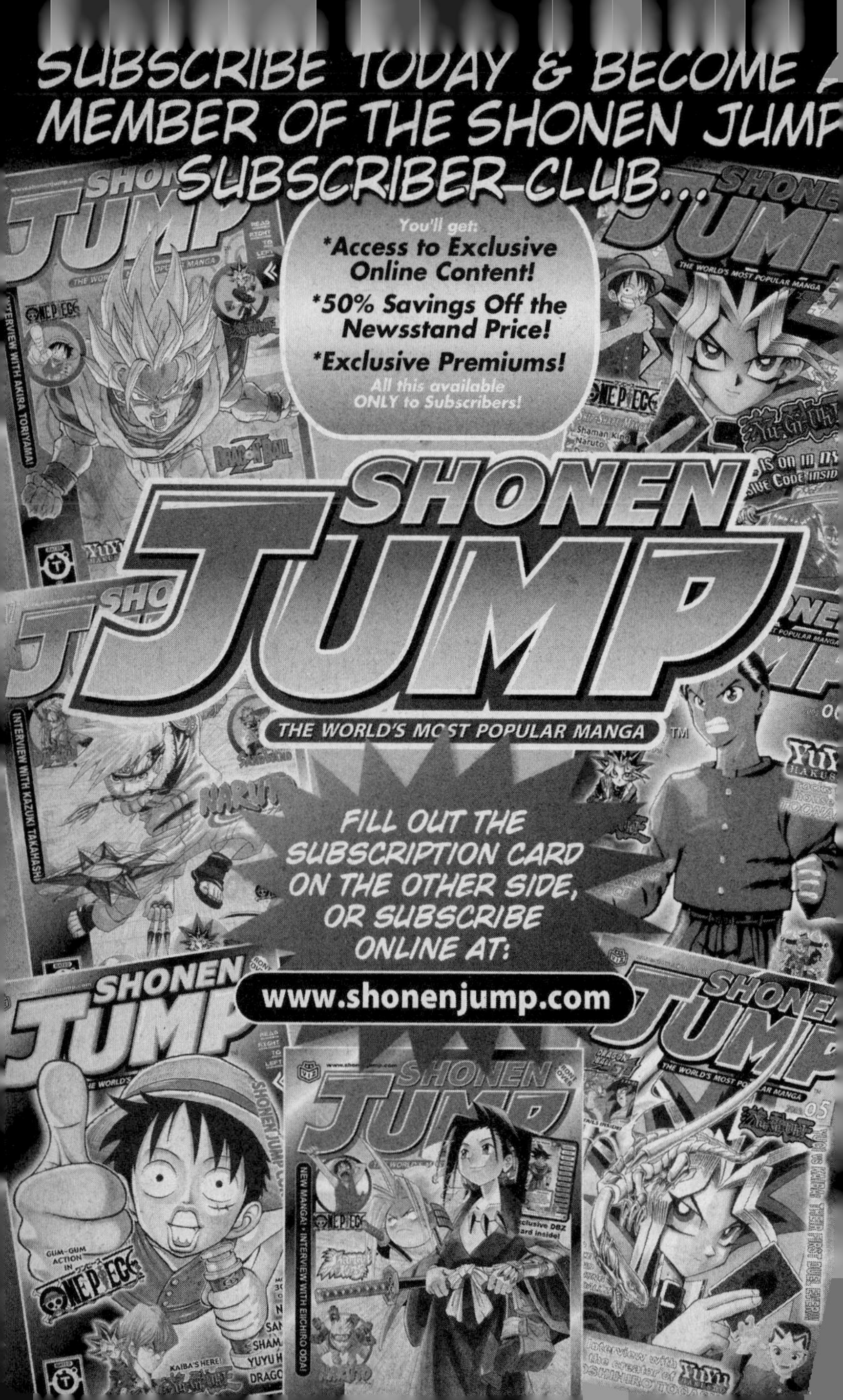
SUBSCRIBE TODAY & BECOME A MEMBER OF THE SHONEN JUMP SUBSCRIBER CLUB...
You'll get:
*Access to Exclusive Online Content!
*50% Savings Off the Newsstand Price!
*Exclusive Premiums!
All this available ONLY to Subscribers!
SHONEN JUMP
THE WORLD'S MOST POPULAR MANGA
FILL OUT THE SUBSCRIPTION CARD ON THE OTHER SIDE, OR SUBSCRIBE ONLINE AT:
www.shonenjump.com